"DISAPPEARANCES"
AND
POLITICAL KILLINGS

HUMAN RIGHTS CRISIS OF THE 1990s

A MANUAL FOR ACTION

"DISAPPEARANCES" AND POLITICAL KILLINGS

HUMAN RIGHTS CRISIS OF THE 1990s

A MANUAL FOR ACTION

AMNESTY INTERNATIONAL

Amsterdam, 1994

AI Index: ACT 33/01/94

ISBN: 90 6463 095 x

CIP

First published: February 1994

Amnesty International Dutch Section
Keizersgracht 620
1017 ER Amsterdam

Typeset at systemText, de Wijk
Printed by: Ten Brink Meppel bv
Design: Wim ten Brinke bNO, Hilversum
Cover photos: above, Kurdistan Koreme (summer 1992), copyright by Argentine Team of
Forensic Antropology (EAAF); under, Silent march in France for the "disappeared", copyright
by Driquet, France.

Copyright: Amnesty International Dutch Section

Original language: English

Several chapters of this report were originally prepared as papers for an expert seminar held by
Amnesty International at Old Jordans, near Beaconsfield, United Kingdom, 15-17 November
1991. Revised versions of the papers were presented at the International Conference on
"Disappearances" and Political Killings organized by Amnesty International's Dutch Section at
Noordwijkerhout, the Netherlands, 4-6 September 1992.

This report was prepared under the direction of Eric Prokosch in collaboration with Richard
Carver, Christopher Keith Hall, Elizabeth Hodgkin, Susan Lee, Hania Mufti, Elizabeth Nissan,
Jonathan Sugden and Wilder Tayler, all members or former members of staff of the International
Secretariat of Amnesty International.

TABLE OF CONTENTS

LIST OF ABBREVIATIONS AND ACRONYMS

Abbreviation/Acronym	Full title
Basic Principles	Basic Principles on the Use of Force and Firearms by Law Enforcement Officials
Body of Principles	Body of Principles for the Protection of All Persons under Any Form of Detention or Imprisonment
Declaration on Disappearances	Declaration on the Protection of All Persons from Enforced Disappearance
EU	European Union
ICRC	International Committee of the Red Cross
Principles on Extra-Legal, Arbitrary and Summary Executions	Principles on the Effective Prevention and Investigation of Extra-Legal, Arbitrary and Summary Executions
Standard Minimum Rules	Standard Miminum Rules for the Treatment of Prisoners
UN	United Nations
Working Group on Disappearances	Working Group on Enforced or Involuntary Disappearances

LIST OF UN DOCUMENT NUMBERS

In the notes to this report, certain UN documents are cited as shown below.

The annual reports of the *Special Rapporteur on summary or arbitrary executions* (SRSAE, 1984-1992), the *Special Rapporteur on extrajudicial, summary or arbitrary executions* (SRESAE, from 1993) and the *Working Group on Enforced or Involuntary Disappearances* (WGEID) are issued as documents for the corresponding sessions of the UN Commission on Human Rights, as follows:

Report	*UN document No.*	*Date*
SRSAE,	1990 report E/CN.4/1990/22	23 January 1990
SRESAE,	1993 report E/CN.4/1993/46	23 December 1992
WGEID,	1981 report E/CN.4/1435	26 January 1981
WGEID,	1990 report E/CN.4/1990/13	24 January 1990
WGEID,	1992 report E.CN.4/1992/18	30 December 1991
WGEID,	1993 report E/CN.4/1993/25	7 January 1993

The reports on *country visits* by the Working Group on Enforced or Involuntary Disappearances are issued separately as annexes to the Working Group's annual reports, as follows:

Country	*Date of visit*	*UN doc. No.*	*Date*
Guatemala	5-9 October 1987	E/CN.4/1988/19/Add.1	21 December 1987
Philippines	27 Aug.-7 Sept. 1990	E/CN.4/1991/20/Add.1	10 January 1991
Sri Lanka	7-18 October 1991	E/CN.4/1992/18/Add.1	8 January 1992
Sri Lanka	5-15 October 1992	E/CN.4/1993/25/Add.1	30 December 1992

The annual reports of the *Human Rights Committee* set up under the International Covenant on Civil and Political Rights are published each year as Supplement No. 40 to the Official Records of the UN General Assembly, as follows:

Year	*UN document No.*
1982	A/37/40
1983	A/38/40
1985	A/40/40
1988	A/43/40

The reports of the *Director of the ONUSAL Human Rights Division*, the UN human rights monitoring mission in El Salvador, are issued as joint documents of the UN General Assembly (A/-) and the UN Security Council (S/-), as follows:

Report	*UN document No.*	*Date*
First report	A/45/1055 and S/23037	16 September 1991
Second report	A/46/658 and S/23222	15 November 1991
Third report	A/46/876 and S/23580	19 February 1992
Fifth report	A/46/955 and S/24375	12 August 1992
Sixth report	A/47/912 and S/25521	5 April 1993

INTRODUCTION

> *"Many of the events described in this report will be hard to believe. This is because the men and women of our nation have only heard of such horror in reports from distant places. The enormity of what took place in Argentina, involving the transgression of the most fundamental human rights, is sure, still, to produce that disbelief which some used at the time to defend themselves from pain and horror. In so doing, they also avoided the responsibility born of knowledge and awareness, because the question necessarily follows: how can we prevent it happening again?"*
> – Nunca Mas (*Never Again*), the report of the Argentinian National Commission on Disappeared People[1]

The events described in the report of the Argentinian National Commission[2] have been reproduced many times elsewhere. People have been taken prisoner by agents of the state and held in secret, while the authorities have denied any knowledge of their whereabouts or fate. People have been murdered in detention, assassinated in the street, or killed in cold blood under the guise of law enforcement or the conduct of armed hostilities.

These "disappearances" and extrajudicial executions are not private affairs, or the result of the legitimate exercise of police and military powers. They are crimes committed by order of governments or with their acquiescence.

More than a million people have been victims of "disappearances" and extrajudicial executions during the past 25 years. Many others have been deliberately and arbitrarily killed by opposition groups.

A *"disappearance"* occurs whenever there is reason to believe that a person has been taken into custody by agents of the state, and the authorities deny that the victim is in custody, thus concealing his or her whereabouts and fate. *Extrajudicial executions* are unlawful and deliberate killings, carried out by order of a government or with its acquiescence. *Political killings* include both extrajudicial executions and *deliberate and arbitrary killings by armed opposition groups*.

"Disappearances" and political killings may be hard to believe because their authors have tried to conceal their true nature. Those responsible for the crimes will try to avoid being called to account for them through lies, cover-ups and the propagation of misleading explanations and excuses. Making the facts known is one of the main tasks of those who wish to stop the atrocities.

"Disappearances" and political killings may be hard to believe because the very thought of committing them is so opposed to notions of human decency, human rights and the rule of law. The past 15 years have seen unprecedented accomplishments by the community of nations in adopting standards for the prevention of "disappearances" and extrajudicial executions and creating mechanisms for tackling these problems internationally. A great task of those who wish to end "disappearances" and extrajudicial executions is to make the standards known and ensure that they are enforced.

This book is dedicated to the courageous people around the world who are working to stop "disappearances" and political killings. Drawing on the experiences and accomplishments of the past 15 years, it is designed to provide tools for use in the effort. It is intended also to remind both governments and opposition groups of their obligation to put an end to "disappearances" and political killings and to repair the damage done. Just as "disappearances" and political killings are the result of decisions by governmental authorities and the leaders of armed opposition movements, so is their eradication a matter of political will.

Chapters 1 to *6* of this report are *country case studies.* These chapters describe patterns of "disappearances" and extrajudicial executions in selected countries and the experience of trying to combat them.

Chapter 7 discusses the *concepts* of "disappearances" and extrajudicial executions, analyzes *how they are carried out* and gives examples of their occurrence since the 1980s.

Chapter 8 describes the development of *international human rights standards* since the Second World War and discusses the prohibition of "disappearances" and extrajudicial executions under these standards.

Chapter 9, 10 and *11* deal with *prevention, investigation* and *bringing the perpetrators to justice.* They cite the relevant international standards and give practical measures drawn from the experience of the international human rights movement and the recommendations of intergovernmental bodies.

Chapter 12 describes the work done through the *United Nations* and other intergovernmental bodies to tackle the problems of "disappearances" and extrajudicial executions.

Chapter 13 discusses Amnesty International's policy and action against *deliberate and arbitrary killings by armed opposition groups* and gives examples of their recent occurrence.

Chapter 14 discusses the work of *relatives of the "disappeared", human rights organizations and other governments* to stop "disappearances" and political killings.

The texts of relevant international instruments and of Amnesty International's 14-Point Programs for the Prevention of "Disappearances" and Extrajudicial Executions are given in the *appendices* to the report.

This report is meant to provide activists around the world with the latest ideas and tools for working to eradicate "disappearances" and political killings. As the effort continues, new insights and recommendations are sure to be added to the list.

CHAPTER 1

IRAQ:
THE WORLD WOULD NOT LISTEN

It is always hard to know where to begin in trying to describe Iraq's human rights record. There are numerous examples of gross and consistent human rights violations coming under all parts of Amnesty International's mandate. This is not new in Iraq's history, but the past 13 years have been marked by the especially brutal suppression of all forms of internal dissent, with no end in sight. Judging by the reactions of the international community, however, one cannot help forming the impression that outside the country, Iraq's appalling human rights record is a recent discovery.

Until Iraq invaded neighbouring Kuwait on 2 August 1990, the perceived political and strategic interests of those states which were in a position to exert pressure on Iraq resulted in the international community effectively turning a blind eye to the atrocities being committed by the Iraqi Government throughout the 1980s. The same interests dictated those states' actions after the restoration of Kuwait's sovereignty in 1991 and the mass uprising in Iraq which followed.

In publishing its report in December 1990 on human rights violations by Iraqi forces in occupied Kuwait, Amnesty International said:

> "Those violations which have been reported since 2 August [1990] are entirely consistent with abuses known to have been committed in Iraq over many years... Amnesty International has repeatedly placed such information on the public record, and regrets that until the invasion of Kuwait, the international community did not see fit to apply serious pressure in an attempt to put an end to these abuses."

Unfortunately, since 1991 the world's attention has once again shifted away from the human rights crisis in Iraq. Amnesty International's proposals for action to prevent further human rights violations have gone largely unheeded.

"Disappearances"

As in other countries, the issue of "disappearances" in Iraq has always been one of the most difficult areas to investigate and on which to mobilise effective action. The scale of "disappearances" remains difficult to gauge precisely. Even today, when parts of Iraq have become more accessible to international agencies, it is impossible to put an accurate figure on the number of victims. It would be safe to say, however, that several hundred thousand people "disappeared" in Iraq during the 1980s. The victims include a wide variety of people and groups: Kurds, Arabs, Turcomans, Assyrians; Sunni and Shi'a Muslims, Christians and others; men, women and children; members of prohibited political parties and their families; military personnel and deserters; disaffected members of the ruling elite; relatives of deportees; Iraqis returning from abroad to benefit from officially-declared amnesties and others. The list of victims appears endless.

Once a person has "disappeared", it is virtually impossible in most cases to discover his or her fate or whereabouts. Usually the families of the "disappeared" remain ignorant of their fate until they are either released or confirmed to have been executed. In the latter case, the bodies of the victims are sometimes returned to the families. In such cases families are frequently forced to pay a fee to cover "state expenses" – including the cost of the bullets used in the execution. In other instances, however, the bodies are never returned, and families live for years in hope of seeing alive "disappeared" relatives who are long since dead.

To exacerbate the problem, the question of using the courts or other domestic remedies in the search for the "disappeared" does not apply in Iraq. The average Iraqi family would not dare to make inquiries with the authorities about those who have gone missing, for fear of meeting the same fate. At best, Iraqi officials deny holding the persons in question in their custody, even in cases where there were eyewitnesses to the arrests. When Amnesty International submitted to the authorities a list of "disappeared" persons in the early 1980s, asking for information about them, the government responded that the names were fictitious.

The government's responses over the years, together with the recent discoveries of mass graves in both northern and southern Iraq, have led Amnesty International to fear that many victims of "disappearance" have been killed, including thousands who "disappeared" *en masse* in specific incidents. Perhaps the best known of these was the "disappearance" of an estimated 8,000 Kurds of the Barzani clan in 1983. All were males between the ages of 8 and 70; all were arrested during the first 10 days of August 1983 in the province of Arbil and have not been seen since. One month after their unacknowledged arrests, President Saddam Hussain said in a speech that "those people were severely punished and went to Hell...".

In the spring of 1988, whole Kurdish families "disappeared" from hundreds of villages after they were rounded up by government forces – ostensibly to be transferred to areas which offered improved living conditions. Many of the villagers had surrendered to the authorities in order to benefit from officially-declared amnesties. The information available today suggests that this wave of arrests – commonly referred to as Operation Anfal – resulted in the "disappearance" of over 100,000 Kurdish civilians in the space of three to four months (some Kurdish estimates place the figure higher, at between 150,000 and 180,000 victims). Amnesty International has obtained the names of over 17,000 of them (almost 6,000 of these names were obtained by Amnesty International from relatives of the "disappeared" during a research visit to only six refugee camps in Iran in May 1990).

During negotiations with the Iraqi Government for greater autonomy in 1991, the opposition Iraqi Kurdistan Front demanded information on the fate and whereabouts of the 8,000 "disappeared" Barzanis and of the victims of Operation Anfal. The Front was reportedly made to understand by Iraqi Government negotiators that they were no longer alive.

However, it emerged after the March 1991 mass uprising in Iraq that many other people who had "disappeared" in the 1970s and 1980s were still alive. During their brief control of major cities and towns in northern and southern Iraq, opposition forces broke into prisons and detention centres, releasing the inmates. Hundreds of them had been held in secret underground detention centres with no entrance or exit visible to the outside world. Among them were people who had been arrested in the 1970s during the presidency of Ahmad Hassan al-Bakr, before President Saddam Hussain came to power.

Since the crushing of the uprising, many other people have "disappeared" after being arrested on suspicion of having participated in the uprising. They include scores of Shi'a Muslim clerics and students of religion from southern Iraq.

Extrajudicial executions

As with "disappearances", the issue of extrajudicial executions in Iraq has been difficult to investigate and to put a figure on; but it can be estimated that, in addition to those of the "disappeared" who were executed or otherwise killed, hundreds of thousands of other people have been the victims of extrajudicial executions during the 1980s. The killing of an estimated 5,000 civilians through the use of chemical weapons in the Kurdish town of Halabja in March 1988 was the most notorious example, rapidly hitting the world headlines because the authorities in neighbouring Iran were able to take journalists into the border town. The news reached the rest of the world, but within Iraq it was another matter altogether. Many Iraqis did not realise the extent of the massacre, and were not able to learn of the devastation that was wreaked in Halabja until after the March 1991 uprising.

There have undoubtedly been a number of Halabja-type killings in Iraq's recent history, some of which are only now coming to the surface. Still other incidents which Amnesty International and others placed on the public record were either disbelieved or ignored. For example, chemical weapons had been used on Iraqi civilians as early as April 1987 (and, earlier, against Iranian soldiers during the Iran-Iraq war of 1980-1988)[1], albeit on a smaller scale. Even after world-wide condemnation of the Halabja massacre, Iraq continued to use chemical weapons against its civilians, culminating in the August-September 1988 offensive which triggered the exodus of over 50,000 Kurds to southern Turkey.

In Iraq over the years, the perpetration of extrajudicial executions has been developed into a fine art. The methods used include the use of chemical weapons against civilians; mass executions by firing squad; burying people alive or tying heavy weights to their feet and pushing them into rivers while alive; poisoning through the use of thallium (a substance used in rat poison) and other poisons; bleeding prisoners and detainees to death; assassinations by shooting; and "accidental deaths" supposedly occurring in car accidents or helicopter crashes. In addition, thousands of people have died in custody in unknown circumstances, or as a result of torture.

The victims are from the same categories as those listed above with regard to "disappearances". The problems encountered in the investigation of extrajudicial executions are also the same: no domestic remedies available to relatives; a lack of access to Iraq by outside investigators; and a state of fear pervading every level of society in Iraq, preventing the victims' families and others concerned about human rights from making even the simplest inquiries.

Since the March 1991 uprising, however, more information has come to light about the nature and scale of atrocities committed in previous years. Sources of information have included thousands of documents, videotapes, films, photographs and other material seized by government opponents from intelligence and security forces buildings during the uprising. Iraqi intelligence and security personnel, many of whom were trained by advisers from the secret police of the former German Democratic Republic, the Stasi, were in the habit of recording for posterity the atrocities they committed. Some of the videotape material, for example, shows officials including government ministers talking in no uncertain terms about their plans to eliminate individuals or groups of people.

Another important source of information has been the series of mass graves recently discovered in northern Iraq. The absence of government forces in parts of the Kurdish region in the north has enabled some qualified international human rights organisations to investigate the graves. (Mass graves in southern Iraq could not be investigated because government forces remain in control there.) One mass grave on the outskirts of the Kurdish city of Arbil contained the remains of 107 Kurdish villagers killed in 1987: they were among a group of some 360 people who had survived chemical weapons attacks and had later been arrested after seeking medical treatment in Arbil's hospitals. Amnesty International had reported in 1988 that they were said to have been executed.

Amnesty International's appeals: falling on deaf ears

Over the years Amnesty International has repeatedly pressed the Iraqi Government to stop extrajudicial executions, torture, the use of the death penalty and other human rights violations and to clarify the fate of the "disappeared". Many Amnesty International members around the world have sent appeals, and trade unions, religious groups, many members of the public, and some governments have lent their support. These appeals have been consistently rebuffed by the Iraqi authorities through misinformation and blanket denials.

Only once, in 1983, was Amnesty International able to send a high-level delegation to Iraq for talks with the government. The visit was unproductive. No information of significance was obtained by Amnesty International; the government did not respond positively to any of Amnesty International's concerns; while the fact that Amnesty International visited Iraq was cited repeatedly by the government in later years as proof of its supposed openness.

Since 1985, Amnesty International's public profile on Iraq has gradually increased in line with the deterioration in the human rights situation in the country. Major documents were issued on matters such as torture (1985), the death penalty (1987), and human rights violations against children (1989). Amnesty International members around the world sent appeals to the Iraqi authorities and sought to publicize the organization's concerns.

Although these efforts helped to raise public awareness outside the country, this was small comfort to those at the receiving end of human rights abuses in Iraq. The problem did not lie in the lack of effort on Amnesty International's part: it was simply that the odds stacked up against it were too high.

In its work for human rights in Iraq, Amnesty International was facing a government that continued to sanction atrocities as a matter of policy. It was facing an apathetic United Nations (UN) that failed, through any of its machinery, to issue a single statement criticizing or condemning Iraq prior to 2 August 1990. It was facing a multitude of states whose perceived geo-political interests at the time did not accommodate any intervention with Iraq on human rights issues. During the Iran-Iraq war, the United States of America (USA) and other major Western powers, as well as their Arab allies (the Gulf States in particular), deemed it imperative to continue supporting Iraq for a variety of reasons, most important of which was to contain the spread of what they perceived as Islamic fundamentalism emanating from Iran. In addition, Iraq remained a lucrative market for the arms industry (as did Iran). After the cessation of hostilities in July 1988, there were prospects of investment to look forward to. The benefits of rebuilding a shattered economy were too great to resist, and the human rights factor was submerged by such considerations.

Attitudes changed after the invasion of Kuwait, when Amnesty International was suddenly inundated with inquiries and requests relating to the nature of the Iraqi regime and the human rights violations it had committed. This newly-found interest in human rights did not last long, however, as evidenced by the absence of a human rights component in the UN-sponsored cease-fire agreement of April 1991, as well as in the subsequent Memorandum of Understanding negotiated between the UN and the Iraqi Government. Furthermore, as the international community stood by while thousands of Iraqi civilians were being killed by their government's helicopter gunships as they fled towards Iran and Turkey in the aftermath of the uprising which followed the cease-fire, it was clear that human rights considerations had once again sunk to the bottom of the international agenda, and with remarkable speed.

The UN Commission on Human Rights: calls for action repulsed

Amnesty International has also tried to draw attention to Iraqi human rights violations at the UN and other intergovernmental organizations. Since 1986 Amnesty

International's concerns in Iraq have been repeatedly mentioned in oral statements at the annual sessions of the UN Commission on Human Rights and its Sub-Commission on Prevention of Discrimination and Protection of Minorities, but with little result.[2]

- At the 1986 session of the Commission on Human Rights, Amnesty International decried arbitrary arrests, torture and executions in Iraq. The statement caused a stir at the Commission and received some attention in the news media, but the Commission did not take any action.

- At the 1988 session of the Commission on Human Rights, Amnesty International drew attention to mass extrajudicial executions in Iraq. The statement was delivered two weeks before the Halabja killings. No action was taken by the Commission.

- At the 1988 session of the Sub-Commission on Prevention of Discrimination and Protection of Minorities, Amnesty International drew attention to extrajudicial executions perpetrated over the previous 18 months, including specific instances of mass killings of detainees and unarmed civilians by firing squad as well as the use of chemical weapons against civilians. The statement cited several chemical attacks, beginning in April 1987 and culminating in the Halabja killings.

What was unusual about this statement was that it expressed concern not only about past human rights violations but also about further violations which might be perpetrated if no action was taken. This point was prompted by fears that once Iraq's war with Iran had ended, the Iraqi Government might turn its full attention to its opponents at home. Amnesty International warned of further chemical weapons attacks and urged the Sub-Commission in the strongest terms to take action. However, the Sub-Commission did not do so.

Exercising his right of reply, the Iraqi member of the Sub-Commission said he failed to see how Amnesty International could "predict" what might happen in the future. Even as he spoke, the Iraqi Government had already launched another chemical weapons offensive in the north, reaching a peak at the end of August and in early September. Some 57,000 Kurds fled across the border into Turkey, while hundreds of others perished.

- At the 1989 session of the Commission on Human Rights, Amnesty International again cited "disappearances" and extrajudicial executions in Iraq. A few days earlier, Amnesty International had published a report detailing human rights violations against children in Iraq, including "disappearances" and killings. Because of the emotive subject of the report, which included photographs, testimonies and lists of victims, it received extensive coverage in the news media and substantially increased the pressure on the Commission to take action on Iraq.

During the debate in the Commission, many government delegations and non-governmental organisations expressed serious concern about human rights in Iraq. A resolution was drafted, supported by eleven UN member states, calling for the appointment of a Special Rapporteur to study Iraq's human rights record. The proposal failed, while at the same time Iraq was dropped from scrutiny under the confidential "1503 procedure" (see Chapter 12) by which the UN examines evidence of a consistent pattern of gross violations of human rights in a given country.

In response, Amnesty International took the unusual step of publicly criticizing the Commission on Human Rights for its failure to act. In a statement to the press, Amnesty International said that "the Commission's decision seemed irreconcilable with a genuine commitment to bring a halt to human rights violations in Iraq" and that the Commission had effectively "sent a signal to victims of abuse and their families that certain human rights situations might be immune from UN concern."

- At the 1989 session of the Sub-Commission, Amnesty International again drew attention to "disappearances" in Iraq. The Iraqi delegate attending the Sub-Commission dismissed Amnesty International's claims as fabrications and emphasized his government's supposed "willingness to cooperate with Amnesty International." In addition, the (governmental) Iraqi Human Rights Commission invited the members of the Sub-Commission to visit Iraq. This move effectively deferred any proposed action by the Sub-Commission.

- At the 1990 session of the Commission on Human Rights, Iraq was one of six countries highlighted in a statement by Amnesty International on extrajudicial executions and the failure of governments to bring perpetrators to justice. The debate at this session was again dominated by Iraq's invitation to Sub-Commission members. No action was taken by the Commission.

- The next session of the Sub-Commission began in August 1990, just four days after the Iraqi invasion of Kuwait. Four members of the Sub-Commission who had accepted the Iraqi Government's invitation to visit Iraq reported back on their findings, but at that juncture it was too little, too late. Iraq's international isolation in the aftermath of the Kuwait invasion dominated the debate, and was clearly of paramount importance in securing the adoption of a resolution recommending that the Commission on Human Rights consider the appointment of a Special Rapporteur on Iraq.

- In 1991 the Commission on Human Rights adopted the Sub-Commission's recommendation and finally agreed to appoint a Special Rapporteur. This decision was made possible by a very changed political climate. Government delegations were vocal in their condemnation of Iraq, although the focus was mainly on human rights violations in Iraqi-occupied Kuwait. Amnesty International and other non-governmental organizations sought to redress the balance by reminding the Commission of similar violations perpetrated in Iraq over many years.

- At the 1991 session of the Sub-Commission, Amnesty International said that steps were urgently needed to protect Kurds, Arab Shi'a Muslims and others at risk of further human rights violations. This point was taken up in a resolution adopted by the Sub-Commission which expressed grave concern at the "flagrant and massive violations of human rights" in Iraq, specifically mentioning the Kurdish and Shi'a Arab populations.[3]

The lack of UN action on Iraq before 1990 can be attributed to the skilful behind-the-scenes efforts of Iraq and the inclination of the majority of governments to put supposed national interest above international human rights concerns. Amnesty International and other non-governmental organizations had urged sympathetic member states to sponsor resolutions on human rights violations in Iraq, and several draft resolutions were introduced at various sessions of the Commission and the Sub-Commission. Until the invasion of Kuwait, Iraq was always able to ensure their defeat through procedural motions not to take a vote on the substantive resolutions, which were introduced by friendly member states, Jordan and Morocco in particular.[4] By the time of the 1990 session of the Commission on Human Rights, no friendly state was willing to do this, and Iraq was forced to introduce the motion itself.

It is also worth noting that, despite Iraq's apparent non-susceptibility to pressure of this kind, it always tried to reconcile the commission of atrocities at home with the maintenance of a "reasonable" image abroad. To ensure that action would be blocked, Iraq's delegates at the UN engaged in intense lobbying behind the scenes, trading votes with other member states who were under scrutiny for human rights violations. At the 1988 Sub-Commission session, the Iraqi representatives even asked Amnesty International to withdraw its statement (after it had been delivered), adding that their information suggested that Amnesty International was "in league with the Iraqi opposition at the highest level in order to overthrow the government".

Amnesty International's proposal for on-site human rights monitoring

Amnesty International's efforts to raise its concerns in the UN were not limited to those UN bodies which traditionally deal with human rights. On 8 September 1988 Amnesty International made an unprecedented appeal to the UN Security Council to act immediately to stop the massacre of Kurdish citizens by Iraqi forces. The appeal was prompted by a drastic deterioration in the human rights situation in Iraq, with thousands of Kurds killed in chemical weapons attacks, coupled with a sense of frustration at the failure of the UN Sub-Commission to act, despite Amnesty International's strong statement to the Sub-Commission in August.

Amnesty International's initiative was widely covered by the news media. It succeeded in re-focusing world attention on the plight of the Kurds, but the interest waned soon thereafter. Several Security Council members responded to Amnesty International, stressing their concern about human rights in Iraq but stopping short of saying they would take the matter further. The UN Secretary-General asked to send a team to Iraq to investigate reports of the use of chemical weapons, but Iraq's summary rejection of the proposal put an end to the matter.

In July 1991, in another unprecedented move, Amnesty International publicly called on the UN to establish an international on-site monitoring operation in Iraq to prevent further torture, killings and other abuses by government forces. It recommended that the special UN operation should be empowered to investigate abuses, ensure protection for victims and work with the government to help enforce international standards for the protection of human rights. Its powers were to include visiting detention centres, interviewing political prisoners and observing trials.

Amnesty International's proposal was sent to the UN Secretary-General. Advance copies were also sent to permanent and non-permanent members of the UN Security Council.[5]

The response was not encouraging. The Secretary-General wrote to Amnesty International reaffirming his concern about the situation in Iraq but saying that the proposal should more appropriately be dealt with by the UN Centre for Human Rights in Geneva.

Amnesty International also approached the UN Secretary-General's Executive Delegate, Prince Sadruddin Aga Khan, who had been responsible for negotiating the UN's April 1991 Memorandum of Understanding with the Iraqi Government. This agreement concerned the provision of humanitarian assistance and relief, in particular to displaced persons and returnees, and the setting up of UN sub-offices and Humanitarian Centres (UNHUCs) in Iraq. An integral part of the agreement was the deployment of a UN Guard contingent of 500 guards, to be assigned as needed to transit centres and UNHUCs. Amnesty International asked Prince Sadruddin and his aides to discuss the extent to which monitoring of the human rights situation was being carried out by this operation or could be incorporated in it. Amnesty International also recommended that the humanitarian assistance being provided should be extended to Iraq's prison population, where it was much needed.

Again, the response was not encouraging. In the face of Iraq's belligerent attitude to all things emanating from the UN, the sense was that nothing could be done on strictly human rights issues through the Memorandum of Understanding. Even so, it is likely that the presence of UN and international non-governmental organization personnel in Iraq helped prevent a massive deterioration in human rights after the crushing of the mass uprising in the spring of 1991.

As Amnesty International pressed for UN action on human rights in the second half of 1991, it became clear that the political climate, hostile to Iraq after the invasion of Kuwait, had once more changed. Those who found Amnesty International's human rights monitoring proposal not feasible were correct in saying that the political will to follow it through did not exist. In fact it had never existed with regard to action on strictly human rights issues. Hence, as mentioned earlier in this chapter, the absence of a human rights component in either the cease-fire agreement reached after the ground war or the Memorandum of Understanding.

In 1992 the UN Special Rapporteur on Iraq, who had visited the country in January, submitted his report to the Commission on Human Rights. Given the limited time and resources of his operation, his efforts were commendable. His recommendations echoed Amnesty International's proposal for on-site human rights monitoring. The Special Rapporteur recommended

> "...that the Commission on Human Rights, confronted with such an intolerable situation, does not confine itself to condemnation alone. In his view, this exceptionally grave situation demands an exceptional response – a response that would have to be considered as disproportionate in most other cases of human rights violations. Specifically, the Special Rapporteur recommends the sending to Iraq of a team of human rights monitors who would remain in Iraq until the human rights situation had drastically improved and who should be able to: (i) move freely in any part of Iraq; (ii) investigate information concerning alleged violations of human rights; (iii) visit, without prior notification and at the time of their choosing, places where persons are deprived of their liberty; and (iv) observe trials and court proceedings."[6]

Even though the Special Rapporteur urged "that no effort be spared to ensure that the monitoring system comes into being as soon as possible"[7], the Commission did not act on this recommendation in 1992. In 1993, however, it adopted a resolution on Iraq (number 1993/74) requesting the UN Secretary-General to send human rights monitors "to such locations as would facilitate improved information flows and assessment" – nearly two years after Amnesty International had made the proposal. The monitoring operation had not been established as of the time of the present report.

It should be mentioned, finally, that Amnesty International's European sections have done considerable work over the years to raise human rights violations in Iraq at the level of the European Community (EC, now known as the European Union). The European Parliament, the parliamentary body of the EC, has normally been less reticent than the UN in condemning Iraq's human rights record. A number of the resolutions adopted by it were based on information provided by Amnesty International. Apart from sending a European Parliament delegation to southern Turkey to investigate allegations of the use of chemical weapons against Iraqi Kurds in the 1988 offensive, these resolutions did not usually lead to action on the part of EC member states. However, at a time when a "conspiracy of silence" about the human rights situation in Iraq prevailed, these public statements at the European level had rather more value than the dozen or so resolutions adopted by the UN Security Council after 2 August 1990.

CHAPTER 2

SRI LANKA: "DISAPPEARANCE" AND MURDER AS TECHNIQUES OF COUNTER-INSURGENCY

"Disappearances" and political killings had reached tragic proportions in Sri Lanka by the late 1980s, after several years of increasing numbers of people falling victim to these gross violations of human rights. In the northeastern part of the country, government forces confronting an armed Tamil separatist movement evolved tactics of "disappearance" and political killings to sow terror and avoid accountability. In the south, where the security forces sought to suppress an armed insurgency within the majority Sinhalese community, tens of thousands of people are believed to have been murdered under the cover of "disappearance" between 1987 and 1990.

Resort by government security forces to widespread extrajudicial executions and "disappearances" in confronting armed opposition is not new in Sri Lanka. But in recent years such violations escalated almost beyond measure, and armed opposition has intensified. Over the years, a progression is evident from the blatant commission of these violations by uniformed personnel to more sophisticated, systematic methods that provided a means of covering up far more widespread abuse of human rights.

Unlike Iraq (see Chapter 1), where the repression over the years has been so pervasive that no expression of democratic opposition was possible, Sri Lanka has retained a system of parliamentary democracy throughout the troubles of the 1980s and 1990s. Its normal legal system contains safeguards which should prevent "disappearances" and extrajudicial executions, but these provisions have been undermined by the fact that the country has been under an almost continuous state of emergency since May 1983. Official emergency measures override the safeguards contained in the normal law and have granted sweeping powers to the security forces. In addition, there has been blatant intimidation of lawyers, relatives and others attempting to take remedial action.

The massive spate of "disappearances" and extrajudicial executions in the south in the late 1980s were illegal and clandestine elements of a counter-insurgency campaign which many in government appear to believe to have been necessary and effective. In 1990 the violence by the armed opposition in the south subsided. The insurgent leaders, together with many thousands of other people, had been wiped out. In the northeast, however, the campaign against Tamil separatists has been markedly unsuccessful. Far from the number of armed separatists falling over the years, the government has lost control of large areas entirely and the main separatist movement, the Liberation Tigers of Tamil Eelam (LTTE), has grown from a small group of armed men in the late 1970s to a fighting force of many thousands of men and women.

The emergence of killings and "disappearances"

In northeastern Sri Lanka, where most people belong to the Tamil minority, Tamil separatists have fought since the late 1970s for secession from the Sinhalese-dominated state. Conflict escalated in mid-1983 after Tamil separatists in the north ambushed and killed 13 government soldiers. There was a wave of retaliatory violence against Tamil people living in the south, and in the north security forces were reported to be killing unarmed Tamil civilians at random, apparently in retaliation for the deaths of their colleagues. Over the next years, further reprisal killings were committed by army and police officers after members of their own forces had been killed by Tamil militants. The reprisal killings were committed openly by men in uniform; "disappearances" were almost unknown at first.

One response of the government forces to the activities of armed Tamil groups was to arrest many young Tamil men. Some were released within a few weeks, and although relatives were not normally informed where the arrested person was being held, many families were able to establish their arrested relatives' whereabouts. However, by late 1984 a new tactic of the security forces was evident: in an increasing number of cases where a person had been arrested by the security forces in front of witnesses, those forces denied holding the prisoner and their relatives were never able to establish their whereabouts. Whole groups of young men, who had been arrested together, simply "disappeared".

This new tactic of "disappearance" developed in Sri Lanka soon after the creation of a new police commando unit, the Special Task Force (STF). Members of this unit, as well as members of the army, were frequently seen taking into custody young men who then "disappeared". Testimony after testimony by witnesses described how the "disappeared" had been rounded up in groups by the army or the STF and taken away. Less frequently police, air force and navy personnel were described as the arresting authority.

Testimonies from released prisoners described the torture and killing of many prisoners in army or STF detention camps, and the secret disposal of bodies, often by burning. "Disappearance" appeared to be used for two purposes: it facilitated torture without accountability, and it concealed the killing of prisoners.

In the northeast the number who have "disappeared" or been extrajudicially executed to date runs into the thousands. From 1984 to mid-1987, Amnesty International recorded over 680 "disappearances" in the northeast. From mid-1987 to March 1990 the Indian Peace Keeping Force (IPKF) was responsible for the security of the northeast under the terms of the Indo-Sri Lanka Accord. During this period Amnesty International recorded 43 "disappearances" there for which the IPKF were believed responsible. After armed conflict resumed between government forces and the LTTE in the northeast in June 1990, the numbers reported to have "disappeared" or been extrajudicially executed reached thousands within months.

After the IPKF took control of the northeast in mid-1987, the Sri Lanka army and the STF were redeployed in the south, where the government was increasingly concerned about mobilization by the *Janatha Vimukthi Peramuna* (JVP), People's Liberation Front, a Sinhalese militant party. The accord between the governments of India and Sri Lanka – which provided for some devolution of power to provincial councils and brought the IPKF to the northeast – provided new momentum for the JVP, which had for years expressed a fear of Indian imperialism. The JVP began to target for assassination members of the ruling party, members of leftist parties which had supported the accord, members of the security forces and others, including relatives of targeted individuals. As their campaign of terror gradually mounted, they were able to command widespread strikes and stoppages, enforced by threats to kill those who refused to obey the strike call.

It was in this context that tactics of counter-terror, mirroring those of the JVP, were increasingly used by the security forces and other groups aligned with the government, and that there was such a massive rise in the numbers of extrajudicial executions and "disappearances". As the number of reported "disappearances" soared, bodies – mutilated or burned beyond recognition – began to be dumped in public places, by roadsides, in cemeteries or in rivers, or burned on pyres of rubber tyres. Some of these bodies may have been those of the "disappeared", but their identities usually could not be established.

Plainclothes pro-government "death squads" appeared under various names, echoing the JVP in issuing death threats to individuals and putting up threatening posters in public places. Like the JVP, they sometimes placed posters by dead bodies, claiming responsibility for the deaths of those whose bodies were dumped.

The government consistently claimed these groups were "pro-government vigilantes" over whom they had no control, and some of the killings were attributed to the JVP. But gradually evidence emerged indicating that, in many cases, the perpetrators were police or military personnel operating in civilian dress.

In addition, the government decided to distribute weapons to a range of civilian groups – including home guards, bodyguards for politicians, as well as members of militant groups with no more than a common enemy to link them to the government – to fight at one remove from direct governmental responsibility. The government provided no measures to ensure adequate control over these forces, and it has failed to hold members of these groups accountable for abuses they have committed. Such proxy forces have thus had much the same degree of immunity from prosecution as that enjoyed by the regular forces of the military and police with which they collaborated.

As in the northeast, many of the southern "disappeared" must be presumed to have been killed in custody. However, whereas in the northeast bodies of the victims were rarely found in the period from 1983 to 1987, in the south unidentifiable bodies, and sometimes severed limbs or heads, were regularly displayed in public as part of the campaign of counter-terror. This pattern of mutilation and display, together with the use of plainclothes squads, was transferred to the east when the military returned there from the south after the resumption of hostilities between the government and the LTTE in June 1990.

A staggering number of people were extrajudicially executed or have "disappeared". Tens of thousands – just how many tens of thousands is not known – "disappeared" in the south between 1987 and 1990, almost certainly the victims of extrajudicial execution, while others are known victims of extrajudicial execution. This period of violence was the most extreme in Sri Lanka's 20th-century history to date, and it was in this period that the so-called vigilante groups appeared. Since June 1990, however, when direct conflict resumed between Sri Lanka government forces and the LTTE over 3,000 people are estimated to have "disappeared", as practices of government forces in the south between 1987 and 1990 were transferred to the east in the initial months of the fighting.

The destruction of domestic safeguards and remedies

Over the years a climate of impunity appeared to develop within the security forces, reinforced by the fact that the government took no action to make security forces personnel accountable for human rights violations. Normal legal safeguards to protect against "disappearances" and extrajudicial executions were eroded by the granting of special powers to the security forces, and many victims and their relatives who attempted to seek redress found themselves intimidated. The government appeared unwilling to prosecute members of the security forces responsible for gross human rights violations, even after an inquiry had been held,[1] and introduced indemnity legislation.

In the face of armed opposition by Tamil secessionists in the late 1970s the Government of Sri Lanka gave extraordinary powers to the security forces. The Prevention of Terrorism Act (PTA) was introduced in July 1979, initially for a period of three years. It was later amended and incorporated into the normal law of Sri Lanka. In addition, a nationwide state of emergency has been in force since 18 May 1983, apart from nearly six months (January to June 1989) when it was lifted by President Ranasinghe Premadasa following his election as President. During a declared state of emergency, which has to be renewed monthly by parliament, the Emergency (Miscellaneous Provisions and Powers) Regulations are in force. These regulations are issued by the President under the Public Security Ordinance.

Both the PTA and the Emergency Regulations give the security forces wide powers to arrest suspected opponents of the government and detain them incommunicado and without charge or trial for long periods – conditions which provide a ready context for deaths in custody, "disappearance" and torture. Many thousands of people have been detained under these provisions. During some periods, Emergency Regulations have also been issued to permit the security forces to dispose of bodies without post-mortem or inquest, thereby enabling them even more readily to cover up their commission of deliberate and unlawful killings. Even when this provision has not been in force, the regulations have provided a special, secret inquest procedure which could be used to facilitate the cover-up of deliberate killings in custody.

The government's willingness to condone the actions of the security forces and government officials, even when they have committed gross abuses, was underlined in December 1988 when the Indemnity (Amendment) Act was passed days before a presidential election was to take place. This act gives immunity from prosecution to all members of the security forces, members of the government and government servants involved in enforcing law and order between 1 August 1977 and 16 December 1988 provided that their actions were carried out "in good faith" and in the public interest. The act also indemnifies any other person who can use the defence that he or she acted "in good faith" under the authority of a government official during this period.

The government's failure to prosecute members of the security forces responsible for human rights violations has contributed to a climate of impunity. Amnesty International does not know of a single case in which a member of the security forces was prosecuted for human rights violations committed in the northeast in the 1980s. In the south after mid-1987, a few cases of torture and extrajudicial execution received widespread publicity and provoked a public outcry; investigations were held and the alleged perpetrators prosecuted, but none of these cases has yet reached a conviction for murder. One of these trials – for the killing of a schoolboy in Teldeniya in June 1989 – was discontinued, and the charges withdrawn, after witnesses failed to appear for the prosecution. Material collected by Amnesty International indicates that they had been murdered or threatened with death if they gave evidence, but no official investigation was held to establish why they failed to appear in court. Only after the international community began to put more pressure on Sri Lanka for its human rights record did the government institute an independent Commission of Inquiry into a massacre by soldiers at Kokkadichcholai in the east in June 1991 – the first inquiry of its kind ever held in Sri Lanka. A military tribunal found the commanding officer guilty of failure to control his troops and illegal disposal of the bodies, and he was dismissed from service. The other 19 soldiers under trial were acquitted. At the time of writing, 23 soldiers had been charged for murdering villagers at Mailanthanai in August 1992, and were being tried by a civilian court. However, the case had been moved to a court some distance from where the killings took place, making it very hard for witnesses to attend.

Victims and their relatives have faced enormous difficulties in seeking redress. No effective legal remedy exists to trace a person who has "disappeared". Hundreds of relatives have filed *habeas corpus* petitions in attempts to trace "disappeared" prisoners, but the procedure has proved slow and ineffective. Lawyers and witnesses in these cases began to be murdered or threatened with death in 1989, and access to *habeas corpus* was effectively closed for many months as lawyers were reluctant to risk taking on such cases.

During the purge of the JVP in the south, the government appeared to become more directly involved in security forces strategies. Some "death squads" were apparently associated with senior members of the ruling party, for example. In the south, the subversive threat came from within the majority community itself: it was close to home and threatened the lives of ruling party politicians and their families. The Tamil separatists, in contrast, did not pose so direct a threat as the JVP to the continuing power of the government and to the lives of ruling party politicians and their families. Similarly, families of members of the security forces came under threat from the JVP.

It was in this context that the government and its security council appears to have encouraged counter-terrorism – state terror to fight opposition terror – as the way to destroy the JVP. There were different phases, with "political" as against "military" approaches predominating at different times. Emergency law was already in place to be applied, and extended, in this new situation.

The fact that such unprecedented numbers of people were victims of "disappearance" and extrajudicial execution in the south between 1987 and 1990 carries various implications, both for the domestic response to the tragedy and for the response of international agencies. Local and international human rights organizations have been overwhelmed by the numbers involved: thorough documentation of the full number of individual cases has so far proved impossible, although details have been recorded in thousands of cases. Pressing for accountability also becomes problematic: what kind of investigation is sought? How can the fate of so many individuals be clarified in practice? And from the government's point of view, the sheer scale of abuse increases the necessity for impunity to be maintained for acts committed in this period, both because such a large proportion of the security apparatus is likely to be implicated and because politicians themselves may be implicated. Indeed, when Amnesty International submitted 32 recommendations for human rights safeguards to the Sri Lankan Government in 1991, the two which the government rejected were both concerned with impunity: the government refused to permit a Presidential Commission of Inquiry into Involuntary Removals to investigate "disappearances" which occurred before 11 January 1991, and it refused to repeal the Indemnity Act.[2]

Violence by the armed opposition and human rights

The context of armed opposition has been crucial in both the northeast and the south. It has provided the government with a rhetorical claim of justification for "excesses in defence of democracy"; it has allowed confusion to be sown over issues of responsibility, particularly within the international community and the media; it has posed problems for local and international human rights organizations, who have been accused of supporting terrorism and of bias when they seek to uphold governmental responsibility under international human rights law.

Violence by the armed opposition has intensified over the years. In the north in the late 1970s and early 1980s, Tamil militants tended to attack a limited range of state targets, as well as other Tamils whom they considered "traitors" by standing as candidates for, or publicly supporting, the ruling party. More generalized attacks against civilian targets by the militants – bombs at bus stands, for example, or attacks on Sinhalese or Muslim communities – came in later years. As the security forces reacted with repressive measures against the Tamil population in general in certain areas, their acts seemed to create more and more of the militants they were ostensibly intended to suppress.

The LTTE were not the only group of armed Tamil separatists at this time: during the 1980s several militant groups formed, with splits and factions developing, and alliances between them changing. Although they were often thought of collectively from the outside as "Tamil Tigers" or Tamil separatists, hostility between certain groups was intense at times. Abuses committed by Tamil militants within the Tamil community – torture of prisoners from rival militant groups, for example, or as disciplinary action within a group – remained closed to public view.

Today, now that one group – the LTTE – has excluded almost all expression of dissent within the area it controls, and has been publicly exposed as guilty of grave abuses of human rights, a small group of concerned Tamils have asked whether this situation might have been prevented if the international human rights community had begun to address abuse by the LTTE earlier. Local human rights workers who had carefully documented "disappearances" and extrajudicial executions by government forces remained silent about abuse within the Tamil community, perhaps sometimes because it would have been too dangerous for them to speak out, but also, according to some, because of fear of tarnishing their community's international image and cause.

In the south, too, the repressive tactics of the security forces may have encouraged the growth of armed militancy for a time. Certainly the JVP, like the LTTE, campaigned on human rights issues, citing the brutality of government forces in support of its anti-governmental stance.

There are several significant differences between the LTTE and the JVP which have implications both for the nature of the government's response to them, as already described, and for human rights organizations which seek to address their abuses. The LTTE is a secessionist movement: it does not seek to overthrow the Colombo government, but to create a separate state structure within a defined area of the country. The JVP, on the other hand, was "the enemy within", originating inside the majority Sinhalese population and seeking to overthrow the government and take power itself.

Unlike the LTTE, the JVP did not have strong international connections. With many thousands of Tamils living abroad, the LTTE has "front" organizations – promoting Tamil culture, lobbying on human rights issues and other themes, as well as providing funds – in several parts of the world. The JVP had no equivalent to this international Tamil lobby. It appears to have been a remarkably self-contained, local organization, armed largely with weaponry it seized itself. Although it brought the country's economy to a standstill at times, it did not reach a point where it sought international recognition for its cause or for its legitimacy.

The international response

Despite the evident intensification of human rights violations in Sri Lanka during the 1980s, the international community was slow to take action on the matter. To highlight the emergence of a new pattern of abuse, in September 1986 Amnesty International launched an international campaign calling attention to the "disappearance" of Tamil youths in the northeast. In March 1987 the UN Commission on Human Rights adopted a weak resolution on Sri Lanka calling on all parties to renounce violence, observe humanitarian norms and reach a negotiated settlement, shortly before the situation in the northeast was dramatically changed by the arrival of the IPKF.

No effective preventive action was taken internationally while tens of thousands of youths in southern Sri Lanka were being killed or "disappearing" in 1989 and 1990. Most concerned foreign ministries appeared to prefer quiet diplomacy to public condemnation in this period, and motions on Sri Lanka failed to gain adequate support in UN bodies. But after the events in the south, at least, when the massive and unprecedented scale of gross governmental abuse became clear and some of the webs of official misinformation had been swept aside, the European Parliament, Western aid donor countries and others were stirred to public denunciation. Western donor countries threatened to withdraw aid on human rights grounds, and this threat in particular has prompted the government to institute various inquiries and procedures concerned with human rights protection. However, the period of greatest abuse remains excluded from the scope of any inquiry so far, and most of the trials and inquiries that are in progress (some after several years) have not reached final conclusions.

During 1989 and 1990, and culminating in another international campaign in September 1990, Amnesty International constantly sought to publicize the intensified human rights violations in the south. For the first time in Sri Lanka, thousands of "disappearances" and extrajudicial executions were being committed by people in civilian dress whom the government falsely claimed to be either "vigilantes" outside their control or members of the JVP. As noted, these so-called vigilantes imitated methods of the JVP and aimed to create a climate of terror to counter the terror the JVP.

Amnesty International's statements and appeals in this period provoked an angry, confrontational response from the government. The Minister of State for Defence accused Amnesty International of being a "terrorist organization", biased against governments and advancing the cause of terrorists. As time went by, confrontation, denial and a refusal to enter into any dialogue gradually gave way to a more conciliatory position as international opinion mobilised around human rights matters. Particularly because of its linkage to aid, the Sri Lankan authorities recognized that they had to address human rights in some visible way.

This recognition, however, has not been made without continued expressions of grievance. Within the country the debate on human rights remains highly politicized. The linkage of human rights with aid has provoked complaint in Sri Lanka, as elsewhere, of neo-colonialism and interference in the country's internal affairs, and the former President Premadasa repeatedly stated his commitment to "poverty alleviation" over and above civil and political rights.

Since the period of greatest abuse in the south, the problem remains of pressing for accountability after the event. The observance of international human rights law depends upon governments upholding human rights standards and providing remedies when violations have been committed. The difficulties of calling to account a government which appears to believe that its actions were justified and necessary are obvious. So far there has been no movement towards redress for the past – for victims of violations in the northeast over the past decade and in the south more recently. Continuing vigilance and action by the international community may be necessary to ensure that steps the government takes with regard to human rights protection for the future are effectively implemented, and are not permitted to exist merely on paper.

The government's response to international pressure has included a signal to the security forces that restraint is required, and a new acknowledgment that gross violations had indeed been committed by government forces. First, in late 1989, the International Committee of the Red Cross (ICRC) was granted access to the country. Then invitations were issued to the UN Working Group on Enforced or Involuntary Disappearances ("Working Group on Disappearances") and to the UN Special Rapporteur on summary or arbitrary executions[3]. In March 1991 Amnesty International was able to visit Sri Lanka for the first time since 1982, and in December 1991 the government announced its acceptance of 30 out of 32 recommendations for human rights protection offered by the organization. By November 1992, however, when Amnesty International visited again to assess the implementation of the recommendations, very few of them had been implemented, and arrests followed by "disappearance" continued to be reported from the east, in particular, although the overall level of "disappearances" was reduced considerably from the previous year[4].

Despite these developments there remains a need for caution in assessing the effect of international pressure on the human rights situation. The situation has certainly improved – but it must be remembered that an appalling record set the baseline for improvement, and the numbers of extrajudicial executions and "disappearances" which continued to be reported in 1992 would be considered high in many other countries. In such situations, where there is clear sensitivity to international opinion, the risk is that a government will create mechanisms ostensibly designed to protect human rights as a palliative to what it sees as an international public relations problem, without making underlying structural, institutional or policy changes which address the causes of human rights violations. In Sri Lanka, the government still has to demonstrate that it is genuinely committed to human rights protection by ensuring that the safeguards it has said it will introduce are implemented in practice, and by fully acknowledging and providing redress for past abuses.

CHAPTER 3

COLOMBIA:
STRATEGIES FOR EVADING
ACCOUNTABILITY

Clandestine military units operating as "death squads" made their first recorded appearance in Colombia in 1978. Coinciding with the emergence of the "death squads" the numbers of political prisoners began to decline while the numbers of recorded "disappearances" and extrajudicial executions increased significantly throughout the 1980s. Extrajudicial executions reached a peak of 3,500 in 1988 and have been perpetrated at a rate of over 1,500 per year since then. Over 1,500 people are believed to have "disappeared" after detention between 1978 and 1992.

Moving beyond the task of fighting to defeat armed opposition groups by legitimate means, the armed forces engaged secretly in the physical elimination of members of a wide spectrum of the legal political opposition and other non-combatant civilians in areas of guerrilla activity. In so doing, they evolved a series of techniques to avoid accountability for their illegal and criminal acts.

Like Sri Lanka, Colombia has remained a formal democracy throughout the 1980s and 1990s. Individuals in the judiciary and the executive and legislative branches of the government have at times acted with independence and initiative in trying to counter the abuses perpetrated by the security forces, but their efforts overall have fallen considerably short of stopping the killings and "disappearances". At the same time, the government has abetted the armed forces by presenting the Colombian situation to the world in ways intended to deflect international criticism. Until sufficient political will is created in the government to confront and control the actions of the security forces, "disappearances" and political killings are certain to continue.

The rise of assassinations and "disappearances" and the proliferation of "death squads" and paramilitary organizations

In 1978 shadowy "death squads" made their first recorded appearance in Colombia, threatening lawyers of political prisoners and members of the Supreme Court who gave dissenting opinions against the anti-terrorist Security Statute enacted in 1978. From 1980, as the number of political detainees began to decline, Amnesty International received increasing reports of torture and killing of peasant farmers in conflict zones by Colombian army counter-insurgency forces and paramilitary groups working with them, and there was a significant rise in "disappearances".

In 1982 most political prisoners were freed under a general amnesty. Coinciding with the freeing of political prisoners, there was a marked upsurge in the number of incidents in which members of political opposition groups, trade unions, and former political prisoners were seized and killed in operations attributed by the security services to supposedly independent "death squads".

After the government embarked on a peace process, culminating in a cease-fire in 1984 with all but one of the major guerrilla movements, the correlation between the declining numbers of political prisoners and increasing numbers of extrajudicial executions and "disappearances" became even more apparent. Resistance to a political solution to the civil conflict was strong within the military, and military officers expressed frustration at the suspension in 1982 of their power to try political prisoners in military courts. While the number of political suspects detained by the army and turned over to the civilian courts remained low, the number of "disappearances" and political killings attributed to phantom "death squads" grew dramatically. Certain left-wing political movements were selected for a campaign of elimination, and many of their members were targeted and killed even before the peace process ended in late 1985.[1]

For such covert and illegal activities to be successful, a means had to be devised by which the army could not be held accountable for its actions. This means was the creation of the supposedly independent "death squads" whose appearance and proliferation coincided with the dramatic increase in "disappearances" and extrajudicial executions in the early 1980's. By 1982 abuses attributed to the "death squad" known as *Muerte a Secuestradores* (MAS), Death to Kidnappers, had spread throughout the country. Although military spokespersons claimed that MAS was an independent group created by the criminal underworld to combat left-wing guerrillas, an investigation by the Colombian Procurator General in 1983 found that 59 serving members of the armed forces had been actively involved in incidents attributed to MAS. In a report to Congress in 1986 the Procurator General referred to MAS as "an authentic paramilitary movement" and said that military officers used it to "do unofficially what cannot be done officially".

In 1987 the Colombian Interior Minister, César Gaviria, who became President in 1990, revealed to Congress the existence of some 140 paramilitary organizations operating in the country. The origin of many of these can be traced to the civilian "self-defence" squads created by the Colombian armed forces to act as auxiliaries to the regular armed forces in counter-insurgency operations. Army brigade commanders and intelligence units attached to brigades and battalions in conflict areas recruited, armed, trained and supported paramilitary "self-defence" squads, while large landowners, industrialists and, later, drug-traffickers lent them economic support.

A legal basis for the formation of paramilitary "self-defence" squads was provided by Law 48 of 1968 which among other things empowered the armed forces to provide military weapons to civilians and to create peasant defence groups. The activities of such groups, however, were not confined to protecting their members' homes and families from guerrilla attacks but included active participation in counter-insurgency "search and destroy" operations in areas where the population was considered sympathetic towards armed opposition groups.[2]

In recent years, the "self-defence" groups have increasingly merged with private armies of gunmen formed by drug-traffickers. There has often been a community of interests between drug-traffickers and local army commanders: both sought to eliminate members of rural communities who might sympathize with or support armed insurgents. The money provided by drug-traffickers to the army's rural paramilitary apparatus permitted the development of a vast paramilitary network capable of coordinated operations throughout the country. In 1988 responsibility for over 80 massacres and hundreds of individual killings of rural workers and left-wing political activists was attributed by independent and official investigators to the paramilitary organizations. In many of these cases evidence also emerged of the direct or indirect participation in the killings of senior military officers.

In 1989 the Colombian Government issued decrees designed to combat "bands of hired killers, groups of self-defence or private justice" and suspended the army's authority to provide military-issue weapons to civilians. However, the decrees were not backed by effective action to disband the politically and militarily powerful paramilitary organizations or to show that the army was itself committed to dismantling the paramilitary structures that had aided its counter-insurgency campaigning. Consequently, paramilitary forces continued to commit widespread human rights violations with impunity. Peace agreements with four guerrilla organizations and the imprisonment of several leading drug-traffickers who had financially supported paramilitary organizations, led to a partial respite in their activities in 1990 and 1991. However, by 1992 the number of serious human rights violations committed by paramilitary forces again increased as several groups were reactivated and new groups were formed with the support of the Colombian armed forces. In some areas of the country, particularly the central Magdalena Medio region, paramilitary forces once again openly engaged in joint operations with counter-insurgency units of the Colombian army.

Patterns of extrajudicial executions

Members and suspected sympathizers of guerrilla groups have not been the only victims of extrajudicial executions. Non-combatant civilians have been massacred during counter-insurgency operations and members of legal opposition groups, union leaders, teachers and peasant and Indian community leaders have been targeted for assassination by both regular armed forces and paramilitary "death squads", apparently because of their leadership role and their political beliefs, real or imputed. In recent years journalists and others attempting to investigate human rights violations, including members of the judiciary and other public officials, have increasingly been singled out for murder.

In urban areas many victims are killed by assailants on high-powered motorcycles or by individual assassins in public places, including restaurants, airports and on board aircraft. Others are gunned down by assailants who break into their homes or are seized in the street and forced into cars, their bodies generally being found hours or days later. Many of the victims abducted are tortured, and their bodies are mutilated or burnt by fire or with acid before being dumped by roadsides or in rivers. Assassins, generally heavily armed men in civilian clothes, almost invariably escape, sometimes in full view of uniformed police or army personnel who do nothing to intervene.

The killing of political and community activists has frequently been the culmination of a campaign of harassment, often in the form of written or telephone threats. In 1987 death threats became so prevalent that "death lists", including the names of many prominent public figures, were published in the national press. Some of those who receive death threats request official protection which, in the case of prominent public figures, is usually provided – at least temporarily. Others leave the country. Judicial and police authorities seem unable or unwilling to try to discover who is responsible for the threats or to give adequate protection to those threatened.

In the countryside, an increasing number of non-combatant civilians in remote areas have been killed during military counter-insurgency campaigns. Some have died during aerial bombardments in which civilian communities appear to have been deliberately targeted. Others have been detained and killed by army infantry patrols who then, frequently, claim the victims were guerrillas, were killed in combat, or were killed by a guerrilla organization.[3] Peasants who refuse to collaborate with paramilitary forces or to pay "taxes" levied by the paramilitary to finance their operations, have also frequently been killed.

Sporadic incidents of multiple killings in the mid-1980s developed from 1988 into a new pattern of attacks on groups of unarmed civilians which left hundreds of people dead throughout the country. Although the likely motives varied, many killings appeared to be part of a campaign to terrify entire communities or sectors of society or to punish them for their perceived party allegiances. Some attacks appeared to be in reprisal for guerrilla attacks against army personnel.

The mode of attack was similar throughout the country. Heavily armed men, at times dressed in military-type uniforms and with faces painted or masked, arrived in convoys of vehicles in remote rural hamlets or small towns. Villagers were sometimes forced to assemble in the town plaza or on a football field, whereupon victims were selected, often from lists, and then taken away and shot. In other instances assailants opened fire on assembled villagers as they participated in community festivals or sports events. Before leaving, the assailants often painted graffiti on village walls claiming the killings in the name of a "death squad", or shouted abuse and anti-communist slogans at villagers. On other occasions graffiti appeared after an attack, warning survivors to remain silent or face a return visit. Many multiple attacks were preceded by threats to clean up the area of "communists and guerrilla sympathizers", appearing in the form of graffiti or pamphlets pushed under people's doors at night.

In the cities people branded as "social undesirables", including homosexuals, prostitutes, minor drug peddlers and addicts, vagrants, "street children", and the mentally retarded have also been killed. Murder operations directed against these people are routinely termed "social clean-up operations" (*operaciones de limpieza social*). They are most frequently attributed to police officers (who in press reports are often characterized as "off-duty") or to collaborators working on information provided by them. Statistics for "clean-up" operations are harder to obtain than for politically connected killings, as the identity of the victims is often unknown. These deaths often go unreported or are not registered, although between April and November 1992, local human rights groups recorded 298 murders attributed to "social clean-up" operations by "death squads".

The large cities including Cali, Bogotá, Medellín and Barranquilla are most affected by these killings. Assailants often gun down their victims from motorcycles or the cabs of trucks. In other cases, victims are rounded up from the streets and forced into trucks; their bodies, frequently tortured or mutilated, are found later dumped by the roadside or in rubbish tips.

Several of the guerrilla organizations active in Colombia have also committed violent abuses and have committed frequent violations of the principles of the international humanitarian law of armed conflict. Victims of deliberate and arbitrary killings by guerrilla movements have included people suspected of being informers for the armed forces, petty criminals, members of rival groups, peasant and local government officials suspected of collaborating with paramilitary organizations and community leaders who refused to accept the authority of the guerrillas in areas they claimed to control. Guerrilla organizations such as the *Fuerzas Armadas Revolucionarias de Colombia*, Revolutionary Armed Forces of Colombia, and the *Ejército de Liberación Nacional*, National Liberation Army, have also executed hostages when ransom demands have not been met.

In poor areas of the large cities, particularly Medellín, Cúcuta and Bogotá, *Milicias Populares*, Popular Militias, believed to be backed by the guerrilla organizations have been responsible for numerous execution-style killings. Among those targeted by the Militias are local drug-dealers, police and army informants and people accused of crimes against the shanty town residents.

"Disappearance" as a means of ensuring impunity

The use of the technique of "disappearance" to evade accountability has been well described by the Colombian Procurator General, Dr Carlos Arrieta Padilla:

> "Perpetrators plan the criminal act [of 'disappearance'] with premeditation, leaving no trace, sign or evidence that would permit the circumstances surrounding the act to be established. They calculatedly rely on the mantle of impunity and on the fear of relatives and witnesses preventing them denouncing the 'disappearance' themselves, preferring to do it through third parties; all of which means the investigation of this kind of human rights violation is particularly difficult."

Attempting to draw a composite picture of "disappearances" in Colombia is difficult because of the complexity of the phenomenon. However, some common threads can be detected.

- Victims of "disappearance" in rural areas are principally peasant farmers associated with left-wing political movements and civic leaders in rural community organizations in areas where military or paramilitary forces are engaged in counter-insurgency operations. They are likely to have been targeted because of a perceived link with guerrilla organizations, or simply for refusing to cooperate with the army or paramilitary forces.

- Other "disappearances" are a result of the Colombian army's practice of co-opting local peasants as expendable guides or porters who are forced to accompany the patrol for several days or weeks. They may suffer ill-treatment or death at the hands of the troops, or be killed in confrontations with guerrilla forces. Others, captured on suspicion of collaborating with the insurgents, have been forced to wear army uniforms or hoods and to accompany army patrols to villages to identify possible guerrilla sympathizers; these captives are often killed once their usefulness is ended. As military authorities routinely deny any knowledge of captured persons, even of people seized as guides, and as their whereabouts generally remain unknown, the captives "disappear".

- Occasionally groups of "disappeared" prisoners are located by judicial or Public Ministry officials in unacknowledged detention in military bases. However, the vast majority of the "disappeared" are probably executed by regular or paramilitary forces within hours or days of being taken captive. Bodies are dumped in rivers or chasms or transferred to another municipality or province before dumping, where, if found, they are buried as "NN" (*no nombre*, no name). The victims' bodies are frequently mutilated to hinder identification.

- Although the majority of "disappearances" occur in remote rural areas undergoing counter-insurgency operations, a significant number of people have also "disappeared" in Colombia's towns and cities. According to evidence received from survivors, from police and army defectors and from investigations conducted by the Procurator General's Public Ministry, the forces mainly responsible for "disappearances" in urban areas are the National Police Intelligence Unit (F-2) and the Colombian army's intelligence division (E-2).

- There is no evidence to suggest that "disappeared" prisoners are routinely held for long periods, as has happened in some other countries. However, according to survivors who have reappeared, most often after escaping, some of the "disappeared" have been held for days or weeks, usually in isolation, in small farms or in vehicles specially adapted as interrogation centres. There they are subjected to intensive interrogation under torture.

- The decision whether to interrogate at length captives whose detention has been denied or to kill them outright probably depends on whether the victim is thought to have information needed by the intelligence services. Victims of extrajudicial execution whose bodies are found and identified frequently appear to have been killed within hours of their capture. Although they too have often been severely tortured, this does not appear to be meant to extract information; some survivors of attempted murders of this kind have said they were tortured without interrogation. The almost ritualistic brutality with which victims are killed appears rather to be designed as a mechanism of terror.

The reluctance of witnesses and relatives of the "disappeared" to report cases because of intimidation and fear of reprisals is well-founded. Relatives of "disappeared" prisoners attempting to seek redress have themselves been subjected to arbitrary arrest, "disappearance" or killing, and attempts to obstruct the investigation of "dis-appearances" often extends to the intimidation even of judicial and Public Ministry officials.

Techniques of impunity

The attribution of killings to "death squads" and paramilitary forces, and the concealment of evidence through "disappearance", are techniques which have enabled the Colombian security forces to act with impunity, avoiding accountability for their crimes. Other techniques have included denials, misinformation, and the obstruction of attempts to investigate "disappearances" and extrajudicial executions and to bring the perpetrators to justice.

Denials and misinformation are the armed forces' initial line of defence. Victims of extrajudicial executions perpetrated by the armed forces or paramilitary forces are described as guerrillas killed in combat, or the killings are attributed to guerrilla organizations or drug-traffickers. Military commanders claim that accusations against armed forces personnel form part of a campaign of black propaganda orchestrated by guerrilla groups to undermine public confidence in the army and the police. Human rights workers are accused of being tools of subversion used by the armed opposition to attack the forces of law.

When armed forces personnel are implicated during judicial investigations of human rights violations, the military authorities have ignored arrest warrants and other demands of the civilian courts and have claimed military jurisdiction.[4] The result is to abort the investigation.

Over the years the military courts have persistently failed to conduct impartial proceedings or to hold police and military personnel criminally liable for human rights violations, although the military courts are not known to be incompetent when enforcing military discipline over offences and infractions unrelated to counter-insurgency operations. In the vast majority of cases taken over by military courts, charges are dropped or those implicated are acquitted.

It is not only the courts' verdicts which illustrate the way armed forces personnel responsible for gross human rights violations are shielded from justice by their superiors. Military authorities routinely fail to enforce arrest warrants against those implicated, even when – exceptionally – the warrant is issued by a military court. In the case of a much-publicized massacre by the army of a family in Fusagasugá in August 1991, the military court judge took the unusual step of issuing arrest warrants against a sub-lieutenant, a sergeant and five privates. Several months later it transpired that at least one of the soldiers supposedly in custody awaiting trial for the killings in Fusagasugá was not in detention at all. In March 1992 the Colombian press reported that he had been arrested and charged with the killing days before of a further three people, including a pregnant woman, in Bogotá – a crime without apparent political motivation.

Under the Colombian Code of Military Justice civil representation is only permitted in cases under investigation by military courts at the discretion of the judge. In practice this means that victims of human rights violations and their lawyers are rarely party to trial proceedings and have no access to trial documents. At the same time, the 1991 Constitution introduces the concept of "due obedience" by which "military men on active duty" will not be held criminally liable for offenses (including human rights violations) if they can demonstrate that they were following orders. This reduces even further the possibility of bringing perpetrators of extrajudicial executions and "disappearances" to justice.

In cases in which conflicts of jurisdiction have been resolved in favour of the civil justice system, the Colombian armed forces have resorted to practices designed to further delay, obstruct or impede investigations. They range from simple failure to cooperate with investigations to the intimidation, harassment and killing of investigators and witnesses. Among the most common practices are the following:

- Arrest warrants are not enforced.

- Officers under investigation are given promotions, sent on training courses abroad, or transferred to areas of the country outside the jurisdiction of the investigating court. Repeated transfers and the failure to advise the court of the suspect's whereabouts result in serious delays which can lead to investigations being suspended or closed.

- The armed forces commanders refuse to name individual members of the armed forces under investigation or to allow them to testify.

- Evidence is adulterated or destroyed and reports of incidents are falsified.

- Witnesses are harassed or even killed to prevent them from testifying. Relatives and friends of victims are threatened or killed if they persist with their denunciations.

- Judges and other judicial officials are threatened, attacked or killed.

- Armed forces commanders systematically attempt to discredit human rights organizations by labelling their legitimate activities in defence of human rights as "subversive".

In cases where, despite the obstacles, investigations are pursued by the civilian courts, those brought to trial are generally low-ranking members of the armed forces. Investigations routinely fail to establish chain-of-command responsibility for planning and ordering attacks; superior officers are, therefore, seldom charged even when serving members of the armed forces have given evidence against their superiors. And in those exceptional cases where members of the armed forces have been found guilty of human rights violations, convictions have generally been overturned on appeal or perpetrators have "escaped" from custody.

Members of paramilitary groups, too, have generally evaded justice with the help of the Colombian army. The security forces have routinely failed to enforce arrest warrants against members of army-backed paramilitary organizations and have given shelter and protection in military installations to paramilitary group members under investigation. Leaders of paramilitary organizations convicted and sentenced to prison terms *in absentia* have continued to operate freely and openly in heavily militarized areas.[5]

The government's response

Until recently the government's reaction was, like the armed forces', to deny any official responsibility for "disappearances" and extrajudicial executions wherever possible. When confronted with conclusive evidence of responsibility of members of the armed forces for human rights violations the government has responded by admitting individual liability – describing killings and "disappearances" as excesses committed by a few "rogue elements" in carrying out duties – while denying institutional responsibility.

In recent years an increasing amount of evidence has emerged from both independent and official investigations conducted by, among others, the civilian judiciary, the Public Ministry and the Executive's own security agency DAS. As a result, the government has increasingly come to accept and acknowledge that state agents are responsible for numerous human rights violations. It has also publicly acknowledged and condemned the links between the armed forces and the paramilitary and "self-defence" groups. However, despite mounting evidence of the armed forces' involvement in systematic and widespread human rights violations, extrajudicial executions and "disappearances" continue to be committed with virtual impunity.

The mechanisms of impunity in Colombia are varied and complex, but a distinction can be made between two main categories: "political" and "structural" impunity.

Structural impunity can be defined as a breakdown in the rule of law resulting from severe deficiencies in the administration of justice due to insufficient resources, lack of training and specialist personnel and pervasive corruption. The Colombian judicial system, plagued by all these problems for many years, has proved incapable of dealing efficiently with growing crime rates and political violence.

Structural impunity within the civilian justice system was perhaps a factor in the armed forces' decision in the 1980s to turn from legitimate means of combating insurgents to the development of a strategy of "disappearances" and extrajudicial executions. The Colombian Government has, in turn, used deficiencies in the administration of justice to explain and justify the failure to hold members of the armed forces responsible for human rights violations.

The government has recently introduced judicial reforms which it claims will eventually resolve the problem of "structural" impunity. Impunity in Colombia, however, goes beyond deficiencies of the judicial system, real though they are. Attempts to redress the failings of the judicial system, including major international assistance programs, are unlikely to have any major impact in halting human rights violations until the government addresses the issue of *political* impunity by securing the compliance of the armed forces in respect for the principle of judicial accountability. The armed forces' response to attempts to hold its personnel accountable before the law for human rights violations has been to systematically obstruct the course of justice.

Some progress has, however, been achieved in disciplinary investigations.

The Colombian Public Ministry, an autonomous body headed by the Procurator General, has a constitutional responsibility to investigate state agents accused of misconduct and to bring disciplinary proceedings and sanctions where appropriate. It cannot bring criminal charges, but it can provide information to the courts and can supervise criminal investigations.

Despite a chronic lack of resources the Public Ministry has made serious efforts to investigate at least some of the many complaints it receives of human rights violations committed by armed forces and police personnel. However, its efforts have frequently been seriously hampered by opposition from the security forces. Armed forces commanders have repeatedly criticised the Public Ministry for pursuing investigations of human rights violations, investigations which they claim reduce the armed forces' capacity to respond to subversion. Despite the efforts of some Public Ministry officials, very few investigations result in disciplinary sanctions being applied.

One of the difficulties cited by successive Procurator Generals to explain the seemingly derisory sanctions imposed on perpetrators of "disappearances" is the fact that no such offence is included in the Colombian penal code, although it is specifically prohibited under the 1991 Constitution. In 1988 the then Procurator General presented to Congress a draft bill designed to incorporate "disappearances" as an offence in the Colombian Penal Code punishable with two to 10 years' imprisonment. In a letter to the Minister of Justice, the Ministry of Defence immediately objected to the proposed legislation on the grounds that it would "undermine the power of the authorities ... who have as their principal priority the re-establishment of public order and as a consequence, facilitate the action of terrorists, who would use the legislation to accuse the armed forces". The bill was never debated by Congress. A second bill presented to Congress in 1990 suffered a similar fate. A new draft bill was under consideration at the time of writing of this report.

The government has claimed that in response to the failure of the judicial system to hold army and police personnel accountable for human rights violations, it has removed violators from the security forces by executive decree,[6] but it appears that the majority of those dismissed were guilty of offences other than human rights violations. Of those who were dismissed for human rights violations, several were already retired from active service, while in other cases high-ranking military officers implicated in extrajudicial executions and "disappearances" have merely been transferred or have even been promoted to high-ranking posts.

Amnesty International and other international organizations have made numerous recommendations to the Colombian authorities over the years about measures needed to end gross and systematic violations of human rights. Some recommendations have been accepted, but to little avail.

Most of the recommendations which have been accepted by the authorities have been of a technical nature: the creation of a central register of detainees; measures to protect witnesses, lawyers and human rights workers; human rights training for security force personnel; improvements to forensic and investigative procedures. Other recommendations which might have had a more significant impact have been accepted in principle but never put into effect.

However, even if the Colombian Government had accepted and implemented all Amnesty International's recommendations for procedural changes, it is debatable whether these measures alone would have ended the severe human rights violations prevailing in the country. Unless the government summons up the political will to stop human rights violations, the security forces will continue to flout the rule of law. Recommendations which would require of the government a fundamental change in attitude towards the armed forces and its counter-insurgency strategy have been ignored.

The national and international news media have also contributed to the misperception of the situation by failing to report gross violations of human rights or by uncritically reproducing misinformation provided by the security forces. The self-censorship exercised by national media proprietors and editors responds to a policy designed to cover up acts which reflect badly on the government or its armed forces.

It seems increasingly unlikely that national events or the pressure of Colombian opinion alone will lead the authorities to take the necessary steps to ensure that the security forces act within the law. This is likely to be brought about only through the added influence of other governments, international organizations and world opinion. Other governments, however, have tended to be unwilling to speak out and thereby risk undermining what is perceived to be a weak, but democratic, government which is under attack by violent sectors of society.

This perception of the state as a victim of violence has been actively fostered by successive Colombian Governments, which have invested significant resources in misrepresenting the extent and nature of human rights violations in Colombia and in minimizing the degree of official responsibility. A good illustration of the authorities' "smoke screens" is the way in which drug-related violence was portrayed by the Colombian Government as the major form of political violence between 1989 and 1991. In reality, the number of deaths officially attributed to drug-trafficking groups during this period was a very small proportion of the number of politically motivated killings. The presentation of drug-traffickers as the main agents of political violence not only distracted attention from official violence but generated significant international economic and technical assistance for the security forces.

International confusion about the sources of impunity in Colombia has also led to attempts to tackle the problem through judicial assistance programs. These may help to improve the quality of justice, but they are unlikely to go far unless they are backed by the political will of the government.

The greatest challenge for human rights organizations concerned about Colombia is to make the international community aware of the true nature of political violence in the country so that the necessary pressure will be mobilised to put an end to gross violations of human rights.

CHAPTER 4

ZIMBABWE: DRAWING A LINE THROUGH THE PAST

> *"...we were trying to kill each other; that's what the war was about. What I'm concerned with now is that my public statements should be believed when I say that I have drawn a line through the past."*
> – *Prime Minister Robert Mugabe, on retaining the head of Rhodesian intelligence in charge of Zimbabwe's Central Intelligence Organization after Zimbabwe became independent in 1980[1]*

The issue of the accountability of security force personnel for human rights violations is seldom debated in Africa. In Latin America and, more recently, Eastern Europe, the issue of whether to bring officials who violated human rights under past regimes to justice has been a subject of national debate. But in most African countries the choice has been scarcely considered and has tended to be decided by default.

The issue occasionally receives public airing because of the former leaders of dictatorial and repressive African governments who gain refuge elsewhere in the continent. Thus, former presidents Hissein Habré of Chad, Siad Barre of Somalia and Mengistu Haile Mariam of Ethiopia currently enjoy the protection of the governments of Senegal, Nigeria and Zimbabwe respectively. The subject of this chapter is the impunity enjoyed by human rights violators in the transition from white minority to democratic rule. Yet the same issues of principle apply to many other African countries where officials responsible for human rights violations have escaped accountability for their actions.

In Rhodesia (later Zimbabwe) in 1980, a white minority government finally conceded democratic rule to the black majority after decades of political repression which had culminated in a brutal war of counter-insurgency in the 1970s. The army, police and other security agencies had been responsible for widespread extrajudicial executions, "disappearances", torture and other human rights violations which had been thoroughly documented by both domestic and international human rights organizations.

At independence, however, essentially political considerations dictated that not only would past human rights violators not be brought to justice, but they would be retained in their positions in the security apparatus, with no investigation or calling to account for the deeds of the past. This was to have serious consequences which are explored in this chapter.

The 1980 amnesty

Zimbabwe's independence settlement came suddenly. Between September and December 1979 the major parties assembled for a conference at Lancaster House in London chaired by the United Kingdom, the colonial power. These parties were the Rhodesian Government and the leaders of a number of black parties co-opted into an "internal settlement" a year earlier, and the two major nationalist parties, the Zimbabwe African National Union (ZANU), led by Robert Mugabe, and the Zimbabwe African People's Union (ZAPU), led by Joshua Nkomo.[2]

The Lancaster House settlement included an amnesty for all acts carried out in the course of the war. Earlier, the nationalist movement had been vocal in calling for Rhodesian leaders to be brought to trial, yet these demands were not reflected in the agreement reached. The amnesty, along with the entrenched guarantees of land and pension rights, were seen as political imperatives if the independence agreement was to be acceptable to the country's economically important white community.

After independence, the Zimbabwean Government adhered to the provisions of the Lancaster House settlement in a number of other matters which it found obnoxious, such as the maintenance of a racially segregated voters' roll. Arguably it would have been unrealistic to expect the government to break the agreement over the amnesty issue, since it depended on continued international good will. However, the new government went far beyond its Lancaster House obligations on this issue by failing to investigate past human rights violations and by keeping human rights violators in crucial positions in the security apparatus.

There was little expression of disquiet over these developments, and the international community heaped praise on the new Prime Minister, Robert Mugabe, for his "statesmanlike" compromises with the white community. The general view was that the new government, dominated by ZANU – regarded as the more radical of the two main nationalist organizations – could have sought "vengeance" against the white settler population, but had instead opted for "reconciliation".

The amnesty for human rights violators was rationalized by describing all abuses committed before independence as being part of the war effort. This was a serious distortion. Rhodesia had been a system of institutionalized racial domination which depended on systematic and often legalized human rights violations for its maintenance. Robert Mugabe and thousands of other nationalists were detained – and in many cases tortured – not for armed activities but for attempting to express their political views. The Rhodesian security forces carried out many extrajudicial executions of prisoners, civilians or others not taking an active part in hostilities, acts which are prohibited under the international humanitarian law of armed conflict as well as international human rights standards. In one of the clearest examples, in August 1976 the Rhodesian security forces launched raids on a Zimbabwean refugee camp at

Nyadzonia in Mozambique, leaving nearly a thousand dead. A member of the elite Selous Scouts who took part in the massacre later described the pre-raid briefing:

> "We were told that Nyadzonia was a camp containing several thousand unarmed refugees who could be recruited to join the guerrillas. It would be easier if we went in and wiped them out while they were unarmed and before they were trained rather than waiting for the possibility of them being trained and sent back armed into Rhodesia."[3]

This was not a normal armed combat operation. It was a gross human rights violation and a war crime – which found its echo in hundreds of smaller incidents throughout the country and across its borders.

The Lancaster House amnesty can be understood as an act of political expediency. But the victims of Rhodesian human rights violations and their surviving families were not consulted when the decision was made that their tormentors should go unpunished.

The rationale for retaining human rights violators in the security forces was explained by Emmerson Mnangagwa, then Minister of State responsible for security, in an interview with the journalist Joseph Lelyveld in 1983. On starting his job after Zimbabwe became independent, Emmerson Mnangagwa went to visit a room in a police station where he had been tortured while suspended upside down from butcher's hooks. In Lelyveld's words:

> "The day after the independence ceremonies, the butcher's hooks were still on the ceiling, and astonishingly, his former interrogators were now on his staff, as was another official who acknowledged having once sent him a letter bomb. They told him they had just been doing their jobs; he then promised they could start in independent Zimbabwe with a 'clean slate.' Some had later proved to be South African agents, but others still appeared to be loyal officers, the minister said. In the beginning he had no choice but to trust them, he explained. Zimbabwe could not be expected to dismantle its only security agency."[4]

The legal framework for continuing human rights violations in Zimbabwe was provided by the state of emergency which had been in force in Rhodesia since 1965 and was retained for a further 10 years after independence. The broad and often arbitrary legal powers of the security forces under emergency regulations gave a sense that those forces operated beyond the reach of the normal provisions of the law. This perpetuated an atmosphere of impunity. It also meant that law enforcement officials such as police officers failed to gain the basic skills to investigate criminal cases and prosecute offenders in court, since they could choose instead to detain them without charge or trial.

Indemnity and compensation in Rhodesian and Zimbabwean law

In 1975 several victims of torture brought actions for damages in the Rhodesian High Court. The government's response was to introduce the Indemnity and Compensation Act. This indemnified members of the security forces and other government servants for any actions carried out in good faith in defence of national security since December 1972. The act also gave the Minister for Law and Order the authority to terminate actions for damages before the High Court.

The Zimbabwean Government retained the act after independence. A senior government minister, Edgar Tekere, successfully invoked the act when he faced charges of murdering a white farmer in August 1980, with the result that the government was obliged to give way to political pressure and repeal the act. However, it promptly reintroduced almost identical provisions as regulations under its emergency powers – which meant that it avoided any parliamentary scrutiny.

In 1985 the government repealed the regulations after the Supreme Court had ruled unanimously that they were in breach of the constitutional provision allowing a person who is wrongfully arrested to sue for compensation. (The ruling was in response to a suit by a Harare lawyer, Denis Granger, for damages for wrongful arrest by the Central Intelligence Organization, CIO.) But despite the existence of a constitutional guarantee of the right to sue for compensation, in many cases the government has disregarded court rulings. Prime Minister Mugabe told Parliament in 1986:

> "If Government – and I want to say this as a matter of principle
> – were to be awarding damages and paying huge sums of
> money that are involved in these cases, some of which are of a
> petty nature, Government would in my view be using the
> taxpayers' money wrongfully... [W]here people take advantage
> of our liberal situation to go to court and win on technicalities,
> they should not expect that Government is going to use the
> people's resources to enrich them..."[5]

In May 1989 Parliament passed a further indemnity law, this time shielding National Park game wardens and other security force personnel from criminal prosecution for acts carried out in good faith in the course of anti-poaching activities.[6] The Protection of Wildlife (Indemnity) Act was introduced after senior National Park officials had faced criminal charges in connection with the deaths of poachers.[7]

Since then the Protection of Wildlife (Indemnity) Act has apparently encouraged the use of lethal force against poachers, including possible extrajudicial executions. According to official figures, between July 1984 and September 1991 anti-poaching patrols killed 145 suspected poachers.

To summarize: Zimbabwe embarked upon its existence as an independent state by sending a clear message to its security forces that they would benefit from the same impunity enjoyed by their Rhodesian predecessors. Officers responsible for human rights violations had been amnestied without any investigation or accounting for their actions. Many were kept on in similar positions of authority. Members of the security forces were indemnified from future prosecutions for human rights violations and much of the legal apparatus which had provided the framework for abuses in the 1970s remained intact. As a result, respect for the rule of law was weakened and the security forces continued to operate within a culture which saw human rights violations as part of an acceptable method of working. Specific techniques of human rights abuse were passed on from the Rhodesian to the Zimbabwean forces – often practised by the very same people.[8]

The effects of impunity: repression in Matabeleland

From the earliest months of Zimbabwe's independence there was tension and potential insecurity. Three armies were to be integrated to form a single Zimbabwe National Army: ZANLA, the military wing of ZANU; ZIPRA, the military wing of ZAPU; and the Rhodesian Army. While the former Rhodesian army continued to be housed in barracks and draw full army pay, the nationalist guerrillas awaiting integration were housed in makeshift camps in poor conditions. Resentment over these problems aroused latent rivalries between ZANLA and ZIPRA which broke out into open conflict in Entumbane township in Bulawayo, the main town in Matabeleland, in November 1980 and again in February 1981. During the latter round of fighting, Prime Minister Mugabe deployed the Rhodesian air force and the Rhodesian African Rifles against the ZIPRA forces in Bulawayo, killing more than 100. There were a number of reports of killings of civilians and prisoners. In Mzilikazi township, more than two kilometres away from the fighting, three children were killed in an attack by a helicopter gunship. In Bulawayo's industrial area former Rhodesian police reservists reportedly executed five ZAPU officials. A judicial commission of inquiry investigated the events, but its report was never made public.

Many former ZIPRA guerrillas were disillusioned by the government's use of the former Rhodesian military apparatus against them and returned to the bush to continue their armed struggle. Over the next six years the army's counter-insurgency campaign against these former guerrillas, now termed "dissidents", was to provide the occasion for renewed gross violations of human rights.

The government launched the anti-"dissident" campaign in early 1982 when it deployed a task force in Matabeleland North under the command of Lieutenant-Colonel Lionel Dyke, a former officer in the Rhodesian Selous Scouts. The force was composed of former Rhodesian African Rifles and Rhodesian Light Infantry. In the course of its operations there were frequent reports of villagers being beaten, tortured and killed.

The Task Force was later replaced by the Fifth Brigade, an elite unit. In the rainy season of early 1983, and again at the same time in 1984, the Fifth Brigade systematically killed civilians in Matabeleland, the area in southern Zimbabwe from which ZAPU drew much of its support. Unlike other army units, which were integrated, the Fifth

Brigade drew exclusively upon former ZANLA guerrillas from the majority Shona-speaking groups. The Fifth Brigade used crude tribalist stereotypes of the minority Ndebele-speakers to justify its abuse of the civilian population.[9]

A Rhodesian tactic which was widely emulated by the Zimbabwean army was the use of "pseudo-gangs" – groups of soldiers posing as guerrillas, either to expose civilian supporters of the rebels or to commit abuses which could be blamed on the insurgents. Amnesty International documented two clear examples of this tactic in 1985. In April 1985 armed attackers, later officially described as "dissidents", killed seven people at a bar in the Mahamba business centre at Inyathi in Matabeleland North. Earlier the same day the paramilitary Police Support Unit had set up camp only 200 metres from the bar, and armed members of the unit were drinking there just before the attack. The attack was signalled by a single warning shot and the Support Unit members left immediately. Neither they nor the regular police intervened until the attackers had left. The owner of the bar was Micah Bhebhe, a member of the central committee of ZAPU. His son was among those killed.

In the second incident unidentified attackers shot dead Luke and Jean Kumalo, a Methodist headmaster and his wife, at Thekwane School near Plumtree in Matabeleland South in November 1985. Again the government described those responsible as "dissidents". Yet the attackers were wearing combat uniforms, some of which were identified by eyewitnesses as being those of the paramilitary People's Militia. The attackers stayed at the school for more than two hours, shooting and burning buildings, although soldiers at an army camp three kilometres away failed to intervene. Like Micah Bhebhe, Luke Kumalo was a supporter of ZAPU, the party which the authorities usually identified with the "dissidents".

The Zimbabwe Government resisted calls for independent inquiries into these two incidents and the culprits were never identified. It is impossible to know how many other killings officially attributed to "dissidents" may have been the work of the army's "pseudo-gangs".

In 1983 the government set up a commission to investigate allegations of army killings of civilians in Matabeleland. Its findings were never made public.

The official culture of forgetfulness reached its apogee in June 1988, when 75 members of the security forces serving sentences or awaiting trial for human rights violations were amnestied. One of those released was Robert Masikini, a CIO officer who only a week earlier had been found guilty of murdering a political detainee. Also released were four Fifth Brigade soldiers under sentence of death for murder, who were among the very few ever to have been brought to justice for human rights violations.[10]

The government claimed to have a clear political justification for the 1988 amnesty. It was a direct parallel with an amnesty earlier the same year which granted immunity from prosecution to the so-called "dissidents", which in turn followed the signing of a unity agreement between ZANU (PF) and ZAPU.

The amnesty for "dissidents" was successful in bringing peace to Matabeleland, but it created serious public misgivings since some of the rebels amnestied were believed to have been responsible for atrocious crimes, such as hacking to death 16 people, including babies and children, at a Protestant mission in Esigodini in November 1987. However, by its amnesty for security force members, the government appeared to attach no special significance to the fact that their crimes had been carried out when they were charged with the responsibility of protecting the human rights of citizens. Essentially the government's rationale was the same as in 1980, when all past abuses were wiped clean under the pretence of being acts of war.

The debate over impunity

Remarkably few voices were raised within Zimbabwe to criticize the amnesties of either 1980 or 1988. However, particularly after the 1988 amnesty, there has been criticism of the government's failure to explain and learn from past human rights violations. There has also been a tenacious legal struggle by the families of one group of "disappeared" people.

The 1980 amnesty scarcely figured in political debate at the time. Even those who were critical of the new government's alleged failure to fulfil other aspects of its pre-independence program, such as land reform, seemed content to accept the view that a line should be drawn through the past.

The 1988 amnesty did arouse some disquiet, especially the releases already mentioned of CIO official Robert Masikini and the convicted murderers of Lieutenant Ndlovu. In strict terms the issue was rather different from that in 1980. At independence a decision was made not to investigate or make any accounting for past human rights violations. By contrast, some of those released under the 1988 amnesty had already been tried and convicted. Once again, however, there was almost no support in political circles for the notion that there should be a thorough accounting for abuses which took place between independence and 1988. Kembo Mohadi, the ZAPU member of parliament who had successfully sued the government for damages for torture, dropped the case after the unity agreement between his party and ZANU (PF). "I personally don't really accept retrospective condemnation. A new chapter was opened on 22 December [when the unity agreement was signed]," he said. Another ZAPU member of parliament, Sidney Malunga, who had been detained three times and beaten on the soles of the feet, expressed similar sentiments: "I believe political leaders must be magnanimous. We don't want to open up old wounds."

Reaction in Matabeleland was different. Joseph Khumalo from Silobela was interviewed shortly after the unity agreement and amnesty:

> "The memory is very powerful. Even people who I played with disappeared. A friend in our area, Matanda Fuzane, they shot him directly... It was done publicly, that shooting, at night. His father witnessed it. It was the Fifth Brigade. They shot him in front of his family. [The unity agreement] has done to help the souls of the people. The people were suffering, now it has come

to a rest. But you can't just say, 'Gentleman, it's over.' There is
nothing that proves to me that we are over this matter."

An Ndebele lawyer whose brother had been given electric shock torture by the CIO
commented:

> "For those who were untouched, they might as well have been
> reading about Lebanon. Those people have nothing to forget,
> nothing to forgive. But in Matabeleland, every family was
> touched. Every family suffered."[11]

One group of families has tried, with only partial success, to use the legal system to
call the government to account for human rights violations. They are the relatives of
nine men who were detained and "disappeared" from the Silobela area of Midlands
province on the night of 30 January 1985.[12] In 1986 a lawyer for the Catholic
Commission for Justice and Peace in Zimbabwe filed a suit in the High Court on behalf
of nine women from Silobela. In their supporting affidavits the women told how their
husbands had been threatened by ZANU (PF) officials before their "disappearance";
how the abductors did not speak proper Ndebele and appeared to be government
officials rather than people who lived in the bush; how the abductors beat the men
and drove them away in vehicles resembling the Nissan trucks used by the security
forces; and how the police failed to carry out proper investigations into the
"disappearances".

The High Court ordered a police investigation into the case which finally reported
in early 1989. However, the police findings did not go beyond what had already been
stated in the women's affidavits.

In early 1992, the nine men from Silobela were declared dead. Although this resolved
certain financial problems connected with the administration of their estates, the
conclusion of the case was unsatisfactory since it failed to account for the
circumstances of their "disappearance", to assign responsibility or to pay damages to
the families. The security forces had received another assurance of their impunity.

Securing human rights: the need to come to terms with the past

It is important that the discussion of impunity does not oversimplify or exaggerate its
effects. The amnesty for Rhodesian human rights violators was not by itself responsible
for the continuation of the same abuses in independent Zimbabwe. However, it did
provide the environment – and the means – for continuing human rights violations.

The new government consciously used the repressive apparatus of the Rhodesian
state: emergency laws, intelligence personnel, specialized military units and counter-
insurgency tactics. More broadly, it allowed a culture of abuse and impunity to
permeate the security structures.

Many observers were surprised by the ease with which former Rhodesian personnel
worked side by side with nationalist guerrillas in independent Zimbabwe. Yet their

shared military ethos – including the notion that they were beyond the reach of the law – proved stronger than their previous differences.

The paradox is that impunity for human rights violators has flourished in a country which since 1980 has been a functioning multi-party democracy. Zimbabwe has a vigorous independent judiciary and a Declaration of Rights which is enforceable by the courts. In principle it does not lack the institutional means to enforce respect for human rights. However, the government has chosen to place the security forces above the law. The problem is essentially political rather than institutional.

Since 1987 the strengthening of institutions of civil society has created greater pressure on the government to act against human rights violators. The emergence of an independent press has been particularly important. For example, independent newspapers have highlighted the "disappearance" of a woman, Rashiwe Guzha, who was last seen in CIO custody in 1990. The elevation of the case into a *cause célèbre* has forced the government to bring charges against a senior CIO official. There have been calls from the press, academics and human rights groups for an independent commission of inquiry into the whole functioning of the CIO.

It is not too late for the Zimbabwean Government to initiate a thorough process of investigation and truth-telling about past human rights violations. The government should understand that this is part of the process of healing wounds both at the individual level – among the families of the dead and "disappeared" – and nationally. It might be added that the government would be likely to emerge with some credit from such an investigation: since 1987 it has made significant steps to overcome the conditions which have caused human rights violations or allowed them to occur. The danger is that without a proper accounting for past violations, such improvements will not be properly secured.

CHAPTER 5

TURKEY: RESPONSES TO AN EMERGING PATTERN OF EXTRAJUDICIAL EXECUTIONS

The persistence of torture has dominated Amnesty International's work on Turkey for over a decade. Today this continuing pattern of torture is, in southeast Turkey, overshadowed by a new pattern of human rights violations. Scores of people known for their criticism of Turkish Government policies have been the targets of selective assassination. Journalists, human rights activists and supporters of opposition parties and lawful groups associated with Turkey's Kurdish autonomy movement have been victims of political killings, often following a history of short-term arrest and police harassment.

Increasing evidence has come to light that since 1991 Turkey's security forces have engaged in a campaign of extrajudicial executions. These have centred on the 10 provinces under emergency rule in southeast Turkey, where the Turkish state is combating guerrillas of the Kurdish Workers' Party (PKK). Since mid-1991 more than 300 people active in the legal opposition to the government, or suspected of having contacts with the clandestine PKK, have been the victims of execution-style killings in the southeast.

In some cases the evidence has shown direct security force responsibility, while in others the collusion of government forces in the killings is strongly suggested by circumstantial evidence. A pattern of political killings has emerged – a pattern which the official institutions of law and order have done little to end.

The rise of killings in the southeast

Although numerous killings in disputed circumstances by the security forces have been reported in many parts of Turkey[1], it is in the southeastern provinces that the toll of such deaths has been the greatest. Unarmed civilians have been killed by security forces firing indiscriminately on demonstrations, in random firing on Kurdish residential areas in "retaliation" for PKK attacks on troops, or in other recklessly excessive uses of lethal force. This chapter, however, focuses on evidence that Turkish forces are systematically eliminating those openly working for Kurdish rights, as well as active supporters of organizations pressing for Kurdish autonomy, whether members of the armed and outlawed PKK or non-violent advocates of democratic reform.

The wave of extrajudicial executions has been part of a crescendo of violence in southeast Turkey since 1990, when fighting between Turkish security forces and Kurdish guerrillas of the PKK intensified. The guerrillas' original stated aim was to establish an independent Marxist Kurdish state; recent statements by their leader, Abdullah Öcalan, have put forward more modest aims, asking for a cease-fire and some form of limited autonomy within the Turkish state. The guerrillas are trained in Turkey or in bases in Syria, Northern Iraq or Iran. They are heavily armed and usually wear a simple uniform without insignia. They carry out almost daily attacks on security posts in villages and towns.

There have been many reports of human rights abuses by the PKK also, including "executions" of village guards (see below) and alleged informers. In some cases village guards' wives and children have also been killed.

The PKK's manoeuvres are matched by a high level of military activity by government security forces, who make expeditions from the population centres into the rugged countryside to track down guerrilla groups. Since the beginning of the conflict in 1984 an estimated 10,000 people have died, many of them civilians.

The security forces comprise some 60,000 gendarmes (members of the regular armed services carrying out police duties); 34,000 village guards; and an estimated 3,000 members of the Special Teams who are trained for close combat with guerrilla forces and are nominally responsible to the local police commander. The security forces believe, probably correctly, that many in the civilian population are supplying guerrillas in the mountains with food and information, and that the PKK has political and military representatives in villages and towns. Unable effectively to identify and prosecute these representatives, it appears that the security forces have resorted to extrajudicial execution as a method of eliminating people they suspect of collaborating with guerrillas and in order to dissuade others from collaborating in the same way.

Increased allegations of extrajudicial execution began in mid-1991 with the murders of Ramazan Aslan and Vedat Aydın. The two cases exemplify two more or less distinct patterns of killings – one rural and one urban – which probably involve two different groups of perpetrators.

Deaths in the countryside: the killing of Ramazan Aslan

Ramazan Aslan was shot with 14 bullets in the courtyard of his home in Midyat, Mardin province on 13 June 1991. He was headman of the nearby village of Ikizdere and kept a small shop in Midyat. On 20 June 1990 he had been arrested and remanded in custody on charges of membership of the local PKK committee. His father had previously been headman of the same village but had resigned the year before after he was convicted of harbouring members of the PKK. Both Ramazan Aslan and his father opposed the village guard system, and the people of Ikizdere have never joined the village guard corps.

On the eve of Ramazan Aslan's election as headman the gendarmerie visited Ikizdere and said that Ramazan Aslan was an unsuitable candidate because he was "a terrorist".

In spite of this he was elected, and on the morning of 13 June he went to Midyat Gendarmerie Headquarters to present his credentials as village headman. He told his family that he had been welcomed and entertained for several hours with tea and coffee.

That night as he crossed the courtyard of his home he was killed by a burst of automatic fire. The killer was never found.

During the rest of the year there were at least 15 other killings in rural areas of Mardin province, mainly of people who had earlier been arrested on suspicion of having contacts with the PKK, or who had relatives who had joined the guerrillas. Some of the killings were reportedly carried out by security personnel dressed as guerrillas. Sometimes individual soldiers were recognized. Assassination teams travelled in military vehicles, through gendarmerie checkpoints or even in helicopters. A security force "death squad" appeared to be operating in the area.

The distinctive factor common to all of the victims was that they came from villages which had refused to join the village guard corps.

The village guard system was established by the government in 1985 to counter the activities of the PKK. Although many villagers are reluctant to serve as village guards for fear of reprisals from the guerrillas, they equally fear reprisals from the security forces if they refuse. In theory, recruitment into the village guard corps is voluntary, but refusal by individuals or entire villages to participate in the system is usually considered by the local security forces as a sign of active or passive support for the guerrillas.

The pressure from the PKK not to join, enforced by the threat of attack or execution, is plainly intense, and there were hundreds of resignations from the corps during 1991 and 1992. As villages which pull out of the system are seen to expose the flank of nearby villages, any PKK attack against these neighbours may trigger reprisals against villages refusing to belong to the system.

It is widely rumoured in Turkey that the selective assassinations among the Kurdish population are part of a campaign by a clandestine anti-insurgency unit, referred to as the *kontrgerilla* (counter-guerrilla), to intimidate the opposition or provoke it into open rebellion so that it could be wiped out by straightforward military means. But some of the killings could have been instigated or carried out by members of any of the security force units, such as plainclothes members of the Anti-Terror Branch, the Special Teams, the village guards, or a combination of elements from all three, acting on their own initiative but with the passive or active collusion of other parts of the law and order system.

Local people have told Amnesty International that they believe that the Special Teams were involved in many of the killings. The identities, activities and methods of the Special Teams are shrouded in great secrecy. They are sometimes uniformed but are often masked. Many Special Team members know Kurdish, and they may also wear local dress. Unlike other soldiers, they are permitted to wear long hair and to grow a beard or moustache, and they frequently wear trainer-type shoes. Those most frequently implicated in rural killings, however, are the village guards.

Villagers are still being killed by village guards, particularly in the Midyat area where the village guards seem to be out of control. Often the killings are initially attributed to the PKK by local officials and the press.

On 1 December 1992 seven inhabitants of the village of Hakverdi near Kızıltepe in Mardin province were taken from their houses and shot. The Emergency Powers Governor promptly blamed the PKK.

Surviving villagers disputed this. They said that although the attackers were dressed like guerrillas, the victims selected were all relatives of a villager who had been jailed for PKK membership, and although the area was under close surveillance there was no clash with the security forces or pursuit. One villager said: "All those killed were [Kurdish] patriots. Our only crime is membership of HEP" (the People's Labour Party).

There had been a similar incident in April the same year, when eight inhabitants of Çalpınar village, Midyat, were killed and nine wounded in an attack on a minibus. This incident too was described by the Emergency Powers Governor as a PKK attack, but ballistic tests later revealed that the weapons used belonged to neighbouring village guards. Ten village guards were arrested.

The Midyat area is also home to Assyrian Christians and to Yezidis, members of a non-Muslim syncretist faith. Members of both groups have been killed in attacks attributed to village guards and apparently carried out in order to intimidate the Christians and Yezidis from having any contact with the PKK, to extort money, or to encourage the communities to leave their land and flee to Istanbul or Europe.

Yusuf Çakar, a Yezidi, was found shot dead with bound eyes, hands and feet on the morning of 1 December 1992, after having been released from Mardin after 10 days' interrogation. On 13 January 1993 five Assyrian Christians and two Yezidis were killed in an attack on two minibuses. Although the attack was publicly attributed to the PKK, the survivors said they believed the killers were village guards.

In some killings, the victims were detained by officials before being killed. On 10 November 1992 Mehmet Akkan, a 70-year-old shepherd of Altıyol village near Dargeçit, Mardin province, was detained by gendarmes. Later that day fellow villager Mehmet Akkum "disappeared" after he was reportedly seen by children of the same village being taken into custody. On 13 November Mehmet Akkan's body was found near the village with numerous bullet wounds, while on 17 November Mehmet Akkum's body was found bearing extensive marks of torture near Elazığ, which is over 300 kilometres away via roads which are under heavy security.

Urban killings: Vedat Aydın

The killing of Vedat Aydın, President of the Diyarbakır branch of the People's Labour Party (HEP) and board member of the Turkish Human Rights Association (THRA), initiated the wave of urban killings. He was taken from his home on 5 July 1991 by several armed men whom he said he knew and who identified themselves as police officers. His body was found on a roadside three days later with eight bullet wounds, broken limbs and crushed skull.

The year before, Vedat Aydın had been held in prison for two months for giving a speech in Kurdish at the annual general meeting of the THRA. On the day of his abduction he had visited a member of another branch of the THRA who had been injured in a bomb attack the previous week. Certain aspects of the crime as well as the perfunctory nature of the official investigation suggest that the security forces may have been responsible.

In a reply to a Council of Europe report on human rights in Turkey, a parliamentary member of parliament of the Social Democratic Populist Party (SHP) – the junior partner in the coalition government – stated: "The death of Mr Aydın is widely believed to be a crime committed by irresponsible officials. This is the opinion shared by the majority of my party".

In early 1992 the pace of political killings accelerated – in the course of the year there were over 250 urban killings. In some killings, the security forces were directly implicated.

Claims that elements within the security forces have been recruiting local people to carry out killings of members of the Kurdish opposition are supported by an episode which occurred early in 1992. Rıfat Akış, aged 16, was detained in Silvan, Diyarbakır province, on suspicion of membership of the PKK. He later claimed that a captain, commander of Silvan Gendarmerie Post, proposed to him with a combination of threats and bribes that he should assassinate Mehmet Menge, Diyarbakır SHP Board member, and that he was given a Kalashnikov rifle and hand grenades. Rıfat Akış' family appealed to a group of members of parliament who, on the initiative of the Interior Minister, took him to Ankara Police Headquarters. There a telephone conversation between Rfat Ak and the commander of Silvan Gendarmerie Post, a captain, was recorded on tape. Amnesty International does not have the full text of the conversation, but part of it was published in the newspaper *Yeni Ülke* (New Land) of 22 March 1992:

> "Rıfat Akış: Hello, this is Rambo Stes [his codename].
> Captain: Where are you?
> Rıfat Akış: I am in Diyarbakır. I found the man. I'll get rid of him.
> Captain: Do not speak too openly on the telephone. Get rid of him and
>   come here, your 20 million [around £2,000] is ready.
> Rıfat Akış: How shall I do it?
> Captain: Pull the fuse on the grenade and throw it at him. Shoot him in
>   the head no more than three times. Do not worry, we have
>   arranged everything. We'll say terrorists killed him. Your money
>   is ready. I will make a big man of you."

The officer with whom this conversation was held is still at liberty and still on duty, and it would appear that no legal proceedings have been taken against him. Following a parliamentary question on the incident, a reply dated 7 May 1992 from Gendarmerie General Command to the Presidency of the Turkish Grand National Assembly, the Turkish parliament, stated that the Silvan Gendarmerie commander had been "transferred to other duties outside the Emergency Powers Region" and that an internal investigation was being carried out by the Interior Ministry. Amnesty International twice wrote to the Turkish authorities asking about the case, but it had received no reply as of November 1993.

Most of the new wave of political killings were carried out by small groups of assassins (often very young according to eyewitnesses) in the street or similar public places and attributed to Hizbullah – an organization which was hitherto almost unknown and which, before November 1992, was not known to have engaged in any violent activities. This is not the branch of the Lebanese-based Shi'a Hizbullah which carried out acts of political violence in Turkey in the mid-1980s, but a shadowy organization which was established in 1987 in Batman and belongs to the Sunni branch of the Islamic faith, like most of the Muslim Kurdish population in that area. The group is committed to the establishment of a fundamentalist Islamic state in Turkey.

After first denying the existence of Hizbullah when the killings began, the authorities claimed that the killings were part of a feud between religious groupings and supporters of the PKK (nearly 100 alleged Hizbullah supporters were killed in 1992 in attacks generally blamed on the PKK). Nevertheless, there have been persistent doubts about the independence of Hizbullah as an armed force – doubts which have been fuelled by the striking degree of coincidence between the targets of the killings attributed to Hizbullah, and the targets of police harassment, arbitrary detention, ill-treatment and torture.

An incident suggesting official protection of "Hizbullah" gunmen occurred in April 1993 in Silvan, after two people were attacked and killed there. The assassins fled the scene and took refuge in the house of a person reputed to be closely connected with Hizbullah. When a crowd surrounded the house demanding that the attackers be handed over, shots were fired from the house. Police arrived at the scene shortly afterwards and took the killers and the owner of the house into custody. The local chief of police prepared a charge-sheet, but Diyarbakır State Security Court declared its incompetence in the case and shortly afterwards the owner of the house was released without appearing in court. This was the last news item covered by Hafız Akdemir, a journalist for *Özgür Gündem* (Free Agenda), before he was shot to death in a street in Diyarbakır. Reportedly the two alleged assassins were also released at a later date, but Amnesty International has not been able to confirm this.

In Turkey there is a legal parliamentary movement for Kurdish autonomy. The movement was led by HEP, which functioned legally as a parliamentary party until its closure. HEP did not advocate violence, but because its political goals resembled some of those of the PKK, the party was regarded in some quarters as the PKK's "parliamentary wing". In August 1993 HEP was closed by a ruling of the Constitutional Court on the grounds that the party was separatist. Its successor party, DEP, has 17 members of parliament.

In the urban killings, HEP members and officials have been among the main targets. Vedat Aydın, the first urban victim, was president of the Diyarbakır branch of HEP. In the 26 months since the killing of Vedat Aydın, a further 56 officials and members of HEP and its successor, the Democracy Party (DEP), have been killed in attacks which seem to have been a direct response to the party's electoral and organizational success.

The cases of Harbi Arman and Abdurrahman Söğüt were typical. Harbi Arman, an active board member of the Malazgirt local branch of HEP, was found dead under a bridge near the village of Örnek, 24 kilometres north of Diyarbakır, on 18 January 1992. He had been beaten to death.

In September 1991 detainees in Malazgirt had reported that the police threatened to kill Harbi Arman. He was detained briefly some days later and then released. On 14 January he went to Diyarbakır, having been called to appear as a witness at the State Security Court in the trial against those detained in September. The bus driver confirmed that Harbi Arman arrived in Diyarbakır, but he was not seen again until his blindfolded body was recovered by villagers.

Abdurrahman Söğüt, aged 38, a shopkeeper and father of eight children, was shot in the head and chest by three unidentified assailants in Nusaybin, Mardin province, on 18 January 1992. Like Harbi Arman, he was an active member of HEP. Abdurrahman Söğüt had been detained on 2 November 1991 on charges of aiding PKK guerrillas. After his release on 31 December he wrote to Amnesty International, describing the torture he said he had been subjected to at Mardin Police Headquarters.

Another victim was Abdul Samet Sakık, former President of HEP Gaziantep branch and brother of Sırı Sakık, the HEP member of parliament for Muş. On 3 October 1992 he was shot dead, reportedly in the presence of a Special Team unit in a jeep which failed to intervene or pursue the attacker.

Some HEP members of parliament have reported threats directly voiced by the security forces. In April 1992 a British human rights delegation reported that they were present when the Diyarbakır Gendarmerie Commander threatened Leyla Zana, HEP member of parliament for Diyarbakır. He reportedly told her: "I am going to kill you, but first I am going to discredit you."

HEP, and now DEP, members are also frequently detained and interrogated under torture for allegedly supporting the PKK. On 7 April 1992 Tahir Seyhan, HEP board member of Dargeçit, Mardin province, died after four days' interrogation by local gendarmerie. Replying to a parliamentary question concerning the death, the Interior Minister, Ismet Sezgin, said: "Tahir Seyhan fainted and fell to the floor when shown a photograph of himself taken with a militant organization member. When as a result of this fall Tahir Seyhan became ill, the barracks doctor intervened, but his condition worsened and he was moved to Diyarbakır State Hospital." The autopsy report registered death as the result of brain trauma.

A relative has alleged that the officer in charge of the gendarmes who detained Tahir Seyhan said: "You are a dead man now". A member of staff at the hospital where he died reportedly stated: "It is an inhuman case. He was brutally tortured. His body was all in pieces."

The latest killings at the time of writing of this report were those of Mehmet Sincar, DEP member of parliament for Mardin, and Metin Özdemir, Chairman of Batman

DEP. The two men were shot dead by three ⟨…⟩ n in broad daylight in the city of
Batman, southeast Turkey, on 4 Septe⟨…⟩ ⟨…⟩our other people, including
Nizamettin Toğuç, also a DEP memb⟨…⟩ ⟨…⟩re wounded in the attack.
Mehmet Sincar and Nizamettin T⟨…⟩ ⟨…⟩t of a DEP delegation to
the funeral of Habib Kılıç, the ⟨…⟩ ⟨…⟩, who was shot dead
on 1 September.

The killers escaped from the s⟨…⟩ ⟨…⟩ler claiming to
represent the Turkish Revenge Brig⟨…⟩ ⟨…⟩pers saying
that the killings were in retaliation for ⟨…⟩ ⟨…⟩ and that their
intended targets were two other DEP men⟨…⟩ ⟨…⟩ Yurttaş and Leyla
Zana. The TIT further stated that they in⟨…⟩ ⟨…⟩e attacks on Kurdish
members of parliament. (TIT was unknown u⟨…⟩ ⟨…⟩bility was claimed in its
name for abducting and killing Ferhat Tepe, the Bi⟨…⟩ ⟨…⟩rrespondent for the Kurdish-
owned newspaper *Özgür Gündem*, in August 1993. The circumstances of that killing
suggested that gunmen acting in the name of TIT may be linked with the security
forces.)

Again in these latest killings there were circumstantial details suggesting possible
collusion by the police. Other DEP members of parliament who were in Batman at
the time of the killings reported that they were under heavy police surveillance the day
before, followed everywhere by at least two vehicles and many plainclothes police
officers. All foreign observers who have visited the area note that police presence is
particularly heavy in Batman, and that their movements are constantly monitored. It
would normally be almost impossible for such killings to be carried out with complete
impunity in broad daylight in the centre of town. However, the DEP members of
parliament report that all police presence disappeared on the morning of 4 September.

Further grounds for concern are given by the circumstances of the arrest of Nesim
Kılıç, the brother of Habib Kılıç, at the airport when he arrived at Batman with Mehmet
Sincar on 3 September. The arrest was reportedly carried out by police officers
accompanied by a "confessor" (a former PKK member who is collaborating with the
security forces) from Mehmet Sincar's home town, and known to him.

On 8 September Batman police announced that they had caught one of the three
attackers. They said that the prisoner would be held in a "confessor" ward of Diyarbakır
prison. They said they knew the names of the other two; all three, they said, were "close
to Hizbullah". This was denied in a press statement by a Hizbullah spokesperson in
Diyarbakır, who said that the cease-fire between Hizbullah and the PKK was still in
force.

The extent of security force toleration, collusion or complicity in the killings
attributed to Hizbullah is still open to question. There have been more than 30
detentions of alleged Hizbullah activists. However, in some cases attackers apparently
acting in the name of Hizbullah who were reportedly caught in the act were apparently
never brought to trial. In September 1992 Amnesty International wrote to the Minister
of Justice asking for further information about a number of such cases, but it had not
received a reply by November 1993.

At the time of writing of this report, three trials involving 15 alleged Hizbullah activists accused of seven murders are being prepared at Diyarbakır State Security Court. The trials should provide further information about the activities undertaken in the name of this organization. The outcome of the trials will be an important test of the determination of the authorities to halt the killings.

Failure of the prosecution service

An important factor in the emergence and persistence of extrajudicial executions in southeast Turkey is the atmosphere of impunity in which the security forces operate there.

Under the terms of the Emergency Powers Region legislation in force in the southeastern provinces, no complaints brought against members of the security forces of manslaughter, theft, rape, assault, wounding or torture can be taken to court unless permission is given by the local governor's office – the office responsible for security and police affairs. Although the governor's permission is not needed for prosecutions for murder or attempted murder, the legislation gives the security forces a free hand to intimidate family members, complainants and potential witnesses. Cases of prosecutions for deaths in custody are also examined by the governor because the torturers claim they did not intend to go so far as to kill the victim. The Emergency Powers Region legislation has prevented the establishment of a tradition of calling government forces to account for abuses.

Under Turkish law, it is the provincial Chief Public Prosecutor's job to investigate non-political murders and killings by security personnel in disputed circumstances. Political killings by opposition groups are investigated by State Security Court prosecutors and tried in State Security Courts. Prosecutors, and to some extent courts, have shown extreme reluctance to investigate or prosecute members of the security forces for any actions they may commit while on duty – indeed such prosecutions are almost unknown in the area under emergency legislation.

The few replies that Amnesty International has received from the Turkish Government to questions about possible extrajudicial executions have claimed that investigations by local prosecutors are continuing. Families and lawyers, who are told the same, state that they have the impression that prosecutors are actually taking no action at all. They point to numerous cases where, despite strong evidence that local gendarmerie or village guards were involved in a killing, there have been few or no arrests or prosecutions and no convictions.

The tactic of official inactivity and delay, combined with assurances that investigations are continuing, effectively immobilises the families and lawyers of victims. Where allegations have been made against specific perpetrators, they must wait for months before the prosecutor makes a decision – usually to drop the case. The written explanation of the reasoning behind such a decision may be no more than two or three lines stating that there is "insufficient evidence". Where the crime is carried out by an unidentified assailant, the case may remain open indefinitely as an unsolved crime. Meanwhile, the family of the victim has no means of monitoring the case or pressing it forward, since the contents of the preliminary investigation file are secret, and a case of an indefinitely unsolved crime may never proceed beyond the secret, preliminary investigation. In theory there is a channel of appeal to the High Council of Judges and Prosecutors against prosecutors who are negligent, but lawyers who have tried to make such appeals state that they remain unanswered for years.

Lawyers themselves are under pressure – many receive death threats. Since the 1980 military coup, lawyers have experienced more than a decade of failure to achieve results in human rights cases. The experience has left lawyers deeply pessimistic about the prospect of legal remedies for human rights violations. Many believe that the only way to get local prosecutions moving is to develop public and press interest in their cases at home and abroad in order to shame the authorities into action.

Bringing a prosecution against members of the security forces is fraught with difficulty and danger. In May 1991 two Special Team members were indicted for intentionally shooting Mustafa Ilengiz in his home village of Çıiçekalan in the province of Kahramanmara (a province in southeast Turkey which is not under emergency rule) the preceding month. Although the provincial court initially claimed, for reasons that were never made clear, that it was not competent to try the case, a prosecution was eventually brought before the court. However, although the defendants are accused of intentional killing, the indictment prejudices the issue by presenting as fact that the defendants shouted to the victim to stop and fired warning shots into the air – an interpretation of the killing which should rightly have been left to the discretion of the court, and was moreover contested by numerous witnesses. Proceedings in the case appear to have been constantly stalled by the non-cooperation of the accused, who were never detained, and their superiors. The Special Team defendants failed to attend court hearings, even when subpoenas were issued, yet no legal action has been taken against them for their continued refusal to appear. The plaintiff's repeated requests for a court survey of the site of the killing was, in turn, refused on the grounds that the court should first take the defendants' statements. Finally and most disturbingly, the lawyer of the family of Mustafa Ilengiz was subjected to intimidation by the security forces. Other clients of the lawyer have said that they were told during interrogation by the local police and gendarmerie to pass on threats to his life. He continues to receive such threats and to be followed, and visitors to his house have been harassed.

Though plainly worn down by the seeming futility of pursuing official procedures of complaint in cases of torture, deaths in custody and extrajudicial executions, Turkish lawyers persist in following official channels in the hope that a file will eventually find its way to the desk of a prosecutor with integrity.

In southeast Turkey, a large part of a prosecutor's daily workload consists of preparing cases against alleged members of the PKK. In this area of their work, in contrast to their response to allegations of human rights violations, they appear extremely energetic, giving the clear impression that a tough line against separatism is a required characteristic of those appointed to prosecutors' posts in the southeast.

A prosecutor in the area who talked to Amnesty International confirmed this impression: his opening words were that his primary task was to preserve the indivisible unity of the state against separatist activity. While the prosecution service appears to regard combatting separatism as its primary task, movement is slow on cases of mysterious deaths of alleged separatists.

There is a further obstacle to thorough investigation of alleged human rights violations by the security forces. In the southeast, civil servants, and especially those involved in law and order, are at personal risk from the armed opposition. Security considerations throw police and judiciary together in their social as well as their professional lives. Police, prosecutors and judges are largely confined to a sealed-off community of security officialdom. In such a context it is not surprising that few prosecutors pursue allegations against their colleagues.

These factors combine to produce an extremely low rate of prosecutions in cases where there have been allegations of security force involvement in political killings. The Justice Ministry has not responded to Amnesty International's request for information about such prosecutions, but news sources indicate that only nine people to date have faced charges for the more than 300 documented murders of suspected oppositionists since mid-1991.

The passive response of the police to this unprecedented crime wave is striking. Most of the purported Hizbullah members who have been detained either appear to have stumbled into the hands of the police by chance, or were seized by local people. Two of those captured by the local population escaped lynching only when they were rescued by members of the Special Team; another was delivered into the hands of the security forces after he was pursued and repeatedly shot at by the victim's father.

The complacency of the authorities in Batman is particularly remarkable. When questioned by the newspaper *Cumhuriyet* (30 July 1992) about the 38 killings of alleged separatists in Batman since the beginning of the year, the governor, who is responsible for the police, stated, "We have not as yet taken resolute measures in connection with these events", and promised more strenuous efforts in future. But in February 1993, by which time the death toll in Batman had mounted to 184, the same governor said that it would be difficult to tackle the problem before specially equipped teams were developed.

In the intervening time observers compared the daily searches and detentions (often accompanied by torture and deaths in custody) in operations against the PKK with the lack of activity in pursuing gunmen acting in the name of Hizbullah. Of the three alleged Hizbullah supporters taken into custody in Batman, two had been caught by local people, while the capture of the third was highly fortuitous.

Information sources under threat

Among the important sources of information about killings in southeast Turkey are journalists from various publications, and the Turkish Human Rights Association (THRA), which has branches in all the provincial capitals in the area. The harassment and killing of journalists and THRA members threatens to result in a situation where human rights violations will increasingly go unreported.

Journalists and local correspondents working for newspapers and magazines like the Kurdish-owned daily *Özgür Gündem* and its sister publication, the weekly *Yeni Ülke* (now closed), *Gerçek* (Fact) and *2000'e Doğru* (Towards 2000), have been the targets of prosecutions, police harassment, detention, ill-treatment, torture and death threats ever since their publications began. Their declared policy is to investigate and publicize human rights violations committed by the security forces, in particular in the mainly Kurdish southeast provinces under emergency rule where reporting has been severely restricted. Issues of these and similar publications are frequently confiscated.

In 1992 the journalists who had been the targets of official harassment became targets of what the Committee for the Protection of Journalists described as "censorship by the bullet". Twelve journalists researching human rights violations were killed in the Emergency Powers Region between February 1992 and August 1993. Most of them had written about political killings in the area, and several had made specific allegations of links between Hizbullah and the security forces. The alleged killers of two of the journalists have been indicted; their trials are expected to last for a year or more.

On 11 August 1992 the then Prime Minister Süleyman Demirel gave his opinion about the attacks on members of the press: "Those killed were not real journalists. They were militants in the guise of journalists. They kill each other."

The THRA also has been under heavy pressure in the southeast. Branches have been closed, usually temporarily, by the local authorities; members are harassed; meetings are frequently banned; officials have been charged with supporting the PKK and remanded in custody, sometimes on the basis of little or no evidence.

In 1991 there was a bombing campaign against members and premises of the THRA, in which Sıddık Tan, board member of Batman branch of THRA, was blinded in one eye. In December 1991 his son, Rıza Tan, was detained by security forces and shot in the legs, allegedly while attempting to escape. On 19 October 1992 Metin Tan, another son of Sıddık Tan, was shot dead in a street in Batman. In June 1992 Sıddık Tan himself was killed after reportedly being invited to a discussion with Hizbullah representatives on how to end the killings.

On the evening of 21 February 1993 Metin Can, the President of the Elazığ branch of the THRA, received a telephone call after which he and his friend Dr Hasan Kaya drove away in Metin Can's car. Six days later their bodies were found about 100 kilometres away. Both had apparently been tortured and then killed with a bullet to the head.

Action against extrajudicial executions: turning back the tide

Experience suggests that a practice of extrajudicial execution, once established and pervasive, can be hard to stamp out. The Turkish authorities must act with great urgency to confront a situation which until now they have blandly denied.

The first step the authorities must take is thorough investigation. This task cannot be left to local prosecutors. In a highly charged situation of ethnic conflict with daily clashes between guerrillas and armed forces, with all the associated pressures and suspicions from both sides, local prosecutors may be afraid to carry out proper investigations, or may not want to do so. The situation calls for the establishment of an independent expert commission of inquiry as laid down in the UN Principles on the Effective Prevention and Investigation of Extra-Legal, Arbitrary and Summary Executions (see Chapter 10, section 9).

Following public outrage over the assassination of a prominent journalist in Ankara in January 1993 (a killing which – unlike others described in this chapter – has not generally been ascribed to the security forces), a cross-party commission of inquiry into political killings was established by the Turkish Grand National Assembly.

Initially there was some doubt as to whether the commission would also investigate killings in the southeast. However, in July the cross- party commission went to the southeast and in August 1993 it released a report which was damning of the security apparatus.

The report described in detail, for example, an incident in which village guards raided the village of Ormandışı, near Silvan in Diyarbakır province, killing two people, and then claimed that the raid had been carried out by the PKK. The report also stated that so-called "confessors" (former members of the PKK operating on behalf of the security forces – alleged by some informants to be involved in killings) live in police residential blocks and are responsible for "numerous robberies, thefts and similar incidents". The report called for the lifting of the emergency legislation and the immediate end of the village guard system.

To turn back the tide of killings, the Turkish Government must ensure that all levels in the judiciary, local government and the military clearly understand that extrajudicial execution is illegal and must not be used as a tool in the conflict with the PKK. It is the responsibility of the Turkish Government to take all necessary steps to re-establish the rule of law and the right to life in southeast Turkey, where, amid the clash of ideologies, life is becoming cheaper every day.

CHAPTER 6

MOROCCO:
THE "DISAPPEARED" REAPPEAR

Hundreds of suspected government opponents, including over 500 people of Western Saharan origin (Sahrawis) and over 100 Moroccans, have "disappeared" since the 1960s after being arrested by the Moroccan security forces. In 1991, after being held in secret detention for up to 19 years in appalling conditions, more than 300 of these prisoners were released after an international campaign against human rights violations in Morocco. The authorities had persistently denied holding any of the "disappeared". This chapter discusses the phenomenon of "disappearances" in Morocco and assesses some of the factors, including the Amnesty International campaign, which, in 1991, led to the releases of some of the "disappeared".

In some countries "disappearance" is often followed by extrajudicial execution: even if the "disappeared" remain alive for a couple of years, they tend, eventually, to be executed. In Morocco a state of "disappearance" can be ended after weeks, months or years, or it can amount to decades-long secret detention with no prospect of release. The "disappeared" are held in secret centres: villas in residential areas, secret police facilities, isolated farms, former military camps or barracks, and ancient fortresses – *qsour* – found even in the most remote areas of the interior.

Those who were released, after months or years of incommunicado detention, rarely dared speak out on their experiences. Most of the 300 released in 1991 are kept silent by the fear of returning to the limbo of "disappearance". However, some of those released in 1991 and a very few released earlier have spoken of their experiences. This chapter is based partly on their testimonies.

The 1991 release of more than 300 of the "disappeared" was only a partial victory. More "disappeared" – perhaps several hundreds – remain in secret unacknowledged detention. Those who were released and who remain in the country are still restricted in their movements and their freedom of expression. Most of them lack medical attention and they have never received the compensation which is their due. In addition, no one has ever been brought to justice for ordering or being involved in a "disappearance".

"Disappearances": the system

Known "disappearances" in Morocco go back to the early 1960s.

- Mohamed Ben Ali Boulahia Tati, a political activist, was arrested in Casablanca by police in early 1963, but his arrest was never acknowledged. He was seen by a fellow-detainee in Dar al-Mokri, a villa in Rabat used as a secret detention centre, in April 1963. There has been no news of him since. For 30 years his wife has continued to seek information about her husband from the Moroccan authorities, but they deny knowledge of him. He remains "disappeared".

- Abdelhaq Rouissi, a trade union activist, "disappeared" in October 1964. No one saw him arrested, but traces of blood were found in his bedroom. In the 1970s various sources, including released "disappeared" prisoners, confirmed that he had been arrested and held for years in secret detention. His family is convinced he is still alive and continues to struggle for his release.

- In 1965 Mehdi Ben Barka, the leader of the opposition *Union national des forces populaires*, was kidnapped while in France by Moroccan secret service officers; he is believed to have been murdered a few days afterwards. A French court found the Moroccan Minister of the Interior, General Mohammed Oufkir, guilty of ordering his abduction. His death is admitted at the highest level – but no official inquiry has ever been made into his fate.

- Another kidnapped trade union leader, Houcine El Manouzi, "disappeared" while in exile in Tunis in 1972. Three released "disappeared" prisoners have testified that Houcine El Manouzi was held with them in Rabat from 1973 to 1975, when they had escaped together and been recaptured. Where he is now is not known. His family has campaigned for 20 years for his release.

The greatest number of "disappearances" have been of people of Western Saharan origin. Over 200 were reported "disappeared" in the year after Morocco annexed the Western Sahara in November 1975. The full number of those "disappeared" is not known. Amnesty International believes that, including short-term "disappearances", over one thousand Sahrawis have "disappeared" after arrest over the last 15 years. Some were released after months or years of incommunicado detention, more than 300 were freed in June 1991, but up to 500 may remain in secret detention.

Hundreds of the "disappeared" remain unaccounted for. Some families continue, year after year, to make the rounds of prisons and to write to the authorities. The Moroccan Government denies knowledge of them just as, for years, it denied secretly detaining the "disappeared" who were eventually released in 1991. Amnesty International believes that the majority of the "disappeared" may still be alive, hidden away in secret cells, on an isolated farm, or in a villa in a smart quarter of Rabat.

Some may be dead. The names are now known of 48 Sahrawis detained in secret centres who died between 1976 and 1990.

In the remote barracks of Tazmamert a slow death in darkness and isolation was part of the punishment. By the time of the 1991 releases, 31 out of 58 military men taken in 1973 to this secret prison had died. This group, not strictly "disappeared" as the Moroccan Government never denied holding them, were taken from Kenitra Central

Prison in 1973 and vanished into Tazmamert, a prison whose existence, right up to the release of its inmates, was denied by the authorities. Even in September 1991, the month when the detainees were transferred from Tazmamert, the Moroccan Minister of the Interior stated on the radio that "Tazmamert only existed in the minds of evildoers".

Occasionally those who have "disappeared" over the years have been set free. One member of the auxiliary forces who "disappeared" in 1973 was discovered doing forced labour on a remote farm in 1979; students who vanished in 1976 were released without warning or explanation in 1984; other students who "disappeared" in 1981 were freed in 1983 and 1984. Those released in 1991 included the "disappeared" wife, cousin and six children (the youngest only three years old when imprisoned) of a former Minister of the Interior, General Mohamed Oufkir, who died in mysterious circumstances in 1972; more than 300 Sahrawis who "disappeared" between 1975 and 1987; and three brothers who "disappeared" in 1973, who were first held in secret villas in Rabat and then virtually buried alive in Tazmamert. Twenty-seven members of the armed forces (all who were left alive out of the 58 transferred there in 1973) were also released from Tazmamert in 1991.

But those who reappear from "disappearance" are never wholly free. They are told to forget what happened and never to talk about it. Their movements are restricted and their communications monitored. If they talk to outsiders about their experiences they risk rearrest. As one Sahrawi former "disappeared" said, they exchange a lesser prison for a greater one. Only a few, mostly those who have managed to leave the country, have been able to talk about the time they were "disappeared".

One purpose of "disappearance" is to imprison – or eliminate – people against whom the state has no legal charges or has charges which it is unwilling to pursue in a court of law. But "disappearance" as used in Morocco has had, as a further consequence, the creation of an atmosphere of fear which spread through the country. For the family of the victim, "disappearance" may be a greater punishment than execution: death ends the matter, grief heals, life resumes. "Disappearance" punishes a whole family forever – or as long as the "disappearance" lasts, for, since the authorities never admit to holding a "disappeared" prisoner, the family do not know what has happened and whether their relative is alive or dead.

Most cases of "disappearance" were perpetrated during periods when the Moroccan state was perceived to be in danger from internal opposition (not only the attempted coups of the early 1970s, but also the activities of opposition parties, trade unions or local rebels) and the Sahrawi opposition in the late 1970s. But the practice of "disappearance" may be continuing. Sahrawis detained in Qal'at M'gouna state that, until the beginning of 1991, new wings were being added on to the secret detention centre. The 11 villas said to hold "disappeared" prisoners in a radius of 50 kilometres around Rabat are still believed to be in use.

Routes in "disappearance"

Various routes seem to followed in "disappearance" cases. Some "disappearances" are temporary, and the "disappeared" person is released after a few months or years. Sometimes "disappearance" is clearly intended to last forever.

Temporary "disappearance" can be seen as an extension of the legal procedure of keeping the suspect for interrogation for a certain number of days in *garde à vue* (incommunicado) detention without contact with lawyers, doctors and family. In the 1970s *garde à vue* was sometimes illegally prolonged for over two years, during which the detainees had no contact with their families, who were never informed where they were held. Illegal prolongation of *garde à vue* remained frequent throughout the 1980s.

Some Moroccans suspected of being opponents of the government, who should have been brought to court, appeared to drop out of the system for months or years, their whereabouts being unknown even to their families, before being released or brought to trial. One place where detainees were held incommunicado for long periods was the detention, interrogation and torture centre of Derb Moulay Cherif in Casablanca. For Sahrawis "disappearance" appeared to be "normal": only very rarely did the authorities bring before the courts any Western Saharan suspected of opposing Moroccan rule or supporting the Popular Front for the Liberation of Seguia el-Hamra and Rio de Oro, known as the Polisario Front.

Recent testimonies of some of those released after "disappearance" over the last 10 years show that, for many, it was clear from the beginning that a special procedure was in operation: they were abducted by armed men with no semblance of legality, taken at once to a secret centre, saw no one clearly attached to any normal police force, and never had the impression that they were being interrogated for any *procès verbal* (police statement).

Some branches of the security forces may hold "disappeared" prisoners without notifying other services. The *Forces armées royales* (FAR), Royal Moroccan Army, usually hands over civilians arrested during its operations to one or other of the police forces. Intelligence forces, which often carry out the same tasks in competition with each other, include the *Direction de la surveillance de territoire*, Office of Territorial Surveillance (under the Minister of the Interior and involved in many "disappearance" cases), the *Renseignements généraux*, General Intelligence, which has the power to arrest suspects and operates from police stations, but is not known to practise "disappearance", and the *Direction générale des études et documentation*, the General Office of Research and Documentation, which has one division under the direct control of the King and another branch under the Prime Minister. Though technically controlled by the FAR, the *Gendarmerie royale*, Royal Gendarmerie, is in practice directly supervised by the King. Its size and equipment was expanded to counterbalance the army, which was implicated in the 1971 and 1972 coup attempts.

The *Compagnies mobiles d'intervention*, Mobile Intervention Companies, are cited as both guarding and transporting "disappeared" prisoners. There are also said to be "parallel" security services, operating in plain clothes, with a direct chain of command to the Minister of the Interior or loyal officials of King Hassan II, who carry out secret and unacknowledged activities.

The *makhazini* (a local auxiliary force) frequently guard the "disappeared" in the rural areas. Testimonies of released "disappeared" prisoners who were held in outlying provinces describe visits by provincial governors to detention centres guarded by *makhazini*. There is little doubt that, although probably not involved in ordering "disappearances", governors condone and collaborate in the imprisonment of scores of people for decades in secret unacknowledged detention.

Recent testimonies suggest that the reasons for "disappearance" include suspected or actual political opposition activities; disloyalty by state servants, especially those involved in secret services (*makhazini* guarding the "disappeared" Oufkirs who smuggled out letters for the family themselves "disappeared"); and sometimes as a result of involvement in secret financial dealings or as a consequence of personal rivalries. Another member of a family, or even a whole family might be detained and "disappear" as a result of the "crime" of one member. This was the case of the Oufkir family, and the family of the first Polisario prime minister, Mohamed Lamine Leili, 11 of whose relatives were arrested and "disappeared".

Although food and living conditions are sometimes bearable, this has not been the norm. The Bourequat brothers, released in 1991, said that after an initial period of torture they were fairly well treated while in secret detention between 1973 and 1981 in various Rabat villas. But for many, including the Bourequat brothers after 1981 when they were moved to Tazmamert, semi-starvation in extremely harsh conditions appeared to be part of the punishment. This was the case at Tazmamert, where about half the inmates died over a period of 17 years; at Qal'at M'gouna (where about 300 Sahrawis were held, some for over 15 years) until 1985, when conditions improved somewhat; at Agdz, where Sahrawis and 10 Moroccans were held until 1983; and at Ain Jdid, where the Oufkir family were detained between 1977 and 1987.

A 1989 letter from Tazmamert described the "infernal prison of Tazmamert" where detainees had "been buried up to now, without even the rights enjoyed by beasts, totally isolated from each other and from the outside world". The "Complex" in Casablanca, in contrast, where 10 "disappeared" prisoners, including five students, were held for 18 months, bound, blindfold and lying on the floor, as regards food was "a five-star hotel. We received yoghurt, apples and bananas brought from the Avicennes Hospital next door. We even grew fatter. But at Agdz we lost all these reserves in the first week". Detainees at Qal'at M'gouna described how the dogs were fed before the detainees; it was their leftovers which were passed to the "disappeared".

Some prisoners could not bear the conditions of detention and went out of their minds. A detainee in Tazmamert who told a guard, in 1974, that he had been sentenced to three years was told: "Don't say three, say forever". One of those detained in Tazmamert is known to have committed suicide after 18 years of darkness and isolation. Sergeant Mimoun Fagouri hanged himself on 1 June 1990, fifteen years after the expiry of his sentence. He called to those in neighbouring cells: "I am weary. The only way out of Tazmamert is by death". Two of the Sahrawis released in June 1991 had gone mad; so had a Lebanese, detained in secret for over 12 years and left in Qal'at M'gouna when the Sahrawis were freed. His fate and that of a Libyan, also detained there, remain unknown.

Pressure for change

In 1981 Group 214 of Amnesty International's Dutch Section began working on behalf of El Bechir (Abdi) ould Labbat ould Mayara, born in 1937, taking over the case from Dutch Section Group 56. From 1981 the group wrote about 400 letters to King Hassan, the Minister of Saharan Affairs, other government ministers, prisons, hospitals, human rights organizations, local authorities, headmasters, mayors, and the Moroccan Ambassador. Letters were also written by Leiden town councillors and over 1,000 postcards were sent.

In 1982 two identical replies were received from the Moroccan Ministry of Justice stating that "the person cannot be found on any prisoner lists ... searches made by the Ministry have yielded no result". One prison only replied to say that "Mayara is unknown here..."

Abdi Mayara was one of the more than 300 Sahrawi "disappeared" who were released in June 1991, over 15 years after his "disappearance" on 3 February 1976.

Amnesty International has campaigned on "disappearances" in Morocco since the early 1970s through work on cases by groups and in a major campaign on Morocco in 1982 (when "disappearances" were raised and letters smuggled out of Tazmamert were given wide publicity for the first time). Moroccan students who "disappeared" for between one and three years in the 1980s were the subject of urgent appeals while both Moroccan and Sahrawi prisoners were the object of long-term action by Amnesty International groups. One Moroccan who "disappeared" in 1972, Houcine El Manouzi, was adopted by Amnesty International as a prisoner of conscience and his case assigned to a group in 1975, while between 1977 and 1980, the cases of 88 Sahrawi "disappeared" were taken up by Amnesty International groups.

Over the next 12 years Amnesty International groups, like Dutch Section Group 214, wrote thousands of letters and postcards on behalf of those who had "disappeared", with minimal response. Between 1981 and 1991, Group 64 of Amnesty International's German Section sent over a thousand letters and postcards on behalf of Heiba ould Omar ould Mayara, the cousin of Bechir Mayara, and one of the first to be arrested and "disappear" a few days after the annexation by Morocco of the Western Sahara in November 1975. They received a standard reply from the Ministry of Justice, and nine prisons returned letters marked "unknown".

In July 1991, when the first, handwritten list of the Sahrawis who had died was received, it was learned that he had died on 28 September 1977 at Agdz. A fellow "disappeared" prisoner described his death:

"The same day [as another detainee died] Heiba was dead in his cell... The whole prison caught an illness, only one person didn't get it, we called it the 'sickness of the knees'. It attacked all the lower body and led to paralysis. It began by black spots on the soles and the whole foot became dry and later you couldn't move. You had diarrhoea. One of us had studied medicine, he was a student and he said the illness was due to lack of vitamin B12, it was a disease of malnutrition..."

A number of solidarity groups of Moroccan or Sahrawi exiles or sympathizers worked actively from the late 1970s in many countries, mostly in Western Europe, for the release of the "disappeared". They included the *Association de parents et amis des disparus au Maroc* (APADM), Association of Relatives and Friends of the Disappeared of Morocco, and the *Asociación de familiares de presos y desparecidos saharauis* (AFAPREDESA), Association of Families of Sahrawi Prisoners and "Disappeared" People; both organizations compiled lists and details of the "disappeared".

Many of the cases of those later released, as well as of those still "disappeared", were raised by families or non-governmental organizations (including Amnesty International) with the UN Working Group on Disappearances. Thus, for example, the 1984 report of the Working Group referred in paragraph 135 to the "disappearance" of the three Bourequat brothers, who had been arrested in 1973:

"In a letter dated 20 June 1983, the Government of Morocco informed the Working Group of the results of its investigations. With regard to the reported disappearance of three brothers who were said to have been arrested on the same day at their home, the Government stated that the records of the courts, the Ministry of Justice and the prisons had been searched, but that no record of criminal charges or of any other judicial procedures regarding the brothers had been found. In the Government's view, they should be sought outside the country".

On 30 December 1991 the three Bourequat brothers were at last released from over 10 years in appalling conditions in Tazmamert and over 18 years' "disappearance".

Until 1991 only a few, sporadic releases occurred to sustain the hopes of campaigners – for example the release between 1984 and 1986 of a group of 12 students who had "disappeared" in 1983.

Difficulties in campaigning on Moroccan "disappearances"

For the world it was often difficult to believe that people could still be alive in a secret cell after "disappearing" for 15 years or more. Part of the difficulty was the shortage of information. To be sure that a "disappearance" has been perpetrated, the victim needs to have been seen to have been arrested by the security forces – preferably by more than one witness – and the government must have been asked to account for the arrest and have denied holding the person. A clamp-down on information from the Western Sahara made it almost impossible to get this sort of information. The climate of fear meant that even a family might not ask after its "disappeared" members. There were hundreds of reports of "disappearances" between 1975 and 1987 in the Western Sahara; on very few did Amnesty International have information on when, how and by whom the person was arrested, and on even fewer, details of family and life before arrest.

The 88 cases taken up by Amnesty International groups between 1977 and 1980 were put before the UN Working Group on Disappearances in 1988, but the Working Group deemed only two of the cases admissible. Interestingly, the two cases deemed admissible were the only ones subsequently shown to have been of prisoners who "disappeared" only temporarily. One had then been released, the other had been brought to trial, sentenced to four years' imprisonment, and released in 1981 (he was part of a group known as the "Meknes" group, the only group of Sahrawis Amnesty International knew of who, after six months' "disappearance" in secret centres, then went through a normal legal process and were brought to trial).

The reappearance of one of these two released prisoners was discovered by Amnesty International and reported to the Working Group. Although it was later confirmed that he had been released in 1981, the Amnesty International group working on his case had written letters on his behalf for eight years without receiving information on his release from the Moroccan authorities. The case was then used extensively by the Moroccan Government to suggest that Amnesty International's information was bad in every other respect, and that all the others who had allegedly "disappeared" had probably also come out of detention and were living happily elsewhere, perhaps under different names. They suggested that the fluidity of the Sahrawi name structure had helped to confuse Amnesty International; the youth who had "disappeared" and been subsequently tried as Mustapha Lahna had reappeared as a lecturer in the Rabat University Department of English as Mohammed Tamek. Moroccan authorities also stressed Sahrawi nomadism to suggest that those alleged to have "disappeared" were probably in Mauritania or the Polisario camps around Tindouf, Algeria.

At the centre of Amnesty International's 1990 report "Morocco; 'Disappearances' of people of Western Saharan origin" (see below) were the case studies of 27 Sahrawi "disappeared", with details of who they were, the circumstances of their "disappearance" – and the affirmation that the Sahrawi "disappeared" were still alive. The evidence for this assertion included a testimony from a Moroccan, released after a period of "disappearance", who had been in the forts of Agdz and Qal'at M'gouna with Sahrawi prisoners until 1984.

In the summer of 1990 Amnesty International received supporting evidence, in the testimony of a former guard at Agdz and Qal'at M'gouna, who described guarding the "disappeared":

"They got given vegetables, lentils and beans, but they weren't properly cooked. Squashes too. There were guard dogs too, at the *qsar* [fortress]. They gave the same food to the prisoners as to the dogs, exactly the same thing, the same mess-tin. Most of them had no clothes. When they went to the latrines they wrapped blankets around themselves out of modesty.

"As these were special prisons we often beat them, in turn, sometimes for five minutes, sometimes for a quarter of an hour. It was tiring for us too. They'd get out into the yard for a short time and we'd tell them that's where they'd be buried, in that yard. We'd even hang out white shroud material so that they could see it from the yard, to bring it home to them...

"During the years I was there, it was always like that, night and day. No visits, no books, no radio, waiting for death... I stayed until 1983. I met someone not long ago who said it was still the same, except that some were dead... "

In addition, the family of one Sahrawi "disappeared" received letters that had been smuggled out: Amnesty International did not mention this in its report, as the family feared that the source of letters might dry up, but it enabled the organization to pinpoint the secret centre in Laayoune where their relative was kept and to be sure that most of those detained there were still alive.

Other factors also encouraged silence:

- *"Quiet diplomacy versus publicity".* When incontrovertible evidence was obtained that people such as the Oufkir family and the military prisoners of Tazmamart were secretly detained by the government, the off-the-record message from those close to the government was always that these people were likely to be released, *as long as no publicity was given on their cases.* Pressure against publicity was applied, not only on the families of the "disappeared" but also on foreign governments and on Amnesty International. The United States (US) Department of State, for example, appears to have been persuaded to keep silent for years over the one Tazmamert prisoner of concern to it, M'Barek Touil, who is married to an American citizen, and to exert any pressure on the Moroccan Government completely without publicity. Some pressure was certainly exerted, and from 1985 M'Barek Touil, sentenced to 20 years' imprisonment in 1972, was given better conditions: he was allowed to correspond with his wife – a heavily censored correspondence which said nothing about his surroundings – but no public statement on his situation was ever made and his place of detention was not revealed. Other Western governments were similarly discreet.

- *The families' fear.* One of the chief difficulties in campaigning is that "disappearance" may force the family into the conspiracy of silence. There is a fear for the safety of the person "disappeared" as well as of reprisals against other members of the family. As one relative of a "disappeared" prisoner said before Amnesty International's 1991 Morocco campaign: "For myself, I don't mind. But suppose that in a month or six months a cousin dies in a road accident – I'll never be sure whether that was really an accident or my fault for speaking out."

Internal forces for change

Morocco has three principal human rights movements, two of which, the *Association marocaine des droits de l'homme* (AMDH), Moroccan Association of Human Rights, and the *Ligue marocaine des droits de l'homme*, Moroccan League of Human Rights, work together in a coordinating committee. The third is the *Organisation marocaine des droits de l'homme* (OMDH), Moroccan Organization of Human Rights.

The human rights movement was becoming more active and vocal after 1988, its demands reflected in the pages of the press and supported by some opposition political parties and trade unions. (In Morocco an outspoken press and human rights organizations raise questions of torture and political imprisonment with a vigour not found in many other countries in the region.) Political prisoners freely answered letters from Amnesty International groups and wrote numerous communiques about prison conditions which were published in newspapers. But a major difficulty in acting against "disappearances" was a conspiracy of silence (with a few notable and courageous exceptions) about the "disappeared", until relatively recently, within Morocco. The freedom of expression in Morocco does not extend to the institution of the monarchy (for instance by calling for a republic or criticizing the King), the integrity of the nation (for instance, by suggesting that the Western Sahara should be offered self-determination) or Islam. These restrictions on free speech are reflected in the constitutional provision that grants immunity to members of parliament but lifts that immunity when "the opinions expressed challenge the monarchical system, Islam or constitute an insult to the King".

The silence from families, former "disappeared" prisoners and the news media was – and still is – a most important part of the success of the use of "disappearance" by the Moroccan Government as a means to eliminate political opponents. Usually "disappearances" have been regarded as part of the royal prerogative – an issue beyond criticism and strictly not to be mentioned.

This has not been true of all "disappearances". Some of the cases of Moroccans suspected of political opposition or students who "disappeared" were mentioned, but rarely, by a few courageous Moroccan newspapers. Other "disappearances" in cases which had followed direct threats to the King, such as attempted coups where people's "disappearance" may have been presumed to have been ordered by the King, were for a long time never mentioned publicly within Morocco.

Protest against "disappearance" by the families of the Sahrawi "disappeared" was even more muted as Sahrawis were more closely watched and more liable to suffer arrest and "disappearance" for speaking out than Moroccans. One description of how arrests were made was given by a young Sahrawi exile in Spain:

> "This is what they do. They come at night normally, straight to the house of the person [they are after]. Several police dressed as locals enter and take him away on a stretcher, after making him bathe in his own blood. In the morning the families go to the commissariat and inquire about him, and the only reply they get, standard for everyone, is 'If you ask again, you'll disappear [yourself]'..."

The ban on speaking openly was also imposed on foreign journalists and usually accepted by them. When King Hassan was interviewed by French journalists for the French television channel *Antenne 2* in December 1989, the same boundaries were drawn. In particular, the interviewers were ordered beforehand not to mention the Oufkir family, and, although one interviewer made a reference to "certain children", they obeyed.

This silence began to break at last in December 1990 when the families of some of the Tazmamert prisoners wrote a petition to certain ministers, including the Ministers of the Interior and Justice, calling for the conditions of their relatives to be investigated and for those who had completed their sentences to be released. Copies were sent to political parties and newspapers. The trigger for the petition was a batch of letters smuggled out of Tazmamert which reached some prisoners' families in November 1990, making them fear that if they did not speak out now it would be too late.

At the same time another letter, a vivid description of Tazmamert written in 1989, was posted anonymously in December 1990 to a number of people and human rights organizations, including Amnesty International. This letter was published first, in French translation, by the *Association de défense des droits de l'homme au Maroc*, the Association for the Defence of Human Rights in Morocco, a Moroccan human rights group based in Paris. It provided the first information that the Bourequat brothers were alive and held in Tazmamert. The knowledge of the heightened awareness of Moroccan events in the international arena strengthened the readiness first of families, and then of Moroccan journalists and human rights groups to speak openly of things which previously could not be mentioned.

Tazmamert was raised in parliament in December 1990 by the leader of the *Organisation de l'action démocratique populaire* (OADP), Organization of Democratic Popular Action; his question was reported in the OADP newspaper *Anwal* and taken up by other papers sympathetic to the *Union socialiste des forces populaires*, Socialist Union of Popular Forces. In February 1991 the Oufkir family were released and only then were they mentioned in a Moroccan newspaper.

In May and June 1991 Tazmamert and the Oufkirs were openly mentioned in conferences and communiques of the OMDH, the AMDH and the *Association de jeunes avocats*, Young Lawyers' Association. A dossier on Tazmamert was published in a small opposition newspaper, *Hurriyat al-Muwatin* (Freedom of the Citizen).

External forces for change

The timing of Amnesty International's campaign against human rights violations in Morocco was made more effective by external forces which coincided with the campaign, but which themselves gained in importance because they happened in a situation in which human rights in Morocco had become high on the agenda, both internally and internationally.

A visit by an Amnesty International delegation to King Hassan in February 1990, and the subsequent publication of a report, "Morocco; Human rights violations in *garde à vue* detention" (February 1990), contributed to this. This report drew international attention to facts which had been exposed by local human rights groups. In its next report, "Morocco; 'Disappearances' of people of Western Saharan origin" (November 1990), Amnesty International, in reporting on the Sahrawi "disappearances", raised questions which could not be raised by activists in the country.

Factors in the changing international situation included:

- The publication in France of *Notre ami le roi* (Our Friend the King) by Gilles Perrault in September 1990. The book received enormous publicity, partly because of the adverse reaction from the Moroccan Government, which rather clumsily tried to stop publication and then bought up an entire edition. This publicity fed back into the human rights movement as well as popular feeling in Morocco, where copies were smuggled in. It also raised consciousness in France, causing Morocco to cancel plans for a program of events there celebrating Morocco's history and culture. It was less important outside francophone countries as it was not, during the next year, translated into other languages. However, its popularity in France meant that, for a time at least, France, the staunchest supporter of the Moroccan Government, felt obliged to put pressure on Morocco to take some action on human rights concerns.

- Pressure from the Human Rights Committee set up under the International Covenant on Civil and Political Rights, which began the consideration of Morocco's periodic report on its implementation of the Covenant in November 1990 (on the Human Rights Committee, see Chapter 12). For the consideration of Morocco's report, numerous human rights groups submitted information to the Human Rights Committee.

Most of these groups were based in Europe and the US, but they included the OMDH – the first time an Arab human rights organization had presented a report to the

Human Rights Committee on its own government. Amnesty International, according to its normal practice, also made available a summary of its concerns, its report on *garde à vue* detention in Morocco, and a report on "disappearances" in Morocco which was to be made public the same month.

During the session of the Committee the question of the "disappeared" was raised quite strongly. When the Moroccan representative said, in answer to questions about the Oufkirs, that this was within the royal prerogative and an internal matter, Committee members told the Moroccan delegation that Morocco's ratification of the International Covenant placed such questions within the competence of the Human Rights Committee.

Eventually the delegation capitulated and apologized; it recognized the competence of the Committee, but said it did not have the information to reply to their questions; Tazmamert and Qal'at M'gouna were not on any lists of prisons. The members of the Committee did not complete consideration of Morocco's report, and specifically asked the delegation, among other things, to return with information on Tazmamert and Qal'at M'gouna.

This meeting showed the potential for publicity on Human Rights Committee discussions. Because of growing international interest in human rights concerns in Morocco, the Committee's sessions began to receive publicity in the West. The text of the discussions was also serialized in a Moroccan daily newspaper.

- The UN-sponsored settlement of the problem of the Western Sahara in June 1990, which was moving towards the first stage of implementation in the summer of 1991 (the cease-fire was scheduled for 6 September). The settlement envisaged an amnesty for all political prisoners and was almost certainly a factor in the releases of Sahrawi "disappeared" in June 1991.

Other external forces for change should not be ignored. One such force is the heightened international awareness of human rights. In 1990 and 1991 this was reflected in influential news media such as Radio France International (to which many Moroccans listen including, reportedly, King Hassan II), which covered a number of human rights stories every day. At the same time new human rights organizations were being founded in many African countries. In neighbouring Mali a military government fell to be replaced by a government headed by the leader of the newly-formed human rights movement.

Evaluation of Amnesty International's campaign

Amnesty International's campaign on Morocco provides an example of the interweaving of internal and external pressures for change. External pressures on the Moroccan Government, for which Amnesty International was responsible for only a small part, clearly increased the confidence of a growing and increasingly outspoken internal human rights movement. Some external pressures, such as that generated by

Gilles Perrault's book, were coincidental to Amnesty International's campaign, while others, such as those stemming from the Human Rights Committee discussions and the Western Sahara settlement, were taken into account when planning the campaign and influenced the focus of the papers which Amnesty International published.

The dimension added by Amnesty International's campaign was the international force of a human rights movement which could not only flood Moroccan authorities with thousands of letters a day from people in every continent, but also had influence with governments and intergovernmental organizations throughout the world. Visits by Amnesty International sections to Moroccan embassies in their countries were important and the pressure by governments, when exercised, supported Amnesty International's demands. Amnesty International groups in other Arab countries played a particular part in the campaign. In the European Parliament, where concerns over human rights violations in Morocco had been raised for years, Amnesty International's information was quoted in speeches and resolutions.

The timing of the releases of Moroccan and Sahrawi detainees may help to identify some of the most significant pressures:

- The release of the Oufkir family came in February 1991, a month before the launch of Amnesty International's campaign (though the campaign's timing was almost certainly already known in Morocco), but five months after the publication of Gilles Perrault's book and an intensive campaign by human rights groups based in France.

- The releases of more than 300 Sahrawi "disappeared" occurred as moves were being made to implement the UN settlement over Western Sahara and three weeks before the session of the Human Rights Committee to continue consideration of Morocco's report in July 1991.

- The transfer of the 30 surviving detainees from Tazmamert took place in September 1991. In August 1991 a number of non-governmental organizations had spoken at the UN Sub-Commission on Prevention of Discrimination and Protection of Minorities to call for the release of the prisoners of Tazmamert. Amnesty International had extended its campaign for a further three months shortly before, issuing a news release to mark the anniversary of the transfer of detainees to Tazmamert on 7 August 1973.

- Pressure from the USA was also clearly important; the emptying of Tazmamert in September 1991 and the release of three long-term political prisoners in Kenitra Central Prison in January 1992 came in each case just before visits of King Hassan to the USA. The Tazmamert prisoner who was married to a US citizen was released before the others.

- The actual releases of most Tazmamert prisoners, after medical treatment,

were in October 1991, around the time of the final session of the Human
Rights Committee for consideration of Morocco's report.

- Lobbying by members of a European Parliament delegation visiting Morocco
in December 1991 was said to have led to the release of the Bourequat brothers.

The importance of Amnesty International's part in the releases of the "disappeared",
even though other pressures played a significant part, cannot be discounted. All the
releases came immediately before or during the organization's 1991 campaign, and
those released included prisoners featured in the campaign. They included 24 of the
27 "disappeared" prisoners mentioned in the case studies published in "Morocco;
'Disappearances' of people of Western Saharan origin". Moreover, the centres from
which the "disappeared" were released were those mentioned with corroborative detail
in Amnesty International reports: Tazmamert, Qal'at M'gouna and Laayoune. Former
"disappeared" people in Qal'at M'gouna reported that they were told in March 1991
that Amnesty International and other organizations were campaigning for them and
they were going to be released.

The future

More "disappeared" prisoners have been released in Morocco than campaigners dared
hope for. But hundreds more are still unaccounted for. Forty-eight Western Saharans
and 30 detained Moroccan military men have died in custody, but the Moroccan
Government has not even officially informed their families of their deaths. New
information suggests that Amnesty International has consistently underestimated the
numbers of Moroccans who may, at one time or another, have "disappeared" after
detention. There is much still to be done to address the problems of the still unresolved
"disappeared".

Other Sahrawi and Moroccan "disappeared" people in other centres still to be
effectively exposed have not been released. Although some of those who have not been
released are those on whose behalf Amnesty International has been campaigning for
years, like Houcine El-Manouzi, often they are people on whose cases Amnesty
International has had only scanty information. New information, which has confirmed
sightings in secret centres of some of these missing people, like Abdelhaq Rouissi,
should help.

No one can now deny that the "disappearances" described in Amnesty
International's reports and appeals were substantiated. The Moroccan Government
itself has now issued a "List of the persons originating from the Sahara reprieved by
His Majesty King Hassan II following the request of the members of the Advisory
Council for the Saharan Affairs". But although Moroccan authorities have been shown
to have held people in secret incommunicado detention in sometimes appalling
conditions for over 15 years, the Moroccan Government has largely avoided the
worldwide condemnation such practices deserve. When the Bourequat brothers were

released, after these French citizens' 18 years' unacknowledged detention without charge or trial, 10 of them in Tazmamert, there was no remonstrance for past injustice when President Mitterrand of France publicly thanked Morocco for their release.

Internally there may never be any inquiry into what has happened. Like other ex-"disappeared" in Morocco, the recently reappeared prisoners have been stifled by continuing governmental intimidation and restrictions. Those who were released from Tazmamert were told, before they were released, to forget that Tazmamert ever existed and never to talk about their experiences. The released Sahrawis are closely watched and effectively harassed to prevent them from talking. However, for the sake of human rights in Morocco, the campaign for a full inquiry should be continued.

In April 1993 Amnesty International issued another report on "disappearances" in Morocco and Western Sahara, "Morocco; Breaking the wall of silence: the 'disappeared' in Morocco". In May 1993 Amnesty International delegates visited Morocco to discuss the organization's concerns with the *Conseil consultatif des droits de l'homme* (CCDH), Consultative Council for Human Rights. This official government-appointed human rights body accepted that there had been "disappearances" in the past and stated that they wished to "turn a page". Amnesty International discussed at length 17 cases with the CCDH and has since sent lists of other people believed to have "disappeared". Amnesty International urged the CCDH to intervene for the release of all those who remain "disappeared".

Today more Moroccan families are ready to speak out about "disappeared" relatives and more information has been gathered on how "disappearances" are organized in Morocco. Moroccan human rights movements have published lists of the Moroccan "disappeared". But the silence within Morocco on the Sahrawi "disappeared" has not been broken. There are political constraints on local activists who might be expected to speak out on their behalf inside Morocco. However, it is clear that open discussion within Morocco on the fate of the "disappeared" must be the next step as Moroccan human rights activists come to accept that "disappearance" can only be stopped if it is opposed whoever the victim and whatever the circumstances.

CHAPTER 7

THE ANATOMY OF THE ATROCITIES

1   What is a "disappearance"?

The "disappeared" are people who have been taken into custody by agents of the state, yet whose whereabouts and fate are concealed, and whose custody is denied.
– Amnesty International 14-Point Program for the Prevention of "Disappearances"

Amnesty International considers that a "disappearance" has occurred whenever:

- there are reasonable grounds to believe that a person has been taken into custody by the authorities or their agents, and

- the authorities deny that the victim is in custody, thus concealing his or her whereabouts and fate.[1]

Amnesty International puts the term in quotation marks to emphasize that the victim has in reality not simply vanished. The victim's whereabouts and fate, concealed from the outside world, are known by someone. Someone decided what would happen to the victim; someone decided to conceal it. Someone is responsible.

There are several elements to a "disappearance" as described above:

- The victim is *deprived of liberty* and held prisoner.

- The victim is deprived of liberty by *agents of the state.* These may be police officers or soldiers in uniform who carry out the arrest openly; the authorities will later deny that the person has been arrested, or acknowledge the arrest but claim that the victim later escaped or was released. They may be intelligence officers or other members of the security forces who wear plain clothes and refuse to identify themselves to onlookers. They may be people who do not formally belong to the security services but are operating by order of the authorities or with their complicity or acquiescence.

- The victim's whereabouts and fate are *concealed,* and the authorities deny holding the victim. This denial may be in the form of a public statement, a reply to inquiries by the victim's relatives, or a response to a judicial procedure such as *habeas corpus* which has been invoked in an effort to find the victim and ensure his or her safety. The authorities also fail to follow correct procedures for detention such as bringing prisoners promptly before a judicial authority and notifying relatives promptly of their arrest and place of detention.

The phrase *reasonable grounds* is used to emphasize that Amnesty International will act on a case even though some of the details may be obscured. Rapid action is vital, as it is often in the hours and days after arrest or abduction that the "disappeared" may suffer some harm. Relatives, lawyers and domestic human rights organizations endeavour to make inquiries at places where the victim might be held, invoke the power of the courts if these are accessible, and press the authorities to produce the "disappeared" person and ensure his or her well-being. International organizations such as Amnesty International join in the effort by making international appeals to the authorities if it is believed such appeals may benefit the "disappeared" person.

Sometimes the effort succeeds, and the victim reappears after a few days or weeks in secret custody. Occasionally the "disappeared" reappear after many years, as in Morocco in 1991. More often the "disappeared" are never seen again alive. As time passes, the fear will grow that a "disappeared" person has been killed.

"Disappearance", torture and extrajudicial execution often go hand in hand. The victim may be arrested or abducted, tortured for such purposes as obtaining information, and then killed. Sometimes the body is dumped in a public place: it may be found and identified, but the "disappearance" will have helped to conceal the authors and circumstances of the torture and killing. In other cases bodies are mutilated beyond recognition or disposed of secretly: the "disappearance" keeps the key facts of the killing hidden, and the fate and whereabouts of the victim remain unknown. "Disappearance" becomes a cover for extrajudicial execution, and extra-judicial execution perpetuates the state of "disappearance".

"Disappearances" cause extreme agony for the victims and their relatives. The victims are cut off from the world and placed beyond any form of protection. Completely in the power of their captors, they suffer from what is impressed on them as the hopeless certainty that no one outside can help them. They must face the prospect of being killed, and indeed this is often how their life ends.

The relatives of the "disappeared" are kept in ignorance, unable to find out whether the victims are alive or dead. Often the authorities prolong the uncertainty long after the victim has in fact been killed, leaving the relatives unable to start a new life, unable to go through a normal bereavement and unable to deal with legal and practical matters which will remain unresolved as long as the victim's death has not been officially acknowledged. This may mean that a family will be unable to receive the pension due to them through the loss of their breadwinner, or to settle matters concerning property and inheritance. The perpetrators may have washed their hands of the "disappeared", but for the relatives, the "disappearance" continues without end.[2]

2   What is an extrajudicial execution?

Extrajudicial executions are unlawful and deliberate killings, carried out by order of a government or with its complicity or acquiescence.
— Amnesty International 14-Point Program for the Prevention of Extrajudicial Executions

The above description used by Amnesty International serves to distinguish extrajudicial executions from other killings. There are several elements.

- An extrajudicial execution is **deliberate**, not accidental.

- An extrajudicial execution is **unlawful**. It violates national laws such as those which prohibit murder, and/or international standards forbidding the arbitrary deprivation of life, as described in Chapter 8.

Its unlawfulness distinguishes an extrajudicial execution from:

- justifiable killings in **self-defence**;

- deaths resulting from the use of reasonable force in **law enforcement**;

- killings in war which are not forbidden under international laws that regulate the conduct of **armed conflict**;

- the use of the **death penalty**.[3]

- An extrajudicial execution is **carried out by order of a government or with its acquiescence**. This concept distinguishes extrajudicial executions from killings for private reasons, or killings which are in violation of an enforced official policy. If a soldier kills someone for personal reasons and the authorities, learning of it, arrest and punish the soldier, clearly showing their disapproval, it is not an extrajudicial execution. Extrajudicial executions are not the work of individual soldiers or police officers acting in isolation. Someone else, at some level of government, whether national, state or local, has ordered the killings or acquiesced in them.

The combination of unlawfulness and governmental involvement puts extrajudicial executions in a class of their own. An extrajudicial execution is, in effect, a murder committed or condoned by the state.

The concept of extrajudicial executions brings together several types of killings.

- In most of the cases known to Amnesty International worldwide, the victim is being held prisoner or is in the control of the perpetrator at the time of the killing, as when soldiers order people to come out of their homes and then line them up and kill them.

- Some victims are not in custody but are assassinated in the street or murdered by unknown assailants.

- Some killings are committed by officers performing law enforcement functions. These killings involve a use of force which was disproportionate to any threat posed, although the authorities may claim that this use of force was legitimate. The security forces may open fire on a peaceful demonstration and later claim they were facing a life-threatening riot, for example, or shoot down a criminal suspect who threatened physical harm to no one and then pretend that the victim was violently resisting arrest.

- Some victims are civilians not involved in hostilities who are deliberately shot, bombed or shelled in military operations.[4]

Some killings are concealed, or presented by the authorities as the work of someone having no official connection. Others are in disputed circumstances: the authorities acknowledge that official forces committed them, but present them as killings which were justified under the circumstances.

As with "disappearances", Amnesty International does not have to be in possession of the full facts in order to take action. If there is reason to believe that an extrajudicial execution has been committed, Amnesty International calls for an official investigation, as required under the standards laid down in international instruments adopted at the UN and other intergovernmental fora. Such an investigation can yield valuable information, leading to the prosecution and conviction of those responsible for an unlawful killing. If the authorities fail to conduct an impartial and effective investigation, this failure adds to the presumption that a killing was committed with governmental acquiescence.

3   Organizational complexity

> "The phenomenon of disappearances is a complex form of human rights violation that must be understood and confronted in an integral fashion."
> – Inter-American Court of Human Rights, Velásquez Rodríguez judgment[5]

This statement on the complexity of "disappearances" could equally be made about extrajudicial executions. These abuses are never the work of a single person acting alone.

- In a "disappearance", the victim must be taken prisoner, transported to a place of secret detention and held there hidden, with the connivance or acquiescence of public officials.

- An extrajudicial execution involves, at a minimum, the person who carried it out and the officials who ordered, connived or acquiesced in it.

Because "disappearances" and extrajudicial executions are so often connected to a unit or branch of the security forces, where hierarchical organization is a hallmark, the perpetration of a "disappearance" or an extrajudicial execution is likely to involve a chain of command extending from the highest official who orders or acquiesces in the crime to the lowest officer who helps to carry it out. Often one or another of the country's intelligence services will be involved in selecting the victims and tracking them down. Logistical support, too, will be needed: guns and ammunition, vehicles, communications facilities, places to hold prisoners and torture them, or the means of disposing of bodies must be available.

Sometimes "disappearances" and extrajudicial executions are perpetrated in isolated incidents only. Sometimes they are concentrated in certain cities or areas of a country, or in places where certain police or military units are operating. Sometimes they pervade the whole country.

Where there are programs of "disappearances" and extrajudicial executions, the armed forces are frequently involved. As an institution, the armed forces possess certain characteristics which enable them to carry out such a task: centralized command, ability to act rapidly and on a national scale, capacity to use lethal force and to overcome any resistance. In some situations, however, "disappearances" and political killings have been decentralized, localized, or carried out by forces ranging from "death squads" composed of regular police or military personnel to irregular bands which are in the pay of local landowners or other private citizens but operate with official acquiescence.

Whatever the form of organization, the mechanics of official murder and "disappearance" are almost certain to be concealed. The pattern only begins to emerge when many bits of information gathered by relatives, lawyers, journalists and human rights organizations are pieced together. Such research is vital: in order to combat "disappearances" and extrajudicial executions effectively, it is necessary to know how they are organized.

4   Secrecy, cover-ups and excuses

Because "disappearances" and political killings are illegal, those responsible for them – the people who plan, order, carry out and acquiesce in them – will want to avoid being called to account and punished. Secrecy helps to accomplish this. It also helps to allow a program of "disappearances" and extrajudicial executions to continue by confusing and neutralizing the efforts of those who would take corrective action.

"Disappearances" are secret by nature. Extrajudicial executions, too, are often carried out in secret. If they are done in the open, steps will be taken to hide the identity of the killers or the illegal character of the killings. The authorities attribute the killings to opposition forces or shadowy "death squads", or they may try to pass them off as the result of armed encounters with government forces or of attempts by the victims to escape. Concealment, lies and cover-ups are regular features of "disappearances" and political killings.

It is often the intelligence services which carry out "disappearances" and killings or are involved in them. With their secret methods of operation, intelligence services have many of the qualities needed for these tasks.

Where the facts of "disappearances" and extrajudicial executions become known, the authorities try to deflect international criticism by devising convincing excuses:

- In conversations with representative of other governments they may admit to "excesses" by individual soldiers. They may say these troops are understandably hard to control, given the poor training available in what may be an impoverished country and the provocation suffered when soldiers see their comrades fall victim to atrocities perpetrated by the other side. This notion of soldiers out of control may, however, be belied by the strict discipline with which the same soldiers perform normal military operations.

- The authorities may say they lack the resources to eliminate "disappearances" and extrajudicial executions and must put their greatest priority on defending what is – often misleadingly – presented as a fragile democracy threatened by armed opposition or by other violent sectors of society. This excuse obscures the fact that what is most needed to stop "disappearances" and extrajudicial executions is, first of all, for the highest civil authorities and military commanders to issue clear orders that such acts will not be tolerated, and then for them to back up these orders by convincing deeds.

Some governments have developed sophisticated techniques for projecting a favourable international image with the help of advertising agencies and international lobbyists, hoping that pervasive human rights violations will be forgotten or ignored. Other governments have often been all too ready to accept the excuses.

5   The need for impunity

Impunity for the perpetrators is a common feature of governmental programs of "disappearances" and political killings. Secrecy helps to ensure impunity by preventing the facts becoming known. Impunity is achieved also by the passage of immunity laws and by the active obstruction of individuals and institutions attempting to take remedial action.

Even in countries where the rule of law is generally observed, the police and armed forces often resist attempts to expose alleged wrongdoing within their ranks. To avoid antagonizing them, the authorities may turn a blind eye, even in such serious matters as "disappearances" and extrajudicial executions – crimes for which the requirement to investigate and bring to justice is established under international human rights instruments. But when the highest authorities are behind the crimes, passive acquiescence in the wrongdoing of subordinate forces turns to active obstruction of the course of justice.

Impunity may be formalized through such legal devices as the adoption of laws extending immunity from prosecution to members of the security forces for acts committed in the course of official duties. Such laws encourage human rights violations by demonstrating to the security forces that they will be allowed to commit such unlawful acts as "disappearances" and extrajudicial executions without fear of prosecution.

Impunity is achieved also through such means as harassment, death threats, "disappearance", murder and other forms of repression against individuals trying to investigate the facts or take remedial action – including victims' relatives, lawyers, journalists and judges; and through the weakening or destruction of organizations and institutions where action is being or might be taken, including domestic human rights organizations, a free press, an independent judiciary or an effective public prosecution service. A governmental program of "disappearances" and political killings can entail a legacy of destruction of the country's most important institutions for securing the observance of human rights.

6   Programs of "disappearances" and extrajudicial executions and
         their targets

The scope of "disappearances" and extrajudicial executions ranges from the targeting of selected individuals to the wholesale elimination of sectors of the population. Several governmental programs of "disappearances" and extrajudicial executions in the past 30 years have claimed hundreds of thousands of victims.

In *Indonesia,* following an abortive coup attempt in September 1965, the army leadership called for the destruction of the communist party (PKI), which they blamed for the coup attempt. One of the army leaders, General Nasution, was reported to have told an army staff conference that "all of their [PKI] followers and sympathizers should be eliminated" and to have called for the party's extinction "down to its very roots". In a period of less than a year all the leading figures of the PKI, Indonesia's largest political party, together with great numbers of its members and supporters, were killed. At least 500,000 people are estimated to have been killed in the nine months between October 1965 and June 1966. The killings in Indonesia amounted to a transformation of the political map through the physical liquidation of the political opposition.[6]

In *Democratic Kampuchea* (Cambodia) at least 300,000 people are believed to have been killed during the period of *Khmer Rouge* rule (1975-1979), a time which Democratic Kampuchea's Foreign Minister, Ieng Sary, later referred to as one of "class struggle". The victims included officials of the former government, intellectuals, teachers, students, members of ethnic minorities, currents within the ruling movement who were out of line with the leadership, and alleged "counter-revolutionaries".

In *Uganda* at least 100,000 and possibly as many as half a million people were killed by the security forces during the eight years of President Idi Amin's rule from 1971 to 1979. Systematic and deliberate killings by government forces began in the first month of President Amin's military government and the practice was rapidly institutionalized as a means of eliminating opponents and potential opponents. The victims included members of ethnic groups other than those from which Amin drew support, as well as religious leaders, judges, lawyers, students and intellectuals, criminal suspects and foreign nationals. The impunity with which the security forces were allowed to kill political opponents and criminal suspects created the conditions in which many other people were killed by members of the security forces for criminal motives or simply at will.

In *Iraq*, Amnesty International has estimated that several hundred thousand people have "disappeared" and several hundred thousand more have been extrajudicially executed under the government of President Saddam Hussein (see Chapter 1). Many of the victims have been Kurds and Shi'a Muslims, two groups which are distinct from the group from which Saddam Hussein's main support is drawn. Together with the killings in Indonesia, Kampuchea, and Uganda under Idi Amin and successive governments, the "disappearances" and political killings in Iraq rank among the most massive violations of human rights since the Second World War.

In countries where there are political divisions along ethnic lines, political killings and "disappearances" also have often followed these lines.

* Just as Idi Amin's government had killed many members of the Acholi and Langi ethnic groups, so the new national army under the government of President Milton Obote (1980-1985), comprising many Acholi and Langi troops, massacred civilians in West Nile, one of Amin's traditional areas of support, and killed a great many Baganda civilians in the Luwero triangle.

* In *Burundi*, the politically dominant Tutsi group had been threatened by a rebellion in 1972 inspired by the numerically larger Hutu group. The army was assisted by the paramilitary youth movement of the ruling party in a government counter-attack and began killing anyone connected with the uprising as well as other Hutu leaders or potential leaders. In the capital and in the provinces Hutu were loaded into jeeps and trucks, clubbed to death and buried in mass graves. At least 80,000 people are believed to have been killed in just two months – May and June 1972. Further mass killings of Hutus were carried out in 1988, 1991 and 1993.

Where killings are directed against members of particular ethnic groups, the authorities may portray them as examples of one group killing another in intercommunal clashes. Those who accept this often misleading portrayal of the situation as one of ethnic bloodletting fail to see that they are more organized than is suggested, and that frequently government forces are behind the atrocities.

"Disappearances" and political killings are often committed in countries where government forces are fighting an armed opposition movement, or where an armed conflict has broken out. The victims may include captured guerrillas and soldiers, civilians thought to support them, members of dissident groups and many others who are killed on the mere pretext of having a role in the conflict.

The notion that atrocities are inevitable in armed conflict or that "disappearances" and extrajudicial executions are predominantly a feature of conflict must be resisted. Two of the most massive programs of political killings since the Second World War, those in Indonesia and Kampuchea, were not committed in periods of armed conflict; armed resistance was minimal in both countries. The same can be said for the majority of "disappearances" and extrajudicial executions in Iraq.

Other targets of "disappearance" and extrajudicial execution have included so-called "social undesirables" such as street children, prostitutes, vagrants, the mentally disturbed, known or alleged criminals, and indigenous people where others desire their lands. Where certain segments of society are despised or unwanted, it is often unfortunately all too easy for the authorities to take repressive measures against them.

7   "Disappearances" and extrajudicial executions since the 1980s

In the early 1980s, Amnesty International conducted major international campaigns calling for public action to end "disappearances" and political killings by governments. The massive killings of the 1970s in *Kampuchea* and *Uganda* and the systematic program of "disappearances" in *Argentina* were an indelible backdrop, along with continuing killings and "disappearances" in countries such as *El Salvador, Guatemala* and the *Philippines*. Other situations of "disappearances" and killings of current or recent concern included those in *Afghanistan, Angola, Bolivia*, the *Central African Empire* (now the Central African Republic), *Chad, Chile, Colombia, Equatorial Guinea, Ethiopia, Guinea, India, Iraq, Lebanon, Namibia, Syria* and *Zaire*. Amnesty International was also concerned about assassinations of political emigres and government opponents abroad, known or alleged to have been committed by the agents of various countries.

It was to be hoped that "disappearances" and political killings would diminish thanks to these campaigns as well as the efforts of recently established UN mechanisms on these issues – the Working Group on Enforced or Involuntary Disappearances, created in 1980, and the Special Rapporteur on summary or arbitrary executions, established in 1983. But such was not to be the case. The 1980s saw hundreds of thousands of "disappearances" and extrajudicial executions in *Iraq*; renewed killings under successive governments in *Uganda*, where over 100,000 people are believed to have been killed between 1981 and 1986; and the appearance of new patterns of "disappearances" and political killings in a number of countries. Serious situations of "disappearances" and extrajudicial executions were reported in *Chad*, where over 40,000 people are believed to have been victims of extrajudicial executions under the government of President Hissein Habré from 1982 to 1990; *Ethiopia*, where tens of thousands of people "disappeared" or were extrajudicially executed under the government of President Mengitsu Haile-Mariam which was in power from 1974 to 1991; *Lebanon*, where police records indicate that over 17,000 people "disappeared" or otherwise went missing during the civil war of 1975 to 1990; *El Salvador*, where tens of thousands of people were extrajudicially executed and thousands more "disappeared" between 1979 and the signing of a definitive peace accord in January 1992; *Somalia*, where tens of thousands of unarmed civilians were killed by the army from 1988 to the end of 1990 in areas of rebel fighting and the capital, Mogadishu; *Sri Lanka*, where tens of thousands of people in the south of the country are believed to have been murdered under the cover of "disappearance" between 1987 and 1990, while others "disappeared" or were killed in the northeast; *Sudan*, where many thousands of men, women and children from southern ethnic groups have been victims of extrajudicial executions since the outbreak of civil war in 1983; *Peru*, where at least 4,000 people have "disappeared" and thousands more appear to have been extrajudicially executed by government forces since the introduction in December 1982 of emergency measures; *Colombia*, where annual numbers of recorded "disappearances" and extrajudicial executions increased during the 1980s, reaching a peak of some 3,500 extrajudicial executions in 1988; *Burundi*, where at least 5,000 civilians were killed in 1988 during what the government described as a counter-insurgency operation against armed rebels; *China*, where at least 1,000 people were killed in the capital, Beijing, in June 1989 when troops fired into crowds of unarmed protesters and bystanders to suppress pro-democracy protests; *Mynamar*, where soldiers shot dead at least 1,000 unarmed demonstrators taking part in nationwide protests against one-party military rule in 1988; and other countries including *Afghanistan, Bangladesh, Brazil, Haiti, Honduras, India, Indonesia and East Timor, Liberia, Mauritania*, the *Philippines, South Africa* and *Yemen*. In *Iran* at least 2,500 prisoners were summarily executed in 1988; government secrecy made it impossible to determine whether they had received any form of trial.

The end of the Cold War brought hopes of a new world order where nations would live in peace and human rights would flourish. But the disintegration of the old order brought new conflicts and with them, in places such as *Azerbaydzhan, Georgia, Tadzhikistan* and the former *Yugoslavia*, "disappearances" and political killings. Elsewhere, too, great numbers of "disappearances" and political killings have been committed by forces engaged in warfare, and otherwise in political repression.

Since the beginning of 1990 Amnesty International has recorded "disappearances" in more than 30 countries. Over the same period the organization received reports of known or suspected extrajudicial executions in over 60 countries, and of killings in disputed circumstances in a number of other countries. Deliberate and arbitrary killings by opposition groups and opposing factions in armed conflicts were reported in over 30 countries, although in most of these situations the number of victims was a small fraction of those killed by government forces.[7]

Serious situations of "disappearances", extrajudicial executions and deliberate and arbitrary killings by opposing forces have been reported in the 1990s in countries including:

- *Liberia*, where many thousands of civilian non-combatants have been killed by opposing forces since the invasion of the country in December 1989;

- *Somalia*, where thousands of unarmed civilians have been deliberately killed by political groups fighting in the civil war which has fragmented the country since the overthrow of the government of President Siad Barre in January 1991;

- *Zaire*, where several thousand unarmed civilians have been killed by members of the security forces and other supporters of President Mobutu Sese Seko since 1990, while thousands of others have reportedly been killed in intercommunal attacks instigated or condoned by the authorities;

- *Angola*, where many thousands have been deliberately and arbitrarily killed by government forces and forces of the opposition *União Nacional para a Independência Total de Angola* (UNITA), National Union for the Total Independence of Angola, since UNITA decided to resume fighting after the elections held in September 1992, and many other people have "disappeared";

- *Sudan*, where the practice of extrajudicial executions which prevailed in the 1980s has continued with thousands more victims in the Nuba Mountains and parts of southern Sudan, while various factions of the opposition Sudan People's Liberation Army, which holds large parts of southern Sudan, have also been responsible for serious human rights abuses including deliberate and arbitrary killings;

- *Afghanistan*, where deliberate and arbitrary killings by all groups involved in the conflict have been widely reported in the civil war which continues to ravage the country;

- *Burundi*, where tens of thousands of people were massacred in October and November 1993, many of them by the army, including President Melchior Ndadaye and several ministers and officials of the National Assembly who were executed by soldiers;

- *Iraq*, where thousands of Shi'a Muslim civilians in the south of the country were killed by government forces in connection with the March 1991 uprising which followed the end of the 1991 Gulf war;

- *Sri Lanka*, where thousands of people reportedly "disappeared" or were extrajudicially executed in the northeast after armed conflict with the secessionist Liberation Tigers of Tamil Eelam resumed in June 1990;

- *Rwanda*, where a report by an International Commission of Inquiry published in March 1993 implicated the government of President Juvénal Habyarimana in the organization of several thousand political killings of government opponents and members of the Tutsi ethnic group carried out since October 1990 by members of the security forces, armed militias and authorized "vigilante" gangs loyal to the President's party;

- *Bosnia-Herzegovina*, where thousands of civilians and captured or wounded combatants have been deliberately and arbitrarily killed by members of Serb and Croat forces as well as by members of the largely Muslim government forces since fighting broke out in March 1992;

- *Colombia*, where Amnesty International has recorded over 4,000 extrajudicial executions and over 400 "disappearances" since the beginning of 1990;

- *Indonesia*, where an estimated 2,000 civilians have been deliberately killed by government soldiers since the security forces began counter-insurgency operations against an armed resistance movement in Aceh province in northern Sumatra in 1989;

- *Brazil*, where thousands of poverty-stricken children in the country's big cities in recent years have been murdered or made to "disappear" by "death squads", often composed of or run by police officers;

- *South Africa*, where thousands of people have been victims of politically motivated killings, many of them carried out by the security forces or with their acquiescence in assassinations and mass attacks on residents of black townships and squatter camps;

- *Myanmar*, where many unarmed villagers have been deliberately killed in counter-insurgency operations or have been taken against their will to serve the military as porters and have then been beaten to death, extrajudicially executed for disobeying orders or trying to escape, or driven to die from exhaustion and neglect.

"Disappearances" and known or suspected extrajudicial executions have been reported in the 1990s in many other countries including *Algeria, Bangladesh, Chad, Egypt, El Salvador, Guatemala, Haiti, India,* the *Israeli-Occupied Territories, Kenya, Mali, Mexico, Niger, Papua New Guinea, Peru, Senegal, Sierra Leone, Thailand, Togo,*

Turkey, Uganda and *Venezuela*. Amnesty International also received reports of killings in disputed circumstances in countries such as the *United Kingdom*, where there have been persistent allegations of an official policy by the security forces in Northern Ireland to deliberately kill suspected members of armed opposition groups rather than arrest them, and *Jamaica*, where a number of people shot dead by police had allegedly surrendered or appeared to offer no immediate threat of deadly resistance.

As of late 1993 Amnesty International continued to press the authorities to clarify the whereabouts and fate of people who had "disappeared" earlier in countries including *Morocco*, where after the release of over 300 "disappeared" prisoners in 1991, others – perhaps several hundred – are believed to remain in secret detention; *Yemen*, where the government which took power in 1990 has done nothing to resolve several hundred cases of past "disappearances"; and *Honduras*, where more than 100 people who "disappeared" between 1979 and 1989 remain unaccounted for.

"DISAPPEARANCES" AND EXTRAJUDICIAL EXECUTIONS AS VIOLATIONS OF INTERNATIONAL HUMAN RIGHTS

1   The rise of international human rights standards

Everyone has the right to life, liberty and security of person.
– *Universal Declaration of Human Rights, Article 3*

"Disappearances" and extrajudicial executions are not only acts of extreme cruelty, violating the laws of the countries where they are perpetrated; they also violate international standards on human rights. The development of these standards since the Second World War has been one of the great achievements of the world community. These standards have proved invaluable to organizations defending human rights in different countries.

The United Nations, formed at the end of the war, was concerned with human rights from the outset. In the *Charter of the United Nations,* adopted in 1945, the UN member states pledged to work for the achievement of "universal respect for, and observance of, human rights..." – a great new goal.[1] Three years later those rights were spelled out in the *Universal Declaration of Human Rights* ("Universal Declaration"), adopted without dissent and proclaimed by the UN General Assembly on 10 December 1948. Its 30 articles list the rights to which everyone is entitled, set forth "as a common standard of achievement for all peoples and all nations".[2]

The adoption of the Universal Declaration was an immensely important event. By adopting it, the governments of the world, represented at the UN, agreed that everyone is entitled to fundamental human rights.[3] These rights apply everywhere, not just in those countries whose governments may choose to grant them. It follows from this that all governments must protect the rights of people under their jurisdiction, and that a person whose human rights are violated has a claim against the government which violates them.[4] Furthermore, the fact that governments together adopted the Universal Declaration means that violations of human rights are of concern to all governments, not just to the governments of the countries where they occur.

The Universal Declaration states that "Everyone has the right to life, liberty and security of person" and that no one shall be subjected to torture or to arbitrary arrest or detention.[5] These rights had been violated on a massive scale in the Second World War, and a major goal in the UN's human rights effort was to ensure that such atrocities should not be repeated.[6]

Since 1948, international standards for the protection of human rights have been strengthened through the adoption of successive instruments[7] in the UN. The drafting of such instruments is always a matter of intense discussion over what should or should not be included. Amnesty International and other human rights organizations have persistently urged governments to adopt texts giving the strongest possible protection against human rights violations.

In 1966 the UN adopted the International Covenant on Civil and Political Rights and the International Covenant on Economic, Social and Cultural Rights.[8] These two key instruments elaborate on many of the rights contained in the Universal Declaration. The *International Covenant on Civil and Political Rights* reiterates the right to life, liberty and security of person and prohibits, in particular, the arbitrary deprivation of life – a characteristic of the killings described in this report. Unlike the Universal Declaration, the International Covenant on Civil and Political Rights is a treaty, committing the states which become parties to it to respect and to ensure the rights recognized therein.[9]

Over the next decades, the UN adopted further international instruments on particular types of human rights violations or on human rights in relation to particular professions or in particular circumstances. Two of these, adopted recently, are of special importance:

- The *Principles on the Effective Prevention and Investigation of Extra-Legal, Arbitrary and Summary Executions* (cited below as the "Principles on Extra-Legal, Arbitrary and Summary Executions"). These were drafted by the UN Committee on Crime Prevention and Control, adopted by the Economic and Security Council in 1989 and endorsed by the General Assembly the same year. (The term "extra-legal, arbitrary and summary executions" embraces what Amnesty International refers to as extrajudicial executions.)[10]

- The *Declaration on the Protection of All Persons from Enforced Disappearance* ("Declaration on Disappearances"),[11] adopted without a vote by the General Assembly in 1992 after consideration by the UN Commission on Human Rights and its Sub-Commission on Prevention of Discrimination and Protection of Minorities.[12]

Together with the human rights treaties adopted regionally and the international humanitarian law which regulates the conduct of armed conflict (see below), these international instruments firmly establish the prohibition of "disappearances" and extrajudicial executions and specify detailed measures for their prevention.

2   The prohibition of "disappearances" and extrajudicial executions under international standards

No state shall practise, permit or tolerate enforced disappearances.
– UN Declaration on Disappearances, Article 2

Governments shall prohibit by law all extra-legal, arbitrary and summary executions...
– UN Principles on Extra-Legal, Arbitrary and Summary Executions, Article 1

"Disappearances" and extrajudicial executions are clear violations of fundamental rights proclaimed in the earliest human rights instruments adopted by the UN.[13] More recently, the prohibition has been spelled out in the two instruments cited above.

Article 3 of the Universal Declaration of Human Rights states: "Everyone has the right to life, liberty and security of person." These rights are violated when "disappearances" and extrajudicial executions are perpetrated.

- Extrajudicial executions clearly violate the right to life. Other rights also are often violated in cases of extrajudicial executions: often, for example, the victims are made to "disappear" or tortured before being killed.[14]

- "Disappearances" violate the right to liberty and security of person as well as the right not to be subjected to torture or cruel, inhuman or degrading treatment as provided under Article 5 of the Universal Declaration. They also violate or constitute a grave threat to the right to life.[15]

The rights to life, liberty and security of person are reiterated in the International Covenant on Civil and Political Rights. Any state party to the International Covenant which permits its officials to engage in "disappearances" or extrajudicial executions has violated the obligations which it agreed to fulfil in becoming a party to this treaty.

Article 6 of the International Covenant, providing for the right to life, states further: "No one shall be arbitrarily deprived of his life." This prohibition of the arbitrary deprivation of life is important because it helps to distinguish extrajudicial executions from killings which are not, or have not yet been, forbidden[16] under international human rights standards, such as killings resulting from the use of reasonable force in law enforcement (see below, section 3), killings in armed conflict not forbidden under the international laws that regulate the conduct of such conflicts (see section 4), and the use of the death penalty in cases where internationally established procedural safeguards and restrictions are observed.[17]

The International Covenant has the formal force of a treaty: a state's act in becoming a party to it is in effect a promise to other states parties to abide by its provisions.

Although the Universal Declaration does not have the formal force of a treaty, and is therefore not legally binding in and of itself, it has become so widely recognized and accepted since its adoption that it should be regarded as obligatory for all states.[18] Whether or not they are parties to the International Covenant, all states must be regarded as obliged to refrain from "disappearances" and extrajudicial executions as violations of the rights to life, liberty and security of person.

The UN adopted its first resolutions expressing general concern about "disappearances" and extrajudicial executions in 1978 and 1980 respectively.[19] Further discussions over the years led to the adoption of the Declaration on Disappearances and the Principles on Extra-Legal, Arbitrary and Summary Executions, spelling out the prohibition of "disappearances" and extrajudicial executions as quoted above, and providing that "disappearances" and extrajudicial executions must not be committed at any time, including a state of war, a threat of war, internal political instability or any other public emergency.[20]

3   Prohibition of arbitrary killings by law enforcement officials

Law enforcement officials may use force only when strictly necessary and to the extent required for the performance of their duty.
– UN Code of Conduct for Law Enforcement Officials, Article 3

The work of a law enforcement official is fraught with danger. Sometimes an officer is obliged to use force, and sometimes the use of force results in a killing. Some killings by law enforcement officials are unavoidable because of the officers' need to protect their own lives and their mission to protect the lives of others. But as this report shows, many officers in different countries have carried out killings which are unlawful and deliberate.

Some killings are done in secret. Others are presented as lawful, the outcome of the justifiable use of force by officers in the performance of their law enforcement duties. How should such claims be assessed?

An important international standard on the use of force in law enforcement was established by the UN General Assembly in 1978 when it adopted the *Code of Conduct for Law Enforcement Officials.* Article 3 of the Code sets forth two important principles:

- Force should be used "only when strictly necessary". The official Commentary included in the Code says that the use of force should be "exceptional", that force should be used only "as is reasonably necessary under the circumstances" and that it should be used for only two purposes, "the prevention of crime" and "effecting or assisting in the lawful arrest of offenders or suspected offenders".

- The force used should be proportional to the objectives (it should be used only "to the extent required" for the performance of law enforcement officials' duty). The Commentary acknowledges the "principle of proportionality" laid down in national laws and says that the Code should not be taken to authorize the use of force which is "disproportionate to the legitimate objective to be achieved".

The Commentary singles out the use of firearms for special attention. The use of firearms is to be considered "an extreme measure"; every effort should be made to exclude their use, especially against children. The purposes for which firearms may be used are narrower than for the use of force overall: in general, firearms should not be used "except when a suspected offender offers armed resistance or otherwise jeopardizes the lives of others and less extreme measures are not sufficient to restrain or apprehend the suspected offender".[21]

These principles set forth in the Code of Conduct were developed further in the UN *Basic Principles on the Use of Force and Firearms by Law Enforcement Officials*, adopted in 1990. Here the use of firearms is restricted to a series of situations involving the "imminent threat of death or serious injury" or "grave threat to life", and "only when less extreme means are insufficient" to achieve the objectives specified. Furthermore, the "intentional lethal use of firearms" is to be made only "when strictly unavoidable in order to protect life." The phrase "strictly unavoidable" implies that lesser means should be used first and that firearms should not be used before lesser means have proved insufficient to protect life.[22]

The Code of Conduct for Law Enforcement Officials and the Basic Principles on the Use of Force and Firearms by Law Enforcement Officials provide detailed standards against which the facts of a particular killing can be assessed. If the actions of the officer who committed the killing exceeded the limits laid down in these instruments, the killing should be considered arbitrary and in violation of the prohibition of arbitrary deprivation of life as established in Article 6 of the International Covenant on Civil and Political Rights.[23]

4   Prohibition of "disappearances" and extrajudicial executions in war

Grave breaches [of the Convention] ... shall be those involving any of the following acts, if committed against persons or property protected by the Convention: wilful killing...
– Geneva Conventions of 1949[24] (referring to international armed conflicts)

...the following acts are and shall remain prohibited at any time and in any place whatsoever with respect to [persons taking no active part in the hostilities]: (a) violence to life and person, in particular murder of all kinds...
– Article 3 common to the Geneva Conventions (referring to non-international armed conflicts)

Public dismay at the sufferings inflicted in warfare has given rise since the mid-19th century to efforts to restrict the horrors of war through international law. One branch of the laws of armed conflict which have been developed through these efforts deals with the protection of victims of war; it is often referred to as "international humanitarian law". Its most recent expression is in the four *Geneva Conventions* of 1949, supplemented by the two *Additional Protocols* adopted in 1977.[25] The Geneva Conventions and the Additional Protocols are binding on all states which become parties to them.

The Geneva Conventions set forth detailed rules of behaviour to protect actual or potential victims of war. Each Convention covers a specific class of "protected persons" – wounded and sick members of the armed forces on land; wounded, sick and shipwrecked members of the armed forces at sea; prisoners of war, and civilians respectively.

The Geneva Conventions do not outlaw war, but they provide that people not involved in the fighting are to be treated humanely. Enemy soldiers may be killed in combat, but a soldier who has been captured or, having laid down their arms, seeks to surrender, or has been put out of action through sickness, wounding or shipwreck, is protected by the Geneva Conventions and must not be killed. Nor may a country at war kill civilians protected by the Fourth Geneva Convention – nationals of an adversary country who are in its territory or a territory occupied by it.[26]

Extrajudicial executions constitute "wilful killings" and are thus "grave breaches" of the Geneva Conventions under the provisions cited above, if perpetrated in an international armed conflict against persons protected by the Conventions.[27] "Disappearances" also violate various provisions of the Conventions.[28]

Like earlier formulations of the laws of armed conflict, the Geneva Conventions of 1949 apply to international conflicts – wars between nations – but in an important innovation, Article 3, a text common to all four Conventions, extends to "armed conflict not of an international character"[29] a list of fundamental rules for the protection of persons not, or no longer, taking an active part in the hostilities, which each party to the conflict is "bound to apply, as a minimum". "Violence to life and person, in particular murder of all kinds" is prohibited "at any time and in any place whatsoever with respect to the above-mentioned persons". Similarly, Article 4 of Additional Protocol II to the Geneva Conventions forbids the murder of anyone not taking a direct part in hostilities in non-international armed conflicts.

Thus the prohibition of wilful killing of protected persons in *international* wars is extended to the prohibition of killing of people who have ceased taking or do not take an active part in hostilities[30] in *internal* armed conflicts – a category of conflict which can be taken to include some of the worst situations of "disappearances" and political killings. Furthermore, under the terms of common Article 3, this prohibition of deliberate and arbitrary killings in internal armed conflicts applies not only to government forces but to all parties to such conflicts including armed opposition groups. This prohibition is binding on all states parties to the Geneva Conventions; according to common Article 3, other parties to an internal conflict are also bound to apply its provisions, and several such parties in recent conflicts have formally declared that they will do so.

The Geneva Conventions are widely accepted as binding standards of behaviour which must be observed in armed conflict.[31] No government would claim that it has the right to kill prisoners of war or civilians protected under the Geneva Conventions. At the same time, parallel to the development of the laws of armed conflict, successive human rights instruments adopted by the UN have made it clear that certain fundamental human rights, such as the right to life and with it the prohibition of arbitrary deprivation of life, must be respected in time of war as in peacetime. These rights are commonly known as "*non-derogable rights*", a reference to the fact that under the International Covenant on Civil and Political Rights and other human rights treaties, states parties may not derogate from their obligations under these treaties to respect these rights in any circumstances including times of public emergency.[32] Accordingly, the UN Declaration on Disappearances (Article 7) and the UN Principles on Extra-legal, Arbitrary and Summary Executions (principle 1) respectively state that a state of war, threat of war, internal political instability or other public emergency must not be invoked as a justification for "disappearances" or extrajudicial executions.

The laws of armed conflict and the human rights standards developed at the UN reinforce each other. "Disappearances" and extrajudicial executions are prohibited at all times.

5   War crimes, crimes against humanity and genocide

Under certain circumstances "disappearances" and extrajudicial executions may constitute war crimes, crimes against humanity, or acts of genocide. These phrases convey strong condemnation, but what is important in terms of bringing those responsible to justice are the legal consequences if a crime is included in one or another of these categories.[33]

Legal consequences of war crimes, crimes against humanity and genocide include the following:

- The crimes are not subject to any statute of limitations.[34]

- The alleged perpetrators cannot claim asylum in another country.[35]

- Other states may be able, or may even be required, to bring the perpetrators to justice if they are outside the country where the crime was committed and regardless of the nationality of the perpetrator or the victim.[36]

- The perpetrators cannot escape conviction by claiming that they were acting under orders.[37]

The three categories apply to different circumstances.

- *War crimes* consist of violations of the laws of armed conflict. They include the crimes defined as "grave breaches" of the Geneva Conventions of 1949, including "wilful killing" of protected persons as well as "unlawful confinement" and "unlawful deportation or transfer" of protected civilians (see above, section 4).[38]

- *Crimes against humanity* can be committed either in wartime or in peacetime.[39] They include the crimes listed as such in the Charter of the International Military Tribunal set up at the end of the Second World War to try major war criminals of the European axis (the Nuremberg Tribunal), including "murder, extermination, ... deportation and other inhumane acts committed against any civilian population". Since then the concept of crimes against humanity has broadened.[40] The definition of crimes against humanity would appear to include both the systematic practice of "disappearances" and the systematic practice of extrajudicial executions.[41]

- *Genocide* is a type of crime against humanity.[42] Under the Convention on the Prevention and Punishment of the Crime of Genocide ("Genocide Convention"), adopted by the UN in 1948, genocide consists of acts intended "to destroy, in whole or in part, a national, ethnical, racial or religious group, as such", including killing members of the group, causing them "serious mental or bodily harm", or forcibly transferring their children to another group, whether such acts are committed in time of peace or war. This definition would include both extrajudicial executions and "disappearances" if committed with the intention specified above.[43]

Despite the many hundreds of thousands of "disappearances" and extrajudicial executions perpetrated since the Second World War, governments have hitherto made little use of the provisions of international law on war crimes, crimes against humanity or genocide in combating these practices. In May 1993, however, the UN Security Council decided to establish an International Tribunal to prosecute persons responsible for war crimes, crimes against humanity, genocide and other violations of the laws and customs of war in the former Yugoslavia.[44] The Tribunal had not started its work at the time of writing of this report.

6   Regional standards

Complementing the worldwide scope of the United Nations, governments in different regions of the world have created organizations where their representatives meet to discuss matters of regional concern, including human rights. Three of these "regional intergovernmental organizations" have adopted human rights treaties which are legally binding on the states in those regions which become parties to them.[45] They are the *European Convention for the Protection of Human Rights and Fundamental*

Freedoms ("European Convention on Human Rights"), which was signed in 1950 and entered into force in 1953; the ***American Convention on Human Rights***, which was adopted in 1969 and entered into force in 1978; and the ***African Charter on Human and Peoples' Rights***, which was adopted in 1981 and entered into force in 1986.[46]

Like the International Covenant on Civil and Political Rights, all three treaties provide for the right to life and, in particular, the right not to be arbitrarily deprived of life. All three provide for the right to liberty and security of person, the right not to be subjected to torture or cruel, inhuman or degrading treatment or punishment and the right not to be subjected to arbitrary arrest or detention. "Disappearances" and extrajudicial executions are clearly prohibited, just as they are under the Universal Declaration of Human Rights.[47]

Each of the three regional treaties provides for the establishment of institutions to supervise its implementation. The activities of these and other regional institutions in combating "disappearances" and extrajudicial executions are described in Chapter 12.

7   National law

Even if international human rights standards had not been developed, "disappearances" and extrajudicial executions would be unlawful. They violate national law.

Extrajudicial executions violate national laws proscribing murder and other unlawful homicide. Depending on the details of the case, a "disappearance" violates national laws such as those against unlawful detention and kidnapping or abduction. Other laws also are often violated in cases of "disappearances" and extrajudicial executions.

Many countries now have constitutional provisions spelling out basic human rights. "Disappearances" and extrajudicial executions violate certain of these rights, and thus violate these constitutions.

What this all means is that officials who order, carry out, conspire to carry out, acquiesce in, or cover up "disappearances" or extrajudicial executions are violating their countries' own laws. Government officials responsible for "disappearances" and extrajudicial executions are violating the very laws which they are supposed to uphold.

8   The implementation of international standards

We now come to one of the key questions of this report. "Disappearances" and extrajudicial executions violate internationally established human rights – yet these horrendous practices continue. How can they be stopped? To put it another way: how can international standards prohibiting "disappearances" and extrajudicial executions be implemented? How can principles be turned into action? What should be done to ensure that the rules established by the UN and regional intergovernmental organizations and the rules of international humanitarian law are respected?

The UN should not be thought of as merely a source of rules on human rights. The need for action is inherent in the existence of the United Nations. One of the purposes of the UN, listed in Article 1 of the UN Charter, is "To achieve international co-operation ... in promoting and encouraging respect for human rights", while in Article 56 of the Charter, all UN member states "pledge themselves to take joint and separate action" in cooperation with the UN for the achievement of "universal respect for, and observance of, human rights". One of the first results of this international cooperation was the adoption of the Universal Declaration of Human Rights, setting forth basic standards. It is a list of rules, but action also is contemplated; the Preamble to the Universal Declaration calls for every individual and organ of society "by teaching and education to promote respect for these rights" and "by progressive measures, national and international, to secure their universal and effective recognition and observance".

The International Covenant on Civil and Political Rights, setting forth rights which are violated in the perpetration of "disappearances" and extrajudicial executions, includes a requirement that states parties to the Covenant implement the standards contained in that treaty. Under Article 2, each state party undertakes "to respect and to ensure to all individuals within its territory and subject to its jurisdiction the rights recognized in the present Covenant". The word "respect" should be understood to entail a promise not to violate the rights set forth in the Covenant, while the term "ensure" entails a positive obligation to take the necessary measures to prevent the commission of those human rights violations (see Chapter 11, section 6). In particular, each state party undertakes under Article 2 of the Covenant to adopt the "legislative or other measures" needed to give effect to the rights recognized in the Covenant. Moreover, each state party undertakes to ensure that anyone whose rights are violated "shall have an effective remedy, notwithstanding that the violation has been committed by persons acting in an official capacity".

Another important feature of the International Covenant is that it establishes a Human Rights Committee to supervise the implementation of the Covenant. (The work of the Human Rights Committee is described in Chapter 12.)

The first substantial resolutions adopted by the UN on "disappearances" and extrajudicial executions set forth specific actions which governments should take. Resolution 33/173 on disappeared persons, adopted by the General Assembly on 20 December 1978, called upon governments "to devote appropriate resources" to searching for the disappeared, "to undertake speedy and impartial investigations", and to ensure that law enforcement and security agencies are "fully accountable", including "legal responsibility for unjustifiable excesses" which might lead to disappearances.[48] Two years later, a resolution on extra-legal executions adopted by the Sixth UN Congress on the Prevention of Crime and the Treatment of Offenders called on all governments "to take effective measures to prevent such acts".[49]

In its efforts to secure the implementation of human rights standards, the UN has taken a number of approaches.

- It has adopted *instruments* specifying measures which governments should take to protect human rights and prevent specific types of violations. Thus, for example, both the Declaration on Disappearances and the Principles on Extra-Legal, Arbitrary and Summary Executions call on the authorities to conduct impartial investigations into complaints and reports of these abuses, to bring the alleged perpetrators to trial and to establish specific safeguards for the prevention of these abuses. The measures specified in these instruments are phrased as rules ("Governments shall prohibit...", "Each State shall ensure..."), constituting further standards which in turn have to be implemented.

- It has called for the instruments and the provisions therein to be *made known*, to be included in the *training* of the relevant officials, and to be incorporated in *national legislation.*

- It has established *institutions* and *procedures* to monitor compliance with the standards, to make recommendations and to take action.

- It has made resources available through UN *public information* offices and *technical assistance* programs.

These approaches provide many opportunities for non-governmental organizations wishing to combat "disappearances" and extrajudicial executions. One must not forget, however, that the basic responsibility for action is with governments. Just as governments are acting unlawfully in ordering "disappearances" and extrajudicial executions or allowing them to be perpetrated, so governments must be pressed to end this lawless situation and uphold human rights. First and foremost, it is a matter of political will.

CHAPTER 9

PREVENTION

1   The duty of prevention

> *"The State has a legal duty to take reasonable steps to prevent*
> *human rights violations and to use the means at its disposal to*
> *carry out a serious investigation of violations committed within*
> *its jurisdiction, to identify those responsible, to impose the*
> *appropriate punishment and to ensure the victim adequate*
> *compensation."*
>
> *"[The obligation of states parties to the American Convention*
> *on Human Rights to ensure the exercise of the rights recognized*
> *by the Convention]* implies the duty of the States Parties to
> organize the governmental apparatus and, in general, all the
> structures through which public power is exercised, *so that they*
> *are capable of juridically ensuring the free and full enjoyment of*
> *human rights. As a consequence of this obligation,* the States
> must prevent, investigate and punish *any violation of the rights*
> *recognized by the Convention and, moreover, if possible attempt*
> *to restore the right violated and provide compensation as*
> *warranted for damages resulting from the violation."*
> *– Inter-American Court of Human Rights,* Velásquez Rodríguez
> *judgment (emphases added)[1]*

"Disappearances" and extrajudicial executions violate fundamental human rights. The duty to prevent them is a consequence of the duty of governments to respect and to ensure human rights to everyone within their jurisdiction, as set forth in Article 2 of the International Covenant on Civil and Political Rights[2]. This duty of prevention is set forth in the leading UN instruments on "disappearances" and extrajudicial executions – the *Declaration on the Protection of All Persons from Enforced Disappearance* ("Declaration on Disappearances") (Article 1) and the *Principles on the Effective Prevention and Investigation of Extra-Legal, Arbitrary and Summary Executions* ("Principles on Extra-Legal, Arbitrary and Summary Executions") (principles 1-8) respectively. It is reinforced by judgments and decisions of the Inter-American Court of Human Rights and the Human Rights Committee set up under the International Covenant on Civil and Political Rights.[3]

In a narrow sense, prevention consists of measures to be taken so that "disappearances" and extrajudicial executions will not be committed, while investigation and bringing those responsible to justice (the subjects of the next two chapters) are reactions which should follow if they are. In a wider sense, investigation and bringing those responsible to justice contribute to prevention. Public officials who might become involved in programs of "disappearances" and political killings will hesitate to do so if they know that similar deeds by others have been uncovered through investigation and that the perpetrators have been brought to justice. The duty to investigate and the duty to bring those responsible to justice are part of the duty of prevention. These duties are incumbent both on the state and on its officials.[4]

International human rights instruments establish that "disappearances" and extrajudicial executions must be prohibited at all times. It follows that the essential safeguards for their prevention, such as *habeas corpus* or other judicial remedies to locate prisoners and ensure their safety, also must not be suspended under any circumstances, including states of war or other public emergency.[5] Without the essential safeguards in place, prohibition will be largely a dead letter.

In an effort to call attention to the official steps needed to end "disappearances" and extrajudicial executions worldwide, Amnesty International has developed *14-Point Programs for the Prevention of "Disappearances" and Extrajudicial Executions.* Most of the measures in these programs have already been agreed by the world's governments and incorporated in UN instruments, while others are measures which Amnesty International from its experience believes would be effective.

The relevant points from the two programs are cited in this and the following chapters. These points can serve as tests of governmental behaviour – and good will. The extent to which they are implemented is an indication of a government's commitment to end "disappearances" and extrajudicial executions at home and abroad. That commitment should be demonstrated in each country by the adoption of a comprehensive program for the prevention of "disappearances" and extrajudicial executions, with clear goals and timetables.

2   Official condemnation

> *The highest authorities of every country should demonstrate their total opposition to "disappearances" and extrajudicial executions. They should make clear to all members of the police, military and other security forces that "disappearances" and extrajudicial executions will not be tolerated under any circumstances.*
> – From Amnesty International's 14-Point Programs for the Prevention of "Disappearances" and Extrajudicial Executions

The eradication of "disappearances" and extrajudicial executions is a matter of political will. The highest authorities of each country are responsible for exercising that will. This is so because:

- The prevention of "disappearances" and extrajudicial executions is part of the state's obligation to protect human rights. That obligation entails a responsibility on the part of the highest authorities of the state, as well as of lower officials.

- In every country the state assumes responsibility for maintaining law and order. This responsibility entails the obligation to suppress breaches of the law by public officials as well as private citizens. A failure to suppress the commission of the most serious crimes by public officials is a denial of the rule of law, under which public officials are not above the law but must be subject to it just like ordinary citizens.

Where there are strong allegations that "disappearances" or extrajudicial executions have been perpetrated, the highest authorities should clearly and publicly declare their opposition to these practices. If people have been killed by the security forces in disputed circumstances, the highest authorities should make clear that any unlawful and arbitrary killings will not be tolerated. Such statements should be aimed at deterring any member of the security forces from committing a "disappearance" or an extrajudicial execution. Conversely, a public statement which appears to instigate or condone deliberate and unlawful killings by members of the security forces may encourage further such killings. If this happens, the author of the statement will share the responsibility for the killings.

Statements condemning "disappearances" and extrajudicial executions need to be accompanied by convincing deeds. These include conducting prompt and effective investigations, bringing perpetrators to justice, disbanding organizations which carry out "disappearances" and extrajudicial executions, and repealing emergency regulations which impede normal remedies against "disappearances" and extrajudicial executions or which grant the perpetrators immunity from prosecution.

3   Prohibition in law

Governments should ensure that the commission of a "disappearance" or an extrajudicial execution is a criminal offence, punishable by sanctions commensurate with the gravity of the practice.
– From Amnesty International's 14-Point Programs for the Prevention of "Disappearances" and Extrajudicial Executions

The responsibility of governments to prohibit "disappearances" and extrajudicial executions by law is recognized in international instruments. The UN Declaration on Disappearances (Article 4) and the UN Principles on Extra-Legal, Arbitrary and Summary Executions (principle 1) provide that "disappearances" and extrajudicial executions shall be recognized as offences under the criminal law, punishable by appropriate penalties which take into account the seriousness of such offences.

As stated in Chapter 8, "disappearances" and extrajudicial executions violate national laws proscribing such acts as unlawful detention, kidnapping and murder. But a "disappearance" or an extrajudicial execution involves more than just these acts. The prohibition of "disappearances" and extrajudicial executions involves ensuring that the component parts of the crimes are prohibited.

- Component parts of a "disappearance" are the arrest – which itself is often arbitrary or unlawful – or abduction, the secret detention, the false denial of knowledge of the victim's fate or whereabouts, and the cruel, inhuman and degrading treatment of the victim, often including torture and often leading to the victim being killed.

- An extrajudicial execution involves an unlawful and deliberate killing. It is often accompanied by other human rights violations, including those listed above.

A "disappearance" or an extrajudicial execution is never committed by one person alone. The actions of those who aid in the commission of the crimes and of the higher authorities who order or acquiesce in them include the following:

- ordering or requesting someone to carry out a "disappearance" or a killing;

- deciding on a plan for the crime;

- providing intelligence information which enables the perpetrators to carry out their work, or providing guns, vehicles or other material assistance;

- covering up a crime, by such means as falsifying records;

- turning a blind eye and allowing the crime to proceed, when it is in an official's power to stop it.

In reviewing whether or not a country's laws adequately prohibit "disappearances" and extrajudicial executions, one must review the component parts of these crimes to see whether they are prohibited. The aim must be to ensure that every person at whatever level who is responsible for a "disappearance" or an extrajudicial execution can be brought to justice for violations of the criminal law, and that these violations are punishable by appropriately serious penalties. Offences short of crimes should be punishable by administrative sanctions.

Several countries recently have explicitly prohibited "disappearances" or extra-judicial executions under their constitutions or have established them as specific offences in their penal codes, or are considering doing so.[6] Such prohibitions can be the occasion for designating "disappearances" and extrajudicial executions as crimes against humanity, entailing the legal consequences of universality of jurisdiction, no statute of limitations and no defence of superior orders (see Chapter 8, section 5).

4   Chain-of-command control

Those in charge of the security forces should maintain strict chain-of-command control to ensure that officers under their command do not commit "disappearances" and extrajudicial executions.
– From Amnesty International's 14-Point Programs for the Prevention of "Disappearances" and Extrajudicial Executions

Officials in charge of the security forces have the power and the consequent duty to prevent "disappearances" and extrajudicial executions. They must carry out this duty through the means by which their authority is normally exercised: chain-of-command control.

The duty to maintain strict chain-of-command control for the prevention of "disappearances" and extrajudicial executions is established in the UN Declaration on Disappearances (Article 12) and the UN Principles on Extra-Legal, Arbitrary and Summary Executions (principle 2). Measures through which chain-of-command control should be exercised include the following:

- ensuring that clear regulations and procedures are established governing arrest, detention and such other areas as the use of lethal force, in conformity with international human rights standards;

- ensuring that these regulations and procedures are known and followed;

- ensuring that there is an effective procedure for the investigation of possible breaches of regulations;

- ensuring that breaches of regulations which could contribute to a "disappearance" or an extrajudicial execution are punished by appropriate sanctions;

- exercising effective supervision through being regularly and accurately informed of the activities of those under the officer's command. In particular, the commanding officer should know the whereabouts and conditions of detention of all prisoners held by officials under his or her command.

Officials sometimes try to escape blame for human rights violations by feigning ignorance or claiming that they cannot control the actions of their subordinates; yet a strong chain of command is a basic feature of police and military forces. The principle of chain-of-command responsibility to prevent human rights violations is a means of counteracting such false claims. It points to the fact that commanding officers who genuinely want to stop "disappearances" and extrajudicial executions can do so by issuing the necessary orders and insisting that they must be obeyed.

5 The right and duty to disobey

Members of the security forces should be instructed that they have the right and duty to refuse to obey any order to participate in a "disappearance" or an extrajudicial execution.
– From Amnesty International's 14-Point Programs for the Prevention of "Disappearances" and Extrajudicial Executions

Because "disappearances" and extrajudicial executions are unlawful, it follows that members of the security forces must not participate in them. The need to disobey an order to do so should be seen as a *duty*, taking precedence over the normal duty to obey orders.

By refusing to obey an unlawful order, a soldier or police officer exposes himself or herself to the risk of suffering the – often severe – sanctions normally attached to an act of disobedience by a member of the security forces. To protect the officer from this risk, it is necessary to establish that the duty to disobey an unlawful order entails the *right* to disobey it. This right needs to be made effective through such means as providing an impartial review body to which the soldier or police officer can appeal if he or she is being punished for disobeying such an order.

The right and duty to disobey an order to participate in a "disappearance" or an extrajudicial execution is connected to the principle that an order from a superior officer may not be invoked as a defence for committing such acts (see Chapter 11, section 5).

In recent years the right and duty to disobey an order to participate in "disappearances" and extrajudicial executions has begun to be incorporated in international instruments. The UN Declaration on Disappearances (Article 6) and the UN Principles on Extra-Legal, Arbitrary and Summary Executions (principle 3) recognize this right and duty. Further, the UN Basic Principles on the Use of Force and Firearms by Law Enforcement Officials protect the right to disobey by stating that no criminal or disciplinary sanction should be imposed on law enforcement officials who, in compliance with the Basic Principles and the Code of Conduct for Law Enforcement Officials, refuse to carry out an order to use force and firearms.[7]

Now that governments have incorporated the right and duty to disobey orders to commit "disappearances" and extrajudicial executions in international instruments, they need to make this right and duty effective nationally. The right and duty to disobey needs to be made known to soldiers, police officers and their superiors. The *duty* to disobey needs to be made a practical possibility through the establishment of the necessary institutional means to protect the *right* to disobey.

Governments should ensure that law enforcement officials use force only when strictly necessary and only to the minimum extent required under the circumstances. Lethal force should not be used except when strictly unavoidable in order to protect life.
– Amnesty International 14-Point Program for the Prevention of Extrajudicial Executions

As described in Chapter 8, two important instruments setting standards on the use of force by law enforcement officials have been adopted by the UN – the *Code of Conduct for Law Enforcement Officials* and the *Basic Principles on the Use of Force and Firearms by Law Enforcement Officials* ("Basic Principles"). These instruments establish that force should be used only when strictly necessary, that the use of force should not be disproportionate to the legitimate objective to be achieved, and that firearms should not be used except as an extreme measure in a restricted range of situations. (For relevant extracts from the Code of Conduct and the full text of the Basic Principles, see Appendices 4 and 5).

The adoption of these two instruments implies that they should be implemented. Implementation involves various measures including the following:

- Governments should adopt national standards on the use of force and firearms by law enforcement officials which conform to the standards established by the UN. These national standards need to be incorporated in laws and regulations governing the activities of law enforcement officials.[8] The texts of the relevant standards should be made available to all law enforcement officials, and their provisions should be made known through training.[9]

- The laws and regulations must cover all officials who perform law enforcement functions – prison guards and military police as well as the regular police.[10]

- In dealing with crowd control, prison disturbances and other violent or threatening situations, law enforcement agencies need to develop tactics which use non-violent means as far as possible.[11]

- Law enforcement agencies should be subject to public scrutiny by the judiciary, a review board, or some other independent agency.[12] People affected by the use of force and firearms by law enforcement officials should be able to have recourse to a judicial authority.[13]

The use of firearms needs to be surrounded by special safeguards, as established in the Basic Principles. They include the following:

- Official guidelines should regulate the storage and issuing of firearms, so as to ensure that law enforcement officials are accountable for the firearms and ammunition issued to them (principle 11 (d)).

- The guidelines should specify the circumstances under which law enforcement officials are authorized to carry firearms and the types of firearms and ammunition permitted (principle 11 (a)).

- Wherever possible, law enforcement officials should "...identify themselves as such and give a clear warning of their intent to use firearms, with sufficient time for the warning to be observed..." (principle 10).

- Governments should establish a system of reporting to be followed whenever law enforcement officials use firearms in the performance of their duty. If death or serious injury results from the use of force or firearms, a detailed report should be sent promptly to the administrative and judicial authorities responsible for control and review of the forces concerned (principles 11 (f), 22).

7   Disbanding "death squads"

"Death squads", private armies, criminal gangs and paramilitary forces operating outside the chain of command but with official support or acquiescence should be prohibited and disbanded. Members of such groups who have participated in the perpetration of "disappearances" or extrajudicial executions should be brought to justice.
– From Amnesty International's 14-Point Program for the Prevention of Extrajudicial Executions (adapted)

Groups carrying out "disappearances" and extrajudicial executions exist in various forms. In some places they are "death squads", composed for example of on-duty or off-duty police or military officers. Sometimes they are criminal gangs or private armies which are not part of the regular security forces but operate with official acquiescence. These groups are manifestly illegal and harmful. They must be prohibited and disbanded.

Sometimes "disappearances" and killings are carried out by paramilitary forces which are legally constituted but operate outside the official chain of command. Such arrangements may suit the purposes of military commanders who use the para-militaries to do their dirty work and then disclaim responsibility. Here the authorities must make a clear choice. Any forces which are necessary for the nation's defence must be put firmly under the established chain of command, so that "disappearances" and extrajudicial executions will be prevented through chain-of-command control. If paramilitary forces are outside the chain of command, they should be prohibited and disbanded.[14]

Other "disappearances" and extrajudicial executions are perpetrated by groups of on-duty officers belonging to regularly constituted police or military agencies, but are passed off as the work of "death squads" outside official control. These officers should be brought to justice. If "disappearances" and extrajudicial executions have become pervasive within an established agency of the security forces, there will be a strong case for disbanding the agency itself, as such pervasive lawless behaviour entails a serious institutional corruption which cannot easily be cleared up by internal reforms.

The obligation to disband "death squads" and other groups carrying out "disappearances" and extrajudicial executions has not yet been explicitly incorporated in international human rights instruments. However, UN bodies have recently begun making this demand for specific countries. For example, the UN Working Group on Disappearances noted in its report on its 1990 visit to the *Philippines* that "disappearances" were being perpetrated by – among other agencies – the official paramilitary Citizen Armed Force Geographical Unit (CAFGU), as well as by so-called vigilante groups and civilian volunteer groups backed by military forces. In its recommendations to the Philippine Government the Working Group wrote: "From many quarters ... it has been recommended that the CAFGUs and similar outfits should be disbanded. That would be the Group's preferred option as well. In any event, their deployment should be restricted to defensive action under the continuous supervision of army personnel; strict discipline should be enforced".[15]

The disbanding of "death squads" and security force agencies responsible for "disappearances" and extrajudicial executions has recently been contemplated or attempted in a number of countries.

- In the Philippines, for example, the government in July 1993 began a drive to disband so-called private armies, some 500 of which were believed to exist in the country. Some of these are under the command of local officials and a number of them have been implicated in political killings and "disappearances". However, the program to disband private armies leaves intact the official paramilitary apparatus, CAFGU, which has some 80,000 men under arms. Amnesty International has repeatedly called for the disbanding of CAFGU and government-backed vigilante groups, which have committed a growing proportion of political killings and "disappearances" in recent years.

- In *South Africa*, following the statement by a police investigator in January 1990 that the Civil Cooperation Bureau (CCB), a covert unit under the responsibility of the South African Directorate of Military Intelligence, had been responsible for two political killings in 1989 and other human rights violations, the CCB was formally disbanded in July 1990. (However, later evidence indicated that some former members of the CCB had left South Africa after receiving large redundancy and pension payments from the government, and that other former CCB operatives were working for Military Intelligence or the military's Special Forces.)[16]

The most comprehensive plan yet for disbanding "death squads" and security force units with bad human rights records is in the 1992 Peace Agreement between the Government of *El Salvador* and the opposition *Frente Farabundo Martí para la Liberación Nacional* (FMLN), Farabundo Martí National Liberation Front, ending the armed conflict between them.[17] The Peace Agreement provided among other things for:

- dissolution of the National Guard, the Treasury Police and the military's intelligence apparatus, the National Intelligence Department, and their replacement by a new national civilian police force and an intelligence agency under direct civilian control. These agencies had been implicated in "disappearances" and killings on a massive scale throughout the 1980s;

- disbanding of civil defence units and proscription of any paramilitary forces;

- regulation of private security services, including a system for the public registration of their staff, weapons and offices, cancellation of licenses for private individuals to bear weapons that are for the exclusive use of the armed forces and the immediate recall of such weapons;

- purging of the armed forces, entailing the evaluation by an *ad hoc* commission of the past performance of each officer, including "his record of observance of the legal order, with particular emphasis on respect for human rights, both in his personal conduct and in the rigour with which he has ordered the redress and punishment of unlawful acts, excesses or human rights violations committed under his command, especially if there have been serious or systematic omissions in the latter respect".

The implementation of the El Salvador Peace Agreement is being monitored by the UN. As of the writing of this report, these objectives had only partly been met.[18]

8   **Protection against death threats**

Governments should ensure that anyone in danger of extrajudicial execution, including those who receive death threats, is effectively protected.
– *Amnesty International 14-Point Program for the Prevention of Extrajudicial Executions*

Often "death squads" or other groups acting with official involvement or acquiescence issue death threats against named individuals or groups. Some threats are made openly by security force agencies. The threats may be communicated in written messages or telephone calls; sometimes they appear as lists of names published in newspapers as a warning or an incitement to kill the people named. A threat may be meant initially to intimidate the victim into acting in a certain way or ceasing to carry out activities which are disliked by those who have issued the threat, but if the victim does not comply, there is a danger that the threat will be carried out.

The duty to protect potential victims is part of a government's responsibility to prevent extrajudicial executions. This duty is spelled out in the UN Principles on Extra-Legal, Arbitrary and Summary Executions (principle 4). If "death squads" or acknowledged official bodies are threatening to kill people, the authorities must ensure that these threats are not carried out.[19]

UN bodies have become increasingly concerned about death threats and other forms of intimidation against people involved in human rights matters.[20] In resolution 1991/70, adopted without a vote on 6 March 1991, the UN Commission on Human Rights urged governments to refrain from acts of intimidation or reprisal against individuals and groups who seek to co-operate with the UN and representatives of its human rights bodies, or to use UN human rights procedures. In 1992 the Commission on Human Rights reiterated its appeal, broadening its concern to include relatives of victims and lawyers.[21]

In protecting a person who receives a death threat, the authorities should apprehend and bring to justice the people responsible for the threat and take any other measures necessary to ensure that the threat will not be carried out, including such measures as tracing threatening telephone calls. If the threatened person wishes, he or she should be provided with police protection until the threat is removed. However, some threatened people are reluctant to ask for police protection because they believe the police are behind the threat, or because the presence of police officers would hamper their work. If people who receive death threats believe they and their relatives will be safe only if they leave the area or the country, they should be given assistance to do so until they can safely return.

The authorities should also take steps to stop threats being made, by, for example, banning the publication or broadcasting of death threats.[22]

National organizations have worked in various ways to protect people against death threats. In *Colombia*, for example, the lives and reputations of over 100 human rights workers, trade union and popular leaders were put at risk in July 1993 when the security forces reportedly gave a television station a list of some 150 individuals and institutions deemed by military intelligence to be collaborators or supporters of guerrilla groups. In response, lawyers from the *Comisión Andina de Juristas – sección Colombiana*, Andean Commission of Jurists – Colombian office, presented to the courts an *acción de tutela*, a procedure intended to protect the constitutional rights of individuals. The action requested a judge to prevent publication of the list by the television station or any other public media and to call on the Ministry of Defence and its dependencies to refrain from divulging any information claiming links between individuals or institutions and guerrilla organizations to the news media or to third parties. The action cited rulings of the Constitutional Court which made it clear that information compiled by military intelligence or in the hands of the security forces should not be divulged to the media or to third parties but could only be used by the security forces themselves and in accordance with the constitutional rights of the individuals concerned.

International organizations and UN mechanisms and monitoring operations also have developed methods to help protect people who are at risk of extrajudicial execution.

- As described in Chapter 12, the UN *Working Group on Disappearances* and the UN *Special Rapporteur on extrajudicial, summary or arbitrary executions* have developed procedures for raising cases urgently with governments when they receive reports of intimidation or reprisals against victims' relatives, lawyers, and people who send the UN information or cooperate with UN human rights procedures.

- Through its *Urgent Action* technique, Amnesty International organizes the sending of thousands of appeals from around the world on behalf of people believed to be at risk of extrajudicial execution after receiving death threats. For example, in the first five months of 1993 Amnesty International issued 22 Urgent Action requests for appeals in response to death threats in eight countries. Several other organizations operate similar techniques.

- People from several organizations have travelled to the countries concerned in order personally to *accompany human rights activists* who receive death threats. The hope is that the people behind the threat will not wish to risk the international embarrassment which would follow if nationals of another country witness a killing or are themselves killed.[23]

- The UN human rights monitoring mission in *El Salvador* has raised individual cases with the authorities. In one such case, a 21-year-old woman complained to the UN mission that her life had been threatened by members of a local military detachment in civilian clothes who accused her of belonging to the opposition FMLN. The UN mission transmitted the complaint to the headquarters of the military detachment and were informed in writing that three soldiers would be discharged; it was later confirmed that they had been. Another complaint concerned a soldier who had threatened a community repeatedly, sometimes discharging his service firearm and displaying hand grenades which he said he would throw at the local residents. In response, the military authorities informed the UN mission that the soldier would be punished for unauthorized use of his firearm, and it was later confirmed that he was. However, in other cases raised by the mission the authorities failed to take action, while in still other cases people who received death threats were too frightened to lodge a complaint with the authorities or to name the authors of the threat.[24]

9   Safeguards on the arrest, detention and release of prisoners

The measures described in the above sections of this chapter concern the general prohibition and prevention of "disappearances" and extrajudicial executions, and the safeguards needed to prevent killings outside custody. Those which follow refer to the protection of people who are in custody. It is into custody that people "disappear". Most victims of extrajudicial executions, too, are taken into custody or otherwise apprehended before being killed.

Concern for the well-being of prisoners is reflected in the earliest human rights instruments adopted by the UN. Many of the provisions of the Universal Declaration of Human Rights (1948) concern actual or potential prisoners. Among them are its provisions for the right to life, the right to liberty and security of person, the right not to be subjected to arbitrary arrest or detention, the right not to be subjected to torture or cruel, inhuman or degrading treatment, and the right to a fair trial.

Since 1948 the UN has adopted two comprehensive sets of standards on the treatment of prisoners:

- The *Standard Minimum Rules for the Treatment of Prisoners* (cited below as the "Standard Minimum Rules"), adopted by the First UN Congress on the Prevention of Crime and the Treatment of Offenders in 1953 and endorsed by the UN Economic and Social Council in 1957 and, as amended, in 1977. The Standard Minimum Rules deal mainly with matters such as food, clothing, accommodation, exercise, medical treatment, punishment and discipline, but they also contain several important provisions for the prevention of "disappearances" and extrajudicial executions. Most of the standards set forth in this instrument apply not only to convicted prisoners and prisoners arrested on a criminal charge but to people arrested or imprisoned without charge, as stated in its rule 95.[26]

- The *Body of Principles for the Protection of All Persons under Any Form of Detention or Imprisonment* ("Body of Principles"), adopted by the UN General Assembly in 1988. This instrument contains many important provisions designed to protect prisoners against human rights violations.[27]

Safeguards for prisoners, many of them similar to the provisions of the Body of Principles, are contained also in the UN Declaration on Disappearances and the UN Principles on Extra-Legal, Arbitrary and Summary Executions, as well as the UN *Declaration on the Protection of All Persons from Being Subjected to Torture and Other Cruel, Inhuman or Degrading Treatment or Punishment*, adopted in 1975, and the UN *Convention against Torture and Other Cruel, Inhuman or Degrading Treatment or Punishment*, which was adopted in 1984 and entered into force in 1987.

The safeguards described below are drawn from UN instruments and from other measures which Amnesty International has found to be important. They are meant to protect all prisoners from the moment they are apprehended to the moment of release and beyond.

10   Safeguards at arrest

Arrest and detention should be carried out only by officials who are authorized by law to do so. Officials carrying out an arrest should identify themselves to the person arrested and, on demand, to others witnessing the event. Governments should establish rules setting forth which officials are authorized to order an arrest or detention.
– Amnesty International 14-Point Program for the Prevention of "Disappearances"

The first stage of a "disappearance" and the first stage of most extrajudicial executions consists of a person being apprehended by agents of the state. This action is often done in an irregular way. For instance, people may be detained without proper cause; officers carrying out an arrest may fail to identify themselves; or victims may be abducted by irregular units linked to the security forces, or by others acting with official support or acquiescence.

Irregular arrest facilitates the perpetration of "disappearances" and extrajudicial executions. It helps the authorities to avoid official responsibility for the welfare of the detained person. It helps to hide the facts and thus evade accountability for the crimes. If correct procedures for arrest are followed, the likelihood that a prisoner will "disappear" or be killed is greatly diminished.

Detailed standards for arrest are spelled out in the UN Body of Principles. These standards are designed to protect the right of freedom from arbitrary arrest, recognized in the Universal Declaration of Human Rights,[28] as well as other human rights which may be threatened if a person is arbitrarily deprived of liberty.

The Body of Principles defines "arrest" very broadly to cover virtually any apprehension of a person which derives from an official source. Under the Body of Principles, "'Arrest' means the act of apprehending a person for the alleged commission of an offence or by the action of an authority".

Safeguards established in the Body of Principles include the following:

- Arrest or detention shall only be carried out "strictly in accordance with the provisions of the law" and "by competent officials or persons authorized for that purpose" (Principle 2).[29]

- The authorities which arrest a person "shall exercise only the powers granted to them under the law" (Principle 9).

- Anyone arrested must be informed at the time of arrest of the reasons for the arrest (Principle 10).

- The time of the arrest, the reasons for the arrest and the identity of the law enforcement officials concerned must be recorded, and the records must be communicated to the detained person or to his or her lawyer (Principle 12).

Amnesty International has included these provisions in its recommendations to governments, along with other, more detailed recommendations intended to prevent "disappearances" and extrajudicial executions. Among these are:

- Officials carrying out an arrest should identify themselves to the person arrested and, on demand, to others witnessing the event.

- Police officers and other officials who make arrests should wear name tags or numbers so that they can be clearly identified. Other identifying markings such as the insignia of soldiers' battalions or detachments are also to be recommended.

- Police and military vehicles should be clearly identified as such. They should carry number plates at all times.

- In situations where there is a serious risk of "disappearances" or extrajudicial executions being perpetrated, the authorities carrying out arrests should give certificates of arrest to relatives stating that the individual concerned has been taken into custody, so that there can be no question later about official responsibility for their safe custody.

11   Notification of relatives

Accurate information about the arrest of any person and about his or her place of detention, including transfers and releases, should be made available promptly to relatives, lawyers and the courts.
– From Amnesty International's 14-Point Programs for the Prevention of "Disappearances" and Extrajudicial Executions

The concealment of prisoners, giving rise to "disappearance", needs to be suppressed by establishing a requirement that the authorities must make accurate information about arrest and place of detention available promptly to prisoners' relatives and others concerned. Prisoners themselves must also have the right to notify relatives promptly of their whereabouts.

Both of these principles are recognized in international human rights instruments. The UN Declaration on Disappearances (Article 10) establishes that accurate information on the detention of all persons deprived of liberty "and their place or places of detention, including transfers, shall be made promptly available to their family members, their counsel or to any other persons having a legitimate interest in the information unless a wish to the contrary has been manifested by the persons concerned." The right of prisoners to notify family members or others promptly of their arrest, transfer, and place of detention is set forth in the UN Body of Principles (Principle 16),[30] while the Standard Minimum Rules for the Treatment of Prisoners (rule 92) state that "(a)n untried prisoner shall be allowed to inform immediately his family of his detention".

The implementation of these principles involves several things:

- The authorities must ensure that all prisoners are fully able in practice to avail themselves of the right to notify family members or others promptly of their whereabouts. All prisoners should be informed of this right: If they do not have the financial or technical means to send word to their relatives, the authorities must be ready to communicate the message for them.

- The authorities must ensure that accurate information on the arrest, place of detention, transfer and release of prisoners is available promptly in a place where relatives and others concerned can obtain it. They must ensure that relatives are not obstructed from obtaining this information, and that they know or are able to find out where the information can be obtained.

- Where "disappearances" have been reported, there should be an additional requirement that the whereabouts of prisoners must be made known to a person or organization outside the place of detention who can act to ensure the prisoner's safety, without waiting for someone to request the information. Normally that person will be a relative, but in some situations it can be some other person or organization acting on the prisoner's behalf, such as a lawyer, a member of parliament, or an organization dealing with human rights matters. (In situations of armed conflict where relatives cannot easily be notified, notification may be to an impartial body such as the International Committee of the Red Cross (ICRC), which will inform the relatives.)

The provisions described above should be set forth in official regulations governing arrest and detention. Any infraction of these provisions should be punished by appropriate sanctions.

12   *Habeas corpus* **and other judicial remedies for locating and protecting prisoners**

> *Governments should at all times ensure that effective judicial remedies are available which enable relatives and lawyers to find out immediately where a prisoner is held and under what authority, to ensure his or her safety, and to obtain the release of anyone arbitrarily detained.*
> *– Amnesty International 14-Point Program for the Prevention of "Disappearances"*

As stated in the preceding section of this chapter, accurate information about the arrest and whereabouts of prisoners should be made available promptly to relatives, lawyers and the courts, but often it is not. An essential safeguard against "disappearances" is for relatives and others acting on a prisoner's behalf to be able to invoke the power of the courts to locate the prisoner and ensure his or her safety.

This safeguard is derived from the ancient legal notion of *habeas corpus*. *Habeas corpus* (literally, "that you have the body") is a device in the laws of various countries to test the legality of a detention. Under this procedure, a person can petition a court to issue a writ of *habeas corpus* commanding the authorities to produce the specified prisoner in person (literally, in "body") before the court so that the court can determine the legality of the detention, and to submit to the court's further directives in the matter.

In protecting the right to liberty, *habeas corpus* also helps to protect prisoners against torture, "disappearance" or extrajudicial execution. It does so by requiring the prisoner's physical presentation before a judicial authority, at which time the legality of the detention can be determined and the prisoner's condition verified.

Another relevant legal device is *amparo*, "protection", provided under the laws of many Latin American countries. Its scope is broader than that of *habeas corpus*, as it affords protection not only of the right to liberty but also of other constitutional rights including the rights to life and physical integrity.

Over the years, relatives of the "disappeared" in different countries have filed petitions for *habeas corpus* or *amparo* in thousands of cases. This experience has led to an appreciation of the importance of *habeas corpus* and similar remedies as safeguards against "disappearances", torture and extrajudicial executions. As the Inter-American Commission on Human Rights observed in 1986, "the immediate aim of this remedy [*habeas corpus*] is to bring the detainee before a judge, thus enabling the latter to verify whether the detainee is still alive and whether or not he or she has been subjected to torture or physical or psychological abuse. *The importance of this remedy cannot be overstated*, considering that the right to humane treatment recognized in Article 5 of the American Convention on Human Rights is one of the rights that may not be suspended under any circumstances."[31] (emphasis added) Similarly, the Inter-American Court of Human Rights has referred to the "vital role" of *habeas corpus* in preventing "disappearances", torture and extrajudicial executions.[32]

The principle of being able to challenge the legality of a detention in the courts has long been recognized in international and regional human rights instruments.[33] More recently, the right to an effective judicial remedy to locate and establish the well-being of prisoners has been recognized under the UN Declaration on Disappearances. Article 9 of the Declaration speaks of "(t)he right to a prompt and effective judicial remedy as a means of determining the whereabouts or state of health of persons deprived of their liberty and/or identifying the authority ordering or carrying out the deprivation of liberty". This right "is required to prevent enforced disappearances under all circumstances", including states of war or other public emergency. Moreover, in such proceedings there must be "access to all places holding persons deprived of their liberty and to each part thereof, as well as to any place in which there are grounds to believe that such persons may be found."

The attempt to locate and rescue "disappeared" people by filing petitions of *habeas corpus* and *amparo* has been an important part of the fight against "disappearances". These petitions have helped to document the extent of "disappearances" in different countries. In the vast majority of cases, however, the petitions have been unsuccessful in finding the "disappeared", owing to such factors as official obstruction or failure to respond to the courts' requests; intimidation of petitioners, lawyers and judges; weakness or lack of independence of the judiciary.[34]

The provision of an effective judicial remedy for locating and protecting prisoners involves several things, including the following:

- This remedy needs to be established in the laws of all countries where it does not yet exist.

- In accordance with Article 9 of the UN Declaration on Disappearances, the exercise of this remedy must not be suspended under any circumstances.[35] (In practice, governments often suspend the right of *habeas corpus* during emergencies.)

- Relatives of arrested people need to be genuinely able to use the remedy. They must have easy access to the courts, where they must be able to file petitions quickly and without intimidation or undue or prohibitive expense. The process of applying for the remedy should be as simple as possible. Relatives and others having knowledge of a "disappearance" should be able to apply directly to the courts without having to use the services of a lawyer.

- Because of the risk to prisoners' lives and well-being, the courts must act immediately on receiving a petition. Moreover, if the courts themselves learn that a person may have "disappeared", they must be able to act even if they have not received a petition on the prisoner's behalf. They must have the power to visit any place of detention without prior notice and without any delay, the power to inspect records and the power to summon witnesses and to compel testimony.

- The courts must have the power to determine the legality of a detention, to establish the whereabouts of prisoners, to ensure their safety, and to order the release of anyone arbitrarily detained. They must have the power to compel officials to comply with their orders; and the authorities must ensure that officials do in fact comply with such orders.

- In situations where the courts cannot act effectively in the face of widespread "disappearances", special arrangements should be made to enable relatives to seek help quickly on behalf of "disappeared" people. An extraordinary body should be set up for this purpose, consisting of independent and respected national and/or international figures or members of international organizations. This body should be able to act quickly on the basis of complaints from relatives and other reports of "disappearances". The authorities should cooperate fully.

One example of a law making detailed provision for the functioning of a judicial remedy against "disappearances" is the Act on *Amparo, Habeas Corpus* and Constitutionality (decree number 1-86) which was adopted in **Guatemala** in 1986 and remains in force. The UN Working Group on Disappearances listed features of the law in its report on its 1987 visit to the country. Among these features are the following:

- Application may be made to any court for a writ of *habeas corpus*, in writing, by telephone or orally, by the victim or any other person.

- There is no need for legal representation, and there are no formalities of any kind.

- *Habeas corpus* proceedings may also be instituted automatically by any court which has information that a person has been unlawfully arrested, detained, or in any way deprived or threatened with loss of freedom or subjected to harassment.

- The writ of *habeas corpus* must be issued as soon as the application has been received or the incident giving rise to it is made known.

- The writ will inform the authority or responsible person when the person concerned must be produced within a period of not more than 24 hours.

- A court which has information concerning incidents giving rise to any application for *habeas corpus* must immediately institute proceedings in the place where the victim is to be found, or – if the place is outside the court's jurisdiction – appoint an executing judge or any other authority or person who is qualified to perform such a function.

- If *habeas corpus* is applied for on behalf of missing people, the judge who has ordered the writ of *habeas corpus* has to appear in person at the place where these people are allegedly held, namely a detention centre, a prison or any other place where it has been indicated or suggested that they might be found.

- The court or the executing authority is empowered to conduct a full and immediate investigation into the incidents necessitating the application for *habeas corpus.* The court is, for example, empowered to summon witnesses and experts to the hearing at which *habeas corpus* has been ordered. The executing authority may search for the person concerned in any detention centre or other place where he or she has been told that the person may be found. The executing authority and the court have to do everything in their power to complete the investigation in order to identify those responsible where the facts giving rise to the writ of *habeas corpus* are proved.

- If there is evidence that the person on whose behalf an application of *habeas corpus* was made has "disappeared", the court has to order an immediate investigation of the case, which will continue until the whereabouts of the missing person have been determined.

- It is compulsory immediately to report any wrongful act on the part of officials who fail to comply with orders by the court or by the executing authority, keep the prisoner hidden, refuse to bring the prisoner before the competent court or in any way prevent *habeas corpus* from being guaranteed. Officials who do not observe the provisions of the Act will be punished in accordance with the law.[36]

The Working Group considered the Guatemalan *habeas corpus* procedure "exemplary" in theory but found that it was ineffective in practice, owing to lack of cooperation by military authorities, inability of the judiciary to pursue its aims with the necessary vigour, and failure of witnesses to testify through despondency or fear of reprisals.[37] A recent study on the operation of *habeas corpus* in Guatemala reached similar conclusions.[38]

Like other safeguards for the prevention of "disappearances" and extrajudicial executions, *habeas corpus* and similar remedies depend for their effectiveness both on their technical construction and on the will of the authorities to ensure that they are carried out. As the Working Group on Disappearances observed in its 1990 report (paragraph 346), "*Habeas corpus* ... is potentially one of the most powerful legal tools for unearthing the fate or whereabouts of a disappeared person. The most sophisticated rules governing this institution, however, are rendered inoperative in a situation where cooperation stops at the barracks gate."

13   No secret detention

Governments should ensure that prisoners are held only in publicly recognized places of detention. Up-to-date registers of all prisoners should be maintained in every place of detention and centrally... No one should be secretly detained.
– Amnesty International 14-Point Program for the Prevention of "Disappearances"

One way in which members of the security forces conceal the whereabouts of the "disappeared" is to hold them in private homes or apartments, "safe houses", or other locations which are not authorized places of detention. In other cases prisoners are held secretly in official places of detention, sometimes in separate sections or buildings which are off limits to ordinary security forces personnel. All such practices of secret detention must be stopped.

The requirement that prisoners must be held only in officially recognized places of detention is established in the UN Declaration on Disappearances (Article 10) and the UN Principles on Extra-Legal, Arbitrary and Summary Executions (principle 7). This requirement should be set forth in national laws. Any infractions should be punished by appropriate sanctions.

Up-to-date lists of all officially recognized places of detention should be published in a form that is readily accessible to lawyers and members of the public.

14   Registers of prisoners

> *Up-to-date registers of all prisoners should be maintained in every place of detention and centrally.*
> – Amnesty International 14-Point Program for the Prevention of "Disappearances"

Accurate record-keeping is an essential element of the proper administration of prisons and other places of detention. Official records establish where prisoners are held and who is responsible for them. The existence of official records that are open to review helps to protect prisoners from "disappearing" or being mistreated. If prisoners are missing, official records may help to trace them and to determine who was responsible for their custody.

Registers of prisoners should be kept in all places of detention including prisons, police stations and military bases. They should be kept in the permanent, tamper-proof form of a bound book with numbered pages. Information to be entered in them should include the following:

- the name and identity of each person detained;

- the reasons for his or her arrest or detention;

- the names and identities of the officials who arrested the prisoner or brought him or her in;

- the date and time of the arrest and of the taking of the arrested person to a place of detention;

- the time of the prisoner's first appearance before a judicial authority;

- precise information concerning the place of custody;

- the date, time and circumstances of the prisoner's release or transfer to another place of detention.

The maintenance of records on the admission and release of prisoners is required as an international standard for the administration of places of detention under the UN Standard Minimum Rules as well as the UN Body of Principles.[39] The UN Declaration on Disappearances (Article 10) also provides that registers of all prisoners should be maintained in all places of detention, and it calls for centralized registers as well. It states that the information in these registers must be made available to relatives, lawyers and others.

The requirement of keeping accurate and complete records and making the information available in conformity with UN standards should be incorporated in national laws and regulations. Any breach of these requirements should be punished by appropriate sanctions.

15   Bringing prisoners before a judicial authority

All prisoners should be brought before a judicial authority without delay after being taken into custody.
– *From Amnesty International's 14-Point Programs for the Prevention of "Disappearances" and Extrajudicial Executions*

All prisoners should be brought before a judicial authority in person as a matter of routine whether or not a writ of *habeas corpus* or similar order has been issued. This is a means of ensuring that all detentions are legal and not arbitrary. It is a safeguard against torture: a judge can see if there are any noticeable signs of ill-treatment and can hear any allegations by the prisoner. It is a means of providing independent supervision of detention through judicial control, removing the absolute power which the officials holding a prisoner might otherwise be able to wield.

The requirement of bringing anyone arrested or detained on a criminal charge promptly before a judicial authority is established in the International Covenant on Civil and Political Rights (Article 9 (3)). In the UN Declaration on Disappearances (Article 10) the requirement is extended to cover all persons deprived of liberty, whether or not they have been arrested or detained on a criminal charge.[40]

The word "promptly" is used in the International Covenant and the Declaration on Disappearances. Amnesty International uses the term "without delay" to emphasize that each prisoner should be brought before a judicial authority as soon as possible. Any delay can be an opportunity for a prisoner to be tortured or killed.

Relatives, lawyers and doctors should have prompt and regular access to prisoners.
– From Amnesty International's 14-Point Programs for the Prevention of "Disappearances" and Extrajudicial Executions

Access to prisoners is a key safeguard against "disappearance", extrajudicial execution and torture. Alongside the measures described earlier, it helps to break down the conditions of isolation in which abuses are committed. By visiting prisoners, relatives and others concerned about their well-being can see where they are held, and in what condition, so as to be able to intervene on their behalf if they are being ill-treated. Once a prisoner is seen by concerned people from outside, there is less chance that he or she will "disappear" or be killed.

The right of access to prisoners has been recognized in international human rights instruments. Principle 19 of the Body of Principles states: "A detained or imprisoned person shall have the right to be visited by ... in particular, members of his family...". Rules 37 and 92 of the Standard Minimum Rules recognize the right of prisoners to receive visits from their family and friends. Rules 37 and 92 apply to all categories of prisoners including people imprisoned without charge.

To ensure that visits are an effective safeguard, the following points should be observed:

- Relatives and others should be able to visit a prisoner *promptly* after he or she is taken into custody, and preferably as soon as possible. This is important because it is often in the first hours or days of detention that prisoners are at greatest risk of being tortured, made to "disappear", or killed.[41]

- They should be able to make further visits *regularly*, and preferably whenever they request, to verify the prisoner's continued well-being.[42]

- Not only relatives, but *lawyers* and independent *doctors* should be able to visit: lawyers, to ensure that a prisoner's rights are respected and to help prepare the prisoner's defence; doctors, to ascertain that the prisoner is healthy and not suffering from torture or ill-treatment.[43]

- Prisoners should be able to speak to visitors without having their conversations listened to or recorded. In particular, prisoners should be able to communicate in full confidentiality with their lawyers.[44] If guards are listening, a prisoner is likely to be impeded from disclosing that he or she has been ill-treated or giving information on the ill-treatment, "disappearance" or execution of other prisoners.

- Prisoners should also be able to correspond regularly with their families and friends.[45]

17   Visits of inspection

There should be regular, independent, unannounced and unrestricted visits of inspection to all places of detention.
– From Amnesty International's 14-Point Program for the Prevention of "Disappearances" and Extrajudicial Executions

Visits of inspection are a valuable means of checking the condition of prisoners and ascertaining that places of detention are being run properly. They are an important safeguard against torture, "disappearance" and extrajudicial execution.

National systems of prison inspection exist in a number of countries, while internationally the ICRC has visited prisoners of war and civilian detainees in armed conflicts and situations of internal disturbance and tension. The practice of visits of inspection has now been accepted by the UN as a requirement for the protection of human rights. Principle 29 of the Body of Principles provides that places of detention must be visited regularly by "qualified and experienced persons". These persons should be appointed by, and responsible to, an authority "distinct from the authority directly in charge" of administration of the place of detention.[46] More specifically, the UN Principles on Extra-Legal, Arbitrary and Summary Executions (principle 7) provide for visits of inspection, including unannounced visits, as a safeguard against extrajudicial executions.

In order to be effective in preventing "disappearances" and extrajudicial executions, a system of visits of inspection should meet several conditions.

- The inspectors must be independent of the authorities in charge of the place of detention.

- They must be able to visit all places of detention, including police stations and military camps as well as ordinary prisons.

- They must be able to make unannounced visits.

- They must have access to all detainees and be able to interview them freely and without witnesses.

- They must be able to make return visits whenever they wish. Often a single visit has little positive effect in the long run and is not enough to develop a program of protection.

- As a safeguard against subsequent "disappearances", they must be able to draw up a list of prisoners based on the relevant official records and other information they have gathered.

- Where necessary, they should be able to receive information rapidly from the authorities on all transfers of prisoners.

- They should be able to contact and be contacted by relatives of the "disappeared" without fear of reprisals against the relatives. Such contacts may yield information which they can compare with what they learn from other prisoners.

- They must be able to make recommendations to the authorities concerning the treatment of prisoners.[47]

18   Other safeguards during detention

Other safeguards established under international human rights instruments also help to protect prisoners from the risk of "disappearance" or extrajudicial execution. Among the most important are:

- The prohibition of torture and other cruel, inhuman and degrading treatment. This prohibition must be strictly enforced.

- Prisoners should be promptly told of their rights, including the right to lodge complaints about their treatment.[48]

- Prisoners and their lawyers should be promptly informed of any order of detention and the reasons for it.[49]

- The treatment of prisoners should conform to the standards laid down in the UN Standard Minimum Rules.

19   Safeguards at release

Prisoners should be released in a way that allows reliable verification of their release and ensures their safety.
– Amnesty International 14-Point Program for the Prevention of "Disappearances"

Officials involved in a "disappearance" sometimes try to cover it up by falsely claiming that the victim has been released. To prevent this happening, governments should institute safeguards for the proper release of prisoners, as established in Article 11 of the UN Declaration on Disappearances.

Elements of such safeguards should include the following:

- Prisoners should be handed over to, or released in the presence of, a person or organization that can verify the prisoner's release and assure his or her safety. Normally this will be the prisoner's relatives, but in some situations releases may be made to another person or organization acting to defend the prisoner's vital interests, such as a local human rights organization. In some situations releases are made under the auspices of the ICRC, who can then accompany the released person to a safe place.[50]

- A certificate of release should be issued in duplicate, signed by the releasing authority and the person to whom release is made or who witnesses the release on behalf of the prisoner, with one copy kept by each.

- Prisoners who "disappear" and are later released must be able to exercise their rights fully, including the right to lodge official complaints about their treatment and the right to obtain compensation and redress.

An example of a detailed set of safeguards for the release of prisoners is the Memorandum of Agreement in the *Philippines* among the Philippines Commission on Human Rights, the Department of National Defense, the Department of Interior and Local Government and the Department of Justice. The memorandum was adopted in 1991 in response to information received by the UN Working Group on Disappearances indicating that people supposedly released by the authorities had actually "disappeared". The memorandum specified that all releases were to be witnessed by a relative, the prisoner's lawyer, a representative of the Philippines Commission on Human Rights or any other person chosen by the prisoner, and in addition by the local fiscal or prosecutor or a representative of the Commission on Human Rights, "the parish priest, pastor, imam or religious leader, or by a well-known and respected member of the community". Releases were to be documented: "All releases must be evidenced by a document that must state clearly the name of the detainee/accused/person taken into custody, the exact date and time of his release, the printed name and signature of the person or persons receiving his living body indicating relationship, if any, to the detainee/accused/person taken into custody, and the independent witness, and the custodian, all of whom must sign over the printed names in the document, with specific designation of their position, rank, unit or office, as the case may be."

The memorandum further established that "Where a detainee/accused/person taken into custody is reportedly released from his custodians or captors in the manner not conforming to the foregoing procedure, and such detainee/accused/person taken into custody thereafter disappears or is found dead, the burden is on his custodians/captors to prove that the missing person was released safely, or that the foregoing procedure for his release was in fact observed and duly witnessed." It stated that failure to observe the established procedures for release "shall make the warden, commander or unit head, together with the custodians and captors or persons concerned" liable to administrative or penal sanctions.[51]

20   Dissemination

The Declaration on Disappearances, the Principles on Extra-Legal, Arbitrary and Summary Executions and other instruments for the protection of human rights adopted by the UN and regional inter-governmental organizations need to be made known if they are to be effective. The dissemination of human rights instruments involves several tasks:

- The full text of the instrument needs to be made available in the languages of different countries to those people who will use it or should do so: to lawyers of victims of human rights violations, to prosecutors and judges, to commanding officers in the security services, to officials in justice and defence ministries. It should be readily available for anyone else who wishes to consult it.

- The principles contained in the instrument should be made widely known – to members of the security forces, to victims of human rights violations and their families and to the general public as part of the task of informing them about human rights.

- Dissemination is a form of communication, and communication is a two-way process. It is not enough to hand out printed texts. Teaching, discussion, and other forms of communication must be included in a program of dissemination so that people will come to understand the principles of human rights protection and the reasons for them.

In adopting human rights instruments and in returning to the subject in later years, the UN has often expressed the wish that these instruments should be disseminated. Thus in the resolution adopting the Principles on Extra-Legal, Arbitrary and Summary Executions, the UN Economic and Social Council recommended that the Principles "shall be brought to the attention of law enforcement and criminal justice officials, military personnel, lawyers, members of the executive and legislative bodies of the Government and the public in general", while the preambular paragraphs of the Declaration on Disappearances contain a statement in which the UN General Assembly "(u)rges that all efforts be made so that this Declaration becomes generally known and respected".

The UN has done some work to publicize information on human rights, but much more effort is needed to distribute key information effectively to officials and the public.

- The UN has been conducting a World Public Information Campaign for Human Rights since 1988. A series of free brochures on human rights issues has been produced in the UN *Human Rights Fact Sheets* series as part of the Campaign. Two of the fact sheets, on "disappearances" and extrajudicial executions, describe the corresponding UN mechanisms – the Working Group on Disappearances and the Special Rapporteur on extrajudicial, summary or arbitrary executions. More effort is needed to ensure that the fact sheets reach the people who need them.[52]

- Huge numbers of copies of the Universal Declaration of Human Rights in many languages have been printed for free distribution. The International Covenant on Civil and Political Rights, the Code of Conduct for Law Enforcement Officials and the Body of Principles are also available in free leaflets. Other key instruments also should be issued as free leaflets.

- Other key resources such as the UN *Manual on the Effective Prevention and Investigation of Extra-legal, Arbitrary and Summary Executions* need to be more widely available. Arrangements should be made to distribute them in other languages in addition to the official UN languages.

- UN Information Centres are now located in the capitals of over 60 countries.[53] These centres should conduct programs to disseminate free copies of UN human rights instruments, including those cited above. They should keep important UN documents on human rights and make them readily available for public consultation. These include the annual reports of the Working Group on Disappearances and the Special Rapporteur on extrajudicial, summary or arbitrary executions, the annual reports of the Commission on Human Rights, the Sub-Commission on Prevention of Discrimination and Protection of Minorities and the Human Rights Committee and the Resolutions and Decisions of the General Assembly and the Economic and Social Council.

Even if all this is done, the UN will never have the capacity to disseminate human rights instruments in the multitude of languages spoken around the world. Governments also should disseminate human rights instruments and information as part of their responsibility for promoting human rights.

The importance of governmental action was recognized by the UN Commission on Human Rights in 1992 when it adopted a resolution stating that the Commission "(e)ncourages all Members States ... to accord priority to the dissemination, *in their respective national and local languages*, of the Universal Declaration of Human Rights, the International Covenants on Human Rights and other international instruments, and to provide information and education on the *practical ways in which the rights and freedoms enjoyed under these instruments can be exercised*" (emphases added). The resolution also recognized "the valuable role that non-governmental organizations can play" in improving public knowledge about human rights.[54]

21   **Training**

> *"As it is in the minds of people that human rights violations are conceived, it is in their minds, and hearts, that consciousness about the inherent dignity of the human person must be instilled. Failing that, it will be quite impossible to end disappearances for all time."*
> – UN Working Group on Enforced or Involuntary Disappearances ("Working Group on Disappearances")[55]

> **The prohibition of "disappearances" and extrajudicial executions should be reflected in the training of members of the security forces and in the instructions issued to them.**
> – From Amnesty International's 14-Point Programs for the Prevention of "Disappearances" and Extrajudicial Executions

The knowledge that "disappearances" and extrajudicial executions are prohibited should be transmitted during the formal training courses which all members of the security forces undergo. These courses differ from country to country, but a few general points may be made.

•   The training needs to reach all officials involved in arrest and custody, including police and prison officers, all officials authorized to use lethal force, and all members of the armed forces.

•   The notion of prevention of "disappearances" and extrajudicial executions needs to be related to the positive goals of the security forces, including the promotion of human rights for everyone and the protection in armed conflict of people not involved in hostilities.

•   The training needs to inculcate *knowledge* of the standards of human rights and international humanitarian law,[56] the *conviction* that it is necessary to respect these standards, and *motivation* to uphold them. Motivation should be conveyed through leadership and the attitude of trainers and supervisors.

•   Practical applications need to be brought in. There should be exercises to show the trainee how the prohibition of "disappearances" and extrajudicial executions should be respected in situations likely to arise in the course of his or her duties.

- Training programs must include a long-term, comprehensive follow-up program with clear goals and evaluation criteria to ensure that security force members incorporate the information learned into their behaviour. Training programs should be continually revised and strengthened in light of such follow-up and evaluation.

All members of the security forces need good training, but training alone will not prevent "disappearances" and extrajudicial executions. The prohibition of "disappearances" and extrajudicial executions must be reflected also in the general regulations and instructions issued to members of the security forces concerning such matters as arrest procedures, treatment of people in detention, crowd control and the use of force and firearms, in the orders issued in particular incidents, and in the words and deeds of superior officers and superior authorities. And if prohibition is to be credible, all members of the security forces must know that any official who becomes involved in the perpetration of a "disappearance" or an extrajudicial execution will be punished.

CHAPTER 10

INVESTIGATION

1   The duty to investigate

> *"The State is obligated to investigate every situation involving a
> violation of the rights protected by the [American] Convention
> [on Human Rights]. If the State apparatus acts in such a way
> that the violation goes unpunished and the victim's full
> enjoyment of such rights is not restored as soon as possible, the
> State has failed to comply with its duty to ensure the free and
> full exercise of those rights to the persons within its
> jurisdiction."*
> – *Inter-American Court of Human Rights*, Velásquez Rodríguez
> judgment[1]

> *"Measures taken by Governments to open independent and
> impartial investigations with a view to identifying and bringing
> to justice those responsible for human rights violations constitute
> one of the main pillars of the effective protection of human
> rights. Consequently, a climate of impunity for human rights
> violators contributes to a great extent to the persistence of – and
> sometimes even to an increase in – human rights abuses in a
> number of countries. The Special Rapporteur has received
> many allegations concerning breaches of the obligation to
> investigate violations of the right to life. On repeated occasions,
> he has reminded the Governments concerned of this
> obligation..."*
> – *UN Special Rapporteur on extrajudicial, summary or arbitrary
> executions[2]*

> *"The World Conference on Human Rights, welcoming the
> adoption by the General Assembly of the Declaration on the
> Protection of All Persons from Enforced Disappearance, calls
> upon all States to take effective legislative, administrative,
> judicial or other measures to prevent, terminate and punish acts
> of enforced disappearances. The World Conference on Human
> Rights reaffirms that it is the duty of all States, under any
> circumstances, to make investigations whenever there is reason*

*to believe that an enforced disappearance has taken place on a
territory under their jurisdiction and, if allegations are
confirmed, to prosecute its perpetrators."*
– World Conference on Human Rights, Vienna Declaration and
Programme of Action[3]

*Governments should ensure that all complaints and reports of
"disappearances" and extrajudicial executions are investigated promptly,
impartially and effectively by a body which is independent of those allegedly
responsible.*
– From Amnesty International's 14-Point Programs for the Prevention of
"Disappearances" and Extrajudicial Executions

Investigation is one of the keys to combating "disappearances" and extrajudicial executions. Successful investigation will reveal facts that the perpetrators are trying to hide. These facts can help to save the victims if they are still alive, and to enable victims' relatives to cope with the great problems they face. These facts constitute evidence making it possible to hold those responsible for "disappearances" and extrajudicial executions accountable for their actions and to bring them to justice.

When there are reports that a person has "disappeared" or been extrajudicially executed, Amnesty International calls on the authorities to conduct an investigation. The conclusion of an effective investigation, coupled with a clear public condemnation of "disappearances" and extrajudicial executions, helps to show that the authorities are determined to put a stop to these human rights violations. If there is no investigation or if an investigation is not properly done, there will be strong suspicions that the authorities are already full aware of the details of the case, that they themselves have ordered or acquiesced in a terrible crime, that they have decided to let the perpetrators get away with it and are determined that the truth should be covered up.

The obligation of governments to conduct prompt, thorough and impartial investigations into suspected "disappearances" and extrajudicial executions is established in UN human rights instruments, notably the Declaration on Dis-appearances (Article 13) and the Principles on Extra-Legal, Arbitrary and Summary Executions (principles 9-17). These instruments also contain standards for how investigations should be conducted. The standards in the latter instrument are especially detailed.

The standards of investigation set forth in the UN Principles on Extra-Legal, Arbitrary and Summary Executions are supplemented by the UN *Manual on the Effective Prevention and Investigation of Extra-Legal, Arbitrary and Summary Executions*.[4] This *Manual* has been welcomed by the UN Commission on Human Rights,[5] and it is used by the UN Special Rapporteur on extrajudicial, summary or arbitrary executions as a standard for assessing governmental investigations. It is an invaluable tool for the investigation of extrajudicial executions in different countries. Many of the measures recommended in this chapter are adapted from the UN *Manual* and the *Model Protocol for a Legal Investigation of Extra-legal, Arbitrary and Summary Executions* ("***Minnesota Protocol***") contained in it.[6]

In many countries, valuable investigative work has been done by victims' relatives, local human rights organizations, lawyers, journalists and other private people, often working against severe obstacles and at great personal risk. "Unofficial" investigations such as these have brought key facts to light, setting in motion official investigations, and providing a basis for action. These unofficial investigations are discussed towards the end of the chapter.

Even when official investigations are held, the standards laid out in this chapter are unfortunately often not met. Wishing to avoid accountability for their crimes, those responsible for "disappearances" and extrajudicial executions will block investigations by means of techniques ranging from legal restrictions on the investigative process to non-cooperation, harassment, intimidation, death threats, and further "disappearances" and killings. The authorities responsible for ordering an investigation may have no interest in seeing that the investigation reaches a satisfactory conclusion, or they may be under pressure from the security forces and other powerful interests not to allow it to do so.

In the face of these obstacles, internationally recognized standards of investigation assume importance as a yard-stick of governmental behaviour. The wilful failure to meet these standards adds to the evidence of official acquiescence in the crimes. As the UN *Manual* (page 14) states, "Non-compliance with the standards [for death investigations] can be publicized and pressure brought against non-complying Governments, especially where extra-legal, arbitrary and summary executions are believed to have occurred. If a Government refuses to establish impartial inquest procedures in such cases, it might be inferred that the Government is hiding such executions." The same inference can be drawn from a failure to investigate "disappearances".

2   The impulse to investigate

Governments should ensure that an investigation is started whenever there is either an official complaint or some other reliable report that a "disappearance" or an extrajudicial execution has been perpetrated. Deaths in custody and deaths at the hands of the security forces should be automatically investigated.

- A relative or any other person who has reason to believe that a "disappearance" or an extrajudicial execution has been committed should have the right to submit a complaint to an official body so that it can be investigated.[7]

- In order to avail themselves of this right, relatives and others affected need to know how and where to submit complaints and must be able to do so without fear of reprisals.[8] The authorities should not impose onerous conditions or procedures on victims' representatives who seek to make complaints.

- Even if no formal complaint has been made, an official investigation should be started if there are reports of a possible "disappearance" or extrajudicial execution.[9] These can include reports in the news media and reports from domestic or international human rights organizations. The obligation should always be on the government to show that it needs no prompting to investigate even informal allegations that members of its security services are responsible for "disappearances" or extrajudicial executions.

- All deaths in custody should be investigated, as should all cases where the authorities fail to account for the fate and whereabouts of a person reported to be in custody.[10]

- There should be a system whereby all deaths resulting from the use of force or firearms by law enforcement officials are reported to the judicial and administrative authorities responsible for review and control of the services involved, in accordance with the UN Basic Principles on the Use of Force and Firearms by Law Enforcement Officials (principle 22). An investigation should be initiated whenever there is reason to believe such deaths may have resulted from excessive use of force or may otherwise have been unlawful.

- An investigation should similarly be initiated on the basis of reports of deaths caused by members of the armed forces whenever there is reason to believe such deaths were unlawful.

The obligation to initiate official investigations is established in UN human rights instruments, as noted in the first section of this chapter. This obligation should be set forth in national laws and regulations.

3   Objectives of an official investigation

The main objective of an official investigation is to establish the facts:

- Has a "disappearance" or an extrajudicial execution been perpetrated? If so, by whom?

- If a public official has committed a crime or breach of regulations, was he or she acting under orders or with the acquiescence of other officials?

An investigation of a suspected *"disappearance"* should, in particular,

- determine the whereabouts and fate of the supposed victim, establishing what happened to him or her from the moment of arrest. Such an investigation should have the power to take the necessary measures to protect the victim's life and safety.

An investigation of a possible *extrajudicial execution* should:

- identify the victim;

- determine the cause, manner, and time of death and the identity of the person or persons responsible. (Determining the cause and manner of death involves establishing what brought about death; whether the death was natural, accidental or deliberate; if the latter, whether it was a suicide or a homicide and, if a homicide, whether or not it was in self-defence.)

An investigation which may lead to *prosecution* should collect evidence of any crimes or breaches of regulations, including unlawful arrest or detention, torture or ill-treatment, and unlawful killing. The investigation should recover and preserve any evidentiary material, identify witnesses, and obtain statements from them. Those allegedly responsible for "disappearances" and extrajudicial executions should be identified, arrested, and brought before a competent court.

4   Characteristics of the investigating body

The body carrying out an official investigation into possible "disappearances" or extrajudicial executions should have several characteristics.

- It should be *independent* of those allegedly responsible.

- It should have the necessary *powers* and *resources*.[11]

- Those carrying out the investigation and their staff should be *professionally competent* for the required tasks.

- They should be *protected* against intimidation and reprisals.[12]

Often investigations are ineffective because the investigating body lacks these characteristics. Its members may not be independent. They may lack the power to subpoena evidence or to compel witnesses to testify. They may be bound by procedural constraints which prevent rapid or effective action. They may be denied access to government installations and official records. They may be subjected to murder, threats or other forms of pressure.

The need for *independence* applies both to the individual investigators and to the investigating body as a whole. This body should be separate from any agency suspected of responsibility for the actions under investigation. Its members and staff should not be associated with any person, governmental entity or political party potentially implicated in the matter.

The investigating body should have the *power* to:

- respond immediately to complaints and reports of "disappearances" and extrajudicial executions;

- conduct on-site investigative visits, including the power to enter and search any place believed to be connected to "disappearances" or extrajudicial executions, and conduct interviews in private;

- obtain and compel the production of all necessary physical evidence, including government records and medical records;[13]

- compel the attendance and cooperation of witnesses, and ensure their protection;

- receive evidence from witnesses unable to attend in person, including witnesses located outside the country.

The investigating body should have the *resources* needed to carry out its tasks, such as laboratory facilities, clerical equipment such as typewriters and computers, and resources to travel and to hold hearings. It should be able to use the services of legal counsel and experts in such fields as ballistics, pathology and forensic science, including, where necessary, experts from other countries. It should have adequate investigative, administrative and clerical staff.

5   Characteristics of the investigation

The investigation itself should have several characteristics.[14]

- It should be *impartial*, not weighted in favour of the security services.

- It should be *effective*, obtaining and considering all relevant evidence and reaching conclusions that are as firm as the evidence permits.

- It should be *prompt*. Promptness is necessary to save the victims if possible, and to receive evidence quickly. Undue delays will give rise to fears that the investigation is being blocked or evidence destroyed.

- The *methods* of investigation should be made public in advance and described in the report of the investigation.

- Advance notices should be widely publicized inviting *members of the public* with relevant evidence to submit it to the investigation. Relatives of the victim and anyone else who has relevant information should have an opportunity to present it.

- Relatives should have access to all information relevant to the investigation.[15]

- Anyone called to give testimony should at the outset be informed of the subject and purpose of the inquiry and of their right to legal counsel and other legal rights.

- There should be an opportunity for the effective questioning of witnesses.

- Complainants, witnesses, lawyers and others involved in the investigation should be *protected* from intimidation and reprisals. Where there is a risk of intimidation or reprisals, the means for protecting witnesses should be publicly announced in advance. Where necessary, these may include such measures as keeping the identity of witnesses confidential and using only such evidence as will not present a risk of identifying the witness. Any ill-treatment, intimidation, reprisal or other interference with the investigation should be appropriately punished.[16]

- Officials suspected of responsibility for the alleged "disappearance" or extrajudicial execution should be *suspended* from active duty during the investigation, as a precaution against the possibility of their perpetrating further such acts and to ensure the integrity of the investigation. They should be removed from any position of control or power over relatives, witnesses and others involved in the investigation while the investigation is in progress. These measures should be without prejudice to the outcome of the investigation, to the careers of the officers concerned or to any eventual judgment regarding their suspected involvement.[17]

- The report of the investigation, or at least the findings and recommendations, should be *made public* as soon as the investigation is completed. It should state the evidence on which the findings and recommendations are based.[18]

- Once the report has been submitted, the government should respond promptly, stating publicly what steps will be taken as a result.[19] The findings should be *acted on.*

- An investigation into a suspected "disappearance" should *not be cut short* until the fate of the victim is officially clarified.[20] If the victim has been killed, the killing should in turn be investigated and those responsible should be brought to justice.

144

6   Investigative techniques

Many techniques are needed in investigating "disappearances" and extrajudicial executions. Thus, an investigation into a reported "*disappearance*" should:

- examine arrest records and records of detention in centres where the presumed victim may have been held;

- collect and examine evidence from eyewitnesses and others, as well as material evidence on such matters as the vehicles or equipment used in the arrest;

- interview officials involved in arrest and detention who may have had contact with the victim or other knowledge of what happened;

- if there are fears that the victim has been killed, attempt to establish his or her fate by searching for places where the body may have been disposed of, and by matching physical details of the prisoner against information on unidentified bodies.

An investigation into a death in custody, a suspicious death at the hands of a public official, or other possible *extrajudicial execution* should include:

- detailed expert examination of the scene of death;

- collection and examination of material evidence;

- ballistic examination of ammunition and firearms which may have been used in the killing;

- autopsy of the body of the person killed;

- interviews with witnesses and others having knowledge of the death or the surrounding circumstances;

- examination of any order or authorization for the use of force resulting in a killing.

7   Autopsy

An autopsy is a key technique in the investigation of possible extrajudicial executions. An autopsy can help to establish the identity of the victim. In conjunction with examination of the presumed scene of death, it can help to determine the time, place, cause and manner of death. If the victim was unlawfully killed, the evidence obtained through autopsy can help in bringing the killers to justice.

The UN Principles on Extra-Legal, Arbitrary and Summary Executions have established that in all suspected cases of extrajudicial executions, "(t)he body of the deceased person shall not be disposed of until an adequate autopsy is conducted by a physician..." (principle 12).

An official autopsy in cases of possible extrajudicial executions should have several characteristics.[21]

- The person conducting the autopsy should, if possible, be an expert in forensic pathology. He or she should be professionally competent, impartial, and independent of those allegedly responsible for the death.

- The person conducting the autopsy should have the necessary facilities and resources. He or she should have access to all investigative data, to the place where the body was discovered and to the place where death is thought to have occurred. The body should be available to those conducting the autopsy for enough time to enable a thorough investigation to be carried out.

- The autopsy report should describe all injuries, including any evidence of torture. A copy of the report should be made available immediately to the victim's relatives or their legal representative.

- Relatives of the victim should be entitled to appoint their own doctor to carry out or be present at an autopsy.

- The body should be returned to the deceased person's family or relatives when the autopsy has been completed.

A *Model Autopsy Protocol* is included in the UN *Manual on the Effective Prevention and Investigation of Extra-Legal, Arbitrary and Summary Executions*. The protocol covers such matters as the investigation of the scene of death, external and internal examination of the body, X-ray examination, photography, and storage of material evidence, as well as specialized analyses which should be carried out, such as tests for poisonous substances and histological studies of tissues. It can be used by forensic pathologists and other doctors in conducting autopsies, by governments in establishing proper autopsy procedures, and by non-specialists as a standard for evaluating the thoroughness of official autopsies. As stated in the introduction to the protocol, its use "will permit early and final resolution of potentially controversial cases and will thwart the speculation and innuendo that are fuelled by unanswered, partially answered or poorly answered questions in the investigation of an apparently suspicious death."

In 1993 the UN Commission on Human Rights decided to invite states "to take measures to introduce into their rules and practices" the international standards set forth in the Model Autopsy Protocol.[22]

Relatives and friends often spend years searching for the "disappeared". Sometimes their inquiries lead them to suspect that the victim has been killed and buried in a certain place. Sometimes secret burials come to light: bodies are found, but there is no record of their identity. By scientifically examining unidentified human remains and comparing them with information on prisoners who have "disappeared", forensic anthropology can help to establish the identity of the dead and thence the fate of the "disappeared".

Forensic anthropology is the study of medico-legal questions relating to a deceased person through the examination of his or her skeletal remains, aiming among other things at determining the person's identity and the manner and cause of death. The application of this technique of criminal investigation in a human rights context is one of the most important developments of the past decade in clarifying the fate of the "disappeared". It is valuable also in the investigation of extrajudicial executions.

Forensic anthropology was first used systematically in the investigation of "disappearances" in Argentina, where unidentified human remains were being found in mass graves. Early initiatives by Argentinian investigators in 1983 had resulted in the virtual destruction of evidence from opened graves due to lack of investigative skills of those carrying out the exhumations. In June 1984 forensic specialists from the American Association for the Advancement of Science held seminars in several Argentinian cities, and one of their members, Dr Clyde C. Snow, supervised on-site investigations and training of local professionals. As a result of their work with Dr Snow, a number of young doctors, anthropologists and students formed the *Equipo Argentino de Antropología Forense* (EAAF), Argentine Forensic Anthropology Team, in 1984.[23]

Since its formation the EAAF has scientifically recovered and analyzed more than 500 bodies of victims from both single and mass graves in Argentina, of whom at least 150 have been identified beyond reasonable doubt. The team has also helped to train investigators in Brazil, Chile, El Salvador, Venezuela and the Philippines, and its members have taken part in investigations in Uruguay, Colombia, Panama, Guatemala, Iraqi Kurdistan, Romania, Ethiopia and the former Yugoslavia.[24] The investigations have proved useful not only for the purpose of providing evidence for the courts, on the basis of which many of those responsible have been charged with murder in several countries, but also for the relatives of the victims, who were thus finally able to know the fate of their loved ones.

A 1993 UN report described three tasks performed by forensic scientists in investigating human remains in unmarked graves and other places:

> "First, they conduct interviews and review documents to ascertain the location of the burial sites and the victims whose remains were probably buried in those sites. Scientists interview the people who live in the locality, sometimes grave-diggers

who have been hired to bury the bodies, or civilians who may have heard rumours that a certain area is used as a burial site or who can provide information on other details leading to the identification of the victims. They also review documents, sometimes official records, which indicate where the bodies of certain individuals may have been interred...

"Second, they conduct the exhumation in the appropriate scientific manner in order to be able to obtain the optimal amount of information. Because information from both the remains themselves and from the spatial features of the graves is useful, it is crucial that both be preserved and documented carefully. Hence, archaeological techniques much like those used in excavating prehistoric sites are used. The graves are marked so that the exact coordinates of where each item is uncovered can be identified. The soil and dirt are removed in such a manner as to ensure that no piece of evidence, however minute (e.g., teeth, bullets, etc.), will be missed. More important, the remains are exhumed with the care and deliberation that will ensure the least amount of damage and alteration to the surface and placement of the remains. Failure to employ the proper method of exhumation can lead to the destruction of the evidence...

"Third, they examine the remains to determine the cause and manner of death, and attempt to establish the identity of the victim. Forensic experts analyze the skeletal remains to determine the physical characteristics of the victim, together with the cause, manner, time and place of death with a view to ascertaining the victim's identity. In doing so, they use techniques in pathology, odontology, radiology, etc. For instance, teeth and skeletal X-rays are taken to identify the victim. Also, anthropological studies may be undertaken to determine the skeleton's age at death, sex, race, stature and handedness. The results are then compared to the antemortem characteristics of the deceased. Forensic anthropologists can also distinguish various types of trauma to the bone which help determine the manner and cause of death."[25]

The experience accumulated by forensic investigators since 1984 has yielded many lessons, including the following:

•   When a grave containing the remains of unknown people is discovered, everything should be left in place and protected from disturbance until it can be excavated using sound archaeological techniques. Excavation by untrained people can destroy evidence which, once lost, can never be recovered.

- Careful records of investigations should be kept. The remains should be photographed and their location recorded before they are removed for laboratory examination.

- The identity of the person is established by comparing the remains with information supplied by relatives, including medical and dental records. For example, if the person had a deformity or an old injury, this will often be evident in the skeletal remains. Items such as clothing or jewelry found in the grave can also help to establish the victim's identity.

- Investigators may need to deal with a host of practical problems, including securing the cooperation of local authorities; overcoming official hostility and obstruction; and finding the necessary equipment, personnel and laboratory facilities. Sometimes the personal security of the investigators must be protected.

- Special care and sympathy are needed for dealing with victims' relatives, whose experience is acutely painful.[26] The investigators may need to arrange for appropriate counselling and – on occasion – psychiatric care. They will need to establish an ethically acceptable basis for their work in relation to the relatives' wishes. (As a matter of principle, the EAAF does not investigate the fate of a "disappeared" person if this is opposed by the victim's relatives.)

The UN has recently taken steps to facilitate international cooperation in the forensic investigation of human rights violations. In 1992 the UN Commission on Human Rights decided "that it would be desirable to create, under United Nations auspices, a standing team of forensic experts and experts in other relevant disciplines, to be enrolled on a voluntary basis worldwide, who could be requested by the Governments concerned, through the Secretary-General, to assist, on the basis of professional objectivity and in a humanitarian spirit, in the exhumation and identification of probable victims of human rights violations or in the training of local teams for the same purpose".[27] In 1993 the Commission decided to ask the UN Secretary-General to compile a list of forensic experts who could be asked to give their services.[28] However, there had been little progress in establishing such a team or list at the time of writing of this report.

A useful description of procedures for forensic anthropological investigation may be found in the Model Protocol for Disinterment and Analysis of Skeletal Remains, contained in the UN *Manual on the Effective Prevention and Investigation of Extra-Legal, Arbitrary and Summary Executions.*

Amnesty International often recommends that a government should establish a *commission of inquiry* into human rights violations. Commissions of inquiry should be established when normal procedures for official investigations are not working effectively, or where there is a pattern of human rights violations which is not being tackled effectively on a case-by-case basis.

A commission of inquiry should have all the attributes, powers and resources of an official investigation as described above, but its scope should be broader. Its mandate should include:

- investigating patterns of alleged "disappearances" and extrajudicial executions as well as individual cases;

- making recommendations for the criminal prosecution of those responsible;

- considering the institutional changes needed to prevent further "disappearances" and unlawful killings, including legal changes, changes in administrative practice and procedures, recruitment, training and accountability of personnel;

- considering means of providing adequate compensation and redress to victims and their families.

The mandate should be formulated in such a way that it does not prevent the commission from examining other matters which appear during the inquiry to be material to the issues under investigation.

The work of a commission of inquiry should be publicized so that its findings will have a positive impact.

The need to set up commissions of inquiry into suspected extrajudicial executions in cases where established investigative procedures are inadequate is set forth in the UN Principles on Extra-Legal, Arbitrary and Summary Executions (principle 11). Detailed standards for commissions of inquiry are contained in the Minnesota Protocol, cited above.

In recent years a number of governments have established national *human rights commissions*. Such commissions often have investigative powers, but their role is usually broader than that of a commission of inquiry. They may, for example, be charged with reporting on human rights generally and advising the government on human rights matters.

Amnesty International has prepared a series of standards for the establishment and functioning of national human rights commissions.[29] Such commissions can play an important role in strengthening the protection of human rights, but they can never replace, nor should they diminish, the safeguards and remedies inherent in comprehensive and effective legal structures enforced by an independent judiciary.

In March 1992 the UN Commission on Human Rights endorsed a set of *Principles relating to the status of national institutions.*[30] This instrument contains detailed standards for the responsibilities, composition and methods of operation of national institutions to promote and perfect human rights. In Amnesty International's view, the Principles should be used as basic minimum guidelines for the establishment of national human rights commissions.

10   Investigations by relatives and human rights defenders

Despite the detailed standards adopted by the UN for the official investigation of suspected "disappearances" and extrajudicial executions, there is often no guarantee that they will be followed, or even that there will be any investigation at all. It is for this reason that investigations by relatives, human rights organizations and others are so important.

Domestic human rights organizations in many parts of the world have worked courageously to document cases of "disappearances" and extrajudicial executions in their countries. Not only organizations, but individual journalists, lawyers, and relatives of victims have done valuable investigative work. They have exposed official involvement in individual incidents and patterns of "disappearances" and killings, leading to remedial action. The evidence compiled locally has enabled international human rights organizations and the UN to take action. Often this evidence has been crucial in later official investigations. Such "unofficial" investigations and the procedures developed through them have become vital components of the effort to combat human rights violations nationally and internationally.

Many techniques, often ingenious, have been used in unofficial investigations. There is no single way, but certain minimal kinds of information and evidence should be sought as soon as possible. The aim is to provide as complete a picture of the case as possible.

When a person "disappears", relatives and human rights organizations should immediately try to compile a record of the facts. As part of this process they should obtain personal identity documents, dental records and copies of fingerprints. These precious records often disappear in the course of investigation.

A documented case of a *"disappearance"* should contain:

- the full name of a missing person, with a photograph if available;

- other information through which the missing person's identity may be established, such as physical characteristics or the clothing worn when the person was last seen;

- the date (day, month and year) and time when the person was arrested, abducted or last seen;

- the place where the person was arrested, abducted or last seen;

- names and details of any witnesses to the arrest or abduction;

- information on the identity of the parties believed to have carried out the arrest or abduction or to hold the person in unacknowledged detention, including physical characteristics, clothing and vehicles used, as well as descriptions of others present at the scene, including uniformed security force personnel;

- an indication of whether the arrest or detention has been denied by the authorities;

- information on the action taken by relatives or others to locate the missing person, such as inquiries with the authorities or *habeas corpus* petitions, including sworn statements by any witnesses and copies of any written communications sent to officials or official bodies.[31]

- copies of any newspaper reports on the incident.

A documented case of a suspected *extrajudicial execution* should contain, as a minimum:

- the full name of the victim, or if the victim's identity is not known, a physical description in as much detail as possible, with a photograph if available, as well as other information through which the victim's identity may be established, such as clothing or jewelry worn;

- a record of the sequence and location of events, including the attack and the moment of death. Times should be specified as precisely as possible. The record should indicate how the attack was carried out (if known) and the probable cause of death;

- information on the identity of the person or people believed to have carried out the attack including physical characteristics, clothing and vehicles used, as well as descriptions of others present at the scene;

- names and details of any witnesses to the incident;

- any other evidence indicating that the victim was unlawfully and deliberately killed by a public official, on official orders or with official acquiescence.

If possible, written reports of "disappearances" and killings should be supplemented by photographs of the actual events or of the scene of the events. Dead bodies also should be photographed for purposes of forensic investigation. Photographs should preferably be in colour, as colour photography records details which do not show up in black-and-white photographs. A ruler should be placed alongside bodies or objects when they are being photographed so as to give an indication of scale.

Tools for recording and reporting cases of "disappearances" and suspected extrajudicial executions include the *questionnaires* prepared by the UN Working Group on Disappearances and international, regional and national organizations such as Amnesty International and the *Federación Latinoamericana de Asociaciones de Familiares de Detenidos-Desaparecidos* (FEDEFAM), Latin American Federation of Associations of Families of the "Disappeared".[32]

The investigation of a "disappearance" or a suspected extrajudicial execution does not stop here. Organizations and individuals working to resolve these cases should continue to collect information. *Continuing investigation* involves:

- keeping a file on each case, including any published or official information, including court documents and other legal papers such as sworn statements;

- continuing to make inquiries about the whereabouts and fate of the "disappeared". Notes should be kept on all inquiries and the responses to them;

- placing advertisements in local and national newspapers, and asking radio and television stations to broadcast details of the "disappeared", asking for information and urging witnesses to come forward;

- searching for the "disappeared" in prisons, other places of detention, hospitals and morgues;

- interviewing people released from places of detention where a "disappeared" person is believed to have been held;

- pressing for official investigation by the courts or other competent official bodies, and pressing for investigations already started to be conducted effectively;

- responding quickly to any new evidence that becomes available by recording it, pursuing any leads, and seeking to ensure that it is not destroyed by officials or others implicated in the case;

- if unidentified bodies are discovered, ensuring that they are examined by forensic experts. (If mass graves are discovered, it is imperative to prevent their being disturbed until they can be examined by a person qualified in the techniques of forensic anthropology, so as not to destroy important evidence);

- arranging for expert assistance where forensic investigation or other specialized techniques are needed;

- transmitting information to UN bodies which take action on cases of "disappearances" and suspected extrajudicial executions (see Chapter 12).

11   Piecing together a pattern

Clear evidence of official responsibility for an abduction or a killing is often hard to come by. But if the known details of different cases are examined side by side, common patterns often emerge. These patterns may suggest that the official security apparatus or some part of it is engaging in a systematic practice of "disappearance" or extrajudicial execution. If new cases conforming to the pattern arise, there will be a presumption that these cases were the product of the same practice.

Human rights organizations compiling cases of "disappearances" and extrajudicial executions have learned to look for possible indicators of governmental responsibility. They include the following.[33]

Information about the victims may suggest that the authorities have selected them for "disappearance" or assassination. The investigator might ask:

- Is there reason to believe that the victim is perceived by the authorities as an enemy, or is the victim a relative of someone wanted by the authorities? Was the victim active politically? Could his or her work, study, or other activity have been deemed subversive or illegal? Did the victim belong to an organization which had been the object of repression or criticism by the government? Had he or she witnessed other human rights violations?

- Had the victim previously been detained? Can this previous detention be connected with the victim "disappearing" or being killed?

- Had the victim been threatened publicly or privately by the authorities? Had he or she been identified in published "death lists" or broadcast threats and branded as a subversive, a traitor or a public enemy?

- Had he or she been under official surveillance? Had his or her home been raided?

- Did the authorities later release information identifying the victim as a criminal or a subversive, implying that the "disappearance" or killing was justified? Did they vilify the victim's family or criticize those who sought to investigate the case?

Information on the methods and circumstances of abductions and killings suggestive of official involvement:

- Did the perpetrators use equipment normally associated with the security forces, such as walkie-talkies or particular types of vehicles or firearms? If unmarked vehicles were used, were they able to pass through security checkpoints unhindered?

- Did the perpetrators use the terminology of the security forces or refer to military or police ranks? (Survivors have often said that subordinates addressed the leaders of those detaining or interrogating them by their titles.)

- Are the cause and manner of death consistent with the known methods of the security services?

- Does the body suggest in any other way that the victim had been held in government custody? (In *El Salvador* many victims of killings have been found with their hands bound behind their backs by their thumbs, a traditional detention technique of the Salvadorean security forces. In other countries the bodies of "death squad" victims show signs of having been handcuffed.)

- Can practices resulting in "disappearances" and killings be linked to procedures or tactics set forth in military manuals, police force instructions or written orders?

- Do perpetrators appear to have access to official intelligence information on such matters as the identification of suspects, where to find them and how to get at them? (Sometimes plainclothes hit squads are found to carry photographs and surveillance information emanating from government security services.)

- Do members of the regular, uniformed security forces cooperate or stand by passively while "disappearances" and killings are perpetrated? For example, do "death squads" gain entry without difficulty to guarded public buildings, perhaps by displaying official credentials? Do perpetrators openly carry firearms without being challenged by ordinary security personnel?

Geographical concentrations of "disappearances" and killings which can be correlated with governmental or administrative units or with the presence of particular sections of the security forces or the assignment of certain military or police commanders to certain regions. (Two years after mass "disappearances" and extrajudicial executions began in *Peru* in 1983, all known cases continued to be reported from just 13 of the country's 144 provinces. These 13 adjoining provinces had been placed under a state of emergency and military control shortly before the killings and "disappearances" began. Later, as more provinces were placed under military control, "disappearances" and extrajudicial executions began to be perpetrated there.)

Changes over time which can be correlated with acknowledged changes in official policy – for example, *increases* in "disappearances" and killings in periods when military and police control is increased, as in times of declared public emergency when extraordinary powers are assumed, or *decreases* when the country is under international scrutiny following adverse publicity over human rights violations.

Lack of governmental action to investigate "disappearances" and killings and bring the perpetrators to justice. For example, do the police neglect to go promptly to the scene of abductions, assassinations and bombings, fail to question witnesses or to seek material evidence, or refuse to pursue named suspects? Can their reactions in cases where official involvement is suspected be contrasted with their reaction in similar incidents involving opposition groups? Do they frustrate the legal process by failing to appear in court?

Official condonation of "disappearances" and killings. Do officials speak approvingly of these crimes as examples of "social cleansing" or "fighting fire with fire", or by making statements such as that society has a right to "defend itself"? Do they make statements vilifying the victims and glorifying the perpetrators?

On an individual case, the presence of one or another of the above indicators constitutes circumstantial evidence suggesting official involvement. Often this evidence is not conclusive, but the more evidence there is, the stronger the case becomes. Moreover, among the many cases in which such circumstantial evidence is present, there will often be a few in which there is incontrovertible evidence of state responsibility for "disappearances" or murder.

When cases are examined together, a pattern may emerge of a systematic official practice of "disappearance" or extrajudicial execution. By revealing the pattern, human rights organizations can challenge official denials and break through governmental strategies for avoiding accountability. Well documented information becomes a weapon in the fight against "disappearances" and extrajudicial executions.

CHAPTER 11

BRINGING THE PERPETRATORS TO JUSTICE

1   **The duty to bring those responsible to justice**

Governments should ensure that those responsible for "disappearances" and extrajudicial executions are brought to justice.
– From Amnesty International's 14-Point Programs for the Prevention of "Disappearances" and Extrajudicial Executions

Those responsible for "disappearances" and extrajudicial executions must be brought to justice. There are several reasons why this is so:

*   The application of sanctions for the commission of crimes is a normal function of criminal justice systems throughout the world. The law sets forth sanctions corresponding to different crimes, and the criminal justice apparatus devotes its resources to finding wrongdoers, bringing them to trial and punishing them. If the criminal justice system fails to bring to justice people who have been responsible for human rights violations including atrocious crimes, criminal justice is undermined and the notion of justice, an important basis of the social order, is dangerously distorted.

*   The impunity of public officials responsible for serious human rights violations undermines the rule of law, the doctrine which holds that officials must not be above the law. Bringing such officials to justice is necessary to restore the rule of law.

*   If officials responsible for "disappearances" and extrajudicial executions are not prosecuted and punished, they will remain free to repeat the crimes, and others may do likewise, believing they can violate the law with impunity. Prosecution and punishment break the cycle of crime and impunity. It protects the public from the culprits repeating their crimes and it helps to deter others from committing similar crimes by raising the real threat that they, too, may be caught and punished.

The need to bring the perpetrators of "disappearances" and extrajudicial executions to justice has been established as an obligation under UN human rights instruments.

Provisions to that effect are contained in the two leading instruments on "disappearances" and extrajudicial executions – the UN Declaration on Disappearances (Article 14) and the UN Principles on Extra-Legal, Arbitrary and Summary Executions (principle 18) – respectively.

This is the requirement, but the reality is different. The officials responsible for "disappearances" and extrajudicial executions are so intent on preserving their impunity, and the repressive forces at their command are so strong, that in practice they are very seldom brought to justice. Finding the means to make this happen is one of the great challenges to be met in the effort to eradicate "disappearances" and extrajudicial executions.

2   Overcoming impunity

> *"Perhaps the single most important factor contributing to the phenomenon of disappearances may be that of impunity. The Working Group's experience over the past 10 years has confirmed the age-old adage that impunity breeds contempt for the law. Perpetrators of human rights violations, whether civilian or military, will become all the more brazen when they are not held to account before a court of law."*
> – UN Working Group on Enforced or Involuntary Disappearances ("Working Group on Disappearances")[1]

This statement by the UN Working Group on Disappearances applies equally to extrajudicial executions. Impunity is both a contributing factor and a standard component of any governmental program of "disappearances" or extrajudicial executions. The officials who plan and carry out the crimes will take pains to ensure that the perpetrators are not caught and punished. Their efforts almost always succeed: while investigations by human rights defenders and official bodies have documented many thousands of "disappearances" and extrajudicial executions, very few of the people responsible have ever been brought to justice.

Literally, impunity means exemption from punishment. More broadly, the term conveys a sense of wrongdoers escaping justice or any serious form of accountability for their deeds. Impunity can arise at any stage before, during or after the judicial process: in not investigating the crimes; in not bringing the suspected culprits to trial; in not reaching a verdict or convicting them, despite the existence of convincing evidence which would establish their guilt beyond a reasonable doubt; in not sentencing those convicted, or sentencing them to derisory punishments out of all proportion to the gravity of their crimes; in not enforcing sentences.[2]

It is convenient to distinguish two types of impunity according to the sources which give rise to it. They may be called *legal* and *practical* (or "*de facto*") impunity.[3]

- *Legal* impunity arises from laws, decrees, or other official measures providing that certain officials, classes of officials, or others carrying out official duties will not be brought to justice. Some of these preclude prosecution; they include the many indemnity, immunity or amnesty laws in force in different countries.[4] Often these are enacted during states of emergency or other situations where governments claim there is a special threat to law and order; they have also been enacted to avoid bringing prosecutions for acts committed under a previous government, ostensibly to promote national reconciliation. Other measures such as pardons ensure that officials convicted of involvement in "disappearances" and political killings will not be punished. Justice may be blocked also by placing human rights cases under the jurisdiction of military courts which lack independence and impartiality.

- *Practical* impunity stems from weaknesses in the judicial system and from actions of officials which hinder or obstruct the course of justice. In some countries, for example, the judiciary is weak, corrupt, or lacking in independence. Where the judiciary is independent, impunity may come from the institutional resistance of the security forces to judicial proceedings in cases involving the actions of security force personnel in the line of duty. This resistance can take the form of refusal of security force personnel to attend court hearings; falsification of evidence or refusal to provide it; failure to carry out arrests and other court directives; intimidation of judges, lawyers and witnesses.

Legal impunity must be overcome by repealing those legal provisions which afford it, opposing the passage of such provisions, and opposing the granting of pardons before the full facts are revealed in judicial proceedings and criminal responsibility has been established. Practical impunity must be overcome by combating and preventing the actions which give rise to it.

Ending impunity is fundamentally a matter of political will. Organizations working to stop "disappearances" and extrajudicial executions must put pressure on governments to develop that will.

3   Characteristics of the judicial process

If the process of bringing those responsible for "disappearances" and extrajudicial executions to justice is to have a satisfactory outcome, it must have certain characteristics. Many of these characteristics have been included as standards in UN human rights instruments, notably the Basic Principles on the Independence of the Judiciary, adopted in 1985.[5] In particular, the judicial process should be characterized by:

- *Promptness.* Undue delays can give the impression that nothing will be done, fostering a sense of impunity. Delays in the judicial process can result in valuable evidence being destroyed or lost.

- *Impartiality.* The court must not be biased against the victims and their relatives, or against the accused.[6]

- *Effectiveness.* If the court fails to pursue evidence, or fails to convict the accused despite overwhelming evidence, the judicial process will be regarded as ineffective and biased.

- *Fairness* to the accused. Trials must conform to international norms for a fair trial as laid down in international instruments, notably in Articles 9, 14 and 15 of the International Covenant on Civil and Political Rights.

- *Openness.* Trials should be open to the public, including families of the victims, families of the defendant, national and international trial observers and the press. The date, time and place of court hearings should be made known publicly well in advance.

In addition to these characteristics:

- **Trials should be held in the civilian courts.** If special or military courts have jurisdiction over serious human rights violations where these are rife, it is extremely unlikely that the perpetrators will be brought to trial, or – if brought to trial – that they will be convicted. Such courts often use truncated procedures and lack the professional competence and independence of the regular civilian courts. Military courts tend to lack independence and impartiality because they are under the military command structure – often the same structure which is suspected of carrying out human rights violations.[7]

- *Prosecutors* should be diligent in the exercise of their functions.[8]

- **Victims and their families** should be able to be represented at trials to protect their interests, without prejudicing the rights of the accused.

- The courts must be given the necessary *resources* to carry out their work.[9] The most highly qualified and independent judge cannot function effectively if he or she lacks the necessary material resources, such as clerical assistance, a telephone, or transport to visit key places where this is essential for the trial.

- The *sentences* imposed should be commensurate with the gravity of the crimes. Trivial sanctions imposed for serious crimes can contribute to a continuing atmosphere of impunity and bring the judiciary into disrepute. (The death penalty, however, should never be used. Amnesty International holds that the death penalty violates the right to life and is the ultimate cruel, inhuman and degrading punishment.)

Apart from sentences imposed by the courts for violations of the law, *administrative sanctions* should also be imposed for violations of administrative regulations.

4   Independence of the judiciary

> *"The independence of the judiciary shall be guaranteed by the State and enshrined in the Constitution or the law of the country. It is the duty of all governmental and other institutions to respect and observe the independence of the judiciary."*
> – UN Basic Principles on the Independence of the Judiciary, principle 1

An independent judiciary is one of the key institutions for the protection of human rights. As human rights become codified in legal rules, the judiciary is a key institution for ensuring that these rules are observed. The protection of human rights entails providing remedies for people whose rights have been denied: it is through the courts that such remedies are exercised. An independent judiciary can help to counteract the illegal and abusive actions of other branches of government resulting in human rights violations.

It is because of its importance as a defender of human rights that the institution of the judiciary is so often attacked when human rights are being flagrantly violated. A governmental program of "disappearances" and extrajudicial executions is almost always accompanied by efforts to weaken the judiciary and undermine its independence.

The need for an independent judiciary is recognized in the leading UN human rights instruments.[10] Its importance has come under increased discussion in recent years. One of the first outcomes of these discussions was the adoption of the *Basic Principles on the Independence of the Judiciary* in 1985. Its provisions include the following:

> "The judiciary shall decide matters before them impartially, on the basis of facts and in accordance with the law, without any restrictions, improper influences, inducements, pressures, threats or interferences, direct or indirect, from any quarter or for any reason." *(principle 2)*

> "There shall not be any inappropriate or unwarranted interference with the judicial process, nor shall judicial decisions by the courts be subject to revision. This principle is

without prejudice to judicial review or to mitigation or commutation by competent authorities of sentences imposed by the judiciary, in accordance with the law." *(principle 4)*

"Persons selected for judicial office shall be individuals of integrity and ability with appropriate training or qualifications in law. Any method of judicial selection shall safeguard against judicial appointments for improper motives. ..." *(principle 10)*

5   **Establishing the full scope of liability to prosecution: universal jurisdiction; no statute of limitations; liability of superior authorities; no defence of superior orders**

Governments should ensure that those responsible for "disappearances" and extrajudicial executions are brought to justice wherever such people happen to be, wherever the crime was committed, whatever the nationality of the perpetrators or victims and no matter how much time has elapsed since the commission of the crime.

Officials with chain-of-command responsibility who order or tolerate "disappearances" and extrajudicial executions by those under their command should be held criminally responsible for these acts.

An order from a superior officer or a public authority must never be invoked as a justification for taking part in a "disappearance" or an extrajudicial execution.

– From Amnesty International's 14-Point Programs for the Prevention of "Disappearances" and Extrajudicial Executions

"Disappearances" and extrajudicial executions are crimes of such supreme seriousness that the limitations on prosecution which often apply to other crimes should be removed. Liability to prosecution should be extended fully over *space*, over *time*, and over the *full range of people responsible* – from those who planned, ordered or acquiesced in the crimes to those who carried them out.

Four legal concepts correspond to these respective extensions of liability. These concepts are derived from principles of international law relating to war crimes and crimes against humanity (see Chapter 8, section 5).

•   *Universality of jurisdiction* (extension over space). According to this concept, states other than those where the crime was committed must establish jurisdiction over the crime. If a person allegedly responsible for a "disappearance" or an extrajudicial execution is outside the country where the crime was committed, the authorities must take the person into custody and either extradite the person to another country where he or she can be tried (either the country where the crime was committed or another country where the authorities wish to bring the person to trial), or bring the person to trial themselves. This principle must apply regardless of the nationality of the accused person or of the victim. (However, in accordance with international human rights standards, as discussed in Chapter 14, a person should not be extradited to another country where he or she risks becoming a victim of torture, "disappearance", or extrajudicial execution. In such cases the authorities should take steps to bring the alleged offender to trial in their own courts. In line with its unconditional opposition to the death penalty, Amnesty International also opposes the forcible return of a person to a country where he or she faces the death penalty.)

- *No statute of limitations* (extension over time). The law should provide that there is no time limit on the liability to prosecution of a person responsible for a "disappearance" or an extrajudicial execution. There must be no provision that such a person is no longer subject to prosecution after a certain length of time.

- *Liability of superior authorities.* The officials behind the crimes – those who planned them, gave the orders, and helped organize them – must be liable to prosecution as well as the people who carried them out. This principle applies also to officials who tolerated or acquiesced in the crimes. These are people who, by virtue of their office, knew or should have known that "disappearances" and extrajudicial executions were being perpetrated and did not try to stop them even though it was within their power to do so.

- *No defence of superior orders.* This concept holds that a person who participates in a "disappearance" or an extrajudicial execution may not escape conviction by pleading that he or she was only following orders. It is related to the principle of the right and duty to disobey an order to participate in a "disappearance" or an extrajudicial execution (see Chapter 9, section 5).

In recent years the four concepts have begun to be incorporated in UN instruments relating to "disappearances", extrajudicial executions and other human rights violations, as well as in the Statute of the International Tribunal on war crimes in the former Yugoslavia as adopted by the UN Security Council in 1993.

- *Universal jurisdiction* over extrajudicial executions is recognized as an obligation under the UN Principles on Extra-Legal, Arbitrary and Summary Executions (principle 18). The UN Declaration on Disappearances says that all states should take "any lawful and appropriate action" to bring to justice "all persons presumed responsible for an act of enforced disappearance, found to be within their jurisdiction or under their control" (Article 14).

- The UN Declaration on Disappearances (Article 17) provides that a "disappearance" shall be considered a continuing offence as long as the victim's fate and whereabouts continue to be concealed and these facts remain unclarified. It says that the *statute of limitations* should be suspended as long as remedies for "disappearances" are ineffective, and that such statutes of limitation, where they exist, shall be "substantial and commensurate with the extreme seriousness of the offence".

- The principle of *liability of superior authorities* who failed to prevent extrajudicial executions is recognized in the UN Principles on Extra-Legal, Arbitrary and Summary Executions. Principle 19 states that "...Superiors, officers or other public officials may be held responsible for acts committed by officials under their hierarchical authority if they had a reasonable opportunity to prevent such acts. ..."[11]

- The UN Declaration on Disappearances (Article 6) and the UN Principles on Extra-Legal, Arbitrary and Summary Executions (principle 19) establish respectively that *a superior order may not be invoked* as a justification for a "disappearance" or an extrajudicial execution.[12]

It is important that both the people behind the crimes and those who carry them out should be brought to justice. Whether high or low in the official hierarchy, these people have committed very serious crimes. If the immediate perpetrators are punished while those above them escape punishment, it will be an injustice. If only higher officials are punished, lower officers will understand that the system protects them, giving a sense that they can continue to commit "disappearances" with impunity.

6   Establishing state responsibility: the *Velásquez Rodríguez* case

Not only must the individuals responsible for "disappearances" and extrajudicial executions be brought to justice: the state itself should be held responsible for killings and "disappearances" which it ordered or in which it has acquiesced.

The Human Rights Committee set up under the International Covenant on Civil and Political Rights has found states responsible for violations of specific human rights in several cases of "disappearances" and extrajudicial executions (see Chapter 12). However, the most far-reaching pronouncement to date of the principle of state responsibility has been in the judgment of the Inter-American Court of Human Rights in the *Velásquez Rodríguez* case, delivered on 29 July 1988. In this judgment the Court found that the state of Honduras had violated its obligations to respect and ensure the rights of Angel Manfredo Velásquez Rodríguez (Manfredo Velásquez), a Honduran student who "disappeared" in 1981. The principles affirmed by the Court should be seen to apply equally to thousands of other cases of "disappearances" and extrajudicial executions around the world.

On 12 September 1981, between 4:30 and 5:00 pm, several heavily armed men in civilian clothes driving a white Ford vehicle without number plates kidnapped Manfredo Velásquez from a parking lot in downtown Tegucigalpa, the capital of Honduras. In the Court's judgment, the kidnappers were connected with the Honduran Armed Forces or under its direction. Subsequently there were "the same type of denials by his captors and the Armed Forces, the same omissions of the latter and of the Government in investigating and revealing his whereabouts, and the same ineffectiveness of the courts" in responding to *habeas corpus* petitions and criminal complaints as in other cases of what the Court called "the systematic practice of disappearances" in Honduras, where some 100 to 150 people "disappeared" between 1981 and 1984.[13]

As a member of the Organization of American States, Honduras has been a party to the American Convention on Human Rights ("American Convention") since 1977. "Disappearances" violate various provisions of the American Convention including Articles 4 (right to life), 5 (right to personal integrity) and 7 (right to personal liberty). As discussed in Chapter 12, two institutions established under the Convention are empowered to act on cases of human rights violations: the Inter-American Commission on Human Rights will consider petitions from individuals and groups alleging violations of the Convention by a state party, while the Inter-American Court of Human Rights can issue rulings on the interpretation and application of the Convention in cases submitted to it by the Commission or a state party, if the state party concerned has made a declaration that it accepts as binding the jurisdiction of the Court. Honduras made such a declaration in 1981.

In October 1981 the Inter-American Commission on Human Rights received a petition against the state of Honduras concerning the "disappearance" of Manfredo Velásquez. After protracted consideration, the Commission asked the Court to determine whether Honduras had violated Articles 4, 5 and 7 of the American Convention and to rule that the consequences be remedied and compensation paid to the injured party or parties.

In its judgment, the Inter-American Court decided to rely also on Article 1 (1) of the American Convention, wherein the states parties undertake to respect the rights recognized in the Convention and to ensure the free and full exercise of those rights to all persons subject to their jurisdiction. The Court discussed these two terms:

- Commenting on the obligation to *respect* human rights, the Court said that "...(t)he exercise of public authority has certain limits which derive from the fact that human rights are inherent attributes of human dignity and are, therefore, superior to the power of the State." According to Article 1 (1), the Court wrote, "...any exercise of public power that violates the rights recognized by the Convention is illegal. Whenever a State organ, official or public entity violates one of those rights, this constitutes a failure of the duty to respect the rights and freedoms set forth in the Convention."[14]

- The obligation to *ensure* human rights, in the Court's view, "...implies the duty of the States Parties *to organize the governmental apparatus and, in general, all the structures through which public power is exercised*, so that they are capable of juridically ensuring the free and full enjoyment of human rights. As a consequence of this obligation, *the States must prevent, investigate and punish any violation of the rights recognized by the Convention* and, moreover, if possible attempt to restore the right violated and provide compensation as warranted for damages resulting from the violation."[15]

In the present case, the Court found, "...the evidence shows a complete inability of the procedures of the State of Honduras, which were theoretically adequate, to carry out an investigation into the disappearance of Manfredo Velásquez, and of the fulfilment of its duties to pay compensation and punish those responsible..." (paragraph 178). The "disappearance" of Manfredo Velásquez was carried out by agents acting under the cover of public authority, but even if this fact had not been proven, "the failure of the State apparatus to act" was a failure by Honduras to fulfil its duty under Article 1 (1) of the American Convention to ensure Manfredo Velásquez the free and full exercise of his human rights (paragraph 182). For these and additional reasons, the Court concluded that "the facts found in this proceeding show that the State of Honduras is responsible for the involuntary disappearance of Angel Manfredo Velásquez Rodríguez. Thus, Honduras has violated Articles 7, 5 and 4 of the Convention." (paragraph 185)

The Court accordingly ruled that Honduras was required to pay fair compensation to the next-of-kin of Manfredo Velásquez.[16]

The *Velásquez Rodríguez* judgment was a victory for the petitioners, but the importance of the ruling goes beyond this one case. The ruling lays down principles of state responsibility; these principles should be taken to apply to the observance of human rights around the world. The Court's strictures on the duty to prevent, investigate, punish and redress human right violations should be followed by all governments.

7 Civil suits

The civil law in many countries provides the possibility to sue a public official for damages caused in the commission of human rights violations, although sometimes this possibility has been abridged under immunity or indemnity measures such as those mentioned above in the discussion of impunity. Despite the practical difficulties, relatives of victims have in recent years been turning to the civil courts to obtain reparation for the injuries suffered through "disappearances" and extrajudicial executions. Often civil suits are the only remedy left when criminal prosecution has been blocked.

A civil suit can bring several benefits:

- In the course of the proceedings, important information may be disclosed.

- It can result in the payment of substantial damages, which are of material benefit to the relatives of the victim.

- Even though the authorities may have refused to acknowledge responsibility for a "disappearance" or a killing, the payment of damages amounts to an admission of responsibility. Thus, a successful civil suit can contribute to the relatives' goal of obtaining justice.

The right to sue for damages caused in the commission of human rights violations is a consequence of the right to an effective remedy for human rights violations, as set forth in the leading UN human rights instruments.[17] It entails the principle that both the state and the officials responsible for human rights violations should be held liable at civil law for the harm caused. With regard to "disappearances", this principle has now been established in the UN Declaration on Disappearances. Article 5 of the Declaration states: "In addition to such criminal penalties as are applicable, enforced disappearances render *their perpetrators and the State or State authorities* which organize, acquiesce in or tolerate such disappearances *liable at civil law...*" (emphases added).

In some cases it has proved possible to obtain judgments awarding compensation in international courts or the courts of other countries. Outstanding examples are the *Velásquez Rodríguez* judgment of the Inter-American Court of Human Rights, described above,[18] and the case of *Filártiga v. Peña-Irala* in which a US court, acting under the US Alien Tort Statute, awarded damages to the father and sister of a young man who had been kidnapped and tortured to death in Paraguay in 1976.[19]

8   Compensation, rehabilitation and redress

> *Victims of "disappearance" and their dependants, as well as the dependants of victims of extrajudicial execution, should be entitled to obtain fair and adequate redress from the state, including financial compensation. "Disappeared" people who reappear should be provided with appropriate medical care or rehabilitation.*
> *– From Amnesty International's 14-Point Programs for the Prevention of "Disappearances" and Extrajudicial Executions*

Victims of "disappearances" and extrajudicial executions and their dependants have suffered grievous wrongs at the hands of the state apparatus. Both the state and the perpetrators individually should be held liable to provide redress.

The term "redress" refers to measures taken to set right a situation in which a person has been harmed, and to repair the damage done.[20] There are several forms of redress:

- Financial *compensation*, including payment in money.[21]

- *Rehabilitation*, including medical care and counselling to help the victim cope with the effects of physical and psychological injuries, as well as measures to restore the dignity and reputation of the victim, who may earlier have been branded as – for example – a terrorist or an enemy of the state. Measures such as naming a street or a school after the victim, or building a monument, may help to do this.

- *Restitution*, meaning action taken to restore, to the extent possible, the situation which existed for the victim before the "disappearance" or extrajudicial execution took place. (For a victim who has been killed, restitution is impossible, but for a "disappeared" prisoner who reappears, restitution can include restoring the victim's job or returning property wrongfully seized.)

Other important elements of redress are **verification of the facts** and **full and public disclosure of the truth**; **public acknowledgement of responsibility** for the human rights violations committed; **bringing those responsible to justice**; and **preventing** the perpetration of further such human rights violations.

Not only those victims who are still alive, but their dependants and relatives should obtain redress for the injuries they have suffered as a result of a "disappearance" or an extrajudicial execution.

Along with the right to sue for damages, this right to redress is a part of the right to an effective remedy for human rights violations, as established in the leading UN instruments on human rights, referred to in the previous section of this chapter.

Both the UN Declaration on Disappearances and the UN Principles on Extra-Legal, Arbitrary and Summary Executions recognise the right to obtain redress. The Declaration on Disappearances provides that victims and their family "shall obtain redress and shall have the right to adequate compensation, including the means for as complete a rehabilitation as possible", and it establishes also that the dependants of people who die as a result of "disappearances" shall be entitled to compensation (Article 19). The Principles on Extra-Legal, Arbitrary and Summary Executions call for "fair and adequate compensation" to be provided "within a reasonable period of time" to the families and dependants of victims of extrajudicial executions (principle 20). The right to compensation and redress for human rights violations has also been recognized in the UN Body of Principles for the Protection of All Persons under Any Form of Detention or Imprisonment[22] and the UN Declaration of Basic Principles of Justice for Victims of Crime and Abuse of Power.[23]

As mentioned in the preceding section of this chapter, victims or their dependants in several countries have instituted civil suits in the national courts to obtain compensation for "disappearances" and extrajudicial executions. Judgments of compensation have also been made in response to suits in the courts of other countries and to petitions to the Inter-American Commission on Human Rights, and the Human Rights Committee set up under the International Convention on Civil and Political Rights has made recommendations of compensation in several cases (see Chapter 12).[24] Compensation and other forms of redress may also be an outcome of the work of commissions set up to investigate human rights violations committed under past regimes.[25]

Several points should be made about financial *compensation* and other forms of redress:

- Compensation and other redress should respond to the needs and wishes of the victims.

- Governments should adapt their laws and procedures as necessary to ensure that the right to redress is readily available and takes into account the potential vulnerability of the victims. They should publicize the procedures for obtaining redress so that potential recipients will know how to invoke them, and should ensure that those who are entitled to redress can receive it with as little difficulty as possible. Once official responsibility has been established, redress should follow. The efforts of victims and their dependants should not be obstructed by over-bureaucratic procedures.

- No absolute figures can be given here, but the amount of compensation should be fair and adequate in view of the seriousness of the damage caused.

- Financial compensation is important both materially and symbolically. Not every victim or dependant will want to accept it, but for those who do, it can contribute to the healing process.[26]

- Sometimes the authorities will grant compensation by agreement with the victims and their families as a means of ending judicial proceedings which are likely to lead to a judgment unfavourable to the state. The awarding of compensation does not relieve the state of the need to admit responsibility for human rights violations.[27]

Rehabilitation of victims and their families involves a variety of techniques for addressing the range of problems characteristic of "disappearances" and extrajudicial executions.

- "Disappeared" people who *reappear* have usually been subjected to torture, privation, extreme isolation and the threat of imminent death. Where prisoners are held for a long time, they may develop disorders typical of prolonged periods without exercise, proper nutrition or adequate hygiene, including skin, visual, dental and musculo-skeletal problems.

In such circumstances former "disappeared" people need social support and recognition of the extremely stressful abuse they have experienced. They require careful medical assessment and, where appropriate, medical treatment, as well as measures to address the psychological impact of their experiences.

In some cases men or women reappearing after a period of "disappearance" will manifest symptoms of the type, severity and duration of post-traumatic stress syndrome. Approaches to treatment for severe trauma following torture or other major stresses include psychodynamic psychotherapy, family therapy, group therapy, pharmacotherapy, and behavioural and cognitive therapies.[28]

- The experience of *relatives of the "disappeared"* is one of stressful uncertainty.[29] The absence of news of the loved one allows the worst fears to be felt, especially where there is a known pattern of brutal or lethal ill-treatment of those who are abducted. Where there is an expectation that the "disappeared" person has been killed, the family is unable to grieve because of the lack of evidence of the death. Even to consider that the "disappeared" person could be dead can sometimes induce strong feelings of guilt.[30]

- Relatives of victims of *extrajudicial executions* are likely to suffer profound grief mixed with fear, anger and anxiety. They will benefit from the activities of support groups and from the availability of legal advice and advocacy. The role of human rights organizations can be of great importance here.

At present there are teams of doctors and mental health workers in over 30 countries offering assistance to victims of torture and other state-organized violence including "disappearances" and political killings. Some of these groups continue to deal with the aftermath of "disappearances" carried out in the 1970s and 1980s.

9   Dealing with abuses committed under past regimes

The ending of a repressive regime is one of the most hopeful moments in a country's history. There is much to be done at such times. Institutions for the protection of human rights need to be created, rebuilt or strengthened. The truth of what happened under the former government must be made known and officially acknowledged. Those responsible for human rights violations must be brought to justice. The needs of victims must be addressed.

During the past decade, commissions of inquiry into abuses under former regimes, including "disappearances" and extrajudicial executions, have been set up in several countries as part of an intended process of national reconstruction by new governments or in connection with a transition to a new political order. Four of them are described below.

170

- *Argentina*: The elected government of President Raúl Alfonsín took office on 10 December 1983, ending seven years of military rule. On 15 December the new government established by decree a *Comisión Nacional Sobre la Desaparición de Personas*, National Commission on Disappeared People, whose aim was to clarify events relating to the "disappearance" of people in Argentina and to investigate their fate or whereabouts. (Its task was not to determine responsibility; it would be the job of the courts, receiving the material from the Commission's investigations, to determine responsibility and to try the guilty parties.) Working with a staff of over 60, its 13 members collected several thousand statements and testimonies, visited secret detention centres where "disappeared" prisoners had been held, and compiled over 50,000 pages of documentation.

In its report, submitted to President Alfonsín in 1984, the Commission concluded that after the military coup of March 1976, tens of thousands of people throughout Argentina were illegally deprived of liberty, of whom 8,960 had not reappeared. Many prisoners had been shot dead, drowned at sea, or killed through torture. The report described the methods used to arrest and abduct victims and gave details of torture, with extracts from personal testimonies. It contained detailed descriptions of 118 secret detention centres, with floor plans of some included, and mentioned a number of others. The testimonies reproduced in the report named military and police officers said by victims to have carried out torture, "disappearances" and killings.

The Commission recommended among other things that the courts urgently investigate the allegations received by the Commission; that laws be passed to declare forced disappearance to be a crime against humanity, to provide relatives of "disappeared" people with economic assistance, and to recognize national human rights organizations; that the judiciary be given the necessary means to investigate human rights violations; and that all repressive legislation still in force be repealed.[31]

- *Chile*: President Patricio Aylwin took office in March 1990, ending 16 years of military rule. One of his first official acts was to create the *Comisión Nacional de Verdad y Reconciliación*, National Commission on Truth and Reconciliation, to inquire into "disappearances", executions, and deaths under torture committed under the military government, as well as kidnappings and attempts on people's lives committed by individuals under political pretexts. The Commission was mandated to describe how the repressive apparatus worked, to account for every dead and "disappeared" person, and to recommend measures for redress and prevention. It was not mandated to state conclusions about the responsibility of particular individuals for human rights violations; if the Commission received any information on crimes committed, this information was to be turned over to the courts.

Working with a staff of over 60, the Commission travelled around the country to gather testimonies from victims and their relatives. It received information from over 4,000 complainants and had access to official data such as autopsy reports and travel certificates. It sent a questionnaire to international human rights organizations and Chilean political parties, churches and unions asking for their views on redress and preventive measures, and received over 150 responses.

In its report, submitted to President Aylwin in early 1991, the Commission presented a lengthy and systematic account of the repression practised under the military government. An annex to the report contained individual entries on the victims identified by the Commission, with brief details of what happened and the Commission's conclusions on each case. Out of a total of 2,115 extensively documented cases – some involving multiple victims – the Commission found that 1,068 people had died at the hands of agents of the state or others in their service and 957 had "disappeared".

The Commission recommended monetary compensation and health benefits for relatives of victims;[32] symbolic measures, such as monuments to restore the good names of victims; and preventive measures, including changes in the law and measures to ensure the independence of the judiciary.

- *Chad*: On 1 December 1990 a coalition of armed groups swept into N'Djaména, the capital of Chad, overthrowing the government of Hissein Habré which had held the country in a rule of terror for eight years. On 20 December the new government under President Idriss Déby created a Commission of Inquiry into crimes committed by the Habré government. Its brief included the investigation of kidnappings, murders, "disappearances", torture and other human rights violations.

Composed initially of two magistrates and four police detectives with six support staff, the Commission interviewed over 1,700 people during its 17-month investigation. It exhumed three mass graves near N'Djaména and visited several detention centres and sites of extrajudicial executions.

In its report, published in May 1992, the Commission estimated that over 40,000 people had died in prison or been executed by the Habré government, leaving widows and orphans whose numbers the Commission estimated at over 30,000 and over 80,000 respectively. It identified the branches of the security forces principally responsible for human rights violations. It recommended that agents transferred from one of these agencies into the intelligence service set up by the new government should be immediately removed from the service, and that those implicated in crimes should be taken into judicial custody to await trial. It cited attempts within Chad and by Chadian exiles to oppose the dictatorship, but found that ordinary citizens had become suspicious of everyone, leading to an attitude of powerlessness, indifference and resignation. It concluded that although international humanitarian organizations such as Amnesty International had tried to draw attention to the atrocities, Western countries regarded Hissein Habré as a strong ally and therefore "turned a blind eye to the terrible crimes committed by him, thus allowing the continuation of a despotic and bloody regime".

Among other things, the Commission recommended that the prosecution of those responsible for past human rights violations should begin without delay. A sovereign and independent judiciary should be created, and human rights training should be started in schools, universities, police schools and the army. A monument should be erected for the victims of the repression.[33]

- *El Salvador*: One of a series of agreements between the Government of El Salvador and the opposition *Frente Farabundo Martí para la Liberación Nacional* (FMLN), Farabundo Martí National Liberation Front, ending the armed conflict between them provided among other things for the establishment of a *Comisión de la Verdad*, Commission on the Truth, with the task of "investigating serious acts of violence that have occurred since 1980 and whose impact on society urgently demands that the public should know the truth". Under the agreement, signed in April 1991, the Commission's three members were to be appointed by the UN Secretary-General. The Commission was empowered "to use whatever sources of information it deems useful and reliable", to interview, "freely and in private, any individuals, groups or members of organizations or institutions", to "(v)isit any establishment or place freely without giving prior notice", and to request reports, records or documents from the parties to the agreement and from state authorities and departments. The agreement states that the two parties "undertake to extend to the Commission whatever cooperation it requests of them in order to gain access to sources of information available to them" and that they "undertake to carry out the Commission's recommendations."[34]

Working with an international staff of investigators, legal specialists and other experts, the Truth Commission, whose three members were all non-Salvadorians, received direct testimony concerning 7,000 victims and information from governmental and non-governmental institutions relating to more than 18,000 victims. Many witnesses came forward for the first time. Over 60 per cent of the cases concerned extrajudicial executions and over 25 per cent concerned "disappearances". Personnel of the army, the security forces, and civil defence forces were identified as perpetrators in 60 per cent, 25 per cent and 20 per cent of cases respectively; "death squads" in over 10 per cent of cases; and the opposition FMLN in approximately 5 per cent.

In its report, published on 15 March 1993, the Commission produced overwhelming evidence that former or current high-ranking army officers and other officials had ordered, participated in and covered up extrajudicial executions, "disappearances" and torture. It also established that the FMLN was responsible for a number of arbitrary killings in breach of the international humanitarian law of armed conflict. The report named those responsible for many of the 32 cases it examined in depth.[35] It said, for example, that Major Roberto D'Aubuisson, the man who founded El Salvador's present ruling party, ARENA, had ordered the assassination of Archbishop Oscar Arnulfo Romero in 1980 and that two army generals and five other senior officers had ordered the killing of six Jesuit priests, their housekeeper and her daughter in 1989. It cited the judiciary as bearing a great responsibility for the impunity with which the abuses had been committed.

The Commission made a series of recommendations including removal from office of all military and judicial officials named in the report as responsible for human rights violations; banning those people from public office for 10 years, as well as FMLN members held responsible for abuses; extensive reforms to the judiciary; and setting up a fund to provide financial compensation for the victims of past human rights abuses. However, the Commission said it could not recommend prosecution of those responsible because of serious deficiencies in the current Salvadorian judicial system.[36]

The four commissions described above all did valuable work. Many of the human rights violations described in their reports had earlier been made known by human rights organizations and victims' relatives, but the reports served to confirm officially that those violations had indeed been committed, and to acknowledge the terrible wrongs done to the thousands of victims whose names were listed in the reports.

Once the truth was acknowledged, the perpetrators needed to be brought to justice. Here and in other areas, the actions of the authorities after the publication of the four reports left much to be desired.

In *Argentina* nine former members of the military junta accused of instituting procedures which led to "disappearances" were brought to trial before a civilian court in 1985. On 9 December 1985 five of the nine, including two former presidents, were convicted of offences including aggravated homicide, illegal detention and torture and sentenced to terms ranging from four and a half years' imprisonment to life imprisonment. The other four defendants were acquitted.

But in December 1986 Congress approved a law known as the *Ley de Punto Final*, Full Stop Law, setting a 60-day deadline for the formal initiation of new prosecutions of security force officers accused of past human rights violations, and in June 1987 a *Ley de Obediencia Debida*, Law of Due Obedience, was enacted granting immunity to all but the most senior military officers for crimes committed during the period of military rule. In October 1989 the new President, Carlos Menem, pardoned 39 senior military officers who were to have been tried for crimes committed during the period of military rule, and in December 1991 he pardoned and released the former military leaders convicted in 1985. Out of the thousands of cases of "disappearances" documented by the National Commission on Disappeared People, only five military officers have been brought to justice, and all five have now been pardoned and set free.

In *Chile*, prosecution of officials responsible for "disappearances" and killings was impeded by the fact that the military government in 1978 had issued a decree law providing an "amnesty for people who as authors, accomplices or accessories have been involved in crimes under the State of Siege" (1973-1978) and who were not already undergoing trial or had not been sentenced. In August 1990 the Supreme Court rejected an appeal submitted on behalf of relatives of "disappeared" prisoners arguing that the 1978 Amnesty Law was unconstitutional. The ruling upheld the decision of lower military courts to use the Amnesty Law to close investigations into the "disappearance" of 35 people before criminal responsibility could be determined.

Announcing the publication of the report of the National Commission for Truth and Reconciliation in March 1991, President Patricio Aylwin noted that the Commission had passed information on its findings to the courts. He called on the judiciary to carry out full investigations, and said the Amnesty Law should not be an obstacle to such investigations. However, the military courts continued to claim jurisdiction over human rights cases and to close cases on the basis of the Amnesty Law. Several cases not covered by the Amnesty Law were pending at the time of writing of this report. No one has yet been convicted for a "disappearance" or an extrajudicial execution committed under the military regime.

In August 1993 President Aylwin presented a draft law that would further ensure the impunity of scores of perpetrators of human rights violations committed under military rule through application of the 1978 Amnesty Law. Following local and international protests, the Congress rejected the bill.

In *Chad* no one has yet been prosecuted for killings and "disappearances" committed under the Hissein Habré government, despite the recommendations of the Commission of Inquiry. Hundreds of people in different parts of the country have been victims of extrajudicial executions under the present government and many people have "disappeared". The government has not ordered its security forces to stop violating human rights and has not conducted effective investigations into the abuses committed. Members of the security forces have been granted immunity from prosecution for human rights violations committed under the present government.

In *El Salvador* the publication of the report of the Truth Commission set off a storm of protest among the military and the judiciary. The Defence Minister, General Emilio Ponce, who was named in the Truth Commission's report, described it as "unjust, incomplete, illegal, unethical, biased and insolent". The Supreme Court issued a statement accusing the Commission of acting with partiality, and refusing to resign as the Commission had called for. Other judges and the Salvadorian Lawyers' Association issued statements supporting the court.

Within hours of the publication of the report, a draft amnesty law had been presented by a pro-government party to the Legislative Assembly. One week later, despite widespread protests by opposition parties, the *Ley de Amnistía General para la Consolidación de la Paz*, General Amnesty Law for the Consolidation of Peace, had been passed by the Assembly and ratified by the President.

This sweeping amnesty law, promulgated on 22 March 1993, shields the perpetrators of "disappearances", torture and killings from prosecution. It has resulted in the release of the two military officers convicted of involvement in the killing of the six Jesuit priests referred to above, a major accused of ordering the killing of 10 peasants in 1988, and a former soldier detained for alleged participation in the killing of two peasants during an army operation in 1989, and who later gave testimony about army involvement in "death squads". Two FMLN members acknowledged to have killed two US advisers in 1991 have also been released. Amnesty International has called for the law to be repealed.

Important as the commissions in Argentina, Chile, Chad and El Salvador have been in establishing the truth of what happened, subsequent actions are grounds for disquiet. It is true that some new governments have inherited amnesty laws instituted by their predecessors, as in Chile. It is true that some civilian governments have laboured under the threat of intervention by a still-powerful military: in Argentina, for example, middle-ranking army officers took over an army base in April 1987 in support of a major accused of torture against whom an arrest warrant had been issued, and the Law of Due Obedience was part of the government's response to the rebellion. Yet the cause of justice cannot be served unless the perpetrators of "disappearances" and extrajudicial executions are brought to trial.

A more encouraging outcome of the process of coming to terms with past human rights violations has been that in *Bolivia*, where some 22 people "disappeared" and 52 were victims of extrajudicial executions during the military government of General Luis García Meza, which lasted from July 1980 to August 1981. After a seven-year trial, former President García Meza and 46 others ranging from former government ministers to members of government-sponsored paramilitary groups were convicted by the Bolivian Supreme Court in April 1993 of charges including genocide and assassination of political opponents. They were sentenced by the Supreme Court to prison terms of up to 30 years. An especially important element of the ruling was the Court's rejection of the claim of due obedience argued by some of the defendants.[37] Bolivian citizens took to the streets in spontaneous demonstrations of support for the Supreme Court verdict, which was broadcast live on national television and relayed by loud-speakers in universities and trade union headquarters around the country.[38]

Amnesty International's position is that those responsible for human rights violations must be brought to justice. They must be held to account even if they are officials of a past or current government and regardless of whether they are members of the security forces or of semi-official paramilitary groups. Those accused of human rights crimes should be tried, and their trials should conclude with a clear verdict of guilt or innocence. All trials should be conducted in full conformity with internationally recognized norms for a fair trial.

Amnesty International takes no position on what sentence should be passed, provided that the death penalty is not imposed. However, the systematic imposition of penalties that bear little relationship to the seriousness of the offences brings the judicial process into disrepute and does not serve to deter further human rights violations. Amnesty laws which prevent the emergence of the truth and accountability before the law are not acceptable. This applies whether the law is passed by those responsible for the violations or by successor governments.

It has been argued that the interests of national reconciliation after a period of violence may be served by pardons after conviction: Amnesty International takes no position on this. But it does insist that the truth is revealed and the judicial process completed.

The protection of human rights requires action, not mere words. Allowing the perpetrators to commit abuses, however clearly prohibited by law, without consequences for themselves, perpetuates their crimes. Ensuring that they are brought to justice transmits throughout a society the clear message that human rights violations will not be permitted to continue.

CHAPTER 12

ACTION THROUGH THE UNITED NATIONS AND REGIONAL INSTITUTIONS

1   Intergovernmental action: hopes and obstacles

The UN was formed in the hope that through this organization, governments could work together to resolve their differences peacefully and avoid war, of which memories in 1945 were only too painful. Human rights were a concern from the outset. Human rights had been violated on a massive scale in the Second World War, and violations of human rights had been integral to the policies which brought about the war. Such atrocities were not to be repeated in the new order which the UN was intended to create. The UN Charter contains an implicit assertion which was made explicit in the Universal Declaration of Human Rights three years later: the observance of human rights is of fundamental importance for the stability of the international order.[1]

Since 1945 the UN has taken several kinds of action on human rights:

•   It has adopted treaties, resolutions and other instruments setting forth *standards* on human rights and on the measures to be taken to prevent or remedy violations of these rights. (See Chapter 8.) (This area of activity is often called "standard-setting".)

•   It has adopted resolutions expressing concern about *human rights violations in particular countries* and requesting the government in question to take remedial action.

•   It has set up subsidiary *bodies* and *procedures* for dealing with human rights or has entrusted special assignments to *individual experts* (often called "Special Rapporteurs") or *working groups* of individual experts from outside the UN Secretariat. Depending on their terms of reference, action taken through these means has included studying allegations of human rights violations (sometimes through on-site investigations) and reporting back to the UN, and raising allegations of individual cases of human rights violations with the government concerned.

•   It has set up *programs* for disseminating information about human rights, conducting training sessions and seminars, and advising governments on human rights matters.

•	It has made *studies* of human rights topics, often paving the way for later action.

During the past few years another kind of action has been added:

•	Setting up on-site operations to **monitor** and press for the observance of human rights as part of a peace process designed to prevent or end fighting within a country, or independently of UN peacekeeping activities.

Since the Second World War, intergovernmental organizations[2] whose concerns include human rights have been set up in several regions of the world. Three of them – the *Organization of American States*, the *Council of Europe* and the *Organization of African Unity* – have adopted regional human rights treaties (see Chapter 8, section 6). Other regional intergovernmental organizations whose concerns include human rights are the *European Union*, the *Conference on Security and Co-operation in Europe*, the *League of Arab States*, the *Organization of the Islamic Conference*, the *Commonwealth* and the *Francophonie*. These organizations are enabled to take action on human rights issues in countries in their regions, and sometimes they have acted on human rights issues in countries outside the region also. (In Asia and the Pacific, no similar organizations have yet been created.)

Questions of human rights come up at periodic meetings of UN bodies and regional intergovernmental organizations. Some of these bodies meet annually, some more often. At such meetings the members of these bodies (usually governmental representatives) decide what action to take.

The most important UN organs, those with the greatest decision-making power, are political bodies composed of UN member states, and the representatives of those states who attend them act on the basis of instructions from their home capitals. Many subsidiary tasks are entrusted to individuals or groups of individuals acting in their personal or professional capacity (they are usually called "*independent experts*"). Although some independent experts are in fact obliged by their governments to follow instructions, many are able to bring their own convictions and expertise to bear on a problem without having to sacrifice principle to state interests. Thanks to this independence and to their high qualifications, individual experts and expert groups have made many important contributions to the UN work for human rights.

In the development of activities on human rights in the UN and regional intergovernmental organizations, a key role has been played by "*non-governmental organizations*" (NGOs) – voluntary organizations, human rights groups, professional associations and other non-official organizations. NGOs have eloquently made known their concerns, calling for action. They have supplied the UN with details of many thousands of cases of horrific human rights violations. They have come up with proposals for action which were later adopted in the UN. They have contributed to standard-setting.

At the main UN meetings where human rights matters are considered, NGOs are very much in evidence, voicing their concerns and urging governments to act. Many NGOs having an international scope have been recognized under UN rules as being in "consultative status" with the UN Economic and Social Council, giving them the right to make statements at certain times during the meetings. Even if an NGO is not in consultative status with the Economic and Social Council, its representatives can attend as members of the public and can submit information through established UN procedures as described below.

Governments are naturally loath to have the UN or other inter-governmental organizations take any action implying that they have been deficient in their obligation to respect human rights. From a government's point of view, a public statement by a UN body that human rights have been violated can cause problems. Because of the authority of the UN and the implied censure from other governments, such a statement will be welcome to the government's opponents. It can make other governments wary of close dealings with the government concerned, affecting diplomatic relations, foreign aid and trade. If a UN body takes some action such as the appointment of a Special Rapporteur on the situation of human rights in the country, the matter will come up again at future sessions of the same body, causing further problems.[3] On the other hand, UN attention to particular human rights issues may provide assistance to those within a government who seek to abolish abusive practices, as well as support to victims seeking domestic remedies to human rights violations.

Lacking the means to force a government to comply with its recommendations, the UN works either by persuasion behind the scenes (through confidential communications) or through public action with the attendant implied threat of embarrassment. Governments intent on violating human rights will work hard to block either form of action. If a UN body is considering a draft resolution stating or implying that a country has violated human rights, the government and its allies will try to weaken the resolution or prevent its passage[4]. If human rights violations are being considered under a confidential procedure, the government will try to have the item dropped. The government and its representatives will deny the accusations, denounce those who make them, and fail to cooperate with requests for information from UN bodies. When new instruments for the protection of human rights are being considered for possible adoption, various governments will try to weaken their provisions, fearing that these may one day be used to embarrass them or curtail their powers.[5]

Many people blame the UN for being ineffective. As a general rule, it is not the UN which is at fault: the fault is with its member states, violating human rights, which manoeuvre strenuously to block action, and other member states who side with them, putting perceived national interest ahead of agreed human rights requirements.[6] The UN should be seen credited for its victories for human rights – partial victories often, but victories nonetheless, sometimes in the face of strong resistance from some of its member states.[7]

Discussions of human rights matters in the UN often amount to a battle between certain governments wishing to take action and others determined to block progress. Nationally, governments which engage in "disappearances" and extrajudicial executions ensure impunity by undermining the country's remedial institutions; internationally they escape criticism by undermining the capacity of the UN to act.

2 UN Commission on Human Rights

The *Commission on Human Rights* is the main UN body dealing primarily with human rights. It consists of representatives of 53 UN member states elected to three-year terms. The Commission meets annually in Geneva for six weeks, beginning in late January or early February. The Commission takes certain decisions on its own, while on other matters it forwards its recommendations to its parent body, the Economic and Social Council, for decision.[8]

The Commission on Human Rights was established in 1946 under the terms of the UN Charter.[9] Its first great achievement was the preparation of a draft text of the Universal Declaration of Human Rights, followed by draft texts of the two International Covenants on human rights.

In the 1970s the Commission began turning its attention to categories of severe human rights violations (beginning with torture) and situations of human rights violations in specific countries. On "disappearances" and extrajudicial executions, two of the Commission's key actions have been the establishment of the Working Group on Enforced or Involuntary Disappearances in 1980 and the Special Rapporteur on summary or arbitrary executions in 1982 (see below). Other important actions have included the appointment of Special Rapporteurs on specific countries and the confidential review of country situations under the so-called "1503 procedure".

The fact that the UN can now act in response to individual complaints of human rights violations is a considerable advance. Soon after the UN was established, people began writing to it claiming that their human rights or the rights of others had been violated, but in 1947 the Commission on Human Rights resolved that it had no power to take any action on any complaint, and its view was endorsed by the Economic and Social Council later in the year.[10] This lamentable decision remained in force until 1967, when the Economic and Social Council, in resolution 1235 (XLII), established a procedure on the basis of which the Commission holds a public debate each year focusing on situations of gross human rights violations.[11] Parallel to this new possibility for public action, a confidential procedure for action in response to complaints was established three years later in Economic and Social Council resolution 1503 (XLVIII).

Under the "*1503 procedure*" (so called after the number of the Economic and Social Council resolution which established it), the Working Group on Communications of the Commission on Human Rights' Sub-Commission on Prevention of Discrimination and Protection of Minorities meets each year before the Sub-Commission's annual session to review the complaints of human rights violations received by the UN and select those which "appear to reveal a consistent pattern of gross and reliably attested violations of human rights and fundamental freedoms" to be referred to the Sub-Commission.[12] The Sub-Commission then meets in closed plenary session and decides which of these situations to refer to the Commission on Human Rights.

At its next session the Commission on Human Rights, acting on the recommendations of its Working Group on Situations, listens in closed session to the statements of government representatives on the country situations under review and decides what action to take. Such actions many include conducting a "thorough study" of the situation; setting up an *ad hoc* investigatory body; establishing "direct contacts" with the government through a representative of the Commission or of the UN Secretary-General; dropping its examination of the situation; or transferring its consideration of the situation to the Commission's public procedure, where the Commission can take public action (see below). The 1503 procedure does not provide redress for individual victims of human rights violations.

After the Commission each year has finished its confidential consideration of country situations under the 1503 procedure, the Chairman of the Commission announces publicly which country situations remain under consideration and which have been dropped from consideration. Since 1980 several countries with bad records of "disappearances" and/or extrajudicial executions have been examined under the 1503 procedure.[13]

The comments made by members of the Commission on Human Rights under the 1503 procedure can constitute pressures on the government concerned, but because the procedure is confidential at all stages, it is impossible to judge what effect if any these pressures have in stopping "disappearances" and extrajudicial executions. People who submit complaints under the procedure are never informed what action if any has been taken in response.

Sometimes consideration under the 1503 procedure is followed by **public action** by the Commission on Human Rights, and consideration under the 1503 procedure does not preclude public action being taken at the same time. Forms of public action may include passing a resolution which expresses concern and recommends remedial measures, and the appointment of a Special Rapporteur who may visit the country to examine the situation and report back to the Commission the next year, ensuring further discussion. These authoritative expressions of UN concern reinforce the efforts of human rights organizations to stop human rights violations in a country.

In 1992, for instance, the Commission decided to transfer its consideration of **Myanmar** from the confidential 1503 procedure to the public procedure. (Amnesty International had submitted information under the 1503 procedure and had campaigned in 1990-91 to draw attention to its concerns in Myanmar, including thousands of people being shot dead by soldiers.) Under the public procedure, the Commission adopted a resolution (number 1992/58) expressing concern at "the seriousness of the human rights situation in Myanmar" and deciding to appoint a Special Rapporteur on Myanmar. Speaking immediately before the passage of the resolution, the observer from Myanmar told the Commission that the resolution was totally unacceptable, unbalanced, negative and a blatant attempt to interfere in Myanmar's internal affairs.

In 1993 the Special Rapporteur on Myanmar recommended that an international human rights monitoring team be allowed access to the Myanmar border area "in light of the seriousness of the refugee and repatriation problem, and the grave threat this situation poses to the physical integrity of Myanmar ethnic and racial minorities..." (There were reports of many "disappearances" and arbitrary executions, he noted; some 250,000 Muslims had been forced to flee the country, and the Myanmar authorities were not permitting the UN to monitor the safety of those who had been repatriated, giving rise to "fears of a resurgence of cyclical repression of these Myanmar Muslims".)[14] The Commission on Human Rights did not act on this recommendation, but decided (in resolution 1993/73) to extend the mandate of the Special Rapporteur for another year.

Another example is that of *Sudan*, considered under the 1503 procedure between 1991 and 1993, when the Commission decided to transfer its consideration to the public procedure. Since the 1989 military coup Amnesty International had been publicizing serious and widespread human rights violations in Sudan, including "disappearances" and extrajudicial executions. In a resolution adopted in 1993 (number 1993/60), the Commission called among other things for the authorities to investigate the deaths of Sudanese employees of foreign relief organizations and decided to appoint a Special Rapporteur on Sudan.

In 1993 the Commission on Human Rights also adopted resolutions on, among other countries, *Togo* (number 1993/75), the former *Yugoslavia* (1993/7) and *Zaire* (1993/61). Each of these resolutions referred to situations in which extrajudicial executions have been perpetrated, although none of the resolutions referred to killings explicitly. The Commission also adopted a resolution on *Iraq* in 1993 (number 1993/74) requesting the UN Secretary-General to send human rights monitors "to such locations as would facilitate improved information flows and assessment", a proposal first made by Amnesty International in 1991. But the members of the Commission on Human Rights have failed over the years to agree to take action on other persistent situations of "disappearances" and extrajudicial executions, including those in Colombia and Peru.

The meetings of the Commission on Human Rights are public, except when it meets in closed session under the 1503 procedure. Non-governmental organizations in consultative status with the Economic and Social Council may be present in the meeting room as observers; others wishing to follow the sessions may watch from the public gallery as may the news media. Many human rights organizations attend these meetings to urge the members of the Commission to defend human rights in different countries[15].

3   UN Sub-Commission on Prevention of Discrimination and Protection of Minorities

The *Sub-Commission on Prevention of Discrimination and Protection of Minorities* is a subsidiary body of the Commission on Human Rights. Unlike its parent body, its 26 members (elected to four-year terms) are independent experts serving in their individual capacity. Originally formed in 1947 to deal with the two issues described in its title, the Sub-Commission has expanded its role over the years to become one of the most productive UN bodies dealing with human rights.

Starting in 1954, the Sub-Commission has made a series of *studies* on specific human rights questions.[16] Typically the task is entrusted to a member of the Sub-Commission. Using information from governments and other sources, the author analyzes the problem in depth and makes recommendations such as measures to be taken or a new instrument to be developed. Sub-Commission studies of importance for the prevention of "disappearances" and extrajudicial executions have included those on the independence of the judiciary (by L.M. Singhvi and by Louis Joinet), on states of emergency (by Nicole Questiaux and by Leandro Despouy), on amnesty laws (by Louis Joinet), and the recently completed study on the right to restitution, compensation and rehabilitation (by Theo van Boven).

The Sub-Commission has also prepared *drafts* of instruments on human rights for eventual adoption by the UN, although the drafts are sometimes weakened when they come under scrutiny by higher UN bodies attended by official representatives of governments.[17] The UN Declaration on the Protection of All Persons from Enforced Disappearance ("Declaration on Disappearances") is an example.

Another important function of the Sub-Commission is to refer situations of gross violations of human rights to the Commission on Human Rights under the "1503 procedure", as described above. The Sub-Commission also adopts *resolutions* concerning human rights violations in particular countries.

The Sub-Commission meets annually for four weeks, beginning in early August. As with the Commission on Human Rights, its meetings are public except when it meets in closed session under the 1503 procedure. Non-governmental organizations in consultative status with the UN Economic and Social Council may be in the meeting room as observers and may make statements, while others wishing to follow the session may watch from the public gallery as may the news media. Many human rights organizations from around the world attend each year to observe the meetings and urge the Sub-Commission members to take up their concerns.

4   UN Working Group on Disappearances

In the half century since the founding of the United Nations, "disappearances" are generally considered to have emerged as a serious human rights problem with the advent of this terrible practice in Guatemala in 1966.[18] It was not until the late 1970s that the problem came under sustained discussion at the UN, chiefly through the reports of the Commission on Human Rights' Working Group on the situation of human rights in Chile (where many people "disappeared" after the 1973 coup) and in response to the reports of "disappearances" in Argentina which began to reach the outside world after the military coup of 1976. In 1978 the UN General Assembly adopted a resolution which among other things requested the Commission on Human Rights "to consider the question of disappeared persons with a view to making appropriate recommendations".[19] The Commission at its next session (1979) was unable to resolve its members' divergent views on what to do about the problem, but the Sub-Commission on Prevention of Discrimination and Protection of Minorities, meeting later in the year, came up with a proposal to create a group of experts empowered to contact the governments concerned. In 1980, after a tense debate, the Commission on Human Rights decided to establish a *Working Group on Enforced or Involuntary Disappearances*.[20] Since then this group has become one of the most innovative UN bodies dealing with human rights violations.

The Working Group on Disappearances consists of five people serving as experts in their individual capacity. The group has a broad mandate "to examine questions relevant to enforced or involuntary disappearances of persons". In carrying out its mandate, the group is to "seek and receive information from Governments, intergovernmental organizations, humanitarian organizations and other reliable sources". It reports annually to the Commission on Human Rights.[21]

Since its inception the Working Group on Disappearances has developed a range of activities.

- The group meets to receive and examine *reports on individual cases of "disappearances"* submitted by relatives of missing persons or organizations acting on their behalf. After determining whether these reports comply with certain formal criteria, the Working Group transmits individual cases to the governments concerned, requesting them to carry out investigations and to inform the group about their results.

- In order to avoid any delays in its endeavour to save lives, the Working Group has devised an *"urgent action procedure"* by which its chairman is authorized between sessions of the group to transmit reports to governments in cases of "urgent reports ... requiring immediate action".[22]

- If a government responds, the Working Group may send the response to the original complainant for their comments.

- In response to growing intimidation and harassment of relatives, lawyers and members of human rights organizations, the Working Group has recently established a procedure of "*prompt intervention*" in "cases of intimidation or reprisal concerning relatives of missing persons, lawyers in cases of disappearance, witnesses to such cases, non-governmental organizations which regularly provide the Working Group with information on disappearances, and persons involved in the identification of corpses found in unmarked graves which are alleged to be those of missing persons."[23]

- In transmitting cases to governments, the Working Group mentions the possibility of a *visit* by members of the group to the country concerned. Such visits have been described by the Working Group as "a preferred option for assessing the overall situation of disappearances in a given country".[24] Its most recent reports on country visits contain analyses of the institutional and legal framework which facilitates the perpetration of "disappearances", along with evaluations of the successes and shortcomings of governmental initiatives to tackle the problem.[25] The Working Group's reports on country visits can lead to attempts in the Commission on Human Rights to take further action regarding the countries in question.

Since its formation the Working Group has visited Peru (in 1985 and 1986), Guatemala (in 1987), Colombia (in 1988), the Philippines (in 1990) and Sri Lanka (in 1991 and 1992).

- The Working Group meets representatives of governments of the countries to which it has sent cases. It has also held *meetings with representatives of national groups* and international human rights organizations concerned about "disappearances". In its annual reports to the Commission on Human Rights the Working Group gives an account of what was said at these meetings, and in its first two reports it annexed reports or excerpts of statements by national groups.[26]

- The Working Group has made valuable *comments* on general aspects of "disappearances", such as the problem of impunity and the need for effective *habeas corpus* procedures.[27] It has contributed to the development of international standards on the prevention of "disappearances", including the UN Declaration on Disappearances.

The Working Group's annual *reports* to the Commission on Human Rights give many details of the Group's activities. The reports convey a sense of the problem worldwide, although the number of cases received by the Working Group is inevitably only a fraction of the true total of "disappearances" perpetrated. In its 1993 report, for example, covering the year 1992 the Working Group disclosed that it had received allegations of "disappearances" from 58 countries since its formation in 1980 and that it was currently following up 31,106 unresolved cases. During 1992, it had continued to process a backlog of some 12,000 reports submitted to it in 1991 and had received some 10,000 new cases from 36 countries. The report contained individual entries on 58 countries with information on its efforts to obtain clarification from the

186

governments concerned, including statistics for each country on the number of new cases, the number of outstanding cases and the number of cases clarified by the government's responses or by non-governmental sources.[28]

The Working Group has repeatedly stressed the right of families to learn what has happened to their relatives. In line with this humanitarian concern, the group has refrained from accusing governments, adopting instead a non-judgmental approach to secure the cooperation of governments in clarifying the facts.[29] Yet the group has not refrained from naming the governments contacted and giving details of cases in its reports to the Commission on Human Rights. The ability to combine humanitarian action with public disclosure is a tribute to the skill of the Working Group over the years.

5   UN Special Rapporteur on extrajudicial, summary or arbitrary executions

UN attention to the problem of extrajudicial executions came slightly later than on "disappearances". The first substantial action was the adoption of resolution 5 on "extra-legal executions" by the Sixth UN Congress on the Prevention of Crime and the Treatment of Offenders in 1980. In this resolution the Congress deplored and condemned the killing of political opponents or suspected offenders by governmental agencies or others acting with their support, and called on governments to prevent such acts.[30] By then the massive killings perpetrated in Uganda, Democratic Kampuchea (Cambodia) and other countries in the 1970s were becoming widely known.[31] Later in 1980, the General Assembly adopted a resolution on "arbitrary or summary executions" urging UN member states to observe internationally recognized procedural safeguards and restrictions in death penalty cases.[32] These two concerns – extrajudicial executions and executions in death penalty cases in violation of international standards – came together in 1982 when the Commission on Human Rights decided to recommend the appointment of a Special Rapporteur to examine questions related to "summary or arbitrary executions". The recommendation was accepted by the Economic and Social Council later in the year and the first Special Rapporteur on summary or arbitrary executions, S. Amos Wako, was appointed.[33] In 1993 the Special Rapporteur's title was changed to *Special Rapporteur on extrajudicial, summary or arbitrary executions.*

Since 1982 the Special Rapporteur has developed a range of activities similar to those of the Working Group on Disappearances:

- Receiving complaints of extrajudicial executions and of executions or death sentences in violation of international standards, and *sending the complaints* to the government concerned with a request for clarification;

- Sending *urgent messages* to the government concerned in cases of "an imminent extrajudicial, summary or arbitrary execution [or] death threats";[34]

- *Visiting* countries where there have been allegations on matters within his mandate, and reporting to the Commission on Human Rights on his findings and recommendations. The Special Rapporteur has visited Suriname (in 1984 and 1987), Uganda (in 1986), Colombia (in 1989) and Zaire (in 1991). In 1992, together with the UN Special Rapporteur on the former Yugoslavia, he visited the former Yugoslavia, and in the first half of 1993 he visited Rwanda and Peru;

- *Commenting* on general aspects of the problem of extrajudicial executions;

- Contributing to the development of *international standards* for the prevention of extrajudicial executions.

Like the Working Group on Disappearances, the Special Rapporteur submits a long **report** to the Commission on Human Rights each year, full of details of his activities. His 1993 report, for example, contained individual entries on 75 countries with information on his communications with the governments concerned, often giving details of individual cases. Although many governments did not reply to his inquiries, others did, indicating for example that they had arrested and brought charges against people allegedly responsible for "disappearances" and killings and had provided police protection for people receiving death threats concerning whom the Special Rapporteur had made inquiries.[35] In several of the country entries the Special Rapporteur offered his own observations on the replies received from governments and on the measures taken by them. These observations indicate that the Special Rapporteur will not be satisfied by a government merely giving vague general answers to specific allegations of extrajudicial executions.[36]

The Working Group on Disappearances and the Special Rapporteur on extra-judicial, summary or arbitrary executions are often referred to as "*theme mechanisms*". In contrast to the Special Rapporteurs on individual countries appointed by the Commission on Human Rights, they deal with issues or "themes" on a worldwide basis. Like the Special Rapporteurs on countries, they report back to the Commission, but they also have means of action which are set in motion when reports of human rights violations reach them. (Other theme mechanisms include the Special Rapporteur on torture, created by the Commission in 1985, and the Working Group on arbitrary detention, created by the Commission in 1991.)

6   Human Rights Committee

As stated in Chapter 8, section 2, the International Covenant on Civil and Political Rights is a treaty under which the states parties agree to respect and ensure the human rights set forth in it, including certain fundamental rights which are violated when "disappearances" and extrajudicial executions are perpetrated. The first Optional Protocol to the Covenant is a related treaty establishing a procedure whereby individuals can submit written complaints alleging that their rights under the

Covenant have been violated. Any state party to the Covenant may become a party to the Protocol.[37]

Part IV of the Covenant provides for the establishment of a **Human Rights Committee** whose task is to monitor the implementation of the Covenant. Under the first Optional Protocol, a state party to the Protocol recognizes the competence of the Human Rights Committee to consider complaints from individuals under its jurisdiction claiming that they are victims of a violation by that state of any of the rights set forth in the Covenant.[38]

The Human Rights Committee consists of 18 individual experts elected to four-year terms. It meets three times a year in three-week sessions in New York or Geneva.

The Human Rights Committee has two main functions:

- It examines the *periodic reports* which states parties to the Covenant are required under Article 40 of the Covenant to submit on the measures they have taken which give effect to the rights recognized in the Covenant and on progress made in the enjoyment of those rights. Such reports must be submitted one year after a state becomes a party to the Covenant and thereafter every five years.[39] Each such report is examined at a public session during which the members question the representative of the state submitting the report. (For example, Committee members have asked for information on any laws or regulations concerning the circumstances in which members of the security forces may open fire in such situations as riots, political disturbances, arrests and escapes from prison, on how they were enforced and what safeguards existed against the arbitrary use of firearms.)[40] The state's report and summaries of the Committee members' questions and comments and the governmental representatives' replies are available as public documents in the Committee's annual reports.[41]

- The Committee also considers *complaints* submitted to it under the first Optional Protocol. If a complaint is found to be admissible, the Committee forwards it to the state concerned, which is required under Article 4 of the Protocol to submit to the Committee within six months "written explanations or statements clarifying the matter and the remedy, if any, that may have been taken by that State". After considering all the information, the Committee forwards its views on the case to the state party and the person who submitted the complaint.

All documents pertaining to the Committee's work under the Protocol are confidential, and they are examined in closed meetings. The texts of final decisions of the Committee, however, are made public.[42]

Two of the most important decisions of the Human Rights Committee in response to individual complaints of "disappearances" have been those given in the cases of Eduardo Bleier and Elena Quinteros Almeida, who were arrested in Uruguay in 1975 and 1976 respectively and then "disappeared". The cases were brought by the daughter and wife of Eduardo Bleier and by the mother of Elena Quinteros. In both cases (*Bleir v. Uruguay* and *Quinteros v. Uruguay*) the Human Rights Committee found that Uruguay had violated Article 9 of the International Covenant on Civil and Political Rights, providing for the right to liberty and security of person. In both cases the Committee held that Uruguay should take effective steps to establish what happened to the victims, to bring to justice those responsible for the "disappearances", to pay compensation for the wrongs suffered, and to ensure that similar violations do not occur in the future.[43]

Another case considered by the Human Rights Committee concerned the extrajudicial execution of 13 prominent civilians and two army officers in Suriname in December 1982; the authorities had claimed they were killed while trying to escape. The case (*Baboeram et al. v. Suriname*) was submitted to the Committee by the relatives of eight of the victims. The Committee found that "the victims were arbitrarily deprived of their lives contrary to article 6 (1) of the International Covenant on Civil and Political Rights". It urged the state of Suriname to take effective steps to investigate the killings, to bring those responsible to justice, to pay compensation to the surviving families and "to ensure that the right to life is duly protected in Suriname".[44]

From time to time the Human Rights Committee also issues *general comments* on various articles of the International Covenant. These comments provide valuable and authoritative interpretations of the meaning and scope of the Covenant's provisions.

Individuals, human rights organizations and the news media may observe all public meetings of the Human Rights Committee. The Committee has no formal procedure for receiving information from individuals and organizations (other than complaints under the first Optional Protocol), but it is possible to send information informally to individual Committee members.[45]

In recent years, national human rights groups have increasingly travelled to New York or Geneva to observe sessions of the Human Rights Committee when their country's periodic report has been under review. By making the Committee members' comments known back at home and encouraging their national news media to attend and report on the proceedings, they can build pressure on states parties to the International Covenant on Civil and Political Rights to comply with their obligations under the Covenant.[46]

7   UN Centre for Human Rights

The Centre for Human Rights is the branch of the UN Secretariat which provides services for the UN human rights program and for the committees which monitor the implementation of human rights treaties such as the International Covenant on Civil and Political Rights. It is located at the UN headquarters in Geneva, with a small outpost at UN headquarters in New York. Its professional and clerical staff assist UN Special Rapporteurs and expert groups in carrying out their work. They make arrangements for meetings of UN human rights bodies and treaty-monitoring bodies and prepare documents for those meetings. The Centre also coordinates the UN program of advisory services and technical assistance in the field of human rights[47] and the informational program called the World Campaign for Human Rights.

The Centre for Human Rights is headed by the Under-Secretary-General for Human Rights, who reports to the UN Secretary-General in New York.

Unfortunately, the United Nations' work for human rights has been hampered for many years by a severe shortage of staff and material resources at the Centre for Human Rights. Established programs fail to meet expectations because the staff at the Centre cannot service them adequately. Both the Working Group on Disappearances and the Special Rapporteur on extrajudicial, summary or arbitrary executions have drawn attention to this problem in their latest reports.[48]

Under-funding is a chronic problem in the UN, but the human rights program has suffered especially. Each year at the Commission on Human Rights, UN member states agree on a program of activities, but at the General Assembly later in the year they fail to provide adequate resources for it. By withholding funds, member states effectively ensure that the UN human rights program will be limited.[49] As one author has written, the General Assembly has clearly "kept Secretariat staff who are responsible for the protection of human rights on a tight budget leash."[50] A significant increase in financial and staffing support is needed if the UN human rights program is to fulfil its crucial role in defending human rights around the world.[51]

8 How to send complaints of "disappearances" and extrajudicial executions to the UN

As mentioned above, the UN was unable for many years to act on the basis of complaints of human rights violations submitted to it by individuals because member states refused to give the Commission on Human Rights the power to take such action. Today it can act, thanks to the establishment of mechanisms such as the Working Group on Disappearances and the Special Rapporteur on extrajudicial, summary or arbitrary executions. Individuals can also complain to the Human Rights Committee if their human rights have been violated by a state which is a party to the International Covenant on Civil and Political Rights and to its first Optional Protocol. They can also complain to the Inter-American Commission on Human Rights, the European Commission on Human Rights or the African Commission on Human and Peoples' Rights if the violation was committed by a member state of the Organization of American States, the Council of Europe or the Organization of African Unity (see below, section 10).[52]

The table on page 194-196 shows the chief avenues by which allegations and complaints of "disappearances" and extrajudicial executions may be submitted to the UN.

The address of the UN Centre for Human Rights is:
>Centre for Human Rights
>UN Office at Geneva
>1211 Geneva 10
>Switzerland
>Facsimile: +41 22 733 98 79
>Telex: 41 29 62
>Cable address: UNATIONS Geneva

A person considering sending an individual complaint or other information on "disappearances" or extrajudicial executions to the UN or another international or regional inter-governmental institution will want to consider a number of factors, including the urgency of the matter, the desired outcome and the chances of success.[53]

9   Human rights monitoring operations and other UN activities

One of the most promising UN initiatives in recent years has been the establishment of *on-site human rights monitoring operations.*

- Some of these are components of *peacekeeping* operations designed to implement peace agreements among hitherto warring parties. Such components can help to end human rights abuses for which governments or other sides in a conflict are responsible. They can help to repair the damage done, and to strengthen or build institutions to protect human rights. They are a way of forging the link between human rights and peace which was recognized in the preamble to the Universal Declaration of Human Rights, as mentioned at the beginning of this chapter[54]

- Other human rights monitoring operations have been established independently of UN peacekeeping activities.

The UN has recently conducted or made plans to conduct operations in a number of countries where "disappearances" or political killings have been perpetrated:

- One of a series of agreements between the Government of *El Salvador* and the opposition *Frente Farabundo Martí para la Liberación Nacional* (FMLN), Farabundo Martí National Liberation Front, ending the armed conflict between them was an Agreement on Human Rights, signed in July 1990. This document incorporated a commitment to stop political killings and "disappearances". Under the Agreement the two parties pledged themselves to take all necessary steps immediately "to avoid any act or practice which constitutes an attempt upon the life...of the individual" and "to eliminate any practice involving enforced disappearances".

The Agreement provided for the establishment of a UN human rights monitoring mission whose purpose is to investigate violations of human rights committed after its establishment and "to take any steps it deems appropriate to promote and defend such rights". The Agreement gave the mission wide powers including the power to receive complaints from any individual or group in El Salvador and the power "(t)o visit any place or establishment freely and without prior notice". The two parties agreed to grant the mission whatever facilities it might need and to ensure the security of its members or of others who gave it information.[55]

The human rights monitoring mission in El Salvador was launched in 1991 with an international staff of human rights observers, legal, military and police advisers and administrative support staff working from regional offices around the country. Between August 1991 and January 1993 the mission received and declared admissible 273 complaints concerning summary executions or arbitrary killings, 382 complaints of death threats and 32 complaints of possible "disappearances". It pursued individual cases, making its own inquiries and raising the cases with judges, police and military officers, the office of the Attorney General, and FMLN commanders as appropriate.

In its published reports the mission recommended immediate measures as well as institutional reforms needed to protect human rights in El Salvador.[56] However, many of these recommendations had not been implemented as of early 1993.[57]

- The Agreement on a Comprehensive Political Settlement of the Cambodia Conflict gives an extensive role to the UN Transitional Authority in *Cambodia* (UNTAC) during a transitional period which began in October 1991 and was to continue until a new government was formed after elections. UNTAC's mandate includes general human rights oversight, and it is empowered to carry out the investigation of human rights complaints and take corrective action.[58]

- The UN Mission for the referendum in *Western Sahara* (MINURSO) has among its tasks the organization of a referendum in cooperation with the Organization of African Unity. The settlement plan requires the UN Special Representative to take all steps to ensure the release of all political prisoners before the referendum campaign. In accordance with this requirement, Amnesty International has urged the UN to address "disappearances" of Western Saharans which remain unclarified.

- It was announced in February 1993 that agreement had been reached for the deployment by the UN and the Organization of American States of a joint International Civilian Mission in *Haiti* (MICIVIH) to monitor respect for human rights. This large mission was expected to play an important role in tackling the serious human rights problems, including many killings, which have persisted in Haiti especially since the military coup of September 1991.

Table: Avenues for submission of complaints of "disappearances" and extrajudicial executions to the UN

Subject	Complaint can be sent to	Who can send a complaint	Information to be sent	Action to be taken
"Disappearance"	Working Group on Enforced or Involuntary Disappearances, c/o UN Centre for Human Rights (see address above)	Family or friend of victim, or an organization acting on their behalf	Name of victim; date and place of "disappearance"; who is believed responsible; information on steps taken to determine the victim's fate or whereabouts	The Working Group tries to determine the fate and whereabouts of the missing person. If a complaint is admissible, the Working Group sends it to the government asking for a response. In urgent cases the Working Group acts immediately.
Extrajudicial execution, threat of extrajudicial execution	Special Rapporteur on extrajudicial, summary or arbitrary executions, c/o UN Centre for Human Rights	Any person or group with reliable knowledge of the facts	Names of victims or intended victims; date, place, circumstances and background of killings; who is believed responsible	If the information appears credible, the Special Rapporteur sends it to the government asking for clarification. In urgent cases he acts immediately.

"Disappearances", extrajudicial executions and other acts indicating a pattern of gross human rights violations	UN Centre for Human Rights	Any person or group with clear evidence of the facts	The relevant facts; list of human rights violated; information on exhaustion of domestic remedies[1]	Consideration by the Commission on Human Rights under the confidential "1503 procedure". This procedure is not designed to redress individual grievances.[2]

1   A communication will not be admitted if it runs counter to the principles of the UN Charter, if it shows political motivations, or (usually) if it uses abusive language. Anonymous communications are inadmissible, as are those based only on reports in the news media. Domestic remedies must have been exhausted unless it can be shown convincingly that solutions at the national level would be ineffective or unreasonably protracted.

2   All communications alleging human rights violations received by the UN are processed under the 1503 procedure unless they fit under a more specific mechanism such as the Working Group on Disappearances or the Special Rapporteur on extra judicial summary or arbitrary executions. A person submitting information under the 1503 procedure will receive an acknowledgement from the UN Secretariat but nothing thereafter. If a communication meets the established criteria, the Secretariat sends a copy to the government concerned, inviting it to respond. Because of the confidentiality of the procedure, it is impossible to learn which of the communications submitted are ultimately considered when the Commission on Human Rights examines a country situation.

Subject	Complaint can be sent to	Who can send a complaint	Information to be sent	Action to be taken
"Disappearances", extrajudicial executions	Committee on Human Rights, c/o UN Centre for Human Rights	A person with authority to act on behalf of the victim, where the victim's human rights have been violated by a state party to the first Optional Protocol to the International Covenant on Civil and Political Rights[3]	The relevant facts; information on exhaustion of domestic remedies	After examining the information submitted by the complainant and the government, and giving each side a chance to comment on the other's arguments, the Human Rights Committee issues a public statement of its views on the merits of the complaint. It may recommend redress or preventive measures.

3   The Human Rights Committee cannot examine a complaint if the same problem is being examined under another international procedure of investigation or settlement such as the European Commission on Human Rights or the Inter-American Commission on Human Rights (but not the UN Commission on Human Rights or its Working Groups and Special Rapporteurs). Furthermore, certain states parties to the first Optional Protocol have made reservations saying that the Human Rights Committee cannot consider a complaint against them if the same matter has already been examined by another such international procedure.

- In March 1993 the UN Commission on Human Rights decided to request the UN Secretary-General to send monitors to areas where they could independently verify the human rights situation in *Iraq*.[59]

Amnesty International and others have recommended the establishment or strengthening of UN on-site human rights monitoring in several other countries:

- Following the conclusion in October 1991 of a General Peace Agreement between the Government of Mozambique and the opposition *Resistência Nacional Moçambicana* (RENAMO), Mozambique National Resistance, Amnesty International called for strengthened human rights promotion and monitoring in the UN peacekeeping operation in *Mozambique* (ONUMOZ). Amnesty International welcomed the UN Secretary-General's proposal for the deployment of UN police monitors to monitor the neutrality of the Mozambican police. It also suggested the establishment of an independent human rights monitoring body.[60]

- In resolution 1993/86, adopted on 10 March 1993, the UN Commission on Human Rights requested the UN Secretary-General to assist his Special Representative for *Somalia* in developing a long-term program of advisory services, with a view to reestablishing the rule of law in the country. The Commission also urged the Secretary-General to establish a unit within the UN operation in Somalia to assist in the promotion and protection of human rights. Amnesty International has proposed the creation of an independent group of civilian human rights monitors in Somalia to receive and investigate complaints of human rights violations and where appropriate to transmit them to the relevant UN or other authority for further investigation and prompt corrective action.[61]

- Amnesty International has also called for the establishment of a substantial on-site human rights investigative and monitoring operation in the former *Yugoslavia*.[62]

The director of the UN human rights monitoring mission in El Savador has described human rights verification as

> "a systematic investigatory procedure designed to gather objective evidence to corroborate the existence of human rights violations. It is carried out through a process comprising various phases: first, the receipt of complaints or the reporting of a violation on the Mission's own initiative; second, the investigation or inquiry proper, which comprises a detailed follow-up of the facts, police and judicial investigations and the

exercise of the Mission's fact-finding powers; third, if the facts are corroborated and it is found that there was no violation of human rights, the case is closed, but if verification reveals the opposite, recommendations are made either for compensating the injury done or for rectifying the situation which gave rise to or facilitated the violation; fourth, throughout the process, active verification involves using the Mission's good offices to contribute to the transparency and efficiency of police investigations, due process, safety of witnesses, etc., and its power of initiative to assist in overcoming existing situations of human rights violations."[63]

Additional important functions are monitoring the implementation of recommendations and reporting publicly on the findings and activities of monitoring missions.

In addition to human rights monitoring operations and the avenues for action described earlier in this chapter, there are several other channels through which the UN can take action on human rights matters:

- Through his "*good offices*" role, the Secretary-General can approach governments (usually confidentially) over cases or situations of human rights concern.[64]

- The *Security Council* can take action, including the adoption of resolutions concerning particular countries.

- The Secretary-General can send *fact-finding missions* to troubled areas, including areas where human rights have been violated. His increasing use of such missions is a step towards an early-warning procedure, which might enable the UN to act more expeditiously to defuse and contain conflict.[65]

10   **Action through regional institutions**

As mentioned in Chapter 8, section 6, governments in different regions of the world have created organizations where their representatives meet to discuss matters of regional concern, and in three regions there are human rights treaties similar to those adopted through the UN, under which "disappearances" and extrajudicial executions are forbidden. Several of these regional organizations and their subordinate bodies have taken action against "disappearances" and extrajudicial executions, sometimes in response to complaints concerning individual cases.

- The *Organization of American States* (OAS) comprises 35 states in the Americas. Its General Assembly meets at least once each year. One function of the General Assembly is to adopt new human rights treaties which can then be ratified by OAS member states. At present the General Assembly is considering a draft convention on "disappearances".[66]

- The *Inter-American Commission on Human Rights* was established in 1960 and is the OAS body primarily responsible for promoting the observance and protection of human rights.[67] It consists of seven independent experts elected to four-year terms. As set forth in the American Convention on Human Rights, the Inter-American Commission has the power to prepare a report on the human rights situation in any OAS member state on its own initiative, and to make recommendations to governments on the measures they should take to secure the observance of human rights. It may visit countries to make on-site observations of the human rights situation with the agreement of the government concerned.[68]

The Inter-American Commission also receives petitions, which as stated in the American Convention may be lodged by "(a)ny person or group of persons, or any nongovernmental entity legally recognized in one or more [OAS] member states", alleging that a member state has violated its human rights obligations.[69] Such complaints are admissible only if domestic remedies have been exhausted and the matter has not been previously studied by the Commission or another international organization and is not being examined "in another international proceeding for settlement".[70] After examining and investigating the matter, the Commission may make a decision on the merits of the complaint, together with recommendations to the state concerned.[71]

Another important OAS body is the *Inter-American Court of Human Rights.* This court, established under the American Convention on Human Rights, consists of seven judges elected to six-year terms. Unlike the Inter-American Commission, whose decisions are not binding on OAS member states, the Inter-American Court of Human Rights can issue binding rulings in individual cases referred to it by the Inter-American Commission or by a state party to the American Convention on Human Rights, if the state concerned has made a declaration that it accepts the jurisdiction of the Court in such cases. Individual petitioners cannot invoke the Court's jurisdiction.[72]

- The *Council of Europe* comprises all Western European states and an increasing number of Eastern European states which began to join it after the end of the Cold War. Its Committee of Ministers and its Parliamentary Assembly can make recommendations about what they consider the governments of member states should do to prevent human rights violations. Both sometimes also adopt statements concerning human rights violations outside the territories of the member states.

All Council of Europe member states are parties to the European Convention on the

Protection of Human Rights and Fundamental Freedoms ("European Convention on Human Rights") or have signed the Convention, indicating their intention to become parties. This Convention provides for the establishment of a *European Commission of Human Rights* consisting of one member from each state party to the European Convention. The Commission is empowered to hear complaints from individuals alleging that the human rights set forth in the Convention have been violated. If the Commission is not able to reach a friendly settlement, it will make a decision on the case and then could also refer it to the *European Court of Human Rights* (also established under the Convention) if the state concerned has accepted the jurisdiction of the Court.[73]

- The *Organization of African Unity* (OAU) comprises nearly all the states of continental Africa and the adjoining islands. The corresponding human rights treaty is the African Charter on Human and Peoples' Rights, adopted by the OAU in 1981. Almost all OAU member states are parties to the African Charter.

The African Charter provides for the establishment of an *African Commission on Human and Peoples' Rights* "to promote human and peoples' rights and ensure their protection in Africa" (Article 30). This Commission consists of 11 individual experts elected to six-year terms. Like the Human Rights Committee set up under the International Covenant on Civil and Political Rights, the African Commission reviews periodic reports submitted by states parties on the measures they have taken to implement the Charter. The Commission is also required under Article 55 of the African Charter to consider complaints from individuals and organizations and to send its confidential observations on these complaints to the OAU Assembly of heads of state and government, which meets once a year in June. If the complaints "apparently relate to special cases which reveal the existence of a series of serious or massive violations of human and peoples' rights", the OAU Assembly may then request the Commission to undertake an in-depth study and issue a factual report with conclusions and recommendations. Unlike the American and European systems, there is no human rights court which the Commission can ask to issue a binding decision, but the Commission has potentially far greater powers to promote and protect human rights than the other regional institutions.[74]

Several other intergovernmental organizations are already active in human rights matters or are likely to become increasingly active, although most of them have not yet addressed the problems of "disappearances" and political killings.

- The *European Union* (EU), formerly known as the European Community, is the outgrowth of several organizations established after the Second World War to coordinate the economic activities of member states and create a common market among them. Twelve countries, all in Western Europe, currently belong to the EU.[75]

EU institutions include a Commission, a Council of Ministers, a Court of Justice, an Economic and Social Committee and a European Parliament whose members are elected directly by the voters of EU member states.

The governments of EU member states often act together on human rights matters outside the EU by issuing joint statements which may express concern and call for specific measures to be taken by the government in question, and by taking other diplomatic steps.[76] The European Parliament also is very active. It adopts resolutions on human rights within and outside the EU, and its members can raise human rights concerns with delegations of third countries. In urgent cases, resolutions can be passed quickly under the European Parliament's procedure for urgent matters.[77] The European Parliament also has a system for examining petitions from EU citizens concerning human rights.[78]

- The *Conference on Security and Co-operation in Europe* (CSCE) comprises all countries in Europe, central Asian republics which have emerged from the former USSR, the USA and Canada. At present the CSCE is creating new institutions and mechanisms in response to the changes in East-West relations of the past decade. The recently established biennial human dimension implementation meeting, where all CSCE states will focus on the implementation of their human rights commitments, should be able to deal with serious human rights violations such as "disappearances" and extrajudicial executions in member states.

One of the CSCE's recent activities has been to send fact-finding missions and longer-term monitoring missions to areas of political turbulence. The existence of these missions should be used by the CSCE Committee of Senior Officials to press for adherence to human rights obligations in the countries to which the missions are sent.

- The *League of Arab States* (often referred to as the Arab League) is a 21-member intergovernmental organization founded in 1945, with its headquarters in Cairo. In 1968 it established a permanent Arab Commission on Human Rights consisting of governmental representatives. It has defined its mandate broadly to include all matters relating to human rights on the Arab or international level. Perhaps its most important contribution so far has been the preparation of a draft Arab Charter on Human Rights. The current draft, which has not yet been approved by the League of Arab States, falls short of other international and regional standards.

- The *Organization of the Islamic Conference*, based in Jeddah, Saudia Arabia, was established in 1971 and has over 40 member states. It conducts summit conferences at the head of state level roughly every three years and annual meetings at the foreign minister level. Its Charter does not expressly refer to human rights, but it has raised human rights violations against Muslims in non-member states at the UN Security Council and the UN General Assembly. It also adopted in August 1990 at the foreign minister level the Cairo Declaration on Human Rights in Islam.[79] The Cairo Declaration, which has not been approved at the head of state level, is significantly weaker than other international and regional standards.

- The *Commonwealth* is an intergovernmental organization of 50 states, including the United Kingdom and its former colonies or states with other ties to the UK. It meets every two years in Commonwealth Heads of Government Meetings which issue final communiques addressing human rights matters as well as other issues. Its Secretariat, located in London, has a Human Rights Unit which provides assistance to Commonwealth countries in promoting human rights. The Commonwealth has a group of observers in South Africa which monitors human rights violations.

- The *Francophonie* comprises 32 member states, including France, plus associate member states and two Canadian provinces. It meets at the head of state level every two years and is dedicated to political and cultural issues related to francophone countries. The *Agence de coopération culturelle et technique* (ACCT), Cultural and Technical Cooperation Agency, based in Paris, acts as its Secretariat. The ACCT has provided assistance to strengthen judicial institutions and has organized conferences related to human rights.

11   Towards a stronger UN role

> *"...if standards and procedures [on human rights] exist for normal situations, the United Nations has not been able to act effectively to bring to an end massive human rights violations. Faced with the barbaric conduct which fills the news media today, the United Nations cannot stand idle or indifferent. The long-term credibility of our Organization as a whole will depend upon the success of our response to this challenge."*
> – *UN Secretary-General Boutros Boutros-Ghali, 1992*[80]

UN standards and mechanisms for the eradication of "disappearances" and extrajudicial executions have proliferated in the past 15 years. Much effort has gone into these developments, yet the killings and "disappearances" persist in the face of obstruction or indifference by many governments. The UN is often criticized for its weakness, but it cannot be strong if its member states are unwilling. The best human rights standards will be meaningless if governments flout them. The best human rights machinery will be powerless if governments refuse to cooperate.

Governments accused of "disappearances" and extrajudicial executions have obstructed UN action in various ways:

- Failing to respond to queries on individual cases, or responding with inaccurate or incomplete information. For example, the Special Rapporteur on extrajudicial, summary or arbitrary executions noted in his 1993 report (paragraph 692) that 28 countries did not respond at all to the allegations he transmitted to them that year. Three of these countries – Haiti, South Africa and Zaire – had not provided any information since the establishment of the Special Rapporteur in 1982;

- Harassing and vilifying individuals and organizations who inform the UN about human rights violations, and attempting to exclude them from participating in the work of the UN;[81]

- Attempting to prevent the UN from taking any public action on human rights in their country;

- Refusing to allow the UN to send a representative to their country to inquire into human rights matters;[82]

- Trying to prevent or discontinue their country's human rights situation being considered under the confidential "1503 procedure".

The annual sessions of the Commission on Human Rights have been replete with disappointments for individuals and organizations who travel to Geneva to press their human rights concerns. Time and again governments with abysmal human rights records have been able to win the support of enough other governments, acting in their perceived self-interests, to block action. Through such concerted obstruction, the UN system for human rights protection is undermined. Not only does a government intent on "disappearances" and extrajudicial executions undermine its own institutions for ensuring the rule of law, it seeks to paralyse the machinery which the UN has created to protect human rights internationally, evading accountability at home and censure abroad.

There is much that could be done to strengthen the existing UN institutions for the protection of human rights. For example, the "theme mechanisms" such as the Working Group on Disappearances and the Special Rapporteur on extrajudicial, summary or arbitrary executions should set time limits for responses from governments, which should be much shorter in the case of urgent appeals. If there is no reply or no cooperation within the time limit, the theme mechanism should be able to treat information which it has received from reliable sources as valid and act upon it. When a considerable number of serious allegations have been raised with a government or where a pattern or violations is revealed and the government persistently refused to cooperate, the full dossier should be transmitted to the Commission on Human Rights for further action. Also, the theme mechanisms should continue to work on relevant cases after they have been clarified or after the immediate danger has passed, in order to ensure that victims and their dependants are offered redress and are not penalized for having made or been the subject of a complaint to the UN.[83]

Over the years, the work of UN bodies dealing with "disappearances" and extrajudicial executions has improved, and it is to be hoped that further improvements will follow.[84] Yet despite the improvements, the UN has thus far had little impact in curtailing serious patterns of "disappearances" and political killings. As the Special Rapporteur on extrajudicial, summary or arbitrary executions wrote in his 1993 report (paragraph 705) "10 years of the existence of a [UN] mandate on extrajudicial, summary or arbitrary executions have not led to the abolition of the phenomenon." Governments may be willing to cooperate over a few cases, but the political cost of disregarding UN requests and appeals is still not high enough to make them reverse their illegal and immoral policies.

Despite the advances of the past 50 years, the UN human rights program has fundamental shortcomings. Because of the intransigence or indifference of many member states, the UN today is critically failing to address some of the most fundamental violations of human rights which are still occurring on a horrifying scale around the world, including "disappearances" and extrajudicial executions.

At the World Conference on Human Rights convened by the UN in Vienna in June 1993, in an attempt to strengthen UN human rights work, Amnesty International called for a major initiative in the form of the establishment of a UN *High Commissioner for Human Rights*. This would be a high-level position with sufficient authority and responsibility to respond to human rights problems on his or her own initiative, including emergencies and possible impending crises. The High Commissioner would maintain an overview of all UN human rights activities and their relation to other program areas; formulate and oversee the human rights components of other UN operations such as peace-keeping activities; ensure that appropriate attention is given to human rights concerns in any country; and develop programs on neglected issues. The High Commissioner would not be expected to replace existing UN mechanisms but rather to draw on their expertise and resources in carrying out his or her own mandate effectively.[85]

Another means of strengthening the international protection of human rights would be the creation of an *international criminal court* able to try people allegedly responsible for "disappearances", extrajudicial executions and other serious human rights violations.[86]

CHAPTER 13

DELIBERATE AND ARBITRARY KILLINGS BY ARMED OPPOSITION GROUPS

Opposing deliberate and arbitrary killings, whether by governments or armed opposition groups, is based on the moral imperative that all parties to a conflict observe basic standards of humane behaviour. These standards are to be found in fundamental provisions of human rights law, the laws of armed conflict (humanitarian law), and the dictates of public conscience...

Impartiality being a cardinal principle of the work of human rights organizations, it should be made clear to parties in a conflict and to public opinion that reporting abuses or patterns of abuses by armed opposition groups does not imply a condemnation of the groups as such; neither does it affect the legal status or otherwise constitute recognition of such groups; and that this is in consonance with the practice that opposing human rights violations does not imply passing judgment on the legitimacy of governments which commit them.

Further it should be made clear that by expanding their work into this field human rights organizations in no way imply that the responsibility of states for the observance of human rights law is diminished. Therefore, the mandate and effectiveness of the human rights mechanisms of the United Nations and of other intergovernmental organizations should not be diluted by taking on abuses by armed opposition groups, and the legitimate choice of other human rights groups to continue to monitor only government violations should be respected.

– Declaration of Amnesty International's International Conference on "Disappearances" and Political Killings, 4-6 September 1992 (extracts)

The previous chapters of this report have dealt with human rights violations perpetrated by state agents, and with the measures needed to combat them. But political groups which are not governments also often commit abuses which are similar to the human rights violations committed by governments. How should organizations working for human rights react to these abuses by non-governmental agents? What can be done to stop them?

In 1991 Amnesty International decided to expand the scope of its work against abuses by opposition groups. This chapter examines Amnesty International's evolving policy and techniques of action.

Not all human rights organizations will want to follow the direction taken by Amnesty International. The discussion in this chapter may help to show some of the pitfalls and possible ways to avoid them.

1   Amnesty International's policy: the 1991 decision

Like many other human rights organizations, Amnesty International began as an organization dedicated to fighting certain specific human rights violations committed by governments. For many years it was reluctant to take a position or take action on abuses by non-governmental political groups, fearing that such a position or such action could dilute its work, drain its resources and be misused by governments for their own ends.

Over the years this policy changed as Amnesty International decided to condemn the torture or killing of prisoners by opposition groups and to express its concerns directly to those opposition groups which had some of the features of governments, exercising exclusive and effective authority over the population in territories which they controlled. Such major decisions about Amnesty International's scope of work are always taken by the organization's International Council, a body comprising representatives of all Amnesty International sections around the world.

In 1991 Amnesty International's International Council decided on a significant expansion of the organization's work on non-governmental abuses. Several elements of this decision should be noted here:

- The decision recognized "the seriousness of the human suffering caused by acts against individuals, in contravention of fundamental international standards of humane behaviour, that are perpetrated by political non-governmental entities". This phrase made it clear that – as with human rights violations perpetrated by governments – Amnesty International's concern was for the suffering inflicted on individuals through the practices which the organization opposes.

- The International Council decided "that Amnesty International should continue to regard human rights as the individual's rights in relation to governmental authority". This statement drew an important distinction – discussed below – between the obligations of a government towards individuals, which are violated when a government violates human rights, and the fundamental standards of humane behaviour which an opposition group contravenes when it commits abuses such as the torture or killing of prisoners.

- Under the new policy Amnesty International opposes the following abuses by non-governmental entities:

  - torture;

- the taking of hostages;

- the killing of prisoners;

- "other deliberate and arbitrary killings, for example killings of people under the non-governmental entity's immediate control at the time and killings carried out solely by reason of the victims' ethnic origin, sex, colour, language, religion or political views or other beliefs".

- Amnesty International will oppose such acts with any such armed political organization which is accessible to approaches, whether or not that organization has the attributes of a government.

2   Armed opposition groups

Amnesty International's policy and practice since the 1991 decision is to oppose specific abuses perpetrated by armed political entities other than governments. Several points should be noted here.

- The policy addresses abuses by entities ranging from groups which are small, limited in power and devoid of authority to organizations that in practice exercise virtual governmental powers, including those with a limited degree of international recognition as governmental authorities. These include organizations controlling territory and organizations fighting in civil wars where central authority has broken down.

- The actions of armed political organizations that work in association with or with the connivance or tolerance of governments – for example, as paramilitary militias, "death squads" or vigilantes – are opposed through Amnesty International's work to halt governmental violations of human rights, not under this policy. To the extent that governmental responsibility can be determined, such acts entail Amnesty International mandate concerns relating to the obligations of governments. But through its policy on abuses by non-governmental armed groups Amnesty International monitors and acts upon abuses by armed political organizations with suspected but uncertain governmental links, pending confirmation of such links, at which point it will hold the government accountable.

- Whether large or small, the armed groups covered by Amnesty International's policy have a *political* dimension which distinguishes them from uniquely criminal organizations. This political dimension is indicated by a range of criteria including the stated or apparent purpose of the organization and the nature and motivation of its activities.

The term "political" is used here in a broad sense and is not intended to have any value connotation or to confer any particular status on the organizations in question. It is used as a working term to distinguish those organizations within the scope of Amnesty International's concerns.

- Outside Amnesty International's range of concerns are isolated, politically motivated acts by individuals, as well as acts by groups of individuals where actions cannot be attributed to a specific and clearly defined political entity, no clear focus of authority can be discerned, or there is no clear structure of political responsibility or military command.

- Also outside Amnesty International's scope of concerns are the acts of criminal groups whose activities have no overt political dimension. Criminal organizations outside Amnesty International's scope of concerns may be distinguished by such criteria as a lack of a political program or a lack of a stated ideology, combined with a dedication primarily to the illicit pursuit of profit for its members.

- Amnesty International offers no special recognition or status to the organizations it monitors or addresses. Amnesty International's appeals and contacts are purely humanitarian in nature – they carry no connotation of recognition.

In this report the term "armed opposition group" is used to refer to entities other than governments committing abuses opposed by Amnesty International. Other possible terms are "political armed opposition group" or "political armed group". The term "armed opposition group" is used to distinguish these groups from the many other opposition groups, such as political parties, which do not resort to arms and do not commit abuses opposed by Amnesty International.

3   Deliberate and arbitrary killings

Amnesty International opposes the killing of prisoners and other deliberate and arbitrary killings by armed opposition groups. These include summary executions, assassinations, and other wilful killings of civilians and of others who are or have been rendered defenceless.

The killings which Amnesty International opposes have several characteristics:

- They are *deliberate*, not accidental.

- They are *arbitrary*, in that they are not countenanced by any internationally recognized standard of law. They flout even minimum standards of humane conduct applicable to governments and armed opposition groups alike. Their

208

arbitrary character distinguishes them from killings in self-defence or the defence of others from an immediate threat, and from a range of killings in armed conflict which may occur as a consequence of an attack on or a defence of a military objective, such as killings in the course of clashes between violent opposing forces, killings in cross-fire, or attacks in general on military and security personnel.

- They are committed *on the authority of an armed opposition group* and in accordance with its policy at some level deliberately to eliminate specific individuals, or groupings or categories of individuals, or to allow those under its authority to commit such abuses. This concept distinguishes deliberate and arbitrary killings from killings for private reasons which are shown, for example through preventive measures and disciplinary action, to have been the acts of individuals in violation of enforced higher orders. The involvement or acquiescence of the group's leadership in the killings renders the group accountable for them.

The victim of a deliberate and arbitrary killing may be targeted individually, or he or she may be the victim of an attack on a particular population group or of random attacks on members of the civilian public at large. Such arbitrary killings include killings solely by reason of the victim's ethnic origin, sex, colour, language, views or beliefs, as well as other criteria which might appear less overtly political.

The killings which Amnesty International opposes are arbitrary under international standards, but Amnesty International has not brought into its range of concerns all arbitrary killings in war. Amnesty International's opposition to deliberate and arbitrary killings by opposition groups and to extrajudicial executions by governments does not extend to all types of killings forbidden under the laws of war. Amnesty International does not, for example, apply these terms to killings which are a by-product of clashes between opposing armed forces. Nor does Amnesty International have a general position on the use of weapons of mass destruction which may inevitably lead to civilian casualties.

Both governments and opposition groups sometimes maintain that deliberate attacks on civilian populations were legitimate attacks on military objectives. When large numbers of civilians are killed in disputed circumstances, Amnesty International will assess the merits of claims that an attack was against a military objective. This could include situations where many civilians are killed merely on a presumption that some individual combatants are among them. Amnesty International is not generally in a position to assess whether the use of military force is disproportionate, but the organization would condemn acts where intention was clearly to kill civilians.

In armed conflicts, people who take no active part in the hostilities must be distinguished from those who do. Civilians, who can be defined as those not taking part in hostilities, must be distinguished from military personnel and others who are directly involved, may influence the course of the conflict, and offer a permanent threat of violence and harm to their adversaries. The deliberate killing of people taking no active part in hostilities and offering no other immediate threat of violence is clearly arbitrary.

Similarly, the deliberate killing of anyone who has been detained, incapacitated, or – having ceased to offer resistance – seeks to surrender to the forces of a government or an opposition group is always arbitrary. Members of fighting forces in such cases are *no longer* taking part in hostilities. The *circumstances* of a killing, and in particular whether the victim had ceased to resist and sought to surrender, will be an important factor in determining whether a killing was deliberate and arbitrary. Such circumstances will be of particular importance in assessing killings of nominal civilians who play a limited security role.

In opposing deliberate and arbitrary killings by opposition groups, Amnesty International neither supports nor condemns the resort to violence by opposition groups in itself, just as Amnesty International neither supports nor condemns a governmental policy of using military force against armed opposition movements or against other states. The issue of whether insurgency or war is morally justified has no bearing on Amnesty International's central task, which is to bring relief to individual victims of abuse.

4   International standards

Just as "disappearances" and extrajudicial executions are prohibited in all circumstances, so do deliberate and arbitrary killings contravene minimum standards of humane behaviour which apply everywhere and at all times. These standards are expressed in several bodies of law.

- The universal prohibition of murder is expressed in national *criminal laws.* Like extrajudicial executions by governments, deliberate and arbitrary killings violate these laws.

- Deliberate and arbitrary killings are prohibited under the laws of armed conflict dealing with the protection of victims of war, known as *international humanitarian law* and contained principally in the four Geneva Conventions of 1949 supplemented by the two Additional Protocols of 1977. As discussed in Chapter 8, "wilful killings" of persons protected by the Geneva Conventions are prohibited under the Conventions in international armed conflicts, while Article 3 common to the four Conventions prohibits "murder of all kinds" of protected persons in non-international armed conflicts.

- International *human rights* instruments recognize inherent **human rights**, including the right to life and the right to security of person. Deliberate and arbitrary killings, torture and other abuses by opposition groups attack and destroy these rights.

Article 3 common to the Geneva Conventions is especially relevant to the prohibition of deliberate and arbitrary killings. *Common Article 3* has a number of important provisions:

- It applies to "armed conflict not of an international character occurring in the territory of one of the High Contracting Parties".[1] (Today virtually all states are parties to the Geneva Conventions.)

- It follows the same approach as the Geneva Conventions themselves by defining a class of protected persons and then establishing rules for the treatment of these people. Protected persons under common Article 3 are "(p)ersons taking no active part in the hostilities, including members of armed forces who have laid down their arms and those placed *hors de combat* by sickness, wounds, detention, or any other cause".

- Acts against protected persons prohibited under common Article 3 include "violence to life and person, in particular murder of all kinds", the "taking of hostages" and "mutilation, cruel treatment and torture". These acts "are and shall remain prohibited at any time and in any place whatsoever with respect to the above-mentioned persons".[2]

- The provisions of common Article 3 are stated to be binding on "each Party" to a non-international armed conflict. This means that not only are states parties to the Geneva Conventions bound to respect the provisions of common Article 3 in an internal armed conflict, but the other parties to such a conflict, such as insurgent groups, should also be bound to respect the provisions of common Article 3.[3]

- The parties to non-international armed conflicts "should further endeavour to bring into force, by means of special agreements, all or part of the other provisions" of the Geneva Conventions. What this does is to set up a mechanism whereby parties to an internal armed conflict can declare that they intend to apply the provisions of the Geneva Conventions, including the ban on "wilful killings", even if they are not states and are therefore not formally parties to the Conventions.

- Common Article 3 also says that the application of the preceding provisions "shall not affect the legal status of the Parties to the conflict." States are usually reluctant to have any official "recognition" conferred on opposition movements fighting against them, as they fear it could bolster claims of legitimacy of the opposition movement's cause. This provision of common Article 3 allows for the protection of victims of conflicts to be extended without being held up by arguments over "recognition".[4]

The coincidence between basic rules of international humanitarian law and fundamental human rights which may never be derogated from, including the right to life and the right not to be subjected to torture, makes it possible to speak of *minimum standards of humane behaviour* which must be observed in all circumstances.[5] To put the point in another way: the prohibition of torture and deliberate and arbitrary killings, as expressed in various bodies of law, rests on an international consensus that these acts must never be committed.[6] When an armed opposition group tortures its prisoners or commits deliberate and arbitrary killings, it is flying in the face of the principles of humanity and the dictates of the public conscience, just as a government is when it commits torture, "disappearances" or extrajudicial executions.

Although the scope of international humanitarian law and human rights law converges on these important points, the historical origins and general approach of these two bodies of law are very different.[7] International humanitarian law comprises rules imposing, in the interest of humanity, restraints on the behaviour of combatants. In the formulation of these rules, balances are struck between humanity on the one hand and what is often called "military necessity" on the other. Human rights doctrine, in contrast, starts from the notion that human rights are inalienable attributes of every human being: the Preamble of the Universal Declaration of Human Rights refers to "the inherent dignity" and "the equal and inalienable rights of all members of the human family". In spelling out these rights, international human rights instruments constrain governmental behaviour so that these rights will not be infringed on, and they set forth measures which governments should take to ensure that everyone can enjoy these rights.

International humanitarian law imposes restraints on the behaviour of combatants. The Geneva Conventions and other instruments of international humanitarian law are binding on the states parties to them, but other combatants which are not parties or are not states can also declare their intention to respect the provisions of these instruments. Moreover, insofar as the provisions of international humanitarian law reflect a universal consensus of the obligation in armed conflict to respect the principles of humanity and the dictates of the public conscience, any opposition group or other organization which engages in armed conflict should be considered bound to respect those provisions. It is in this sense that the prohibition of torture, murder and other acts set forth in common Article 3 is stated to be binding on all parties to an armed conflict, including those that are not states.[8]

International human rights treaties, in contrast, constitute undertakings among the states parties to them to respect and ensure human rights. Legally, when a state engages in torture or extrajudicial executions or permits its officials to do so, that state has violated its obligation to respect and ensure the corresponding rights under international and regional human rights treaties as well as any applicable national constitutions or other instruments.

The term *human rights violation* carries the connotation of a violation of a legal obligation. Amnesty International uses the term to refer to acts of torture, "disappearance", extrajudicial execution and other violations of the internationally established human rights obligations of states. It uses the term *abuses* to refer to torture, deliberate and arbitrary killings and other acts committed by armed opposition groups. These acts, too, contravene the minimum standards of humane behaviour reflected in national laws, international humanitarian law and international human rights instruments.

The difference between the terms "violation" and "abuse" does not imply any judgment about the suffering caused or the moral reprehensibility whether these acts are committed by the state or by an armed opposition group. The difference in terminology is intended rather to reflect the difference in legal status between states and other kinds of organizations.

5 The scope of the killings

In recent years Amnesty International has received many reports of deliberate and arbitrary killings by armed opposition groups in different countries.

- In the *Indonesian* province of Aceh, for example, an armed group called *Aceh Merdeka* has been fighting for independence since the mid-1970s. Since the re-emergence of armed conflict in 1989, its members have committed human rights abuses, including arbitrarily killing civilians they alleged were informers.

- In *Mozambique,* armed units of the *Resistência Nacional Moçambicana* (RENAMO), Mozambique National Resistance, have murdered and mutilated prisoners and attacked and killed thousands of civilians for nearly two decades. The leadership of RENAMO has consistently refused to acknowledge these abuses or to take action to halt them.

- In *South Africa,* the opposition African National Congress (ANC) was found responsible for torture, ill-treatment and executions in its detention camps over a 12-year period in the late 1970s and 1980s. Many of the victims were members of the ANC's military wing who had opposed aspects of ANC policy. The abuses took place in several African countries, notably Angola, Zambia, Tanzania and Uganda – sometimes with the active collaboration of the government concerned. Following an ANC inquiry, ANC President Nelson Mandela accepted the organization's full responsibility for the abuses.

- In *Peru* the armed opposition *Partido Comunista del Perú (Sendero Luminoso)* (PCP), Communist Party of Peru (Shining Path), has summarily killed hundreds of municipal election candidates, mayors and other local and regional state officials and administrators. The PCP has also deliberately killed members of non-governmental human rights organizations; journalists; priests, nuns and other attached to the Roman Catholic and evangelical churches; political activists from across the political spectrum; and leaders of popular organizations not in sympathy with the PCP's aims and methods. In addition, the organization has summarily killed thousands of peasants accused of collaborating with the counter-insurgency forces or who refused to support the PCP.

- In *Colombia*, guerrilla organizations such as the *Fuerzas Armadas Revolucionarias de Colombia* (FARC), Revolutionary Armed Forces of Colombia, and the *Ejército de Liberación Nacional* (ELN), National Liberation Army, have carried out numerous attacks in which civilians have been deliberately killed. Scores of people have been kidnapped and held to ransom: some have been killed in captivity.

- In *India*, armed opposition groups have committed numerous human rights abuses in many states. In the state of Punjab, armed separatists have deliberately killed thousands of civilians. In Jammu and Kashmir, armed separatist groups have captured and killed civilians, taken hostages, tortured prisoners and raped women in their custody. In Andhra Pradesh, they have killed or mutilated alleged "informers".

- In *Sri Lanka*, Tamil militants of the Liberation Tigers of Tamil Eelam, seeking independence for the northeast of Sri Lanka, have committed numerous gross abuses of human rights including the massacre of hundreds of non-combatant Muslim and Sinhalese civilians in attacks on their communities and in attacks on buses and trains. They have tortured and killed prisoners, and abducted people for ransom. They have also executed prisoners whom they accused of being traitors.

- In the *United Kingdom*, members of the Irish Republican Army (IRA) have killed civilians in Northern Ireland and Britain, and have killed captive suspected informants. Other abuses have been committed in Northern Ireland by Protestant groups such as the Ulster Volunteer Force and the Ulster Defence Association. They have killed members of the minority Catholic community in random attacks they said were "reprisals" for IRA violence, as well as suspected informants.

- In *Spain*, members of the Basque separatist organization *Euskadi Ta Askatasuna* (ETA), Basque Homeland and Liberty, have deliberately killed civilians as well as members of the security forces in attacks.

- In *Turkey*, during 1993 alone, the Kurdish Workers' Party (PKK) carried out more than 200 "executions" of prisoners – including teachers, members of the government-organized village guard corps, and people suspected of being police informers. Members of the organization *Devrimci Sol*, Revolutionary Left, have also killed several of their own members who were suspected of being informers.

- In *Algeria* and in *Egypt*, killings of police and civilians by militant Islamic groups have coincided with drastic clampdowns by the government and a sharp deterioration in respect for human rights. Some victims have been targeted by opposition groups solely on account of their views. In Egypt, for example, Farag Foda, a writer and vocal opponent of Islamic militant groups, was shot dead by two men in June 1992: responsibility for the killing was claimed by the opposition group *Al-Gama'a al-Islamiya*.

- In *Lebanon*, various militias have for years committed deliberate and arbitrary killings, especially during the civil war of 1975 to 1990.

- In the *Israeli-Occupied Territories*, Palestinians – including members of armed political groups – have killed hundreds of people in recent years. From January to May 1993, Palestinians killed up to 14 Israeli civilians and about 50 Palestinians, many of them suspected of "collaborating" with the Israeli authorities. Some of the victims were interrogated and tortured before being put to death.

- In *Iraq*, deliberate and arbitrary killings have been committed by opponents of the Iraqi government, notably in northern Iraq in areas under the control of the Iraqi Kurdistan Front (IKF) and, since July 1992, the Council of Ministers for the Kurdistan Region. In October 1991, for example, armed Kurdish units (*Pesh Merga*) summarily executed about 60 unarmed Iraqi soldiers in Sulaimaniya. An IKF investigation into the killings identified 14 Kurds as the suspected perpetrators, most of whom were affiliated to Kurdish political organizations. However, the suspects were released in 1992 after the IKF decided not to pursue the investigation.[9]

6   The attitude of governments

The clashes between governments and armed opposition groups involve not only force but also a battle of ideas. Just as an opposition group attempts to obtain legitimacy in the eyes of the public by decrying the policies and actions of the government, so will a government depict the aims and practices of an armed opposition group as "criminal" and "subversive".

The propaganda war extends to the atrocities perpetrated by the two sides. Opposition groups committing deliberate and arbitrary killings may present these as heroic deeds, the just actions of an "oppressed people". Governments, condemning the same actions as morally reprehensible, may use the threat as a pretext for their own harsh and unlawful practices – arbitrary arrest, torture, "disappearance", extrajudicial execution. Opposition groups likewise may use governmental human rights violations as an excuse for committing similar atrocities.

An organization attempting to combat human rights abuses is likely to find itself caught up in the propaganda war. Even though it tries to be impartial and objective, either side may say it is not. If it draws attention to human rights violations by government forces, the government may call on it to condemn the aims of the other side and accuse it of hypocrisy if it does not.

This governmental attack is intended to serve several purposes. If human rights organizations can be discredited, the government will find it easier to violate human rights without fear of exposure. The notion that human rights violations are justifiable reactions to non-governmental abuses, if accepted, will obscure the international obligation of governments to respect fundamental human rights in all circumstances. The notion that governmental human rights violations and opposition group abuses somehow cancel each other out can obscure the many situations where the former are far more numerous than the latter. It may also obscure situations in which most of the victims from both sides are from among the same people, their "crime" having been to remain neutral or simply to be caught, defenceless, between implacable enemies.

Organizations working for human rights in different countries do so from a variety of perspectives. Some of those working to expose and combat extrajudicial executions have decided also to oppose deliberate and arbitrary killings by opposition groups. Others have chosen to focus their limited resources exclusively on the human rights obligations of governments, recognizing that governments are the authors and the addressees of the instruments setting forth international human rights standards.

Either decision should be respected. The valuable efforts of organizations and individuals around the world to document and combat "disappearances" and extrajudicial executions in their countries must be acknowledged and supported, not attacked and suppressed.

7   Action against deliberate and arbitrary killings

Armed opposition groups should take steps to ensure that their forces comply with minimum standards of humane behaviour. This should be reflected in the training of their forces and in the instructions issued to them. Armed opposition groups should:

- order their fighters to treat humanely prisoners, the wounded and those seeking to surrender, whether such people are civilians or members of the armed forces, and never to kill them;

- prohibit deliberate and arbitrary killings of non-combatants under any circumstances;

- conduct proper investigations into alleged abuses by their combatants in order to determine responsibility;

- ensure that individuals suspected of committing or ordering deliberate and arbitrary killings are removed from any position of authority or duties which bring them into contact with prisoners or others at risk of abuse.

Various means of action are open to non-governmental organizations working to end deliberate and arbitrary killings and other abuses by opposition groups:

- gathering objective information on these abuses and making it known;

- publicizing minimum standards of humane behaviour and the importance of adhering to them;

- appealing directly to leaders of armed opposition groups through such means as exchanges of correspondence, direct contacts and public appeals.

With armed groups which are well established and have achieved some degree of external recognition, contacts may be possible with their representatives in different countries or at the UN. With groups which are clandestine and have no office or postal address, indirect means of appeal must be sought, such as appeals through the news media.

Governments and others who provide support to opposition movements from abroad should convey to them the need to respect minimum standards of humane behaviour and not commit deliberate and arbitrary killings.

CHAPTER 14

INTERNATIONAL ACTION

1 The need for international action

A governmental program of "disappearances" and extrajudicial executions is very hard to combat. Even in isolated incidents where the extent of official backing for the actions of individual officers may be in doubt, the authorities often will be loath to take corrective measures for fear of weakening the prestige and power of the security forces. When "disappearances" and extrajudicial executions become systematic, the official resistance to stopping them will be all the stronger.

Locally, victims' relatives, human rights organizations and many others have tried to combat "disappearances" and extrajudicial executions. Their achievements are often remarkable, but they normally have immense difficulties in trying to reverse an official policy and obtain a full accounting for the abuses committed. Often the perpetrators strike back, neutralizing their efforts and even putting their lives in danger. International action is needed to increase the pressure for human rights observance on the governments concerned and to support national activists at risk.

The UN and regional inter-governmental organizations are vehicles for international action, but their efforts are seldom enough. Other governments must put pressure directly on the governments concerned to uphold human rights and stop "disappearances" and extrajudicial executions. Individuals and non-governmental organizations also have important roles to play in this international effort.

2 Action by other governments

Governments should use all available channels to intercede with the governments of countries where "disappearances" and extrajudicial executions have been reported.
– From Amnesty International's 14-Point Programs on "Disappearances" and Extrajudicial Executions

The eradication of "disappearances" and political killings should be a part of every country's foreign policy. In its bilateral relations with other countries and in intergovernmental bodies, each government should work to stop "disappearances" and extrajudicial executions and to protect those at risk.

The need to act against human rights violations internationally is a part of the duty of governments to strive to ensure universal respect for human rights. This need has been recognized as an obligation in international human rights instruments. Thus the UN Principles on Extra-Legal, Arbitrary and Summary Executions states,

"Governments shall make every effort to prevent extra-legal, arbitrary and summary executions through measures such as diplomatic intercession ... and public denunciation" (principle 8), while according to the UN Declaration on Disappearances (Article 2 (2)), "States shall act at the national and regional levels and in cooperation with the United Nations to contribute by all means to the prevention and eradication of enforced disappearance."

Each government should instruct its diplomatic representatives to:

- seek information on any suspected "disappearances" or extrajudicial executions, as well as on any laws or practices which facilitate these abuses;

- meet local human rights organizations to gather information on alleged "disappearances"and extrajudicial executions;

- express concern with the host government over allegations of "disappearances" and extrajudicial executions;

- intercede with the host government to locate "disappeared" prisoners and ensure their safety, to protect people at risk of "disappearance" or extrajudicial execution, and to protect members of human rights organizations threatened because of their work;

- in urgent cases, offer shelter to people at risk of "disappearance" or extrajudicial execution;

- send observers to trials of people allegedly responsible for "disappearances" and extrajudicial executions, as a sign of their own government's wish to see those responsible brought to justice;

- report back on these matters so that the home government can take the situation of human rights into account in formulating policy.

Action by other governments for the eradication of "disappearances" and political killings also includes:

- public criticism of the practice of governments which engage in "disappearances" and extrajudicial executions or abet political killings by opposition groups;

- efforts through the UN Commission on Human Rights and other inter-governmental bodies to act multilaterally against "disappearances" and extrajudicial executions;

- technical assistance contributing to the eradication of "disappearances" and extrajudicial executions, including expert assistance in investigative techniques;

- action to ensure that transfers to other countries of equipment, know-how, training or doctrine for military, security or police use do not facilitate or encourage "disappearances" or extrajudicial executions;

- pressure on opposition groups with which they have ties to stop deliberate and arbitrary killings.

3   Non-refoulement

No one should be forcibly returned to a country where he or she risks becoming a victim of "disappearance" or extrajudicial execution.
– From Amnesty International's 14-Point Programs for the Prevention of "Disappearances" and Extrajudicial Executions

People at risk of "disappearance" or extrajudicial execution by their own government sometimes find themselves in other countries. They may have fled, or they may have been abroad when political changes made it unsafe for them to return. These people should not be deported, extradited, or otherwise sent back against their will to the country where they are at risk.

The duty of governments not to return a person forcibly to a country where he or she risks becoming a victim of "disappearance" or extrajudicial execution is established in the UN Declaration on Disappearances (Article 8) and the UN Principles on Extra-Legal, Arbitrary and Summary Executions (principle 5). This duty follows from the prohibition on *refoulement*[1] which, as set out in Article 33 of the 1951 Convention relating to the Status of Refugees, prohibits the forcible return of any person to a country where that person's life may be threatened "on account of his race, religion, nationality, membership of a particular social group or political opinion".[2] Over 110 states are parties to this Convention. Moreover, it is widely recognized that the *non-refoulement* obligation is a principle of customary international law binding on all states. While the 1951 Convention allows some exceptions to the principle as set forth in its Article 33, the prohibitions on forcible return in the Declaration on Disappearances and the Principles on Extra-Legal, Arbitrary and Summary Executions are absolute, emphasizing the grave nature of these human rights violations and the need to take all possible steps to prevent them. Similarly, Article 3 of the UN Convention against Torture and Other Cruel, Inhuman or Degrading Treatment or Punishment ("Convention against Torture") prohibits the forcible return of a person to another country where there are substantial grounds for believing that he or she would be in danger of being tortured.

Many people at risk of "disappearance" or extrajudicial execution face difficulties in trying to flee to safety in another country. The Universal Declaration of Human

Rights proclaims the right of everyone to seek and enjoy *asylum* from persecution,[3] but countries where people may wish to seek asylum often obstruct this right through their application of immigration control policies which are often indiscriminate and obstruct the entry of people in need of protection. In many cases people fleeing political killings have been stopped at borders and not admitted because their documents or visas are not in order.

To ensure that people at risk of "disappearance" or extrajudicial execution are not sent back, governments must allow people claiming asylum an opportunity for a full and fair examination of their claim.

- Asylum-seekers often find themselves in a strange environment, apprehensive of the authorities and unable to speak the language of the country. The government should ensure that they receive the assistance of lawyers and that competent interpreters are provided. They should also receive assistance from specialized non-governmental agencies.

- The officials who make decisions on asylum claims should be able to rely on the services of a documentation office that draws on information about human rights in the country of origin from the widest possible range of sources, in particular information from independent and non-governmental sources. Amnesty International has urged the establishment of such offices.

- If an application for asylum is turned down, asylum-seekers must be allowed to appeal against the decision and to remain in the country pending the outcome of the appeal.

Non-governmental organizations, lawyers and human rights activists in countries where people seek asylum can play a crucial role in helping to protect people from being sent back to countries where their lives are at risk. By providing information to support an individual case, they can help to overcome any prejudicial tendency by the authorities to disbelieve the person's story. Their involvement can help to ensure that the asylum-seeker's legal rights are fully respected and that the applicant understands the procedures involved.

Besides providing such support in individual cases, human rights organizations and others often engage in public education to counter attitudes hostile to asylum-seekers. By making known the risk of repression in the countries which people flee, they can overcome common misconceptions about asylum-seekers, such as that they are motivated solely by the desire for material gain.

Occasionally an asylum-seeker is alleged to have been responsible for human rights violations in the country which he or she has fled. If such a person is at risk of "disappearance" or extrajudicial execution if returned home, the person should not be returned, but granting protection to him or her should not preclude an investigation into the alleged crimes.

4   Action by human rights organizations and organizations of relatives of the "disappeared"

"In our efforts to build a culture of human rights, we must not forget the importance of human rights workers and non-governmental organizations, nor the courage shown by many who risk their lives and security for the rights of others."
– UN Secretary-General Boutros Boutros-Ghali[4]

"...over the past decade, non-governmental human rights organizations have played a vital role in protecting and promoting the human rights of the most vulnerable sectors of society, in difficult and sometimes tragic circumstances. Quite a number of human rights activists were forced to go into exile, and some even lost their lives in the course of their work. Human rights organizations have been among the few organizations to investigate human rights violations and to protect their victims."
– From the second report of the Director of the UN human rights monitoring mission in El Salvador (paragraph 9), referring to the work of human rights organizations in El Salvador

"The World Conference on Human Rights recognizes the important role of non-governmental organizations in the promotion of all human rights and in humanitarian activities at national, regional and international levels. The World Conference on Human Rights appreciates their contribution to increasing public awareness of human rights issues, to the conduct of education, training and research in this field, and to the promotion and protection of all human rights and fundamental freedoms. While recognizing that the primary responsibility for standard-setting lies with States, the Conference also appreciates the contribution of non-governmental organizations to this process. In this respect, the World Conference on Human Rights emphasizes the importance of continued dialogue and cooperation between Governments and non-governmental organizations. Non-governmental organizations and their members genuinely involved in the field of human rights should enjoy the rights and freedoms recognized in the Universal Declaration of Human Rights, and the protection of the national law. ... Non-governmental organizations should be free to carry out their

human rights activities, without interference, within the
framework of national law and the Universal Declaration of
Human Rights."
– World Conference on Human Rights, Vienna Declaration and
Programme of Action, part I, paragraph 38.[5]

Much of this report has concerned the measures which governments must take to fulfil their obligations to eradicate "disappearances" and extrajudicial executions and redress the wrongs caused. To say that they must do so is one thing, but experience shows that it will not happen automatically. Much of the credit for improvements belongs not to the authorities but to the pressures created by unofficial organizations working, often under great difficulties and at great risk, in defense of human rights.

Some of these are organizations of relatives of the "disappeared". Such organizations often appear spontaneously. Mothers, wives and others, visiting police stations, army barracks and government offices to inquire about their missing relatives, meet others there whose plight is the same; they exchange experiences, discuss their problems and then – sometimes – decide to act together. In Sri Lanka and the Philippines, in Chad, in Chile, Argentina, Guatemala and other countries, relatives' organizations have searched for the "disappeared" and acted to confront the practice of "disappearance".[6]

Other organizations also are active on human rights matters at the local and national levels. Such organizations vary in their mandates and methods of action. Some have their base in the structures of established religious organizations; others are affiliated with trade unions, political parties or professional associations while still others are independent. Some are primarily legally oriented, working through the judicial system; others rely mainly on publicity and other forms of action.

Relatives' organizations and national human rights groups work in various ways, including the following:

- making inquiries and pressing the authorities to disclose information about the whereabouts and fate of the "disappeared";

- pursuing individual cases in the courts through such means as *habeas corpus* petitions, criminal denunciations and civil suits;

- providing material and moral support to victims' relatives, and to victims of "disappearance" who reappear;

- investigating individual cases and documenting the extent of the practice;

- informing the public of their rights under national law and international human rights standards.[7]

Complementing the work of national organizations, other organizations tackle "disappearances" and political killings internationally.

Amnesty International is an independent movement for human rights, with an active worldwide membership comprising more than one million members, subscribers and supporters in over 150 countries and territories. It has been working to stop "disappearances" and political killings since the 1970s.

Amnesty International's activities include:

- sending fact-finding missions to make on-the-spot investigations and meet government officials;[8]

- publishing reports of "disappearances" and political killings with recommendations on the measures needed to end them;

- through its worldwide Urgent Action network, sending urgent appeals to the authorities on behalf of individuals who have "disappeared" or are at risk of extrajudicial execution;

- assigning individual cases of "disappeared" people or of victims of extrajudicial execution to one or more Amnesty International groups for long-term work;

- conducting international campaigns against "disappearances" and political killings in different countries to mobilize public opinion and put pressure on government authorities and on opposition groups responsible for political killings;[9]

- working for stronger international action and improved international instruments at the UN and regional inter-governmental organizations.

The *International Committee of the Red Cross* (ICRC) is an independent institution which works to protect and assist military and civilian victims in international and internal armed conflicts and internal disturbances and tensions. It is a part of the International Red Cross and Red Crescent Movement, whose other components are national Red Cross and Red Crescent Societies and the world federation of national societies known as the League of Red Cross and Red Crescent Societies. Its work is based on the Geneva Conventions of 1949 and the two Additional Protocols of 1977, which confer on the ICRC the right to take action and to make proposals to states. The Movement's Statutes recognize that the ICRC has a right of humanitarian initiative in situations not covered by the Conventions or the Additional Protocols.

From its headquarters in Geneva and through the delegations which it sets up in conflict areas around the world, the ICRC works against "disappearances" and political killings in several ways:

- visiting places of detention, interviewing without witnesses the people held there and registering their names (see Chapter 9, section 17);

- operating a Central Tracing Agency which traces people who have "disappeared" or whose families have no news of them. At the request of family members, the ICRC may prepare lists of "disappeared" people for government authorities, asking them to clarify the fate of the victims. If ICRC delegates identify a detainee as a person who has been reported to have "disappeared", the family is informed;

- reminding the parties to armed conflicts of their obligation to respect international humanitarian law, under which "disappearances" and political killings are prohibited;

- in cooperation with national Red Cross and Red Crescent Societies, promoting understanding of the laws of war by helping to train national instructors whose task is to make the principles of these laws known to members of the armed forces;

- providing material assistance to families of the "disappeared".[10]

Other international non-governmental organizations also work against "disappearances" and political killings.[11] International trade unions, international religious organizations and organizations of journalists, for example, have taken up cases of members of their constituent organizations who have been victims of "disappearance" or extrajudicial execution, and have acted in other ways against these abuses.

The contribution of non-governmental organizations to the international protection of human rights is increasingly being recognized in the UN. Thus the Special Rapporteur on extrajudicial, summary or arbitrary executions in his 1993 report (paragraph 690) thanked the non-governmental organizations which sent him information, and wrote that "without their efforts, very little could have been done". The Working Group on Disappearances has for many years cited the work of non-governmental organizations and organizations of relatives of the "disappeared" in its reports. The UN General Assembly has repeatedly recognized the constructive role that non-governmental organizations can play in relation to national institutions for the protection and promotion of human rights.[12]

Non-governmental organizations make vital contributions to the protection of human rights worldwide. By working on behalf of victims and their relatives, these organizations help to protect individuals against abuses of state power. By investigating and denouncing human rights violations, they keep watch for human rights, helping to maintain a state of vigilance which needs to be permanent, as there will always be a risk that the powers wielded by state officials will be abused. It is through working for human rights and making human rights known that the universal and effective recognition and observance of human rights can be secured, as called for in the Universal Declaration of Human Rights.[13]

5   Action by individual citizens

The organizations working for human rights around the world are made up of individuals. Often these organizations have come into existence because of the needs and wishes of victims, victims' relatives, and others concerned about human rights. Out of the desperate experience of relatives of the "disappeared" and the killed, out of the fearsome and anguishing knowledge of these atrocities has come action.

Where "disappearances" and political killings are perpetrated, relatives and others have courageously pursued the truth, sought to find the "disappeared" and ensure their well-being, and joined others to take action in the face of the atrocities.

Outside the country, people horrified by the atrocities have joined others to make the facts more widely known, and have sought means of action from their country which would help to find the "disappeared" and to stop "disappearances" and political killings. Through their efforts, human rights become a matter of public international concern, transcending national boundaries.

The efforts of people confronting "disappearances" and extrajudicial executions lead to exposure of these human rights violations. Out of exposure comes awareness: awareness of internationally agreed human rights standards; awareness of human rights violations, of their human cost, of the means by which they are perpetrated; awareness of the proper remedies and how they can be invoked. Exposure provokes horror, indignation and outrage, leading to a determination that "disappearances" and political killings must be stopped. Out of this determination comes action.

This report contains many possibilities for action, but there is no single formula for success. Different measures will be tried in different places, with varying results. Out of these efforts will come more ideas for action. The experience of confronting "disappearances" and political killings must be one of resourcefulness in the face of adversity.

The doctrine of human rights and the institutional machinery for human rights observance are designed to protect individuals from the egregious misuse of the awesome power of the state. The minimum standards of humane behaviour discussed in Chapter 13 apply everywhere and at all times, to states and armed opposition groups alike. Individuals must defend these rights and these standards, for themselves and for others, for their dearest relatives and for strangers in other countries, for the sake of the common humanity of all. It is through these means that "disappearances" and political killings can be defeated.

NOTES

Introduction

1. *Nunca Más; Informe de la Comisión Nacional Sobre la Desaparición de Personas*, Editorial Universitaria de Buenos Aires, Buenos Aires, 1984. English-language edition: *Nunca Mas (Never Again); A Report by Argentina's National Commission on Disappeared People*, Faber and Faber, London and Boston, 1986.

2. See Chapter 11, section 9.

Chapter 1   Iraq: The world would not listen

1. The use of poisonous gases in warfare is forbidden under the Geneva Protocol of 1925, adopted in reaction to the horrors of gas attacks in the First World War. In attacking soldiers with chemical weapons, Iraq was violating its obligations under international law as a party (with Iran) to the Geneva Protocol of 1925. The relative lack of international protest over these attacks must have encouraged President Saddam Hussein to believe there would be little outcry if he turned the same weapons against his own citizens.

2. The annual sessions of the Commission on Human Rights in February and March and the Sub-Commission on Prevention of Discrimination and Protection of Minorities in August are the major events in the UN calendar of human rights discussions. The workings of these two UN bodies are described in Chapter 12.

3. Other UN-related bodies and procedures where human rights violations in Iraq have been considered are the Special Rapporteur on torture, the Working Group on arbitrary detention, the confidential 1503 procedure of the Commission on Human Rights, and the Human Rights Committee established under the International Covenant on Civil and Political Rights in its consideration of Iraq's periodic reports under the Covenant. In particular, "disappearances" and extrajudicial executions in Iraq have been taken up by the thematic mechanisms which report to the Commission on Human Rights, notably the Special Rapporteur on extrajudicial, summary or arbitrary executions and the Working Group on Enforced or Involuntary Disappearances. The latter has taken up the largest number of cases, many of which remain unresolved. Sadly, these cases represent only a tiny fraction of the actual number of "disappearances" perpetrated in Iraq. It was interesting to note that in the Working Group's report to the 1992 session of the Commission on Human Rights, Sri Lanka was said to have the highest number of "disappearances" of any country in the world, 12,000 such cases having been recorded since 1983 by the Working Group, which visited the country in 1991. Should the Working Group ever gain access to Iraq, its members would find that 12,000 "disappearances" represent the average for a "good" year there.

4. Morocco itself had been eliminating real or suspected dissidents through "disappearance" (see Chapter 6).

5. The proposal was published as Amnesty International, "The need for further United Nations action to protect human rights in Iraq", AI Index: MDE 14/06/91, 15 July 1991.

6. UN Commission on Human Rights, *Report on the situation of human rights in Iraq, prepared by Mr. Max van der Stoel, Special Rapporteur...*, UN document No. E/CN.4/1992/31, 18 February 1992, paragraph 156.

7. *Ibid.*, paragraph 157.

Chapter 2   Sri Lanka: "Disappearance" and murder as techniques of
                   counter-insurgency

1. In 1979, for example, there was an isolated incident of killings and "disappearances" days after a state of emergency had been declared in the Jaffna district. The mutilated bodies of two young Tamil men who had been arrested by police the day before were found near a bridge. Three other young men who had also been arrested that day "disappeared".

The government established a Parliamentary Select Committee to investigate. The report, which was only made public four years later, concluded that in at least two of the cases there was evidence that the men had been taken to a police station. The Committee recommended that a special team of investigators be appointed. Instead, the government ordered the police to investigate themselves, and the police found no evidence of the men's whereabouts. One of the police officers named in the inquest into the death of one of the victims was later promoted.

The chairman of the Committee later became Minister of Internal Security. Violations committed during his term of office failed to be investigated.

2. For the recommendations, see Amnesty International, "Sri Lanka – the Northeast; Human rights violations in a context of armed conflict", AI Index: ASA 37/14/91, September 1991.

3. The Working Group visited Sri Lanka in both 1991 and 1992. The Special Rapporteur has yet to take up his invitation.

4. These findings are documented in Amnesty International, "Sri Lanka; An assessment of the human rights situation", AI Index: ASA 37/1/93, February 1993.

Chapter 3   Columbia: Stratregies for evading accountability

1. Although the Colombian authorities described the "death squads" as independent groups of right-wing extremists over which they had no control, their true characteristics soon became apparent. In 1980 five army officers formerly attached to the *Batallón de Inteligencia y Contra-Inteligencia "Charry Solano"*, the Colombian army's chief military intelligence group, wrote to Amnesty International giving details of a clandestine assassination unit operating from within the battalion. The five alleged that they had been ordered by the intelligence battalion to torture political detainees and they named battalion personnel who had been detailed to serve as a "terrorist group" called the Triple A which had recently murdered several members of the political opposition and bombed three Bogotá periodicals.

2. On entering a civilian community in an area of guerrilla activity, army patrols take a census of inhabitants in which community leaders and political activists are identified. Paramilitary forces which arrive in the wake of the army have in their possession the list of activists; many

have subsequently been forced to leave their homes and land, while others have been killed.

3. Before entering civilian communities, counter-insurgency units of the armed forces regularly disguise themselves as guerrillas with the intention of identifying and eliminating guerilla sympathizers among the local population.

4. Before 1991 in those cases in which civilian court judges challenged the military courts' right to jurisdiction, the conflict was resolved by either the Disciplinary Tribunal or the Supreme Court of Justice. Both the Colombian Constitution and the Code of Military Justice establish a special military jurisdiction for offences committed by members of the Colombian armed forces "in connection with military duty". In the 1991 Constitution military jurisdiction was extended to the national police. The contrasting interpretation placed on the concept of "in connection with military duty" has led to contradictory resolutions in jurisdictional conflicts. With the introduction of the new Constitution in 1991 the resolution of jurisdictional conflicts was assumed by a new body, the Supreme Council of the Judiciary.

5. In 1990 two army officers and six civilian members of a paramilitary organization were convicted of killing 12 members of a civilian judicial commission of inquiry in 1989 in La Rochela, Santander department. The two officers were sentenced to eight and 12 years' imprisonment respectively for "aiding and abetting terrorist activities" after the court found them guilty of providing information and weapons to the paramilitary group which carried out the killings. One officer escaped from the army battalion headquarters where he was being held shortly before the trial ended; later, both officers' convictions were overturned on appeal.

6. In April 1992 a representative of the Colombian Government told members of the Human Rights Committee set up under the International Covenant on Civil and Political Rights that more than 200 police agents had been dismissed in recent months for human rights violations.

Chapter 4   **Zimbabwe: Drawing a line through the past**

1. Quoted in Ken Flower, *Serving Secretly; An Intelligence Chief on Record; Rhodesia into Zimbabwe; 1964 to 1981*, John Murray, London, 1987, page 3.

2. At this stage ZANU and ZAPU were linked in an alliance known as the Patriotic Front (PF). At independence the Patriotic Front broke up and the two organizations contested the elections separately. ZANU (PF) – as it became known – won a majority of seats and formed the government, with a minority of ZAPU ministers. Most ZAPU ministers were dismissed in 1982 with the worsening of political tensions. In December 1987 the two parties agreed to unite and now form the government under the name of ZANU (PF).

3. Quoted in David Martin and Phyllis Johnson, *The Struggle for Zimbabwe; The Chimurenga War*, Faber and Faber, London, 1981, page 241.

4. Joseph Lelyveld, *Move Your Shadow; South Africa, Black and White*, Times Books, New York, 1985, page 213.

5. Speech of 16 July 1986, cited in G. Feltoe, *A Guide to Zimbabwean Cases Relating to Security, Emergency Powers and Unlawful Arrest and Detention*, Legal Resources Foundation, Harare, 1988, page 8.

6. This indemnity does not apply to civil proceedings for compensation and is therefore not affected by the Supreme Court ruling in the Granger case.

7. There were widespread allegations that the charges had been fabricated by police personnel who were themselves involved in elephant poaching and eventually the charges were dropped.

8. The legacy of Rhodesian human rights violations was not confined within Zimbabwe's borders. Many Rhodesian personnel left the country at independence and placed themselves beyond the reach of Zimbabwean law. A proper truth-telling might have inhibited further abuses. Many ex-Rhodesians ended up in the service of the South African state, some actively engaged in subverting Zimbabwe's security. Others found employment with the nominally independent black "homelands" within South Africa. Among the most prominent, Ron Reid-Daley, head of the Selous Scouts who were responsible for gross abuses including the Nyadzonia massacre, became commander of the Transkei Defence Force. Many other Rhodesians also found senior positions in the Transkei security apparatus. During Reid-Daley's period in Transkei there were frequent reports of armed attacks on neighbouring Lesotho by the South African-backed Lesotho Liberation Army and the Transkei Defence Force itself. Rhodesia also bequeathed to South Africa an entire institution dedicated to the abuse of human rights – RENAMO, *Resistência Nacional Moçambicana*, Mozambique National Resistance. The Rhodesian CIO created RENAMO in the mid-1970s as a means of countering ZANLA, the military wing of ZANU, which operated from rear bases inside Mozambique. The organization grew into a fully fledged opposition to the Mozambican Government and engaged in widespread killing, mutilation and enslavement of that country's rural population. RENAMO was initially recruited from among the Shona-speaking Ndau, who straddle the Zimbabwe-Mozambique border. At Zimbabwean independence in 1980 control of RENAMO "was transferred lock, stock and barrel" to the South African military, according to its creator, Ken Flower, who became Robert Mugabe's trusted security adviser. Flower later wrote: "I began to wonder whether we had created a monster that was now beyond control." (Flower, *op. cit.*, pages 261-2)

9. In 1984 Operation Turkey, a counter-insurgency tactic inherited from the Rhodesian army, was revived by the Fifth Brigade in Matabeleland South, then in the grip of a three-year drought. As before, food supplies were destroyed, shops closed and food confiscated from travellers. A strict curfew was imposed and curfew breakers were shot. There were reports that food relief was only supplied to those who produced a ZANU (PF) party card.

10. Probably the reason why they were charged in the first place was that one of their four victims was an off-duty army officer, Lieutenant Edias Ndlovu. The inquest had found that "the deceased were tied with pieces of fibre, were got down on the ground and repeatedly stabbed with bayonets, much as a hunter slaughtering a wounded animal with a spear."

11. This and the preceding quotations are from interviews carried out by Bill Berkeley, Zimbabwe, 1988.

12. Dozens – possibly hundreds – of people "disappeared" in Matabeleland and Midlands in the space of a few weeks in January and February 1985. Most were abducted at night by armed men driving vehicles without registration plates. The victims were overwhelmingly Ndebele-speaking – although Midlands has a mixed population of Shona and Ndebele-speakers – and many were local ZAPU officials. The government alleged that the "disappeared" had slipped across the border to Botswana to join the "dissidents". Quite aside from the inherent improbabilities in this account – many of the "disappeared" were elderly and there are no reported instances of "dissidents" driving vehicles – it remains a fact that when the amnesty for "dissidents" was

declared in 1988 not a single person reappeared of those who had gone missing in January and February 1985.

Chapter 5	Turkey: Responses to an emerging pattern of extrajudicial executions

1. Since June 1991, 43 people have been killed in a succession of police operations against safe houses of Devrimci Sol (Revolutionary Left – Turkey's principal urban guerrilla organization). These raids were marked by a high mortality rate and considerable evidence suggesting that the police were shooting to kill without giving a warning or an opportunity to surrender.

Chapter 7	The anatomy of the atrocities

1. For a discussion of the definition of the term "disappearance", see *'Disappearances'; A Workbook*, Amnesty International USA, New York, 1981, Chapter VII. See also the description in the third paragraph of the UN Declaration on Disappearances, reproduced in Appendix 6 of this report.

2. The UN Working Group on Enforced or Involuntary Disappearances ("Working Group on Disappearances") has drawn attention to the wide circle of victims caused by a "disappearance":

> "Family members and other relatives or dependants suffer the immediate consequences of a disappearance. Not only are they subjected to agonizing uncertainty about what happened to their parent, child or spouse, but in many cases also economic hardship and social alienation may be part of their sorry lot. The psychological effects on children are found to be severe, even devastating at times. Children born during the captivity of their disappeared mothers constitute a category all by themselves." (WGEID, 1990 report, paragraph 339)

3. As in Article 2 of the European Convention on Human Rights, the use of the death penalty can be described as the execution of a death sentence imposed by a court on a prisoner convicted of a crime for which this penalty is provided by law. International human rights instruments and the international humanitarian law of armed conflict set forth standards to be followed in all death penalty cases, including norms for a fair trial (see *When the State Kills... The Death Penalty v. Human Rights*, Amnesty International Publications, London, 1989). As was noted in Amnesty International's first general report on extrajudicial executions,

> "When a government lives up to these standards in imposing a death sentence, the execution is not extrajudicial. However, in some cases governments have formally imposed the death penalty but failed to comply with the procedural safeguards prescribed in international law. In such cases, the government has clearly violated international law, and has illegally and arbitrarily deprived a person of his or her life.
>
> "Whether such cases constitute extrajudicial executions, however, is more difficult to decide. The spectrum ranges from cases with only a single procedural defect to those with such pervasively defective procedures that the accused can be said to have had a trial in name only. There are strong arguments for excluding all such

cases from the category of extrajudicial executions. The existence of judicial procedures must be recognized as positive, no matter how defective they may be. International legal standards exist against which the procedures may be judged and pressure can be exerted on a government if it fails to live up to those standards. Institutional structures for dealing with such cases in the country may improve as a result. If, on the other hand, rudimentary or inadequate procedures are dismissed and the resultant executions included in a broad category with government killings where no procedures have been followed, the opportunity to build on and improve existing procedural structures has been lost."

(*Political Killings by Governments*, Amnesty International Publications, London, 1983, pages 89-90)

4. For example, in July 1993 Amnesty International wrote to the leader of Serb forces in Bosnia-Herzegovina expressing concern about reports of the deliberate and arbitrary killing on 12 July of 12 people waiting in a queue to collect water in the Dobrinja district of Sarajevo. On the basis of press reports there appeared to be little doubt that the group of unarmed citizens queuing for water was deliberately targeted and that they were the victims of a mortar shell fired from Serbian positions several hundred yards away.

5. Inter-American Court of Human Rights, Series C, Decisions and Judgments, No. 4, *Velásquez Rodríguez Case; Judgment of July 29, 1988*, Secretariat of the Court, San José, Costa Rica, 1988, paragraph 150.

6. *Political Killings by Governments*, pages 23-24, 34-38.

7. For examples of deliberate and arbitrary killings by armed opposition groups, see below and Chapter 13, section 5.

Chapter 8   **"Disappearances" and extrajudicial executions as violations of
                     international human rights**

1. Charter of the United Nations, Articles 55-56. Article 1 of the Charter establishes that one of the purposes of the UN is "(t)o achieve international co-operation ... in promoting and encouraging respect for human rights".

2. Universal Declaration, Preamble.

3. "Everyone is entitled to all the rights and freedoms set forth in this Declaration..." (Universal Declaration, Article 2).

4. Article 8 of the Universal Declaration of Human Rights proclaims the right of everyone to an effective remedy before the national courts for violations of such fundamental rights as have been "granted him by the constitution or by law". The International Covenant on Civil and Political Rights goes further by providing for the right to an effective remedy for violations of the internationally recognized human rights set forth in the Covenant. See below, section 8.

5. The provisions of the Universal Declaration and other international instruments relating to "disappearances" and extrajudicial executions are reproduced in the appendices to this chapter. The texts of the Universal Declaration and the two International Covenants are widely available; they are reproduced, for example, in "The International Bill of Human Rights", *Human Rights Fact Sheets* series, No. 2, UN Centre for Human Rights, Geneva, 1988, and in UN Centre for

Human Rights, *Human Rights; A Compilation of International Instruments*, UN Sales No. E.88.XIV.1, United Nations, New York, 1988.

6. As Nigel S. Rodley has written, "assaults on the inherent dignity of human beings were recognized as being relevant to the stability of the international order" in the linking of references to the determination of the peoples of the United Nations "(t)o save succeeding generations from the scourge of war" and "to reaffirm faith in fundamental human rights". Rodley points out that after the Second World War "It became clear to the Allied Powers who founded the United Nations that no peace could be secure where governments were free to break and obliterate their own people. Where there is no restraint at home, no limit to the exercise of official power, there need be none such abroad either. And law could not just rest at addressing the behaviour of a state beyond its frontiers. International law could no longer just be the law regulating behaviour between states, it had also to concern itself with what went on within them." Nigel S. Rodley, *The Treatment of Prisoners under International Law*, UNESCO, Paris, Clarendon Press, Oxford, 1987, pages 1-2.

7. In this report, the term "international instrument" refers to documents setting forth rules of behaviour which have been officially adopted by the UN or other intergovernmental organizations such as the Organization of American States or the Council of Europe. They range from resolutions *recommending* certain behaviour to treaties which *require* states parties to comply with them. The term "international standard" is used in this report to refer to the rules of behaviour contained in international instruments.

8. The two International Covenants entered into force in 1976.

9. An important related treaty is the first Optional Protocol to the Covenant which provides for individuals to submit complaints to the Human Rights Committee of violations of the rights set forth in the Covenant. These and other mechanisms for the international enforcement of human rights are described in Chapter 12. As of 2 September 1993, 120 states were parties to the International Covenant and 74 were parties to the first Optional Protocol. Amnesty International regularly urges all states to become parties to the Covenant and the first Optional Protocol, as well as to its second Optional Protocol, which provides for the abolition of the death penalty.

10. While most of the leading instruments on human rights have emerged through the UN Commission on Human Rights, several important instruments including the Principles on Extra-Legal, Arbitrary and Summary Executions have been developed by UN bodies responsible for criminal justice matters – the former Committee on Crime Prevention and Control and the quinquennial Congresses on the Prevention of Crime and the Treatment of Offenders. The Congresses bring together police and prison officials, prosecutors, judges and other national officials dealing with criminal justice, as well as non-governmental organizations. Human rights instruments adopted through these bodies can be considered to have the backing, not only of governments, but more specifically of the officials who are professionally responsible in their countries for seeing that the law is carried out. (For more information on the UN criminal justice program and its work on human rights, see Manuel Lopez-Rey, *A Guide to United Nations Criminal Policy*, Cambridge Studies in Criminology, No. 54, Gower, Aldershot, UK and Brookfield, Vermont, USA, 1985; Rodley, *op. cit.*)

The initiative for the drafting and adoption of the Principles on Extra-Legal, Arbitrary and Summary Executions came from non-governmental organizations, particularly the Minnesota

Lawyers International Human Rights Committee, which had developed a model protocol for the investigation of suspected extrajudicial executions. Amnesty International contributed suggestions on measures for the prevention of extrajudicial executions. The background to the development of the Principles is described in UN Centre for Social Development and Humanitarian Affairs, *Manual on the Effective Prevention and Investigation of Extra-Legal, Arbitrary and Summary Executions*, United Nations, New York, 1991, UN Sales No. E.91.IV.I. The text of the Principles and other important standards for the investigation of suspected extrajudicial executions is reproduced in the *Manual.*

11. "Disappearances" are usually referred to in UN texts as "enforced disappearances" (or "enforced or involuntary disappearances" in earlier texts).

12. The initiative for the Declaration came from a number of non-governmental organizations which believed there was a strong need for an international instrument to address specifically this grave form of human rights violation. The Declaration was drafted by the Working Group on Detention of the Sub-Commission on Prevention of Discrimination and Protection of Minorities. The Working Group on Disappearances contributed suggestions. The fact that the Declaration was adopted by the General Assembly without a vote is a sign of strong agreement, in that no UN member state wanted to go on record as opposing it.

13. Article 1 of the Declaration on Disappearances states that any act of enforced disappearance "is condemned as a grave and flagrant violation of the human rights and fundamental freedoms proclaimed in the Universal Declaration of Human Rights..." The 1989 UN resolution whereby the Principles on Extra-Legal, Arbitrary and Summary Executions were adopted states that "...extra-legal, arbitrary and summary executions contravene the human rights and fundamental freedoms proclaimed in the Universal Declaration of Human Rights" (Economic and Social Council resolution 1989/85 of 24 May 1989 on the effective prevention and investigation of extra-legal, arbitrary and summary executions).

14. In that the victim is executed without any judicial proceedings, he or she can be said to have been deprived of the right to a fair and public trial as provided in the Universal Declaration of Human Rights, Article 10. More broadly, an extrajudicial execution entails the violation of all human rights, since a person deprived of the right to life is no longer able to exercise any other right.

15. These rights are cited in Article 1 of the Declaration on Disappearances. The Declaration also cites the right to recognition as a person before the law. Like the right to life and the right not to be subjected to torture or to cruel, inhuman or degrading treatment or punishment, the right to recognition as a person before the law may never be derogated from under the International Covenant on Civil and Political Rights (see below, section 4).

The UN Working Group on Disappearances has stated that "enforced or involuntary disappearances constitute the most comprehensive denial of human rights of our time." (1990 report, paragraph 338) The Working Group has pointed out that "practically all basic human rights of a disappeared person are infringed in one way or another following an abduction. ... Likewise, the Working Group has drawn attention to the wide circle of victims caused by a disappearance." (*ibid.*, paragraph 339)

16. One scholar, in a discussion of the meaning of "arbitrary" deprivation of life, has proposed four principles which can be invoked to assess claims that a deprivation of life is justified under

international standards. First, the deprivation must purport to have a legal basis; second, it must be a proportionate response in the circumstances; third, the question of justification of a deprivation of life must be subject to an independent judicial process; fourth, deprivation of life may be justified only in defence of life. C.K. Boyle, "The Concept of Arbitrary Deprivation of Life", in B.J. Ramcharan, ed., *The Right to Life in International Law*, Nijhoff, Dordrecht, the Netherlands, 1985, pages 221-244.

17. International safeguards and restrictions on the death penalty are set forth in Article 6 of the International Covenant and in the Safeguards Guaranteeing Protection of the Rights of Those Facing the Death Penalty, adopted by the UN Economic and Social Council in 1984 (reproduced in *Human Rights; A Compilation of International Instruments, op. cit.*). However, Amnesty International holds that the death penalty itself violates the right to life as well as the right not to be subjected to torture or cruel, inhuman or degrading treatment or punishment. See *When the State Kills...* , cited in Chapter 7. Article 6 of the International Covenant, while not prohibiting the death penalty, states that "Nothing in this article shall be invoked to delay or to prevent" the abolition of the death penalty.

18. According to the Proclamation of Teheran, adopted and proclaimed by the International Conference on Human Rights, convened by the UN in Iran in 1968, "The Universal Declaration of Human Rights states a common understanding of the peoples of the world concerning the inalienable and inviolable rights of all members of the human family and *constitutes an obligation for the members of the international community*" (emphasis added; for the text of the Proclamation of Teheran, see *Human Rights; A Compilation of International Instruments*). Moreover, the fact that the Universal Declaration has been accepted by so many states gives it considerable moral and political weight. The provisions of the Universal Declaration have been cited as the justification for numerous UN actions and have inspired or been used in many international conventions and national constitutions and laws. See "The International Bill of Human Rights", *op. cit.*, pages 8, 16-20; also "Human Rights; Questions and Answers", UN Department of Public Information, New York, 1987.

19. See Chapter 12, sections 4, 5.

20. Declaration on Disappearances, Article 7; Principles on Extra-Legal, Arbitrary and Summary Executions, principle 1.

21. The text of the Code of Conduct for Law Enforcement Officials is reproduced in *Human Rights; A Compilation of International Instruments*. Article 3 and the Commentary to it are reproduced in Appendix 4 of this report.

22. For further discussion of international standards on the use of force by law enforcement officials, see *Political Killings by Governments, op. cit.*, pages 90-92; Rodley, *op. cit.*, pages 148-152, 282.

The Basic Principles also contain valuable provisions on the issuing of firearms and on controls over their use. See Appendices 5 for the text of the Basic Principles.

23. The link between the disproportionate use of force and the arbitrary character of a killing was established by the Human Rights Committee set up under the International Covenant on Civil and Political Rights in the case of *Guerrero (Camargo) v. Colombia* (45/1979). The case concerned a woman who was one of seven people shot dead by police in a house in Colombia in 1978. In its decision issued in 1982 the Committee found that the police action "was apparently

taken without warning to the victims and without giving them any opportunity to surrender...",
and it found "no evidence that the action of the police was necessary in their own defence or
that of others, or that it was necessary to effect the arrest or prevent the escape of the persons
concerned". The Committee concluded that the police action "was disproportionate to the
requirements of law enforcement in the circumstances of the case and that she was arbitrarily
deprived of her life contrary to article 6 (1)" of the International Covenant. (Human Rights
Committee, 1982 report, Annex XI, paragraphs 13.2, 13.3; Rodley, *op. cit.*, pages 149-150)

24. This identical language appears in the First Geneva Convention, Article 50, the Second
Geneva Convention, Article 51, and the Third Geneva Convention, Article 130. The Fourth
Geneva Convention, Article 147, contains the same text with the additional word "present"
before the word "Convention" ("... protected by the present Convention").

25. Like the Universal Declaration of Human Rights, the Geneva Conventions of 1949 were an
outgrowth of the horrors of the Second World War. Additional Protocol I of 1977 develops the
protection of victims of international armed conflicts, while Additional Protocol II develops
and supplements the provisions for the protection of victims of internal armed conflicts
contained in common Article 3 of the Geneva Conventions.

For an account of the development of international humanitarian law and its philosophical
basis, see Geoffrey Best, *Humanity in Warfare; The Modern History of the International Law of
Armed Conflicts*, Weidenfeld and Nicolson, London, 1980. For an introduction to the Geneva
Conventions and Additional Protocols, see Frits Kalshoven, *Constraints on the Waging of War*,
International Committee of the Red Cross, Geneva, 1987.

26. The death penalty is not excluded, but its use is surrounded by stringent restrictions and
safeguards, including a six months' delay in the carrying out of a death sentence. The provisions
of the Geneva Conventions and the Additional Protocols relating to the death penalty are
reproduced in *When the State Kills...*, *op. cit.*, Appendix 6, pages 247-249.

27. "Grave breaches" of the Geneva Conventions are war crimes. See below, section 5.

28. The "disappearance" of a prisoner of war would violate various provisions of the Third
Geneva Convention, including the prisoner's right to notify his or her family and the Central
Prisoners of War Agency (in practice, the Central Tracing Agency of the International
Committee of the Red Cross, located in Geneva) immediately upon capture or transfer to
another camp (Article 70), the right of correspondence (Article 71), and – ultimately – provisions
for the prisoner's release and repatriation after the cessation of active hostilities (Article 118).
The "disappearance" of a civilian protected by the Fourth Geneva Convention would probably
be considered "unlawful confinement" and possibly also "unlawful deportation or transfer",
constituting a grave breach of the Convention (Rodley, *op. cit.*, page 198). (The scope of transfers
prohibited in the Fourth Geneva Convention is enlarged in Article 85 of Additional Protocol I
of 1977.) Other acts prohibited in the Geneva Conventions may also be involved in cases of
"disappearances", including "wilful killing, torture or inhuman treatment", which are forbidden
as grave breaches of the four Conventions. If these provisions did not suffice, "disappearances"
as well as extrajudicial executions would be banned under Article 1, paragraph 2 of Additional
Protocol I: "In cases not covered by this Protocol or by other international agreements, civilians
and combatants remain under the protection and authority of the principles of international
law derived from established custom, from the principles of humanity and from the dictates of
public conscience."

236

29. The notion of "non-international" or internal armed conflict typically applies to armed confrontations between governmental armed forces and organized, armed opposition groups which occur exclusively within the territory of a particular state. Such conflicts also include those in which two or more armed factions within a country engage in hostilities without the involvement of governmental forces, such as when the established government has dissolved or is too weak to intervene.

30. Persons protected by common Article 3 include wounded, sick or captured combatants as well as civilians taking no active part in the hostilities.

31. Virtually all states are parties to the Geneva Conventions, and the majority are parties to the Additional Protocols. As of 15 June 1993, 181 states were parties to the Conventions, 125 to Additional Protocol I and 116 to Additional Protocol II. (A list of states parties to the Conventions and the Additional Protocols is published each year in the Annual Report of the International Committee of the Red Cross (ICRC), available from the ICRC in Geneva.) UN bodies have cited the Conventions and Additional Protocols and have urged states to ratify or be guided by them. See "International Humanitarian Law and Human Rights", *Human Rights Fact Sheets* series, No. 13, UN Centre for Human Rights, Geneva, 1988.

32. Under Article 4 of the International Covenant on Civil and Political Rights, states parties may derogate from certain obligations under the Covenant "(i)n time of public emergency which threatens the life of the nation", but no derogation is permitted from Article 6, which provides for the right to life and prohibits the arbitrary deprivation of life; from Article 7, prohibiting torture and cruel, inhuman and degrading treatment or punishment; or from Article 16, guaranteeing the right to recognition as a person before the law. Under the European Convention on Human Rights and the American Convention on Human Rights, the right to life, the right not to be tortured and certain other rights are non-derogable. (The African Charter on Human and People's Rights does not have a provision for derogation.) Furthermore, the UN has adopted resolutions affirming that fundamental human rights must be respected in situations of armed conflict.

33. A crime in any of these categories is a crime under international law. Different bodies of international law designate various crimes as crimes under international law and specify how they should be prosecuted.

34. The Convention on the Non-Applicability of Statutory Limitations to War Crimes and Crimes against Humanity, adopted by the UN General Assembly in resolution 2391 (XXIII) of 26 November 1968, provides that no statutory limitation shall apply to war crimes or crimes against humanity as defined in the Convention, or to genocide as defined in the Convention on the Prevention and Punishment of the Crime of Genocide. The text of the Convention on the Non-Applicability of Statutory Limitations is reproduced in *Human Rights; A Compilation of International Instruments.*

35. The Declaration on Territorial Asylum, adopted by the UN General Assembly in resolution 2312 (XXII) of 14 December 1967, states: "The right to seek and to enjoy asylum may not be invoked by any person with respect to whom there are serious reasons for considering that he has committed a crime against peace, a war crime or a crime against humanity..." Similarly, the 1951 UN Convention relating to the Status of Refugees excludes from the category of refugees covered by the Convention "any person with respect to whom there are serious reasons for

considering that: (a) He has committed a crime against peace, a war crime, or a crime against humanity..." The texts of these two instruments are reproduced in *Human Rights; A Compilation of International Instruments.*

36. On crimes against humanity, there are provisions for cooperation between states in the Principles of International Co-operation in the Detection, Arrest, Extradition and Punishment of Persons Guilty of War Crimes and Crimes against Humanity adopted by the UN General Assembly in resolution 3074 (XXVIII) of 3 December 1973 (the text is reproduced in *Human Rights; A Compilation of International Instruments*). The Principles state that the alleged perpetrators shall "as a general rule" be tried "in the countries in which they committed those crimes", but they do not exclude trial in another country.

37. This principle was established in Article 8 of the Charter of the Nuremberg Tribunal. For further discussion of the legal consequences of "disappearances" and extrajudicial executions under international law, see Rodley, *op. cit.*, pages 154-158, 205-207.

38. The Geneva Conventions have special provisions regarding the crimes designated as "grave breaches" of the conventions. States parties to the Conventions are required to provide effective penal sanctions in law for these crimes, to "search for persons" alleged to have committed or ordered them, and to bring the alleged offenders, regardless of nationality, before their own courts or to hand them over for trial to another state party (Kalshoven, *op. cit.*, page 68). In other words, grave breaches of the Geneva Conventions are subject to universal jurisdiction – the possibility of bringing those responsible to justice wherever they are.

39. The Convention on the Non-Applicability of Statutory Limitations to War Crimes and Crimes against Humanity applies to crimes against humanity "whether committed in time of war or in time of peace as they are defined in the Charter of the International Military Tribunal, Nürnberg, of 8 August 1945 and confirmed by resolutions 3 (I) of 13 February 1946 and 95 (I) of 11 December 1946 of the General Assembly". Thus, in adopting this Convention, the General Assembly expressly recognized as a principle of international law that crimes against humanity could be committed in peacetime.

Although the above-mentioned International Military Tribunal interpreted its jurisdiction over crimes against humanity under its Charter to extend only to crimes committed during time of war, nothing in the Charter, the Judgment of the Tribunal or the two 1946 UN General Assembly resolutions endorsing the principles of law established in the Charter and the Judgment of the Tribunal should be read to suggest that crimes against humanity cannot be committed during peacetime. Other military tribunals set up after the Second World War under Allied Control Council Law No. 10 to try Axis defendants convicted some of them for crimes against humanity committed before the Second World War. Furthermore, international conventions against *apartheid* and genocide, both of which are considered crimes against humanity, apply to acts committed during peacetime as well as wartime.

40. The 1968 Convention on the Non-Applicability of Statutory Limitations to War Crimes and Crimes against Humanity includes genocide and inhuman acts resulting from *apartheid* in the list of crimes against humanity. See also M. Cherif Bassiouni, *Crimes against Humanity in International Law*, Nijhoff, Dordrecht, the Netherlands, 1992.

According to the UN Secretary-General's report on the legal basis for establishing an international war crimes tribunal for the former Yugoslavia, "Crimes against humanity refer to inhumane acts of a very serious nature, such as wilful killing, torture or rape, committed as part of a widespread or systematic attack against any civilian population on national, political, ethnic, racial or religious grounds. In the conflict in the territory of the former Yugoslavia, such inhumane acts have taken the form of so-called 'ethnic cleansing' and widespread and systematic rape and other forms of sexual assault including enforced prostitution." (UN Security Council, *Report of the Secretary-General pursuant to paragraph 2 of Security Council resolution 808 (1993)*, UN document No. S/25704, 3 May 1993, paragraph 48)

The Statute of the International Tribunal on war crimes in the former Yugoslavia, as set forth in the same document (paragraph 49) and approved by the Security Council in resolution 827 of 25 May 1993, lists under the heading *Crimes against humanity* "the following crimes when committed in armed conflict, whether international or internal in character, and directed against any civilian population: (a) murder; (b) extermination; (c) enslavement; (d) deportation; (e) imprisonment; (f) torture; (g) rape; (h) persecutions on political, racial and religious grounds; (i) other inhumane acts."

41. In a resolution adopted on 17 November 1983, the General Assembly of the Organization of American States declared that "the practice of the forced disappearance of persons in the Americas .... constitutes a crime against humanity" (Resolution 666 (XIII-0/83) on the Annual Report of the Inter-American Commission on Human Rights). This position was supported by the Parliamentary Assembly of the Council of Europe, which in resolution 828 adopted on 26 September 1984 called for the adoption of a UN declaration recognizing enforced disappearances as a crime against humanity. However, the final text of the UN Declaration on Disappearances goes only so far as to say that the systematic practice of enforced disappearances is "of the nature of" a crime against humanity.

42. Convention on the Non-Applicability of Statutory Limitations to War Crimes and Crimes against Humanity, Article I (b).

43. One weakness of the Genocide Convention is that political and other groups are not included among the listed categories of potential victims. For an account of the drafting of the Convention, see Leo Kuper, *Genocide*, Penguin Books, London, 1981.

44. Security Council resolution 827 (1993), adopted unanimously on 25 May 1993. The categories of crimes covered by the Tribunal are set forth in Articles 2-5 of the Tribunal's Statute as approved by the Security Council (*Report of the Secretary-General...*, *op. cit.*, S/25704). Amnesty International has made a series of recommendations aimed at enabling the Tribunal to carry out its task fairly and effectively. See Amnesty International, "Memorandum to the United Nations: The question of justice and fairness in the international war crimes tribunal for the former Yugoslavia", AI Index: EUR 48/02/93, April 1993. In Amnesty International's view, the Tribunal should be a step towards establishing a permanent international criminal court able to try cases involving gross violations of human rights and the international humanitarian law of armed conflict wherever they occur (see Chapter 12, section 11).

45. Two other regional intergovernmental organizations have begun drafting human rights instruments. The League of Arab States is drafting an Arab Charter on Human Rights in the form of a treaty with a supervisory body, but it has not yet been adopted. The Organization of the Islamic Conference has drafted the Cairo Declaration of Human Rights in Islam, which is a declaration of principles rather than a legally binding treaty. It has been approved at the foreign

minister level but has not been approved at the head of state level. Both instruments in their current form would provide significantly less protection for human rights than other regional and international instruments.

46. The regional organizations corresponding to these treaties are the Council of Europe, the Organization of American States (OAS) and the Organization of African Unity (OAU). All states belonging to the Council of Europe either are parties to the European Convention on Human Rights (having ratified or acceded to it) or have signed it, indicating their intention to become parties. As of mid-May 1993, 24 member states of the OAS had ratified or acceded to the American Convention on Human Rights and 49 OAU member states were parties to the African Charter on Human and Peoples' Rights.

47. "Disappearances" and extrajudicial executions are also forbidden under the American Declaration of the Rights and Duties of Man. Article 1 of the American Declaration states: "Every human being has the right to life, liberty and the security of his person." The Declaration was adopted in 1948 at the international conference in Bogotá which created the Organization of American States (OAS). The rights set forth in it are normative standards for all OAS member states whether or not they are parties to the American Convention on Human Rights.

48. For the text of this resolution, see 'Disappearances'; A Workbook, op. cit., Appendix, pages 167-168.

49. See Chapter 12, section 5.

Chapter 9   **Prevention**

1. The passages quoted are from paragraphs 174 and 166 respectively. The *Velásquez Rodríguez* judgment is cited in Chapter 7.

2. See Chapter 8, section 8.

3. In the case of Manfredo Velásquez Rodríguez, who "disappeared" in Honduras in 1981, the Inter-American Court of Human Rights ruled that the right to physical integrity and the right of detainees to treatment respectful of their human dignity as provided under the American Convention on Human Rights "require States Parties [to the Convention] to take reasonable steps to prevent situations which are truly harmful to the rights protected" (paragraph 187). Similarly, the right to life and the right not to have one's life taken arbitrarily "imply an obligation on the part of States Parties to take reasonable steps to prevent situations that could result in the violation of that right" (paragraph 188). The *Velásquez Rodríguez* judgment is discussed further in Chapter 11.

The obligation to prevent "disappearances" and extrajudicial executions is implied also in a decision of the Human Rights Committee set up under the International Covenant on Civil and Political Rights in the case of *Herrera Rubio v. Colombia*. The decision concerned José Herrera and Emma Rubio de Herrera, who "disappeared" in Colombia in March 1981 and were killed soon after. The case was brought by their son. The Committee found that Colombia had violated Article 6 of the International Covenant because it had not taken appropriate measures to prevent the "disappearance" and killing of the two and had not conducted an effective investigation into the responsibility for the killings. (Human Rights Committee, 1988 report, Chapter VII.B)

4. The responsibility of superior authorities to prevent extrajudicial executions is laid down in

240

principle 19 of the UN Principles on Extra-legal, Arbitrary and Summary Executions. It has been incorporated also in the Statute of the International Tribunal on war crimes in the former Yugoslavia. See Chapter 11, section 5.

5. See below, section 12. Several of the safeguards described in this chapter have been included as rights which should never be suspended, even in time of emergency, in the initial draft Guidelines for the Development of Legislation on States of Emergency prepared by the Special Rapporteur on states of emergency of the UN Sub-Commission on Prevention of Discrimination and Protection of Minorities. In his fourth report, the Special Rapporteur proposed that such legislation

> "should provide that nothing done pursuant to a state of emergency may affect the following rights:
>
> (a) No person deprived of liberty for whatever reason shall be denied of the following:
>
> > (i) the right to be informed of the reasons for detention promptly and in writing, in a language which he or she understands;
> > (ii) the right to have his or her family informed of the detention without delay, and to receive visits;
> > (iii) the right of prompt and regular access to a lawyer of his or her choice;
> > (iv) the right to challenge the legality of the deprivation of liberty before a court of law by *habeas corpus* or other prompt and effective remedy."
>
> (UN Sub-Commission on Prevention of Discrimination and Protection of Minorities, *The administration of justice and the human rights of detainees: Question of human rights and states of emergency; Fourth annual report...presented by Mr Leandro Despouy, Special Rapporteur...*, UN document No. E/CN.4/Sub.2/1991/28, 24 June 1991, Annex I, article 8)

6. For example:

Colombia: "No one shall be subjected to enforced disappearance, torture, or cruel, inhuman or degrading treatment or punishment." – Constitution of Colombia, 1991, Article 12.

Paraguay: "No one shall be subjected to torture or to cruel, inhuman or degrading treatment or punishment. Genocide, torture, enforced disappearance and politically motivated kidnapping and murder are not subject to a statute of limitations." – Constitution of Paraguay, 1992, Article 5.

Peru: "The civil servant or public official who deprives someone of their liberty, ordering or carrying out actions that result in their duly proven disappearance, will be punished with imprisonment of no less than 15 years and rendered unfit for duty" (Decree Law No. 25592, which was published on 2 July 1992 and came into effect on the same day).

7. Basic Principles, principle 25. For the text of the Basic Principles, see Appendix 5.

8. Principle 1 of the Basic Principles states that governments and law enforcement agencies should adopt rules and regulations on the use of force and firearms by law enforcement officials. Also, the Human Rights Committee set up under the International Covenant on Civil and Political Rights has emphasized the importance of limiting by law the circumstances in which

a person may be deprived of life by the authorities. According to the general comment on Article 6 of the International Covenant, adopted on 17 July 1982 by the Human Rights Committee, "The deprivation of life by the authorities of the State is a matter of the utmost gravity. Therefore, the law must strictly control and limit the circumstances in which a person may be deprived of his life by such authorities."

9. In resolution 35/70 on the Code of Conduct for Law Enforcement Officials, adopted on 15 December 1980, the UN General Assembly called on all states "(t)o make the text of the Code of Conduct available to all law enforcement officials in their own language" and "(t)o instruct, in basic training programmes and in all subsequent training and refresher courses, law enforcement officials in the provisions of the national legislations which are connected with the Code of Conduct and other basic texts on human rights".

The resolution of the Eighth UN Congress on the Prevention of Crime and the Treatment of Offenders adopting the Basic Principles states that the Basic Principles should be "brought to the attention of law enforcement officials". Principles 18 to 21 refer to matters to be covered in training, including issues of police ethics and human rights and alternatives to the use of force and firearms.

10. The Commentary to Article 1 of the Code of Conduct for Law Enforcement officials reads, in part:

> "(a) The term 'law enforcement officials' includes all officers of the law, whether appointed or elected, who exercise police powers, especially the powers of arrest or detention.
>
> (b) In countries where police powers are exercised by military authorities, whether uniformed or not, or by state security forces, the definition of law enforcement officials shall be regarded as including officers of such services."

11. See the Basic Principles, principles 2 to 4 and 12 to 17, which refer among other things to the use of non-lethal incapacitating weapons and the principles to be followed in policing unlawful assemblies and people in detention. See also the UN Standard Minimum Rules for the Treatment of Prisoners, rule 54, which states: "Officers of the institutions shall not, in their relations with the prisoners, use force except in self-defence or in cases of attempted escape, or active or passive physical resistance to an order based on law or regulations. ..."

12. In resolution 34/169 of 17 December 1979, whereby the Code of Conduct for Law Enforcement Officials was adopted, the UN General Assembly stated that "the actions of law enforcement officials should be responsive to public scrutiny, whether exercised by a review board, a ministry, a procuracy, the judiciary, an ombudsman, a citizens' committee or any combination thereof, or any other reviewing agency".

13. Basic Principles, principle 23.

14. Civil defence forces, which are a type of paramilitary force, have recently come under scrutiny by UN bodies. In its 1992 report the Working Group on Disappearances stated that the question of civil defence units abusing their powers was of concern to it, "particularly as they are reported to be involved in many cases of disappearance and other abuses." (paragraph 378) It noted: "Reports of abuses by such groups are more frequent in situations where civil defence units are seen to be operating without adequate supervision by government forces, or, on the other hand, precisely where they do act in close cooperation with the army or police, for example during

combat or search and seizure operations. ... On the whole, the training, discipline and accountability of such outfits are poor, if not lacking. Recruitment and lines of command are often haphazard." (paragraph 379)

The Working Group went on to state its view that

> "if abuses by civil defence units, especially disappearances, are to be prevented, the law must lay down a number of minimum conditions for their operations and effective measures must be taken to implement them. First of all, the only objective of civil defence deployment should be self-defence; units should not be involved in operations which would normally be carried out by army or police units, such as combat, search and seizure, 'fishing expeditions', etc. Secondly, recruitment into civil defence must be on a genuinely voluntary basis only, rather than on the basis of conscription. Civil authorities should exercise effective control over recruitment, guarding against any form of duress, real or perceived. Thirdly, public forces should constantly supervise training, arming (if any) and discipline of the units, as well as all operations they carry out. Clear lines of command should be established, as well as levels of responsibility. Fourthly, criteria for accountability should be unequivocal and should be explained to the members. Breaking the rules should be met with disciplinary punishment; abuses, particularly human rights violations, should be pursued before the civil administration of justice with all the necessary vigour." (paragraph 381)

In 1992 the UN Commission on Human Rights recognized "that action by civil defence forces has in some cases jeopardized the enjoyment of human rights and fundamental freedoms" (resolution 1992/57, adopted without a vote on 3 March 1992). The matter remains under discussion by the Commission.

15. WGEID, *Report on the visit to the Philippines...*, 1991, paragraph 168.

16. For further details see *South Africa; State of Fear; Security Force Complicity in Torture and Political Killings, 1990-1992*, Amnesty International Publications, London, 1992, pages 12-17.

17. Peace Agreement, signed in Mexico City on 16 January 1992, in *El Salvador Agreements: The Path to Peace*, United Nations, New York, Department of Public Information, DPI/1208, 1992.

18. See *Endgame; A Progress Report on Implementation of the Salvadorean Peace Accords; December 3, 1992*, Hemisphere Initiatives, Cambridge, Massachusetts, USA, 1992.

19. The duty of the authorities to suppress the activities of groups issuing death threats has been pointed out by the Director of the UN human rights monitoring mission in El Salvador. In his second report the Director referred to repeated death threats issued by members of a clandestine organization and stated (in paragraph 38) that "effective measures by State agencies are needed to put an end to the activities of these groups, which seem to be operating without restraints of any kind. *The passivity shown by the authorities in these matters is tantamount to a clear dereliction of duty* on the part of public officials and could also act as an incentive to the authors of such threats to persist in their activities, which are a breach of human rights." (emphasis added)

20. In his 1990 report the UN Special Rapporteur on summary or arbitrary executions referred to the practice of death threats and subsequent assassinations as a "heinous practice of terror" (paragraph 448) and took note of "a particularly alarming trend" of death threats directed in particular against human rights defenders and people working for social and criminal justice

in a society (paragraph 472). He reported that he had received more appeals than in previous years for urgent intervention in cases of death threats (paragraph 447):

> "According to the appeals made to the Special Rapporteur, in most cases the authorities had taken no effective measures to protect those who had received death threats or to undertake appropriate investigations. The appeals also indicated the involvement of the Government concerned, either directly, by orders given to officials or the employment of individuals or groups under the control of the Government, or indirectly by connivance in or collusion with such death threats by private individuals or groups. Absence of official investigation, prosecution and/or punishment of those responsible for such threats was the rule rather than the exception." (paragraph 453)

21. In resolution 1992/59, adopted without a vote on 3 March 1992, the Commission among other things:

> "1. Urges Governments to refrain from all acts of intimidation or reprisal against:
> (a) Those who seek to cooperate or have cooperated with representatives of United Nations human rights bodies, or who have provided testimony or information to them;
> (b) Those who avail or have availed themselves of procedures established under United Nations auspices for the protection of human rights and fundamental freedoms and all those who have provided legal assistance to them for this purpose;
> (c) Those who submit or have submitted communications under procedures established by human rights instruments;
> (d) Those who are relatives of victims of human rights violations;
> "2. Requests all representatives of United Nations human rights bodies as well as treaty bodies monitoring the observance of human rights to continue to take urgent steps, in conformity with their mandates, to help prevent the hampering of access to United Nations human rights procedures in any way;
> "3. Also requests all representatives of United Nations human rights bodies, as well as treaty bodies monitoring the observance of human rights, to continue to take urgent steps, in conformity with their mandates, to help prevent the occurrence of such intimidation and reprisals..."

22. In his fifth report the Director of the UN human rights monitoring mission in El Salvador, where armed forces "hit lists" have appeared in the news media, recommended that the authorities should "adopt regulations prohibiting the radio or television broadcasting of threatening messages, without prejudicing the liberty of the press." (paragraph 94)

23. See Laurie S. Wiseberg, "Protecting Human Rights Activists and NGOs: What More Can Be Done?", *Human Rights Quarterly*, vol. 13, No. 4, November 1991, pages 525-544.

24. Third report of the Director of the UN human rights monitoring mission in El Salvador, paragraphs 15-27, 35-36.

25. In the present report and in Amnesty International's 14-Point Programs, the term "prisoner" refers to anyone detained or imprisoned, whether or not the person has been arrested on a criminal charge and whether or not the person is serving a sentence of imprisonment imposed by a court.

26. The text of the Standard Minimum Rules is reproduced in the UN publication *Human Rights; A Compilation of International Instruments,* cited in Chapter 8.

27. The text of the Body of Principles is reproduced in the *Amnesty International Report 1989,* Amnesty International Publications, London, 1989, Appendix IX.

28. "No one shall be subjected to arbitrary arrest, detention or exile." – Universal Declaration of Human Rights, Article 9.

29. This safeguard is spelled out in more detail in the UN Declaration on Disappearances (Article 12).

30. Principle 16 (1) of the Body of Principles provides:

> "Promptly after arrest and after each transfer from one place of detention or imprisonment to another, a detained or imprisoned person shall be entitled to notify or to require the competent authority to notify members of his family or other appropriate persons of his choice of his arrest, detention or imprisonment or of the transfer and of the place where he is kept in custody."

Principle 16 also provides that detained foreigners may communicate with a consul or diplomatic mission of their country; refugees may communicate with the international organization which protects them; and the authorities must themselves make the notification if the prisoner is a juvenile or is incapable of understanding the right of notification.

Principle 16 (4) states: "Any notification referred to in this principle shall be made or permitted to be made without delay. The competent authority may however delay a notification for a reasonable period where exceptional needs of the investigation so require." Even in exceptional circumstances, however, "communication of the detained or imprisoned person with the outside world, and in particular his family or counsel, shall not be denied for more than a matter of days" (Principle 15).

31. The passage quoted is from the Inter-American Commission on Human Rights' request to the Inter-American Court of Human Rights for an advisory opinion on whether or not the remedy of *habeas corpus* as provided for under the American Convention on Human Rights could be suspended by states parties to the Convention. (Inter-American Court of Human Rights, Series A: Judgments and Opinions, No. 8, *Advisory Opinion OC-8/87 of January 30, 1987; Habeas Corpus in Emergency Situations...*; Organization of American States, Inter-American Court of Human Rights, Secretariat of the Court, San José, Costa Rica, 1987, paragraph 12)

32. The Inter-American Court stated that "*habeas corpus* performs a vital role in ensuring that a person's life and physical integrity are respected, in preventing his disappearance or the keeping of his whereabouts secret and in protecting him against torture or other cruel, inhumane, or degrading punishment or treatment." (*Ibid.,* paragraph 35)

33. Article 9 (4) of the International Covenant on Civil and Political Rights provides that anyone deprived of liberty "by arrest or detention shall be entitled to take proceedings before a court", so that the court can decide on the lawfulness of the detention. The court must make its decision "without delay" and it must order the prisoner's release if the detention is not lawful. The European Convention on Human Rights and the American Convention on Human Rights contain similar provisions. (Nigel S. Rodley has pointed out that although the International Covenant refers only to proceedings being taken by a person who has been deprived of liberty, "no interpretation aimed at effectiveness would deny to others the power to initiate the

proceedings on behalf of that person." Rodley, *The Treatment of Prisoners under International Law*, page 267)

34. For early examples of the failure of *habeas corpus* or *amparo* in finding the "disappeared", see *'Disappearances'; A Workbook*, pages 153-161.

35. The Inter-American Court of Human Rights also has stated that *habeas corpus* should never be suspended. In the advisory opinion of 30 January 1987 cited above, the Court referred to several articles of the American Convention on Human Rights: Article 7 (6), setting forth the right of *habeas corpus*; Article 25 (1), setting forth the right to judicial protection against human rights violations; and Article 27 (2), under which the right to juridical personality, the right to life and the prohibition of torture may never be suspended. The Court stated that "writs of habeas corpus and of amparo are among those judicial remedies that are essential for the protection of various rights whose derogation is prohibited by Article 27 (2) and that serve, moreover, to preserve legality in a democratic society" (paragraph 42). Its unanimous opinion was "That, given the provisions of Article 27 (2) of the American Convention on Human Rights, the legal remedies guaranteed in Articles 7 (6) and 25 (1) of the Convention may not be suspended because they are judicial guarantees essential for the protection of the rights and freedoms whose suspension Article 27 (2) prohibits." (paragraph 44)

36. WGEID, *Report on a visit to Guatemala...*, 1987, paragraphs 14-17.

37. *Ibid.*, paragraphs 77, 79.

38. Comisión para la Defensa de los Derechos Humanos en Centroamérica (CODEHUCA), *El Habeas Corpus en Centro América*, Doctrina Sobre Derechos Humanos, Serie Jurídica No 2, CODEHUCA, San José, Costa Rica, 1992, pages 178-179.

39. Rule 7 of the Standard Minimum Rules states:

> "(1) In every place where persons are imprisoned there shall be kept a bound registration book with numbered pages in which shall be entered in respect of each prisoner received:
>
> > (a) Information concerning his identity;
> > (b) The reasons for his commitment and the authority therefor;
> > (c) The day and hour of his admission and release.
>
> "(2) No person shall be received in an institution without a valid commitment order of which the details shall have been previously entered in the register."

Under rules 4 and 95 of the Standard Minimum Rules, the requirement set forth in rule 7 applies to all categories of prisoners, untried or convicted, including people detained without charge. Principle 12 of the Body of Principles states:

> "1. There shall be duly recorded:
>
> > (a) The reasons for the arrest;
> > (b) The time of the arrest and the taking of the arrested person to a place of custody as well as that of his first appearance before a judicial or other authority;
> > (c) The identity of the law enforcement officials concerned;
> > (d) Precise information concerning the place of custody.
>
> "2. Such records shall be communicated to the detained person, or his counsel, if any, in the form prescribed by law."

40. Similarly, the UN Body of Principles states: "A person shall not be kept in detention without

being given an effective opportunity to be heard promptly by a judicial or other authority. ..."
(Principle 11)

41. Principle 18 (3) of the Body of Principles provides for the right for prisoners to be visited by their legal counsel without delay. Principle 18 (3) states: "The right of a detained or imprisoned person to be visited by and to consult and communicate, without delay or censorship and in full confidentiality, with his legal counsel may not be suspended or restricted save in exceptional circumstances, to be specified by law or lawful regulations, when it is considered indispensable by a judicial or other authority in order to maintain security and good order."

The Basic Principles on the Role of Lawyers, adopted by the Eighth UN Congress on the Prevention of Crime and the Treatment of Offenders in Havana on 7 September 1990, also provide for the right of detainees to prompt access to a lawyer. The Basic Principles on the Role of Lawyers are reprinted in the *Amnesty International Report 1991*, Amnesty International Publications, London, 1991, Appendix X.

42. Rule 37 of the Standard Minimum Rules states: "Prisoners shall be allowed under necessary supervision to communicate with their family and reputable friends at regular intervals, both by correspondence and by receiving visits."

43. See the Body of Principles, Principle 18, on the right of a prisoner to be visited by and to communicate with his or her legal counsel; also the International Covenant on Civil and Political Rights, Article 14 (3)(b) and the Standard Minimum Rules, rule 93 on communications with lawyers, and the Standard Minimum Rules, rules 24 and 91 on visits by doctors.

44. Principle 18 (4) of the Body of Principles states: "Interviews between a detained or imprisoned person and his legal counsel may be within sight, but not within the hearing, of a law enforcement official."

45. Standard Minimum Rules, rule 37 (quoted above); also rule 92. Principle 19 of the Body of Principles also provides for the right of prisoners to correspond with their families.

46. Principle 29 of the Body of Principles states:

> "1. In order to supervise the strict observance of relevant laws and regulations, places of detention shall be visited regularly by qualified and experienced persons appointed by, and responsible to, a competent authority distinct from the authority directly in charge of the administration of the place of detention or imprisonment.

> "2. A detained or imprisoned person shall have the right to communicate freely and in full confidentiality with the persons who visit the places of detention or imprisonment in accordance with paragraph 1, subject to reasonable conditions to ensure security and good order in such places."

47. These recommendations are drawn largely from the conditions for ICRC visits as described in Philippe de Sinner and Hernan Reyes, "Visits by the International Committee of the Red Cross to Persons Deprived of their Freedom", ICRC Division for Detention Matters, September 1992.

48. Body of Principles, Principles 13, 33.

49. Body of Principles, Principle 11.

50. Sometimes prisoners' relatives, fearing reprisals, may prefer to have the prisoner released to, or in the presence of, a representative of a reliable non-governmental organization or a

reliable public figure such as a member of parliament. The ICRC sometimes receives released prisoners, for example in situations of armed conflict where prisoners' relatives are not able to be present.

51. The full text of the memorandum is reproduced in, *Philippines; The Killing Goes On*, Amnesty International Publications, London, 1992, Appendix V. As of the time of writing of this report it was not clear how vigorously the memorandum was being implemented.

52. For more on the UN campaign, see "World Public Information Campaign for Human Rights", *Human Rights Fact Sheets* series, No. 8, UN Centre for Human Rights, Geneva, 1989.

53. A list of UN Information Centres is available from the Department of Public Information at the UN Secretariat, United Nations, New York, NY 10017, USA.

54. Resolution 1992/38, adopted on 28 February 1992.

55. WGEID, 1990 report, paragraph 365.

56. One expert involved in training programs on the laws of war conducted by the ICRC has written: "This teaching by the dissemination of the law of war cannot be simply a mental or psychic exercise, but must be carried out so that the law of war is effectively observed. In this sense, there is a general feeling that *good knowledge of these norms is an essential factor for its effective application...* It is a fact that the norms of the law of war will be a dead letter if they are not known, and it is a proven truth, repeated on many occasions, that the majority of the transgressions of proper wartime conduct are not carried out in bad faith, but simply because the norms were not known..." José Luis Fernández-Flores, "The Dissemination of the Law of War", in International Institute of Humanitarian Law, *Yearbook 1989-90*, Milan, Guiffrè Editore, 1992, page 12; emphasis added.

Chapter 10 **Investigation**

1. Paragraph 176. The *Velásquez Rodríguez* judgment is cited in Chapter 7.

2. SRESAE, 1993 report, paragraph 686.

3. Vienna Declaration and Programme of Action, adopted on 25 June 1993 by the World Conference on Human Rights (Vienna, 14-25 June 1993), United Nations, New York, Department of Public Information, DPI/1394-39399, 1993, part II, paragraph 62.

4. Cited in Chapter 8.

5. UN Commission on Human Rights, resolution 1993/71, adopted without a vote on 10 March 1993.

6. The Minnesota Protocol is named after the Minnesota Lawyers International Human Rights Committee, which developed it. The Protocol contains a detailed list of techniques for the investigation of suspected extrajudicial executions and detailed standards for commissions of inquiry.

7. The right to submit complaints follows from the right of anyone whose human rights are violated to have an effective remedy, as established in the International Covenant on Civil and Political Rights, Article 2. It is recognized explicitly in the UN Declaration on Disappearances, Article 13 (1), and implicitly in the UN Principles on Extra-Legal, Arbitrary and Summary Executions, principles 9, 15 and 16.

8. The Declaration on Disappearances (Article 13 (3)) and the Principles on Extra-Legal, Arbitrary and Summary Executions (principle 15) provide that complainants should be protected from intimidation.

9. Declaration on Disappearances, Article 13; Principles on Extra-legal, Arbitrary and Summary Executions, principle 9.

10. Principle 34 of the UN Body of Principles for the Protection of All Persons under Any Form of Detention or Imprisonment calls for an investigation to be held whenever a prisoner dies or "disappears" and also when a former prisoner dies or "disappears" shortly after release. Principle 34 states:

> "Whenever the death or disappearance of a detained or imprisoned person occurs during his detention or imprisonment, an inquiry into the cause of death or disappearance shall be held by a judicial or other authority, either on its own motion or at the instance of a member of the family of such a person or any person who has knowledge of the case. When circumstances so warrant, such an inquiry shall be held on the same procedural basis whenever the death or disappearance occurs shortly after the termination of the detention or imprisonment. ..."

11. Declaration on Disappearances, Article 13 (2); Principles on Extra-legal, Arbitrary and Summary Executions, principle 10.

12. Declaration on Disappearances, Article 13 (3); Principles on Extra-legal, Arbitrary and Summary Executions, principle 15.

13. The importance of having adequate authority to obtain evidence is shown by the results which can be obtained when such authority is exercised. One such experience was that of the Commission of Inquiry regarding the Prevention of Public Violence and Intimidation, set up in South Africa in 1991 under the chairmanship of Mr Justice R.J. Goldstone. The Commission stated that it would investigate fully any evidence implicating senior members of the South African security forces in political violence and intimidation. The Commission was given extensive powers of search and seizure, and its staff was reinforced by international police experts seconded from European Community countries.

On 11 November 1992, largely as a result of strong support from these international experts, the Commission with police reinforcements raided a building housing a large operations unit of Military Intelligence and seized five files from a vast store of documentation. The seized files indicated the existence of a secret unit which appeared to be the coordinating structure for a range of clandestine military projects. The files also showed that the chief of staff of Military Intelligence had authorized the hiring in 1991 of a notorious former member of a covert military unit, the Civil Cooperation Bureau (CCB), to run a task force aimed at destabilizing the opposition African National Congress and its military wing. The CCB had been officially disbanded in 1990 after damning evidence had been presented to a judicial commission of inquiry indicating that the unit had been responsible for political killings carried out in the 1980s.

The Goldstone Commission promptly published the findings of the raid, thus pre-empting the possibility that its discoveries would be hushed up. However, the State President of South Africa intervened and ordered an army and a police general to take over further investigation of the seized documents, in coordination with the Commission, thus effectively preventing the

Commission from carrying out its own independent investigation. The appointment of such senior army and police investigators prompted fears of an official cover-up. Although 23 military officers were subsequently forced to take early retirement, no prosecutions have been brought against the officials alleged to have committed unlawful acts. Furthermore, the secret unit appears to be still in operation.

14. Most of these characteristics are included in international instruments adopted by the UN. Both the UN Declaration on Disappearances (Article 13) and the UN Principles on Extra-Legal, Arbitrary and Summary Executions (principles 9, 15-17) call for prompt, thorough and impartial investigation.

15. Principles on Extra-legal, Arbitrary and Summary Executions, principle 16.

16. Declaration on Disappearances, Article 13 (3, 5); Principles on Extra-legal, Arbitrary and Summary Executions, principle 15.

17. Declaration on Disappearances, Article 16; Principles on Extra-legal, Arbitrary and Summary Executions, principle 15.

18. Principles on Extra-legal, Arbitrary and Summary Executions, principle 17. With reference to commissions of inquiry, detailed proposals for what should be included in the report are given in the Minnesota Protocol, section D (15).

19. Principles on Extra-legal, Arbitrary and Summary Executions, principle 17.

20. Declaration on Disappearances, Article 13 (6).

The UN Working Group on Disappearances has stated in its 1990 report (paragraph 362):
> "Under its terms of reference, the Group will continue to deal with cases as long as they have not been clarified. It believes that the need to insist on investigation of all cases of disappearances lies at the heart of its mandate. It does so bearing in mind the interest of those who will suffer anguish and bitterness as long as they cannot be assured of the fate or whereabouts of their loved ones."

21. Most of the characteristics listed here are included in the UN Principles on Extra-Legal, Arbitrary and Summary Executions (principles 12-14, 16).

22. Commission on Human Rights, resolution 1993/33, adopted without a vote on 5 March 1993.

23. For a history of the work of the EAAF, see Christopher Joyce and Eric Stover, *Witnesses from the Grave; The Stories Bones Tell*, Little, Brown and Ballantine Books, New York and Bloomsbury, London, 1991; also Mauricio Cohen Salama, *Tumbas Anónimas; Informe sobre la Identificación de Restos de Víctimas de la Represión Ilegal...* (Unmarked Graves; Report on the Identification of Remains of Victims of the Illegal Repression), Catálogos Editora, Buenos Aires, 1992.

24. In a recent example of a forensic investigation, a forensic team from the US organizations Middle East Watch and Physicians for Human Rights exhumed 27 male skeletons from two graves in Koreme, a Kurdish village in northern Iraq, in 1992. All 27 of the victims appeared to have died from gunshot wounds. The team examined the location and trajectory of the bullet wounds and concluded that the evidence was consistent with witnesses' accounts of a massacre of 27 men and boys during the Iraqi armed forces' 1988 campaign against the Kurds of northern Iraq. (Middle East Watch and Physicians for Human Rights, *The Anfal Campaign in Iraqi Kurdistan; The Destruction of Koreme...*, Human Rights Watch, New York, 1993, pages 45-50, 97-99)

25. UN Commission on Human Rights, *Report of the Secretary-General on human rights and*

forensic science..., UN document No. E/CN.4/1993/20, 5 February 1993, paragraphs 8-11.

26. The EAAF has found that most relatives need a constant flow of information from the investigators. This enables the relatives to accept the final truth emerging from the investigation whether or not it confirms their expectations. Also, the process of accepting the truth appears to be less traumatic when the relatives are given an active role in the investigation. The task most frequently taken on by them is the gathering of information about the "disappeared" person. This information can be vital for the identification of the remains.

27. Resolution 1992/24, adopted without a vote on 28 February 1992.

28. Resolution 1993/33, adopted without a vote on 5 March 1993.

29. Amnesty International, "Proposed standards for national human rights commissions", AI Index: IOR 40/01/93, January 1993.

30. Resolution 1992/54, adopted by consensus on 3 March 1992. The text of the Principles is reproduced in Amnesty International, "Proposed standards for national human rights commissions", *op. cit.*

31. Five essential pieces of information – name, date and place of "disappearance", parties considered responsible, and information on steps taken to determine the victim's fate or whereabouts – are minimum elements which a report of a "disappearance" submitted to the UN Working Group on Enforced or Involuntary Disappearances should contain. The Working Group urges those submitting reports to furnish as many details as possible on the identity of the victim (including identity card numbers if available) and the circumstances of the "disappearance". Missing details should not prevent the submission of reports, but the Working Group can only act on clearly identified individual cases containing the five minimum elements described above. ("Enforced or Involuntary Disappearances", *Human Rights Fact Sheets* series, No. 6, UN Centre for Human Rights, Geneva, 1988, pages 10-11, 13-14)

32. The UN Working Group on Disappearances has prepared a four-page questionnaire which local groups and individuals can use in sending reports of "disappearances" to the Working Group. Spaces are provided for details to be filled in under the five heading described above. Copies of the questionnaire may be obtained from the UN Centre for Human Rights in Geneva (for address, see Chapter 12).

33. For a discussion of the problems of establishing official involvement in the face of governmental denials, see Michael McClintock, "Establishing Accountability for State Violence", in *Human Rights in the Twenty-First Century: A Global Challenge*, proceedings of a conference held in Banff, Alberta, Canada, 1990.

Chapter 11   **Bringing the perpetrators to justice**

1. WGEID, 1990 report, paragraph 344.

2. For examples of impunity in different countries, see Amnesty International, "Crime without punishment", AI Index: ACT 33/52/93, August 1993.

3. Similarly, the 1993 progress report on impunity prepared for the UN Sub-Commission on Prevention of Discrimination and Protection of Minorities distinguishes two paths of impunity: "firstly, de facto impunity resulting from the dysfunction of the institutions concerned, which is either directly or indirectly encouraged, or even organized by the authorities; and secondly,

impunity legitimized by provisions borrowed from the rule of law and diverted from their purpose." (UN Sub-Commission on Prevention of Discrimination and Protection of Minorities, *Progress report on the question of impunity of perpetrators of human rights violations...*, UN document No. E/CN.4/Sub.2/1993/6, 19 July 1993, paragraph 29) See also the discussion of "structural" and "practical" impunity in Colombia in Chapter 3 of this report.

4. In India, for example, Section 6 of the Armed Forces (Special Powers) Act reads: "No prosecution, suit or other legal proceeding shall be instituted, except with the previous sanction of the Central Government, against any person in respect of anything done or purported to be done in the exercise of the powers conferred by this Act." The act in question gives the security forces wide powers to shoot to kill. It is currently in force in several Indian states where there is armed insurgency. Another Indian law, adopted in 1991, protects government officers from any prosecutions for actions taken in the course of duty in states which are under direct rule from the central government. ("Legally sanctioned impunity", in *India; Torture, Rape & Deaths in Custody*, Amnesty International Publications, London, 1992, pages 59-61) The decision of the government of newly independent Zimbabwe to grant immunity from prosecution for acts in connection with the war for independence is another example (see above, Chapter 4). Amnesty International has frequently drawn attention to legal provisions preventing the prosecution of officials for human rights violations in different countries and has called for these provisions to be repealed.

5. The Basic Principles on the Independence of the Judiciary were adopted by the Seventh UN Congress on the Prevention of Crime and the Treatment of Offenders (Milan, 26 August – 6 September 1985) and endorsed by the UN General Assembly in resolutions 40/32 of 29 November 1985 and 40/146 of 13 December 1985. They are reproduced in *Human Rights; A Compilation of International Instruments*.

6. See the Basic Principles on the Independence of the Judiciary, principle 2, quoted in the next section of this chapter.

7. With regard to "disappearances", Article 16 (2) of the UN Declaration on Disappearances establishes that alleged perpetrators should not be tried in special or military courts. More generally, principle 5 of the Basic Principles on the Independence of the Judiciary states: "Everyone shall have the right to be tried by ordinary courts or tribunals using established legal procedures. Tribunals that do not use the duly established procedures of the legal process shall not be created to displace the jurisdiction belonging to the ordinary courts or judicial tribunals."

In a comment on the second periodic report of Egypt under the International Covenant on Civil and Political Rights, the Human Rights Committee set up under the Covenant has stated: "...military courts should not have the faculty to try cases which do not refer to offences committed by members of the armed forces in the course of their duties." (Human Rights Committee, *Consideration of reports submitted by states parties under Article 40 of the Covenant*, UN document No. CCPR/C/79/Add.23, 9 August 1993, paragraph 9)

Similarly, the UN Working Group on Disappearances has stated: "...the Working Group wishes to reiterate that military tribunals should be reserved exclusively for those members of the security forces who commit military crimes, a category from which such serious human rights violations as enforced disappearances must be clearly and explicitly excluded." (WGEID, 1992 report, paragraph 367)

In its 1990 report (paragraph 345) the Working Group stated: "Military courts contribute significantly to impunity, in the Working Group's experience. A recurrent theme in times of internal crisis or under the doctrine of national security is that military personnel attested to have engaged in gross misconduct, are almost invariably acquitted or given sentences that are disproportionate to the crime committed. ..."

8. Guideline 15 of the UN Guidelines on the Role of Prosecutors states: "Prosecutors shall give due attention to the prosecution of crimes committed by public officials, particularly corruption, abuse of power, grave violations of human rights and other crimes recognized by international law and, where authorized by law or consistent with local practice, the investigation of such offences." The Guidelines on the Role of Prosecutors were adopted in 1990 by the Eighth UN Congress on the Prevention of Crime and the Treatment of Offenders.

9. Principle 7 of the Basic Principles on the Independence of the Judiciary states: "It is the duty of each Member State to provide adequate resources to enable the judiciary to properly perform its functions."

10. Article 10 of the Universal Declaration of Human Rights states: "Everyone is entitled in full equality to a fair and public hearing *by an independent and impartial tribunal*, in the determination of his rights and obligations and of any criminal charge against him." (emphasis added) A similar provision appears in Article 14 (1) of the International Covenant on Civil and Political Rights.

11. The principle of criminal responsibility of those behind the crimes is incorporated in the Statute of the International Tribunal on war crimes in the former Yugoslavia, cited in Chapter 8. The Statute also establishes (as did Article 7 of the Charter of the Nuremberg Tribunal) that a person cannot escape prosecution on the grounds of his or her official capacity, including that of head of state. Article 7 of the Statute states, in part:

> "1. A person who planned, instigated, ordered, committed or otherwise aided and abetted in the planning, preparation or execution of a crime referred to in articles 2 to 5 of the present Statute, shall be individually responsible for the crime.
>
> "2. The official position of any accused person, whether as Head of State or Government or as a responsible Government official, shall not relieve such person of criminal responsibility nor mitigate punishment.
>
> "3. The fact that any of the acts referred to in articles 2 to 5 of the present Statute was committed by a subordinate does not relieve his superior of criminal responsibility if he knew or had reason to know that the subordinate was about to commit such acts or had done so and the superior failed to take the necessary and reasonable measures to prevent such acts or to punish the perpetrators thereof."

12. The concept of no defence of superior orders is contained also in the UN Basic Principles on the Use of Force and Firearms by Law Enforcement Officals (principle 26) and in the Statute of the International Tribunal on war crimes in the former Yugoslavia. Article 7 (4) of the Statute states:

> "The fact that an accused person acted pursuant to an order of a Government or of a superior shall not relieve him of criminal responsibility, but may be considered in mitigation of punishment if the International Tribunal determines that justice so requires."

13. *Velásquez Rodríguez* judgment, paragraph 147. The *Velásquez Rodríguez* judgment is cited in Chapter 7.

14. *Ibid.* The passages quoted are from paragraphs 165 and 169 respectively.

15. *Ibid.*, paragraph 166; emphases added.

16. *Ibid.*, paragraph 194. For an extensive discussion of the responsibility of states for human rights violations, see Menno T. Kamminga, *Inter-state Accountability for Violations of Human Rights*, University of Pennsylvania Press, Philadelphia, 1992.

17. Universal Declaration of Human Rights, Article 8; International Covenant on Civil and Political Rights, Article 2 (3).

18. The Inter-American Court's judgment of compensation in the *Velásquez Rodríguez* case was based on Article 63 of the American Convention on Human Rights. This article establishes the power of the Inter-American Court of Human Rights to order compensation to the injured party when a right protected by the Convention has been violated.

19. The judgment of damages was awarded by the US Eastern District Court in New York in 1984 against Americo Norberto Peña-Irala, who as Inspector General of Police in Asunción, Paraguay, had kidnapped and tortured Joelito Filártiga to death. However, the plaintiffs have hitherto been unable to collect the damages. (*Filártiga* v. *Peña-Irala*, 577 F Supp. 860 (E.D. N.Y. 1984), on remand from *Filártiga* v. *Peña-Irala*, 630 F.2d 876 (2d Cir. 1980), excerpted in Frank Newman and David Weissbrodt, *International Human Rights*, Anderson, Cincinnati, 1990, pages 596-601, 651-654)

In 1992 the United States adopted a law, the Torture Victim Protection Act, under which any victim of torture, as well as the legal representative or other person who may be a claimant in an action for the wrongful death of a victim of extrajudicial killing, may file a claim in a US court against any individual who "under actual or apparent authority, or color of law, of any foreign nation" took part in the torture or extrajudicial killing. (See Robert F. Drinan and Teresa T. Kuo, "Putting the World's Oppressors on Trial: The Torture Victim Protection Act", *Human Rights Quarterly*, vol. 15, No. 3, August 1993, pages 605-624. See also Richard B. Lillich, "Damages for Gross Violations of International Human Rights Awarded by US Courts", *Human Rights Quarterly*, vol. 15, No. 2, May 1993, pages 107-229.)

20. The term "redress" comes from the French word *redresser*, meaning "to straighten". The UN Special Rapporteur on the right to restitution, compensation and rehabilitation for victims of gross violations of human rights and fundamental freedoms ("Special Rapporteur on the right to restitution") has used the alternative term *reparation*, meaning "repairing". As defined by the Special Rapporteur:

"The word 'reparation' in this study denotes all types of redress, material and non-material, for victims of human rights violations. Consequently, the terms 'restitution', 'compensation' and 'rehabilitation' cover particular aspects of reparation."

(UN Sub-Commission on Prevention of Discrimination and Protection of Minorities, *Study concerning the right to restitution, compensation and rehabilitation for victims of gross violations of human rights and fundamental freedoms; Final report submitted by Mr. Theo van Boven, Special Rapporteur*, paragraph 13, footnote)

21. Under proposed basic principles and guidelines concerning reparation to victims of gross violations of human rights prepared by the UN Special Rapporteur on the right to restitution,

"Compensation shall be provided for any economically assessable damage resulting from human rights violations, such as:

    (a) Physical or mental harm;

    (b) Pain, suffering and emotional distress;

    (c) Lost opportunities, including education;

    (d) Loss of earnings and earning capacity;

    (e) Reasonable medical and other expenses of rehabilitation;

    (f) Harm to property or business, including lost profits;

    (g) Harm to reputation or dignity;

    (h) Reasonable costs and fees of legal or expert assistance to obtain a remedy."

(*Ibid.*, paragraph 137, principle 9)

22. The Body of Principles establishes a requirement to make compensation for human rights violations and provides that official information needed to claim compensation must be made available. Principle 35 of the Body of Principles states:

"1. Damage incurred because of acts or omissions by a public official contrary to the rights contained in these Principles shall be compensated according to the applicable rules on liability provided by domestic law.

"2. Information required to be recorded under these Principles shall be available in accordance with procedures provided by domestic law for use in claiming compensation under this principle."

23. Article 8 of this Declaration states that "Offenders or third parties responsible for their behaviour should, where appropriate, make fair restitution to victims, their families or dependants. ..." Article 11 states: "Where public officials or other agents acting in an official or quasi-official capacity have violated national criminal laws, the victims should receive restitution from the State whose officials or agents were responsible for the harm inflicted. In cases where the Government under whose authority the victimizing act or omission occurred is no longer in existence, the State or Government successor in title should provide restitution to the victims." Articles 18 to 19 call for restitution and/or compensation to be provided for "acts or omissions that do not yet constitute violations of national criminal laws but of internationally recognized norms relating to human rights."

The Declaration of Basic Principles of Justice for Victims of Crime and Abuse of Power was drafted by the Seventh UN Congress on the Prevention of Crime and the Treatment of Offenders in 1985 and adopted by the UN General Assembly on 29 November 1985 in resolution 40/34. The text is reproduced in *Human Rights; A Compilation of International Instruments*.

24. The Human Rights Committee has held in a number of cases of "disappearances" and killings that the governments concerned should pay compensation. These cases are reviewed in the final report of the UN Special Rapporteur on the right to restitution, *op. cit.*, paragraph 53.

25. In Chile, where the National Commisson on Truth and Reconciliation had recommended that compensation be provided to the families of victims named in its report who had been killed or remained "disappeared" (see the next section of this chapter), a law was enacted in February 1992 creating a *Corporacíon Nacional de Reparación y Reconciliación*, National Corporation for Reparation and Reconciliation, a public agency responsible for overseeing the carrying out of the Commission's recommendations. The law established a monthly pension of

a specified amount, of which fixed percentages were to be allocated to the victim's surviving spouse, mother (or father if the mother was dead), children under 25 years old and disabled children of any age, and father or mother of any natural children. Beneficiaries were also to be entitled to free medical care, and children were to be given educational benefits and exempted from military service if they so requested. The Corporation was also to investigate the cases of further alleged victims of "disappearances" and political violence under the former government; the relatives of those whom it declared to have been victims would be entitled to the same benefits as the relatives of victims named in the Commission's report.

Since then, benefits have been provided in accordance with the 1991 law. The National Commission has completed its investigations and turned the results over to the courts.

26. As one psychologist has noted in a study of psychological aspects of redress for human rights violations, financial compensation is a concrete acknowledgement of responsibility and of the wrongfulness of the harm caused. Yael Danieli, "Preliminary Reflections from a Psychological Perspective," in Netherlands Institute of Human Rights, *Seminar on the Right to Restitution, Compensation and Rehabilitation for Victims of Gross Violations of Human Rights and Fundamental Freedoms; Maastricht, 11-15 March 1992, Studie- en Informatiecentrum Mensenrechten*, SIM Special No. 12, Human Rights Project Group, University of Limburg, Maastricht, the Netherlands, 1992, pages 196-213.

27. The Special Rapporteur on the right to restitution has recommended further that claims relating to reparations for gross human rights violations, including "disappearances" and extrajudicial executions, should not be subject to statutes of limitation. (*Op. cit.*, paragraph 137)

28. For discussion of these issues see Metin Başoğlu, ed., *Torture and its Consequences; Current Treatment Approaches*, Cambridge University Press, Cambridge, 1992.

29. As mentioned in Chapter 12, section 6, the decision in the case of *Quinteros v. Uruguay* taken by the Human Rights Committee set up under the International Covenant on Civil and Political Rights gives formal recognition that a close relative of a "disappeared" person suffers torture or ill-treatment.

30. The experiences of a group of psychotherapists working with families of "disappeared" people in Argentina have been described in Diana R. Kordon, Lucila I. Edelman y Equipo de Asistencia Psicológica de Madres de Plaza de Mayo, *Efectos Psicológicos de la Represión Política*, Sudamericana/Planeta, Buenos Aires, 1986 (English-language edition: Diana R. Kordon, Lucila I. Edelman et al., *Psychological Effects of Political Repression*, Sudamericana/Planeta, Buenos Aires, 1988).

31. Cited in the introduction to this report.

32. See the preceding section of this chapter for information on how this recommendation has been carried out. *Informe Rettig; Informe de la Comisión Nacional de Verdad y Reconciliación* (Rettig Report; Report of the National Commission of Truth and Reconciliation), La Nación and Editiciones del Ornitorrinco, Santiago, Chile, 1991

33. Republic of Chad, Ministry of Justice, *Rapport de la Commission d'Enquête sur les crimes et détournements commis par l'ex-Président, ses co-auteurs et/ou complices*, N'Djaména, May 1992, pages 5, 11, 77, 94-95, 101, 106-108. For a summary of the Commission's work, see Amnesty International, "Chad; Never Again? Killings Continue into the 1990s", AI Index: AFR 20/04/93, February 1993, pages 23-24.

34. Agreement signed in Mexico City on 27 April 1991, in *El Salvador Agreements: The Path to Peace*, cited in Chapter 9.

35. The Commission stated in its report that it decided to name those responsible because "it is not possible to tell the whole truth omitting names... [The Commission] was entrusted with the task of investigating and describing acts of violence of singular importance and of recommending measures intended to prevent a repetition of such acts in the future. This task cannot be fulfilled in the abstract, suppressing information (for example the names of those responsible) when there is faithful testimony..., especially when those identified are high-ranking officials and carrying out official tasks directly related to the violations or covering them up. Not to mention names would reinforce the very cloak of impunity which the Parties charged the Commission with removing."

36. *De la Locura a la Esperanza; La Guerra de 12 Años en El Salvador; Informe de la Comisión de la Verdad para El Salvador* (From Madness to Hope; the 12 Years' War in El Salvador; Report of the El Salvador Commission on the Truth), United Nations, San Salvador and New York, 1993.

37. The Court's rejection of the plea that they were only obeying orders was based on the country's Penal Code which establishes that due obedience is only applicable to orders which are not in contradiction with the Constitution.

38. Former President García Meza escaped the country in 1989 and is still at large. Amnesty International knew of 10 other defendants who were arrested and had begun serving their sentences at the time of writing of this report.

Chapter 12   **Action through the United Nations and regional institutions**

1. Rodley, *op.cit.*, page 1. The Preamble to the Universal Declaration of Human Rights says that "recognition of the inherent dignity and of the equal and inalienable rights of all members of the human family is the foundation of freedom, justice and peace in the world". Earlier, the preamble to the Charter of the United Nations had expressed the determination of the peoples of the United Nations "to save succeeding generations from the scourge of war, which twice in our lifetime has brought untold sorrow to mankind, and to reaffirm faith in fundamental human rights, in the dignity and worth of the human person..."

   In a similar vein, linking human rights with peace and development, the UN Secretary-General wrote in 1992: "Respect for human rights is clearly important in order to maintain international peace and security and to achieve social and economic development." (UN Secretary-General, *Report on the Work of the Organization from the Forty-sixth to the Forty-seventh Session of the General Assembly; September 1992* (UN document No. A/47/1), Department of Public Information, United Nations, New York, paragraph 109)

2. Intergovernmental organizations are international organizations formed by governments, and through which governments can hold consultations and take joint positions and joint actions.

3. As Iain Guest has written, the UN system is ponderous, and the machinery for taking up human rights violations is often slow to get started, but once it starts, "it cannot be turned off at a stroke." (Iain Guest, *Behind the Disappearances; Argentina's Dirty War against Human Rights*

and the United Nations, University of Pennsylvania Press, Philadelphia, 1990, page 101)

4. For example, at the 1992 session of the UN Commission on Human Rights, Portugal and 27 other countries introduced a draft resolution condemning "the unjustifiable action by the armed forces of Indonesia that cost the life of many innocent and defenceless citizens in East Timor", a reference to the massacre at Dili, East Timor on 12 November 1991 in which some 200 peaceful demonstrators had been shot dead by Indonesian troops. Most Asian governments opposed the draft resolution. The Japanese representative made a statement to the Commission referring to the Indonesian Government's "sincere attitude towards the international community's concern" over the incident, while Australia said that the advance report of the Commission of Inquiry set up by the Indonesian Government was "encouraging", although Amnesty International, in a statement made available to Commission members, had said that the Commission's mandate and methods of work were fatally flawed and that its findings were unacceptable. (Both Japan and Australia have important trading links with Indonesia.) After long and intense negotiations the resolution was withdrawn.

Later in the year the Commission's Sub-Commission on Prevention of Discrimination and Protection of Minorities adopted a resolution on East Timor, and in 1993 the Commission adopted a resolution (number 1993/97) regretting the failure of the Indonesian Government to identify clearly those responsible for the Dili killings, and urging the government to invite UN Special Rapporteurs and Working Groups to visit East Timor, including the Special Rapporteur on extrajudicial, summary or arbitrary executions and the Working Group on Disappearances. (Such visits, if allowed, would be important advances in view of the resistance of the Indonesian Government in submitting to international scrutiny of its human rights behaviour in East Timor.) Before the resolution was adopted, Indonesia complained that it was being "targeted" by the Commission and decried the "unfairness" of several articles of the resolution. One of the governments most active behind the scenes in trying to weaken or defeat the resolution was the United Kingdom, a country which had recently been trying to arrange a lucrative deal to sell military aircraft to Indonesia.

5. A case in point is the UN Declaration on Disappearances. When the first draft emerged in 1990 from the UN Sub-Commission on Prevention of Discrimination and Protection of Minorities, a body of independent experts, it contained several important provisions which were weakened or dropped as the text passed through the successive stages of consideration by governmental representatives. Thus the first draft included a statement that the systematic practice of enforced disappearance is "a crime against humanity" and made the perpetration of "disappearances" subject to universal jurisdiction. These provisions would have strengthened the provisions for bringing the perpetrators of "disappearances" to justice. During the later stages of discussion the latter provision was dropped, while the former was replaced by a statement in the preamble to the Declaration that the systematic practice of enforced disappearance is "of the nature of" a crime against humanity, a phrase which carries far less legal weight than the original formulation. The text finally adopted by the General Assembly in 1992 is weaker than the original but still contains many valuable provisions, most of which were first proposed by NGOs.

6. For a detailed account of the efforts of the Argentinian ambassador in Geneva between 1976 and 1983 to block UN action on "disappearances" in Argentina, see Guest, *op. cit.*

7. For proposals on the improvement of the UN's work for human rights, see below, section 11.

8. The Economic and Social Council is one of the principal organs of the UN (the others are the General Assembly, the Security Council, the Trusteeship Council, the International Court of Justice and the Secretariat). Under Article 62 of the UN Charter the Economic and Social Council is empowered to "make recommendations for the purpose of promoting respect for, and observance of, human rights . . . " The Economic and Social Council may decide a matter on its own, or it may forward its recommendations to the General Assembly for decision.

9. Under Article 68 of the UN Charter, the Economic and Social Council had been directed to set up a commission "for the promotion of human rights".

10. John P. Humphrey, the first Director of the UN Division on Human Rights, later wrote that the UN "had been receiving great numbers" of communications alleging violations of human rights "from people and organizations in many countries." Humphrey had a list prepared and drew the attention of the Commission on Human Rights to its existence. One member wanted the Commission to discuss those complaints which came from non-governmental organizations in consultative status with the Economic and Social Council, but other members (including the USA and the USSR) opposed having the Commission review individual complaints. The Economic and Social Council resolution which endorsed the Commission's view that it had no power to act on the basis of complaints also established a complicated procedure to be followed by the Secretariat in handling the communications, a procedure characterized by Humphrey as "probably the most elaborate wastepaper basket ever invented". (John P. Humphrey, *Human Rights & the United Nations: A Great Adventure*, Transnational Publishers, Dobbs Ferry, New York, USA, 1984, page 28; Howard Tolley, Jr., *The U.N. Commission on Human Rights*, Westview Press, Boulder, Colorado, USA, 1987, page 17.)

11. Economic and Social Council resolution 1235 (XLII) authorized the Commission to examine information received by the UN on "gross violations of human rights and fundamental freedoms" and to make recommendations on such situations. Under the terms of resolution 1235 (XLII), this examination and action were to have been based on the communications received by the UN alleging violations of human rights, but since the establishment of the "1503 procedure" in 1970, complaints of human rights violations have been processed under the latter procedure except for those which are referred to one of the "theme mechanisms" such as the Working Group on Enforced or Involuntary Disappearances. The public action contemplated in resolution 1235 (XLII) is now dealt with annually by the Commission on Human Rights under agenda item 12. Under this agenda item Commission members can formally request the Commission to take action on human rights problems in specific countries. For a history and discussion of the "1235 procedure", see Philip Alston, "The Commission on Human Rights", in Philip Alston, ed., *The United Nations and Human Rights; A Critical Appraisal*, Clarendon Press, Oxford, 1992, pages 126-210, at pages 155-173.

12. All communications about alleged human rights violations received by the UN are processed by the UN Secretariat under the confidential procedure established by Economic and Security Council resolutions 728 (XXVII) F of 1959 and 1503 (XLVIII), except those which fit under a more specific UN procedure. Under resolution 728 (XXVII) F, copies of all communications are sent to the government concerned without divulging the identity of the author, and the government may send a reply to the Commission on Human Rights. From 1972 to 1987 over

350,000 communications and several thousand government replies were received by the UN and forwarded to the Working Group on Communications for consideration. For further information see "Communications Procedures", *Human Rights Fact Sheets* series, No. 7, UN Centre for Human Rights, Geneva, 1989 (available free of charge from the UN Centre for Human Rights); Amnesty International, "Summary of selected international procedures and bodies dealing with human rights matters", AI Index: IOR 30/01/89, August 1989.

13. Such countries have included Afghanistan (reviewed in 1980-83), Argentina (1980-84), Bolivia (1980-81), Ethiopia (1980-81), Uganda (1980-81), Indonesia (1980-81, 1983-85), Chile (1981), El Salvador (1981), Guatemala (1981), Haiti (1981-86, 1989-90), the Philippines (1984-86), Iraq (1988-89), Honduras (1988-89), Somalia (1989-93), Myanmar (1988-92), Chad (1991-93) and Sudan (1991-93). For a list of 30 governments subjected to review under the 1503 procedure between 1978 and 1986, see Tolley, *op. cit.*, page 128.

14. UN Commission on Human Rights, *Report on the situation of human rights in Myanmar...*, UN document No. E/CN.4/1993/37, 13 February 1993, paragraphs 228-236, 242.

15. The periodical *Human Rights Monitor* gives details of planned agendas and reports on the results of UN human rights meetings. It is published by International Service for Human Rights, 1 rue de Varembé, P.O. Box 16, 1211 Geneva 20 cic, Switzerland.

16. According to John P. Humphrey, the idea of doing studies came from a staff member in the UN Division of Human Rights. The program of studies made the Sub-Commission "one of the most useful organs in the United Nations", Humphrey wrote. (Humphrey, *op. cit.*, page 168)

17. See above, note 5.

18. *'Disappearances'; A Workbook*, pages 1, 22-24

19. The text of the resolution is reproduced in *'Disappearances'; A Workbook*, Appendix.

20. Rodley, *op. cit.*, pages 193-197.

21. Commission on Human Rights resolution 20 (XXXVI) of 29 February 1980.

22. WGEID, 1981 report, paragraph 30. In 1992, for example, the Working Group transmitted 348 cases to governments under the urgent action procedure, of which 53 were clarified during the year (1993 report, paragraph 23). In its 1990 report (paragraph 351) the Working Group noted that the clarification rate for cases under the urgent action procedure was as high as 25 per cent, compared with an overall clarification rate of about 7 per cent for all cases.

In its 1981 report (paragraph 10) the Working Group characterized its urgent appeals as the action of "the eyes of the international community". Describing the procedure, it stated that "while the Working Group has been in existence, it may well have been realized by those, throughout the world, who contemplated the detention of a person and his disappearance, that the Group was continuously acting as the eyes of the international community, and acting with that sense of urgency which alone can save lives."

23. WGEID, 1992 report paragraph 25. In resolution 1991/70, adopted without a vote on 6 March 1991, the Commission on Human Rights had urged governments "to refrain from all acts of intimidation or reprisal, in any form, against private individuals and groups who seek to co-operate with the United Nations and representatives of its human rights bodies, or who have sought to avail themselves of procedures established under United Nations auspices for the protection of human rights and fundamental freedoms". The resolution requested representatives of UN human rights bodies "to help prevent the occurrence of intimidation or

reprisal as well as prevent that access to United Nations human rights procedures be hampered in any way". The Working Group's "prompt intervention" procedure was developed in response to this request.

In 1992 the Working Group on Disappearances sent "prompt intervention" appeals to the governments of six countries – Brazil, Colombia, Ecuador, Guatemala, Honduras and Peru. See UN Commission on Human Rights, *Cooperation with representatives of United Nations human rights bodies; Report of the Secretary-General...*, UN document No. E/CN.4/1993/38, 8 February 1993, paragraph 20.

24. WGEID, 1990 report, paragraph 352.

25. In its report on a visit to Sri Lanka in 1991, the Working Group made detailed recommendations on the measures which the government should take to prevent "disappearances" and clarify the fate of the "disappeared". (WGEID, *Report on the visit to Sri Lanka...(7-18 October 1991)*, 1992, paragraph 204)

26. As Iain Guest has written, the appendices served as "tangible proof" that relatives of victims "had taken their own campaign to the United Nations and that the United Nations had responded." Displayed at local meetings of relatives' groups back at home, the reports "acted like glue. They had unified a human rights movement across Latin America and linked it to friends outside." (Guest, *op. cit.*, page 359)

27. In 1992 the Working Group wrote to governments and non-governmental organizations asking for their comments on a series of suggested measures needed to overcome impunity for "disappearances". The results are summarized in the Working Group's report for 1992, paragraphs 46-49 and Annex I.

28. *Ibid.*, paragraph 4 and country entries.

29. See Rodley, *op. cit.*, pages 208-214.

30. In its operative paragraphs, this resolution states that the Congress:
> "1. *Deplores and condemns* the practice of killing and executing political opponents or suspected offenders carried out by armed forces, law enforcement or other governmental agencies or by paramilitary or political groups acting with the tacit or other support of such forces or agencies;
> "2. *Affirms* that such acts constitute a particularly abhorrent crime the eradication of which is a high international priority;
> "3. *Calls upon* all Governments to take effective measures to prevent such acts;
> "4. *Urges* all organs of the United Nations dealing with questions of crime prevention and human rights to take all possible action to bring such acts to an end."

The text of the resolution is reproduced in Rodley, *op. cit.*, Annex 7.

31. Attempts had been made by governments and non-governmental organizations to raise concerns about killings in Uganda and Kampuchea at the Commission on Human Rights, but the Commission did not take action. See *Political Killings by Governments*, pages 43, 48.

32. Resolution 35/172 of 15 December 1980. The text of the resolution is reproduced in *When the State Kills...*, *op.cit.*, Appendix 9.

33. S. Amos Wako, a Kenyan lawyer, was Secretary-General of the Inter-African Union of Lawyers. When he resigned as Special Rapporteur in 1992 after his appointment as Attorney

General of Kenya, Bacre Waly Ndiaye, a Senegalese lawyer, was appointed Special Rapporteur.
34. SRESAE, 1993 report, paragraph 26.

Like the Working Group on Disappearances, the Special Rapporteur has sent urgent appeals also in response to allegations of "acts of intimidation or reprisal in violation of the right to life against those cooperating with United Nations human rights procedures and their legal advisors and against relatives of victims of human rights violations" (*ibid.*, paragraph 27). In 1992 he sent such appeals to the governments of 12 countries – Brazil, Chile, Colombia, Cuba, El Salvador, Guatemala, Honduras, Israel, Mexico, Peru, Rwanda and Sri Lanka. (*Cooperation with representative of United Nations bodies...*, *op. cit.*, paragraph 23).

35. Paragraphs 133-139, 226, 425.

36. Paragraph 183.

37. To ensure human rights protection, Amnesty International regularly urges states to become parties to both instruments. The UN also periodically calls for states to become parties to these instruments. Thus, UN General Assembly resolution 46/113, adopted on 17 December 1991 without a vote, states that "The General Assembly ... (a)gain urges all States that have not yet done so to become parties to ... the International Covenant on Civil and Political Rights and to consider acceding to the Optional Protocols to the International Covenant on Civil and Political Rights ... "

38. The texts of the International Covenant and the first Optional Protocol may be found in "The International Bill of Human Rights" and in *Human Rights; A Compilation of International Instruments,* cited in Chapter 8.

39. For a description of the reporting process and the issues to be considered under each article of the Covenant, see UN Centre for Human Rights, *Manual on Human Rights Reporting under Six Major International Human Rights Instruments,* United Nations, New York, UN Sales No. E.91.XIV.1, 1991.

40. See Dominic McGoldrick, *The Human Rights Committee; Its Role in the Development of the International Covenant on Civil and Political Rights,* Clarendon Press, Oxford, 1991, page 331.

41. The Report of the Human Rights Committee is published each year as Supplement No. 40 to the Official Records of the UN General Assembly.

42. A short description of the work of the Human Rights Committee is given in "Human Rights Machinery", *Human Rights Fact Sheets* series, No. 1, UN Centre for Human Rights, Geneva, 1988, pages 12-14. For a more detailed description of the procedure for examining individual complaints, see UN Centre for Human Rights, *United Nations Action in the Field of Human Rights,* United Nations, New York, UN Sales No. E.88.XIV.2, 1988, paragraphs 100-115.

43. The Bleier and Quinteros decisions are given respectively in *Human Rights Committee,* 1982 report, Annex XI and 1983 report, Annex XXII. For an analysis of the decisions, see Rodley, *op. cit.,* pages 192-93, 199, 201, 203 and 205.

In the case of Elena Quinteros, who the Committee found had been tortured, in violation of Article 7 of the International Covenant on Civil and Political Rights, the Committee found that her mother also, who had brought the case, "is a victim of the violations of the Covenant, in particular of article 7, suffered by her daughter". This conclusion flowed from the Committee's understanding of "the anguish and stress caused to the mother by the disappearance of her daughter and by the continuing uncertainty concerning her fate and whereabouts." As Rodley has observed, "In so far as 'in these respects' the mother 'is a victim of the violations...suffered by her daughter', it appears to follow that the article 7 violation of Elena Quinteros's rights stemmed from her 'disappearance' itself, as well as the torture in the detention centre. In any event, the decision gives formal recognition that the close family of the victim of a 'disappearance' is also subjected to torture or other ill-treatment." (Rodley, *op. cit.*, page 201)

As the Uruguayan Government had not taken the steps called for by the Human Rights Committee, the relatives of Eduardo Bleier and Elena Quinteros resubmitted the cases to the Committee in 1988. The Committee has not yet published its new views on the two cases. In 1993, however, during the Committee's review of Uruguay's periodic report under the Covenant, Committee members criticized Uruguay for curtailing the ability of victims of human rights violations to obtain redress.

44. Human Rights Committee, 1985 report, Annex X, pages 187-195.

45. When the periodic report of a state party to the International Covenant on Civil and Political Rights is about to be examined by the Human Rights Committee, well documented information on human rights violations in that country may be useful to Committee members in preparing to question the country's representative. Information should be addressed to the Committee member by name, whose title should be given as "Member of the Human Rights Committee", and sent to him or her c/o Human Rights Liaison Office, United Nations Headquarters, New York, NY 10017, USA if the Committee is to meet in New York and c/o the UN Centre for Human Rights if the meeting is to be in Geneva. It is advisable to send copies to each member of the Committee and to ensure that they arrive no later than one week before the session so that the pre-sessional working group which prepares questions for the full Committee can take this information into account. It is also possible to offer information informally to Committee members during periods when the Committee is in session (although not during the actual meetings). For information on the agendas of future Human Rights Committee meetings and the results of meetings held, see *Human Rights Monitor* (cited above).

46. Recommendations for strengthening the work of the Human Rights Committee are contained in Amnesty International, "World Conference on Human Rights; Facing up to the failures: proposals for improving the protection of human rights by the United Nations", AI Index: IOR 41/16/92, pages 30-39 and in Torkel Opsahl, "The Human Rights Committee", in Alston, ed., *op. cit.*, pages 369-443. See also the recommendations in UN General Assembly, *Effective implementation of international instruments on human rights... Note by the Secretary-General*, UN document No. A/47/628, 10 November 1992.

47. See "Advisory Services and Technical Assistance in the Field of Human Rights", *Human Rights Fact Sheets* series, No. 3, UN Centre for Human Rights, Geneva, 1988.

48. The Working Group on Disappearances, for example, noted in its 1993 report that "the staff servicing the group is not only less than half the size it was in 1980, when the Group started, but it also deals with a task which has grown exponentially over the past 12 years." (paragraph 522) In 1992 the Working Group transmitted twice as many cases to governments as in 1991, but some 8,000 cases still awaited consideration by the Working Group staff (paragraph 521). "At present, the Working Group understands that the members of its staff have reached a point where they can no longer cope with the workload. This means that, unless additional personnel is assigned to the Working Group, an ever-increasing proportion of the cases received by the

Group will not be analyzed, processed and transmitted. The older the backlog, the less likelihood there is that the fate and whereabouts of the disappeared will ever come to light. The dialogue with Governments and non-governmental organizations will be seriously hampered and the Group's main humanitarian function seriously jeopardized. The Group's credibility is bound to dwindle and its activities, as a result, will tend to become marginalized. Unless decisive action is taken...the achievements of the Group since 1980 may be dissipated irretrievably." (paragraph 523)

The Special Rapporteur on extrajudicial, summary or arbitrary executions wrote in his 1993 report (paragraphs 700-701) that in order to discharge his mandate effectively, including country visits, he would need three professional staff and a full-time secretary, rather than the one professional staff then provided by the Centre for Human Rights. He also called attention to the need for better computer facilities at the Centre.

49. Sometimes budget cuts are aimed at specific parts of the human rights program which are understandably disliked by the member states under scrutiny. Iain Guest has told the story of how in 1981 Argentina, which had been prominently mentioned in the first report of the Working Group on Disappearances, persuaded a UN budgetary advisory committee to cut $54,900 from the human rights budget. According to Guest, this was the exact amount needed to finance the Working Group for the next year along with the UN investigation on Chile. Fortunately the Director of the UN Division on Human Rights learned what had happened and was able to persuade member states to reinstate the sum at a later stage in the General Assembly's consideration of the budget. (Guest, *op. cit.*, page 308)

50. Tolley, *op. cit.*, page 217.

51. For a discussion of the functioning of the Centre for Human Rights and the activities of the Secretary-General in human rights matters, see Theo van Boven, "The Role of the United Nations Secretariat", in Alston, ed., *op. cit.*, pages 549-579.

52. There are other avenues also for the submission of complaints. For example, if there is reliable evidence that a person was tortured, a complaint can be sent to the Committee against Torture if the state concerned is a party to the Convention against Torture and Other Cruel, Inhuman or Degrading Treatment or Punishment and has made a declaration recognizing the competence of that Committee to consider individual complaints under Article 22 of the Convention. Such complaints should be sent to the Committee against Torture, c/o the UN Centre for Human Rights.

53. For further information on sending communications to the UN, see UN Centre for Human Rights, *Human Rights Fact Sheets* series, No. 6, "Enforced or Involuntary Disappearances"; No. 7, "Communications Procedures"; No. 11, "Summary or Arbitrary Executions". For more on sending information to UN and other international and regional bodies, see Amnesty International, "Summary of selected international procedures and bodies dealing with human rights matters", *op. cit.*

When considering whether to submit a complaint to the Human Rights Committee or a regional human rights body, it is advisable to consult others, including lawyers, who have had experience in doing so. Organizations which can advise on this matter include

Interights

5-15 Cromer Street

London WC1H 8LS
United Kingdom
Telephone: +44 71 278 3230
Facsimile: +44 71 278 4334

and

International Human Rights Law Group
1601 Connecticut Avenue NW, Suite 700
Washington DC 20009
USA
Telephone: +1 202 232 8500
Facsimile: +1 202 232 6731

54. In the case of El Salvador, for example, human rights was a component in the peace process, as established in the Geneva Agreement of 1990 which stated that the purpose of the process was "to end the armed conflict by political means as speedily as possible, promote the democratization of the country, *guarantee unrestricted respect for human rights* and reunify Salvadorian society". ("Geneva Agreement", section 1, in *El Salvador Agreements: The Path to Peace*, cited in Chapter 9; emphasis added)

A 1993 report by the UN Observer Mission in El Salvador (ONUSAL) commented that the inclusion of respect for human rights in the Geneva Agreement reflected an understanding between the two warring parties of "the interrelationship that exists between the ending of the armed conflict, the consolidation of democracy and respect for the human rights of the population." This understanding "does not assimilate peace with the elimination of the armed conflict." Instead, it recognizes "that the achievement of peace is structurally linked to the adoption of a complex series of undertakings, constitutional and institutional reforms and the adjustment of individual and social conduct, with a view to replacing the culture of violence created by 11 years of armed conflict by a culture of human rights." (UN Commission on Human Rights, *Note by the Secretary-General*, UN document No. E/CN.4/1993/96, 22 February 1993, paragraph 3)

For an assessment of human rights protection in UN operations in different countries, see Human Rights Watch, *The Lost Agenda; Human Rights and UN Field Operations*, Human Rights Watch, New York, 1993.

55. "San José Agreement on Human Rights", paragraphs 1, 13-15, in *El Salvador Agreements...*, pages 7-12. The mission did not, however, have the power to enforce its recommendations.

56. First report of the Director of the ONUSAL Human Rights Division, paragraphs 7-10; second report, paragraphs 18-43; third report, paragraphs 31, 32; fifth report, paragraphs 12, 19, 26; sixth report, annex, page 64.

57. The UN Independent Expert on El Salvador, appointed in pursuance of a decision of the UN Commission on Human Rights, reported that as of early 1993 most of the recommendations of the UN human rights verification mission had not been implemented. (UN Commission on Human Rights, *Report of the Independent Expert on El Salvador...*, UN document No. E/CN.4/1993/11, 9 February 1993, paragraphs 224-241, 268) See also Americas Watch, "El Salvador; Peace and Human Rights: Successes and Shortcomings of the United Nations Observer Mission in El Salvador (ONUSAL)", *News From Americas Watch*, vol. 4, No. 8, 2 September 1992.

58. Article 16 of the Comprehensive Political Settlement of the Cambodia Conflict, adopted at the Paris Conference on Cambodia in October 1991, states that UNTAC "shall be responsible during the transitional period for fostering an environment in which respect for human rights shall be ensured". Annex 1 to the Comprehensive Political Settlement sets forth UNTAC's human rights mandate in greater detail.

By the end of 1992 the Human Rights Component of UNTAC had a professional staff of 10 in the capital, Phnom Penh; some of these officers dealt with monitoring and investigation while others were responsible for training, education and information. A correspondent was assigned to each of the 21 provinces. As of November 1992 the Human Rights Component had received 14 complaints involving wrongful death and had conducted investigations into abductions and killings. (UN Commission on Human Rights, *Situation in Cambodia; Report of the Secretary-General*, E/CN.4/1993/19, 14 January 1993, paragraphs 10-11, 15-19) However, the Human Rights Component was not given access to areas controlled by the Party of Democratic Kampuchea, the "Khmer Rouge".

59. This decision was taken in resolution 1993/74, adopted by the Commission on Human Rights on 10 March 1993. In 1991 Amnesty International had called on the UN to establish an on-site monitoring operation in Iraq to prevent further killings and torture by governmental forces. In 1992 the UN Special Rapporteur on Iraq recommended to the Commission on Human Rights that a team of human rights monitors be sent to Iraq. He reiterated the recommendation in his 1993 report to the Commission.

60. Amnesty International, "Mozambique; The role of the United Nations in the protection of human rights under the General Peace Agreement", AI Index: AFR 41/01/93, January 1993.

61. "Somalia; Update on a disaster – Proposals for human rights", AI Index: AFR 52/01/93, April 1993.

62. Oral statement to the exceptional session of the UN Commission on Human Rights, 30 November – 1 December 1992, AI Index: EUR 48/31/92.

63. Sixth report, paragraph 41.

64. For a brief discussion, see van Boven, *op. cit.*, pages 556-559. See also B.G. Ramcharan, *Humanitarian Good Offices in International Law; The Good Offices of the United Nations Secretary-General in the Field of Human Rights*, Nijhoff, The Hague, the Netherlands, 1983. In resolution 33/173 of 20 December 1978 on disappeared persons, cited earlier in this chapter, the UN General Assembly urged the Secretary-General "to continue to use his good offices in cases of enforced or involuntary disappearances of persons".

65. Guidelines on UN fact-finding missions are contained in the Declaration on Fact-Finding by the United Nations in the Field of the Maintenance of International Peace and Security, adopted by the UN General Assembly on 9 December 1991 in resolution 46/59.

66. A draft Inter-American Convention on the Enforced Disappearance of Persons was prepared by the Inter-American Commission on Human Rights in accordance with a decision of the OAS General Assembly and was published in 1988. Since then the draft has been revised several times. Amnesty International and other human rights organizations have urged that the text of the Convention should contain the strongest possible provisions for the eradication of "disappearances".

67. On the history of the formation of the Inter-American Commission and the later

establishment of the Commission as a principal organ of the OAS under the amended OAS Charter, see Inter-American Commission on Human Rights, *Ten Years of Activities; 1971-1981*, Organization of American States, General Secretariat, Washington, 1982, pages 5-7.

68. In the area of "disappearances" and extrajudicial executions, one of the most important on-site investigations conducted by the Inter-American Commission was its visit to Argentina in September 1979. The Commission received 5,580 complaints of "disappearances", most of which had not reached it before. Its devastating report, published in 1980, described the formation of special units in the armed forces which carried out "disappearances" and said that the authorities "could not have been ignorant of the events as they were occurring and did not adopt the necessary measures to terminate them". The report was angrily rejected by the Argentinian Government. (*'Disappearances'; A Workbook*, pages 12, 138-141; Guest, *op. cit.*, pages 176-177)

69. These obligations involve the observance of the human rights recognized in the American Convention on Human Rights or (for states which are not parties to the American Convention) the American Declaration on the Rights and Duties of Man.

70. For example, by the Human Rights Committee set up under the International Covenant on Civil and Political Rights.

71. American Convention on Human Rights, Articles 41, 44-51; Dinah L. Shelton, "The Inter-American Human Rights System", in Hurst Hannum, ed., *Guide to International Human Rights Practice*, second edition, University of Pennsylvania Press, Philadelphia, 1992, pages 119-132. The article by Shelton gives details on the admissibility of petitions to the Inter-American Commission.

72. Shelton, *op. cit.*, pages 129-130.

73. The procedure for submission and consideration of complaints before the European Commission on Human Rights is described in Kevin Boyle, "Europe: The Council of Europe, the CSCE, and the European Community", in Hannum, ed., *op. cit.*, pages 133-158.

74. The African Commission held its first session in 1987 and has only recently begun reviewing states' reports. The Commission has received over 100 individual complaints under Article 55, but it did not send any of these complaints to the OAU Assembly urging that it request the Commission to conduct an in-depth study until its 13th session in March and April 1993. As the work of the Commission develops, it is to be hoped that a strong role will emerge for it in the protection of the individual against "disappearances", extrajudicial executions and other human rights violations in Africa. See Amnesty International, "The Organization of African Unity and Human Rights", AI Index: IOR 63/01/91, 1991; Cees Flinterman and Evelyn Ankumah, "The African Charter on Human and Peoples' Rights", in Hannum, ed., *op. cit.*, pages 159-170.

75. The European Community (EC) changed into the EU on 1 November 1993 with the coming into force of the Treaty on European Union, signed in Maastricht, the Netherlands, in 1992 and finally ratified by all EC member states by 1 November 1993. The EU is founded on the European Communities supplemented by the policies and forms of cooperation established by the Treaty on European Union establishing political union.

76. These statements are issued in the name of the EU (formerly the EC) and its member states. Recent statements have referred to extrajudicial executions and arbitrary and deliberate killings by opposition forces in Sri Lanka (22 October 1990), the killing of demonstrators in Dili, East Timor by Indonesian forces (13 February 1992), mass killings and "ethnic cleansing" in former Yugoslavia (5 October 1992) and killings in Rwanda (15 February 1992).

Under the EC such joint statements were adopted within the framework of the European Political Cooperation, a process of information, consultation and common action among the EC member states. The country holding the rotating presidency of the EC Council of Ministers was in charge of the European Political Cooperation and played a key role in initiatives taken within its framework.

Since the coming into force of the Treaty on European Union, the European Political Cooperation has been replaced by a Common Foreign and Security Policy. Statements and other diplomatic steps concerning human rights are now presented in the name of the EU.

77. Recent European Parliament resolutions have referred among other things to killings of members of the Tuareg ethnic group in Mali (adopted on 9 July 1992), killings of street children in Colombia (12 March 1992) and Guatemala (9 April 1992), political killings in the Philippines (9 April 1992), "disappearances" in Morocco (27 May 1993), and the assassination of a deputy mayor in Peru by the opposition group the *Partido Communista del Perú* (*Sendero Luminoso*), Communist Party of Peru (Shining Path) (12 March 1992).

78. On individual petitions, see Boyle, *op. cit.*, 1992, pages 154-155. For a discussion of action by EU institutions on human rights inside and outside the EU, see Andrew Clapham, *Human Rights and the European Community: A Critical Overview*, Nomos, Baden-Baden, 1991.

79. UN document No. A/Conf.157/PC/35; also published as UN document No. A/45/421.

80. *Report on the Work of the Organization... September 1992, op. cit.*, paragraph 101.

81. In one incident described by Iain Guest, the Argentinian representative tried to block Emilio Mignone, director of the Argentinian Centre for Legal and Social Studies, from addressing the UN Commission on Human Rights on behalf of the International Commission of Jurists in 1982. The Argentinian representative told the Commission that Mignone, whose daughter had "disappeared" in 1976, "was arrested in Argentina earlier this year on the serious charge of violating state security. He has even called for sanctions against his own government!" After a recess of several hours, the Commission decided to let Mignone speak. (Guest, *op. cit.*, pages 329-331 and Chapter 24, note 22)

82. For example, the Working Group on Disappearances stated in 1984 that it would like to visit Guatemala, where many "disappearances" had been reported, but there was no response to its request until a constitutional government took power in 1986, and it was finally in 1987 that the Working Group visited the country (WGEID, *Report on a visit to Guatemala...*, 1981, paragraphs 1-2).

In the 10 years since the establishment of the Special Rapporteur on summary or arbitrary executions in 1982, the first Special Rapporteur was able to visit only four countries. Since 1992 the pace of visits has increased (see above, section 5). In his 1993 report the Special Rapporteur reiterated the importance of on-site visits and said he would continue to seek invitations (paragraphs 35-37, 88-91, 695).

83. These and other recommendations are presented in Amnesty International, "World Conference on Human Rights; Facing up to the failures...", *op. cit.*, pages 26-30.

84. One important step has been for Special Rapporteurs and Working Groups to return to countries which they have visited before, in order to see how their recommendations are being addressed and to offer further advice and observations. A good example is the 1992 follow-up visit to Sri Lanka by three members of the Working Group on Disappearances who had visited

the country the year before. In the report on their second visit, the three experts noted that the number of "disappearances" had declined but was still of serious concern, and that few of the detailed recommendations offered in their first report had been implemented. (WGEID, *Report on the visit to Sri Lanka... (5-15 October 1992)*, paragraphs 126-131).

Other improvements are reflected in the 1993 report of the Special Rapporteur on extrajudicial, summary or arbitrary executions (paragraphs 79, 694, 696). In requesting governments to clarify cases, the Special Rapporteur now supplies a list of the details needed (an innovation which should encourage governments to be more specific in their replies), and he has taken the initiative to work more closely with other UN mechanisms and procedures dealing with subjects related to his mandate.

Despite the improvements, the efforts of the Working Group and the Special Rapporteur will still fall short of expectations if UN member states fail to provide the necessary funds, do not heed their recommendations, or impose crippling restrictions on their activities. For example, the Special Rapporteur can act only on the basis of information formally submitted to him, and has more than once been unable to act "in a situation where there were serious grounds to believe that extrajudicial, summary or arbitrary executions were being committed in certain countries, sometimes even on a large scale and, on occasion, covered by extensive reports in the [news] media, concerning which he had not received any allegations" (1993 report, paragraph 14).

85. See "World Conference on Human Rights; Facing up to the failures...", *op. cit.*

86. There have been many attempts in this century to establish a permanent international criminal court. After the Second World War the International Law Commission was asked to draft a statute for an international criminal court, but the Cold War stifled progress. The end of the Cold War and the move to establish an International Tribunal for the former Yugoslavia (see Chapter 8, section 5) revived interest in the idea. In resolution 47/33, adopted on 25 November 1992 without a vote, the UN General Assembly requested the International Law Commission to work on preparing a draft statute of an international criminal court, and to submit a progress report to the General Assembly in 1993. (The International Law Commission, established by the General Assembly in 1947, is an expert body which has as its object the progressive development of international law and its codification.)

Chapter 13   **Deliberate and arbitrary killings by armed opposition groups**

1. Noting that the Geneva Conventions do not contain a clear definition of the conflicts covered by common Article 3, the Commentary on the Third Convention published by the International Committee of the Red Cross (ICRC) states the opinion that "the scope of application of the Article must be as wide as possible." (*The Geneva Conventions of 12 August 1949; Commentary published under the general editorship of Jean S. Pictet...; III Geneva Convention...*, International Committee of the Red Cross, Geneva, 1960) The Commentaries have been published by the ICRC in four volumes – one volume on each Convention. The statement quoted above appears also in the Commentary on the Fourth Geneva Convention, and a similiar statement appears in the Commentary on the First Convention.

2. Murder, hostage-taking and torture are prohibited also under Article 4 of Additional Protocol

II to the Geneva Conventions. Additional Protocol II applies to armed conflicts between the armed forces of a state party to the Protocol and "dissident armed forces or other organized armed groups which, under responsible command, exercise such control over a part of its territory as to enable them to carry out sustained and concerted military operations and to implement this Protocol" (Article 1 (1)).

3. The ICRC Commentary on the First Geneva Convention stresses the advantages of an insurgent party to an armed conflict, "in revolt against the established authority", respecting the provisions of common Article 3, even though such an organization does not "represent a legal entity capable of undertaking international obligations". (One such advantage would be the improvement of their image as an organization which respects minimum standards of humane behaviour.) Furthermore, as the Commentary points out with reference to insurgents in revolt against a state party to the Geneva Conventions, "if the responsible authority at their head exercises effective sovereignty, it is bound by the very fact that it claims to represent the country, or part of the country." The same statement appears in the Commentaries on the Third and Fourth Geneva Conventions, and a similar statement appears in the Commentary on the Second Convention.

4. According to the ICRC Commentaries on the First and Fourth Geneva Conventions, this provision of common Article 3 "makes it absolutely clear that the object of the Convention is a purely humanitarian one, that it is in no way concerned with the internal affairs of States, and that it merely ensures respect for the few essential rules of humanity which all civilized nations consider as valid everywhere and under all circumstances and as being above and outside war itself." A similar statement appears in the Commentary on the Third Convention.

5. Recently several attempts have been made to draw up minimum standards of humane behaviour. For example, the participants in an expert meeting convened by the Institute for Human Rights at Åbo Akademi University University in Turku/Åbo, Finland from 30 November to 2 December 1990 adopted a "Declaration of Minimum Humanitarian Standards". The text was forwarded to the UN in a *Working paper submitted by Mr. Theo van Boven and Mr. Asbjorn Eide* to the UN Sub-Commission on Prevention of Discrimination and Protection of Minorities (UN document No. E/CN.4/Sub.2/1991/55, 12 August 1991) and was reprinted in the *International Review of the Red Cross*, No. 282, May-June 1991, pages 328-336. Two earlier sets of proposed minimum standards of humane behaviour are the "Code of Conduct in the Event of Internal Disturbances and Tensions" and the "Draft model Declaration on internal strife", contained in: Hans-Peter Gasser, "A Measure of Humanity in Internal Disturbances and Tensions: Proposal for a Code of Conduct", and Theodor Meron, "Draft Model Declaration on Internal Strife", published in the *International Review of the Red Cross*, No. 262, January-February 1988, pages 38-58 and 59-76 respectively. Like common Article 3, all three of these draft instruments prohibit "murder", and all three also explicitly prohibit "disappearances".

6. As stated in the ICRC Commentaries on the First, Third and Fourth Geneva Conventions, common Article 3 "merely demands respect for certain rules, which were already recognized as essential in all civilized countries, and enacted in the municipal law of the States in question, long before the Convention was signed."

7. See Louise Doswald-Beck and Sylvain Vité, "International Humanitarian Law and Human Rights Law", *International Review of the Red Cross*, No. 293, March-April 1993, pages 94-119.

8. As one expert has written, certain norms stated in common Article 3, including the prohibition

of torture and murder, are "of such an elementary, ethical character, and echo so many provisions in other humanitarian and human rights treaties, that they must be regarded as embodying minimum standards of customary law also applicable to non-international armed conflicts" (Theodor Meron, *Human Rights and Humanitarian Norms as Customary Law*, Clarendon Press, Oxford, 1989, page 34). The importance of a norm's *customary* character is that such a norm is binding on states that are not parties to the instrument in which that norm is restated (*op. cit.*, page 3).

9. For more examples of deliberate and arbitrary killings by armed opposition groups, see Chapter 7, section 7 and *Getting Away with Murder; Political Killings and 'Disappearances' in the 1990s*, Amnesty International Publications, London, 1993, pages 38-48.

Chapter 14   International action

1. The word "refoulement" comes from the French word *refouler*, to turn back. Refoulement means returning a person forcibly to his or her country.

2. The text of the 1951 Convention is reproduced in *Human Rights; A Compilation of International Instruments*, cited in Chapter 8.

3. Article 14, paragraph 1 of the Universal Declaration of Human Rights states: "Everyone has the right to seek and to enjoy in other countries asylum from persecution."

4. *Report on the Work of the Organization...* September 1992, paragraph 104 (*cited in Chapter 12*).

5. *Cited in Chapter 10.*

6. For example, the work of the Chilean Association of Relatives of the Detained-Disappeared (AFDD), formed in 1974, is described in *Disappearances; A Workbook*, pages 113-115. This organization, the Argentinean Mothers of the Plaza de Mayo and the Guatemalan Mutual Support Group for the Reappearance of our Sons, Fathers, Husbands and Brothers are discussed in Jennifer G. Schirmer, "Those Who Die for Life Cannot Be Called Dead: Women and Human Rights Protest in Latin America", *Harvard Human Rights Yearbook*, Harvard Law School, Cambridge, Massachusetts, USA, Volume 1 (1988), pages 41-76. The history of the Argentinean Mothers of the Plaza de Mayo has been described in several books; see, for example, Alfredo Martin, *Les Mères "folles" de la Place de Mai; Maternité, contre-institution et raison d'état*, Reanudot, Paris, 1989.

The *Federación Latinoamericana de Asociaciones de Familiares de Detenidos-Desaparecidos* (FEDEFAM), Latin American Federation of Associations of Families of the "Disappeared", brings together national organizations of relatives of the "disappeared" in Latin America and presses for the resolution of cases of "disappearance" at the regional and international levels. For further information contact FEDEFAM, Apartado Postal 2444, Carmelitas 1010-A, Caracas, Venezuela.

7. For a general analysis of the work of human rights organizations, see Alejandro Artucio, "Los Derechos Humanos y las Organizaciones No Gubernamentales (ONG)", *Revista de IELSUR*, Instituto de Estudios Legales y Sociales del Uruguay, No. 2 (July 1988), pages 13-22.

The organization SOS-Torture is a clearing-house for information on "disappearances", political killings and torture, serving a worldwide network of non-governmental human rights organizations. Organizations wishing to join the network can contact SOS-Torture, Boîte Postale 119, 1211 Geneva, Switzerland.

Directories of human rights organizations in different regions of the world have been published as special issues of the *Human Rights Internet Reporter*. For further information contact Human Rights Internet, c/o Human Rights Centre, University of Ottawa, 57 Louis Pasteur, Ottawa, Ontario K1N 6N5, Canada.

8. One of Amnesty International's earliest missions concerned with "disappearances" was a visit to Argentina in November 1976, eight months after the military coup which marked the beginning of "disappearances" as a systematic practice. Despite official surveillance and a stream of hostile and misleading reports in the national press, the Amnesty International team was able to receive personal testimonies from the relatives of more than 100 missing people who came to see them. The published report described the process by which an alleged 2,000 to 5,000 people had joined the "ghostly army" of the "disappeared" since the coup and gave details of 343 cases recorded by Amnesty International. (Amnesty International, *Report of an Amnesty International Mission to Argentina; 6-15 November 1976, Amnesty International, London 1977*. For an account of the Amnesty International mission, see Guest, *op. cit.*, pages 76-86)

9. In 1993, for example, Amnesty International members in over 30 countries campaigned intensively for an end to political killings and "disappearances" in Chad. They wrote letters calling on the Chadian authorities to fulfil their publicly stated promises to establish safeguards for the protection of human rights, urged the governments of other countries to intercede with the Chadian authorities to the same end, and worked to publicize the little-known human rights tragedy in Chad, where over 600 people have been victims of extrajudicial executions since the present government came to power in December 1990. In recent years Amnesty International has campaigned on other countries where "disappearances" and/or political killings were major concerns, including Sudan in 1989-90, Brazil and Sri Lanka in 1990, Myanmar in 1990-91, Morocco in 1991, Peru in 1991-92, the Philippines in 1992 and Uganda in 1992-93.

10. On the ICRC's work against "disappearances", see "The Fight Against Forced Disappearances" (pages 24-25), in "ICRC Protection and Assistance Activities in Situations not Covered by International Humanitarian Law", *International Review of the Red Cross*, No. 262 (January-February 1988), pages 9-37.

Publications describing the work of the ICRC may be obtained from national Red Cross and Red Crescent Societies or from the ICRC Publications and Documentation Service, 19 avenue de la Paix, 1202 Geneva, Switzerland.

11. Among international organizations working against "disappearances" and extrajudicial executions and on related problems are the International Commission of Jurists, whose headquarters are in Geneva; the Fédération Internationale des Droits de l'Homme, International Federation of Human Rights, whose headquarters are in Paris; Human Rights Watch, based in the USA and comprising five regional Watch Committees (Africa Watch, Americas Watch, Asia Watch, Helsinki Watch and Middle East Watch); the Lawyers Committee for Human Rights, located in New York; Physicians for Human Rights, located in Boston; the Comisión Andina de Juristas, Andean Commission of Jurists, located in Lima.

12. The most recent such statement is in resolution 46/124 on national institutions for the protection and promotion of human rights, adopted by the General Assembly without a vote on 17 December 1991.

13. Artucio, *op. cit.*, pages 15-16.

APPENDICES

APPENDIX 1 **UNIVERSAL DECLARATION OF HUMAN RIGHTS**
(extracts)

Article 3
Everyone has the right to life, liberty and security of person.
Article 5
No one shall be subjected to torture or to cruel, inhuman or degrading treatment or punishment.
Article 9
No one shall be subjected to arbitrary arrest, detention or exile.

APPENDIX 2 **INTERNATIONAL COVENANT ON CIVIL AND POLITICAL RIGHTS** (extracts)

Article 6 (1)
Every human being has the inherent right to life. This right shall be protected by law. No one shall be arbitrarily deprived of his life.
Article 7 (extract)
No one shall be subjected to torture or to cruel, inhuman or degrading treatment or punishment. ...
Article 9 (1)
Everyone has the right to liberty and security of person. No one shall be subjected to arbitrary arrest or detention. No one shall be deprived of his liberty except on such grounds and in accordance with such procedure as are established by law.

APPENDIX 3 **GENEVA CONVENTIONS AND ADDITIONAL PROTOCOLS** (extracts)

a **Geneva Convention for the Amelioration of the Condition of the Wounded and Sick in Armed Forces in the Field of 12 August 1949** (First Geneva Convention)

Article 50 (extract)
Grave breaches to which the preceding Article relates shall be those involving any of the following acts, if committed against persons or property protected by the Convention: wilful killing, torture or inhuman treatment...
[Note: This identical language appears in the First Geneva Convention, Article 50, the Second Geneva Convention, Article 51, and the Third Geneva Convention, Article 130. The Fourth Geneva Convention,

Article 147, contains the same text with the additional word "present" before the word "Convention" ("... protected by the present Convention").]

b   **The four Geneva Conventions of 12 August 1949**
Article 3 common to the four Geneva Conventions

In the case of armed conflict not of an international character occurring in the territory of one of the High Contracting Parties, each Party to the conflict shall be bound to apply, as a minimum, the following provisions:

1   Persons taking no active part in the hostilities, including members of armed forces who have laid down their arms and those placed *hors de combat* by sickness, wounds, detention, or any other cause, shall in all circumstances be treated humanely, without any adverse distinction founded on race, colour, religion or faith, sex, birth or wealth, or any other similar criteria.

To this end, the following acts are and shall remain prohibited at any time and in any place whatsoever with respect to the above-mentioned persons:

(a) violence to life and person, in particular murder of all kinds, mutilation, cruel treatment and torture;

(b) taking of hostages;

(c) outrages upon personal dignity, in particular humiliating and degrading treatment;

(d) the passing of sentences and the carrying out of executions without previous judgment pronounced by a regularly constituted court, affording all the judicial guarantees which are recognized as indispensable by civilized peoples.

2   The wounded and sick shall be collected and cared for.

An impartial humanitarian body, such as the International Committee of the Red Cross, may offer its services to the Parties to the conflict.

The Parties to the conflict should further endeavour to bring into force, by means of special agreements, all or part of the other provisions of the present Convention.

The application of the preceding provisions shall not affect the legal status of the Parties to the conflict.

c   **Protocol Additional to the Geneva Conventions of 12 August 1949, and relating to the Protection of Victims of Non-International Armed Conflicts** (Additional Protocol II)
Article 4 – Fundamental guarantees (extract)

1   All persons who do not take a direct part or who have ceased to take part in hostilities, whether or not their liberty has been restricted, are entitled to respect for their person, honour and convictions and religious practices. They shall in all circumstances be treated humanely, without any adverse distinction. It is prohibited to order that there shall be no survivors.

2   Without prejudice to the generality of the foregoing, the following acts against the persons referred to in paragraph 1 are and shall remain prohibited at any time and in any place whatsoever:

(a) violence to the life, health and physical or mental well-being of persons, in particular murder as well as cruel treatment such as torture, mutilation or any form of corporal punishment...

APPENDIX 4   CODE OF CONDUCT FOR
LAW ENFORCEMENT OFFICIALS (extract)

Article 3

Law enforcement officials may use force only when strictly necessary and to the extent required for the performance of their duty.

> *Commentary:*
>
> (a) This provision emphasizes that the use of force by law enforcement officials should be exceptional; while it implies that law enforcement officials may be authorized to use force as is reasonably necessary under the circumstances for the prevention of crime or in effecting or assisting in the lawful arrest of offenders or suspected offenders, no force going beyond that may be used.
>
> (b) National law ordinarily restricts the use of force by law enforcement officials in accordance with a principle of proportionality. It is to be understood that such national principles of proportionality are to be respected in the interpretation of this provision. In no case should this provision be interpreted to authorize the use of force which is disproportionate to the legitimate objective to be achieved.
>
> (c) The use of firearms is considered an extreme measure. Every effort should be made to exclude the use of firearms, especially against children. In general, firearms should not be used except when a suspected offender offers armed resistance or otherwise jeopardizes the lives of others and less extreme measures are not sufficient to restrain or apprehend the suspected offender. In every instance in which a firearm is discharged, a report should be made promptly to the competent authorities.

APPENDIX 5   BASIC PRINCIPLES ON THE USE OF FORCE AND
FIREARMS BY LAW ENFORCEMENT OFFICIALS
(adopted by the Eighth UN Congress on the Prevention of
Crime and the Treatment of Offenders on 7 September 1990)

Whereas the work of law enforcement officials* is a social service of great importance and there is, therefore, a need to maintain and, whenever necessary, to improve the working conditions and status of these officials,

---

* In accordance with the commentary to article 1 of the Code of Conduct for Law Enforcement Officials, the term "law enforcement officials" includes all officers of the law, whether appointed or elected, who exercise police powers, especially the powers of arrest or detention. In countries where police powers are exercised by military authorities, whether uniformed or not, or by State security forces, the definition of law enforcement officials shall be regarded as including officers of such services.

Whereas a threat to the life and safety of law enforcement officials must be seen as a threat to the stability of society as a whole,

Whereas law enforcement officials have a vital role in the protection of the right to life, liberty and security of the person, as guaranteed in the Universal Declaration of Human Rights and reaffirmed in the International Covenant on Civil and Political Rights,

Whereas the Standard Minimum Rules for the Treatment of Prisoners provide for the circumstances in which prison officials may use force in the course of their duties,

Whereas article 3 of the Code of Conduct for Law Enforcement Officials provides that law enforcement officials may use force only when strictly necessary and to the extent required for the performance of their duty,

Whereas the preparatory meeting for the Seventh United Nations Congress on the Prevention of Crime and the Treatment of Offenders, held at Varenna, Italy, agreed on elements to be considered in the course of further work on restraints on the use of force and firearms by law enforcement officials,

Whereas the Seventh Congress, in its resolution 14, *inter alia*, emphasizes that the use of force and firearms by law enforcement officials should be commensurate with due respect for human rights,

Whereas the Economic and Social Council, in its resolution 1986/10, section IX, of 21 May 1986, invited Member States to pay particular attention in the implementation of the Code to the use of force and firearms by law enforcement officials, and the General Assembly, in its resolution 41/149 of 4 December 1986, *inter alia*, welcomed this recommendation made by the Council,

Whereas it is appropriate that, with due regard to their personal safety, consideration be given to the role of law enforcement officials in relation to the administration of justice, to the protection of the right to life, liberty and security of the person, to their responsibility to maintain public safety and social peace and to the importance of their qualifications, training and conduct,

The basic principles set forth below, which have been formulated to assist Member States in their task of ensuring and promoting the proper role of law enforcement officials, should be taken into account and respected by Governments within the framework of their national legislation and practice, and be brought to the attention of law enforcement officials as well as other persons, such as judges, prosecutors, lawyers, members of the executive branch and the legislature, and the public.

General provisions

1   Governments and law enforcement agencies shall adopt and implement rules and regulations on the use of force and firearms against persons by law enforcement officials. In developing such rules and regulations, Governments and law enforcement agencies shall keep the ethical issues associated with the use of force and firearms constantly under review.

2   Governments and law enforcement agencies should develop a range of means as broad as possible and equip law enforcement officials with various types of weapons and ammunition that would allow for a differentiated use of force and firearms. These should include the development of non-lethal incapacitating

weapons for use in appropriate situations, with a view to increasingly restraining the application of means capable of causing death or injury to persons. For the same purpose, it should also be possible for law enforcement officials to be equipped with self-defensive equipment such as shields, helmets, bullet-proof vests and bullet-proof means of transportation, in order to decrease the need to use weapons of any kind.

3   The development and deployment of non-lethal incapacitating weapons should be carefully evaluated in order to minimize the risk of endangering uninvolved persons, and the use of such weapons should be carefully controlled.

4   Law enforcement officials, in carrying out their duty, shall, as far as possible, apply non-violent means before resorting to the use of force and firearms. They may use force and firearms only if other means remain ineffective or without any promise of achieving the intended result.

5   Whenever the lawful use of force and firearms is unavoidable, law enforcement officials shall:

(a) Exercise restraint in such use and act in proportion to the seriousness of the offence and the legitimate objective to be achieved;

(b) Minimize damage and injury, and respect and preserve human life;

(c) Ensure that assistance and medical aid are rendered to any injured or affected persons at the earliest possible moment;

(d) Ensure that relatives or close friends of the injured or affected person are notified at the earliest possible moment.

6   Where injury or death is caused by the use of force and firearms by law enforcement officials, they shall report the incident promptly to their superiors, in accordance with principle 22.

7   Governments shall ensure that arbitrary or abusive use of force and firearms by law enforcement officials is punished as a criminal offence under their law.

8   Exceptional circumstances such as internal political instability or any other public emergency may not be invoked to justify any departure from these basic principles.

Special provisions

9   Law enforcement officials shall not use firearms against persons except in self-defence or defence of others against the imminent threat of death or serious injury, to prevent the perpetration of a particularly serious crime involving grave threat to life, to arrest a person presenting such a danger and resisting their authority, or to prevent his or her escape, and only when less extreme means are insufficient to achieve these objectives. In any event, intentional lethal use of firearms may only be made when strictly unavoidable in order to protect life.

10   In the circumstances provided for under principle 9, law enforcement officials shall identify themselves as such and give a clear warning of their intent to use firearms, with sufficient time for the warning to be observed, unless to do so would unduly place the law enforcement officials at risk or would create a risk of death or serious harm to other persons, or would be clearly inappropriate or

pointless in the circumstances of the incident.

11 Rules and regulations on the use of firearms by law enforcement officials should include guidelines that:

(a) Specify the circumstances under which law enforcement officials are authorized to carry firearms and prescribe the types of firearms and ammunition permitted;

(b) Ensure that firearms are used only in appropriate circumstances and in a manner likely to decrease the risk of unnecessary harm;

(c) Prohibit the use of those firearms and ammunition that cause unwarranted injury or present an unwarranted risk;

(d) Regulate the control, storage and issuing of firearms, including procedures for ensuring that law enforcement officials are accountable for the firearms and ammunition issued to them;

(e) Provide for warnings to be given, if appropriate, when firearms are to be discharged;

(f) Provide for a system of reporting whenever law enforcement officials use firearms in the performance of their duty.

Policing unlawful assemblies

12 As everyone is allowed to participate in lawful and peaceful assemblies, in accordance with the principles embodied in the Universal Declaration of Human Rights and the International Covenant on Civil and Political Rights, Governments and law enforcement agencies and officials shall recognize that force and firearms may be used only in accordance with principles 13 and 14.

13 In the dispersal of assemblies that are unlawful but non-violent, law enforcement officials shall avoid the use of force or, where that is not practicable, shall restrict such force to the minimum extent necessary.

14 In the dispersal of violent assemblies, law enforcement officials may use firearms only when less dangerous means are not practicable and only to the minimum extent necessary. Law enforcement officials shall not use firearms in such cases, except under the conditions stipulated in principle 9.

Policing persons in custody or detention

15 Law enforcement officials, in their relations with persons in custody or detention, shall not use force, except when strictly necessary for the maintenance of security and order within the institution, or when personal safety is threatened.

16 Law enforcement officials, in their relations with persons in custody or detention, shall not use firearms, except in self-defence or in the defence of others against the immediate threat of death or serious injury, or when strictly necessary to prevent the escape of a person in custody or detention presenting the danger referred to in principle 9.

17 The preceding principles are without prejudice to the rights, duties and responsibilities of prison officials, as set out in the Standard Minimum Rules for the Treatment of Prisoners, particularly rules 33, 34 and 54.

Qualifications, training and counselling

18   Governments and law enforcement agencies shall ensure that all law enforcement officials are selected by proper screening procedures, have appropriate moral, psychological and physical qualities for the effective exercise of their functions and receive continuous and thorough professional training. Their continued fitness to perform these functions should be subject to periodic review.

19   Governments and law enforcement agencies shall ensure that all law enforcement officials are provided with training and are tested in accordance with appropriate proficiency standards in the use of force. Those law enforcement officials who are required to carry firearms should be authorized to do so only upon completion of special training in their use.

20   In the training of law enforcement officials, Governments and law enforcement agencies shall give special attention to issues of police ethics and human rights, especially in the investigative process, to alternatives to the use of force and firearms, including the peaceful settlement of conflicts, the understanding of crowd behaviour, and the methods of persuasion, negotiation and mediation, as well as to technical means, with a view to limiting the use of force and firearms. Law enforcement agencies should review their training programmes and operational procedures in the light of particular incidents.

21   Governments and law enforcement agencies shall make stress counselling available to law enforcement officials who are involved in situations where force and firearms are used.

Reporting and review procedures

22   Governments and law enforcement agencies shall establish effective reporting and review procedures for all incidents referred to in principles 6 and 11 (f). For incidents reported pursuant to these principles, Governments and law enforcement agencies shall ensure that an effective review process is available and that independent administrative or prosecutorial authorities are in a position to exercise jurisdiction in appropriate circumstances. In cases of death and serious injury or other grave consequences, a detailed report shall be sent promptly to the competent authorities responsible for administrative review and judicial control.

23   Persons affected by the use of force and firearms or their legal representatives shall have access to an independent process, including a judicial process. In the event of the death of such persons, this provision shall apply to their dependants accordingly.

24   Governments and law enforcement agencies shall ensure that superior officers are held responsible if they know, or should have known, that law enforcement officials under their command are resorting, or have resorted, to the unlawful use of force and firearms, and they did not take all measures in their power to prevent, suppress or report such use.

25   Governments and law enforcement agencies shall ensure that no criminal or disciplinary sanction is imposed on law enforcement officials who, in compliance with the Code of Conduct for Law Enforcement Officials and these basic

principles, refuse to carry out an order to use force and firearms, or who report such use by other officials.

26   Obedience to superior orders shall be no defence if law enforcement officials knew that an order to use force and firearms resulting in the death or serious injury of a person was manifestly unlawful and had a reasonable opportunity to refuse to follow it. In any case, responsibility also rests on the superiors who gave the unlawful orders.

APPENDIX 6   DECLARATION ON THE PROTECTION OF ALL PERSONS FROM ENFORCED DISAPPEARANCE
(adopted by the UN General Assembly without a vote on 18 December 1992 in resolution 47/133)

The General Assembly,

Considering that, in accordance with the principles proclaimed in the Charter of the United Nations and other international instruments, recognition of the inherent dignity and of the equal and inalienable rights of all members of the human family is the foundation of freedom, justice and peace in the world,

Bearing in mind the obligation of States under the Charter of the United Nations, in particular Article 55, to promote universal respect for, and observance of, human rights and fundamental freedoms,

Deeply concerned that in many countries, often in a persistent manner, enforced disappearances occur, in the sense that persons are arrested, detained or abducted against their will or otherwise deprived of their liberty by officials of different branches or levels of Government, or by organized groups or private individuals acting on behalf of, or with the support, direct or indirect, consent or acquiescence of the Government, followed by a refusal to disclose the fate or whereabouts of the persons concerned or a refusal to acknowledge the deprivation of their liberty, thereby placing such persons outside the protection of the law,

Considering that enforced disappearance undermines the deepest values of any society committed to respect for the rule of law, human rights and fundamental freedoms, and that the systematic practice of such acts is of the nature of a crime against humanity,

Recalling resolution 33/173 of 20 December 1978, by which the General Assembly expressed concern about the reports from various parts of the world relating to enforced or involuntary disappearances, as well as about the anguish and sorrow caused by those disappearances, and called upon Governments to hold law enforcement and security forces legally responsible for excesses which might lead to enforced or involuntary disappearances of persons,

Recalling also the protection afforded to victims of armed conflicts by the Geneva Conventions of 12 August 1949 and the Additional Protocols of 1977,

Having regard in particular to the relevant articles of the Universal Declaration of Human Rights and the International Covenant on Civil and Political Rights, which protect the right to life, the right to liberty and security of the person, the right not to be subjected to torture and the right to recognition as a person before the law,

Having regard further to the Convention against Torture and Other Cruel, Inhuman or Degrading Treatment or Punishment, which provides that States parties shall take effective measures to prevent and punish acts of torture,

Bearing in mind the Code of Conduct for Law Enforcement Officials, the Basic Principles on the Use Of Force and Firearms by Law Enforcement Officials, the Declaration of Basic Principles of Justice for Victims of Crime and Abuse of Power and the Standard Minimum Rules for the Treatment of Prisoners,

Affirming that, in order to prevent enforced disappearances, it is necessary to ensure strict compliance with the Body of Principles for the Protection of All Persons under Any Form of Detention or Imprisonment contained in its resolution 43/173 of 9 December 1988, and with the Principles on the Effective Prevention and Investigation of Extra-legal, Arbitrary and Summary Executions, set forth in the annex to Economic and Social Council resolution 1989/65 of 24 May 1989 and endorsed by the General Assembly in its resolution 44/162 of 15 December 1989,

Bearing in mind that, while the acts which comprise enforced disappearance constitute a violation of the prohibitions found in the aforementioned international instruments, it is none the less important to devise an instrument which characterizes all acts of enforced disappearance of persons as very serious offences, setting forth standards designed to punish and prevent their commission,

1   *Proclaims* the present Declaration on the Protection of All Persons from Enforced Disappearance, as a body of principles for all States;

2   *Urges* that all efforts be made so that this Declaration becomes generally known and respected.

Article 1

1   Any act of enforced disappearance is an offence to human dignity. It is condemned as a denial of the purposes of the Charter of the United Nations and as a grave and flagrant violation of the human rights and fundamental freedoms proclaimed in the Universal Declaration of Human Rights and reaffirmed and developed in international instruments in this field.

2   Such act of enforced disappearance places the persons subjected thereto outside the protection of the law and inflicts severe suffering on them and their families. It constitutes a violation of the rules of international law guaranteeing, *inter alia*, the right to recognition as a person before the law, the right to liberty and security of the person and the right not to be subjected to torture and other cruel, inhuman or degrading treatment or punishment. It also violates or constitutes a grave threat to the right to life.

Article 2

1   No State shall practise, permit or tolerate enforced disappearances.

2   States shall act at the national and regional levels and in cooperation with the United Nations to contribute by all means to the prevention and eradication of enforced disappearance.

Article 3

Each State shall take effective legislative, administrative, judicial or other measures to prevent and terminate acts of enforced disappearance in any territory under its jurisdiction.

Article 4

1. All acts of enforced disappearance shall be offences under the criminal law punishable by appropriate penalties which shall take into account their extreme seriousness.

2. Mitigating circumstances may be established in national legislation for persons who, having participated in enforced disappearances, are instrumental in bringing the victims forward alive or in providing voluntarily information which would contribute to clarifying cases of enforced disappearance.

Article 5

In addition to such criminal penalties as are applicable, enforced disappearances render their perpetrators and the State or State authorities which organize, acquiesce in or tolerate such disappearances liable at civil law, without prejudice to the international responsibility of the State concerned in accordance with the principles of international law.

Article 6

1. No order or instruction of any public authority, civilian, military or other, may be invoked to justify an enforced disappearance. Any person receiving such an order or instruction shall have the right and duty not to obey it.

2. Each State shall ensure that orders or instructions directing, authorizing or encouraging any enforced disappearance are prohibited.

3. Training of law enforcement officials shall emphasize the above provisions.

Article 7

No circumstances whatsoever, whether a threat of war, a state of war, internal political instability or any other public emergency, may be invoked to justify enforced disappearances.

Article 8

1. No State shall expel, return (*refouler*) or extradite a person to another State where there are substantial grounds to believe that he would be in danger of enforced disappearance.

2. For the purpose of determining whether there are such grounds, the competent authorities shall take into account all relevant considerations including, where applicable, the existence in the State concerned of a consistent pattern of gross, flagrant or mass violations of human rights.

Article 9

1. The right to a prompt and effective judicial remedy as a means of determining the whereabouts or state of health of persons deprived of their liberty and/or identifying the authority ordering or carrying out the deprivation of liberty is required to prevent enforced disappearances under all circumstances, including those referred to in article 7.

2. In such proceedings, competent national authorities shall have access to all places holding persons deprived of their liberty and to each part thereof, as well as to

any place in which there are grounds to believe that such persons may be found.

3 Any other competent authority entitled under the law of the State or by any international legal instruments to which a State is a party may also have access to such places.

Article 10

1 Any person deprived of liberty shall be held in an officially recognized place of detention and, in conformity with national law, be brought before a judicial authority promptly after detention.

2 Accurate information on the detention of such persons and their place or places of detention, including transfers, shall be made promptly available to their family members, their counsel or to any other persons having a legitimate interest in the information unless a wish to the contrary has been manifested by the persons concerned.

3 An official up-to-date register of all persons deprived of their liberty shall be maintained in every place of detention. Additionally, each State shall take steps to maintain similar centralized registers. The information contained in these registers shall be made available to the persons mentioned in the paragraph above, to any judicial or other competent and independent national authority and to any other competent authority entitled under the law of the State concerned or any international legal instrument to which a State concerned is a party, seeking to trace the whereabouts of a detained person.

Article 11

All persons deprived of liberty must be released in a manner permitting reliable verification that they have actually been released and, further, have been released in conditions in which their physical integrity and ability fully to exercise their rights are assured.

Article 12

1 Each State shall establish rules under its national law indicating those officials authorized to order deprivation of liberty, establishing the conditions under which such orders may be given, and stipulating penalties for officials who, without legal justification, refuse to provide information on any detention.

2 Each State shall likewise ensure strict supervision, including a clear chain of command, of all law enforcement officials responsible for apprehensions, arrests, detentions, custody, transfers and imprisonment, and of other officials authorized by law to use force and firearms.

Article 13

1 Each State shall ensure that any person having knowledge or a legitimate interest who alleges that a person has been subjected to enforced disappearance has the right to complain to a competent and independent State authority and to have that complaint promptly, thoroughly and impartially investigated by that authority. Whenever there are reasonable grounds to believe that an enforced disappearance has been committed, the State shall promptly refer the matter to that authority for such an investigation, even if there has been no formal

complaint. No measure shall be taken to curtail or impede the investigation.

2   Each State shall ensure that the competent authority shall have the necessary powers and resources to conduct the investigation effectively, including powers to compel attendance of witnesses and production of relevant documents and to make immediate on-site visits.

3   Steps shall be taken to ensure that all involved in the investigation, including the complainant, counsel, witnesses and those conducting the investigation, are protected against ill-treatment, intimidation or reprisal.

4.   The findings of such an investigation shall be made available upon request to all persons concerned, unless doing so would jeopardize an ongoing criminal investigation.

5   Steps shall be taken to ensure that any ill-treatment, intimidation or reprisal or any other form of interference on the occasion of the lodging of a complaint or the investigation procedure is appropriately punished.

6   An investigation, in accordance with the procedures described above, should be able to be conducted for as long as the fate of the victim of enforced disappearance remains unclarified.

Article 14

Any person alleged to have perpetrated an act of enforced disappearance in a particular State shall, when the facts disclosed by an official investigation so warrant, be brought before the competent civil authorities of that State for the purpose of prosecution and trial unless he has been extradited to another State wishing to exercise jurisdiction in accordance with the relevant international agreements in force. All States should take any lawful and appropriate action available to them to bring all persons presumed responsible for an act of enforced disappearance, found to be within their jurisdiction or under their control, to justice.

Article 15

The fact that there are grounds to believe that a person has participated in acts of an extremely serious nature such as those referred to in article 4, paragraph 1, regardless of the motives, shall be taken into account when the competent authorities of the State decide whether or not to grant asylum.

Article 16

1   Persons alleged to have committed any of the acts referred to in article 4, paragraph 1, shall be suspended from any official duties during the investigation referred to in article 13.

2   They shall be tried only by the competent ordinary courts in each State, and not by any other special tribunal, in particular military courts.

3   No privileges, immunities or special exemptions shall be admitted in such trials, without prejudice to the provisions contained in the Vienna Convention on Diplomatic Relations.

4   The persons presumed responsible for such acts shall be guaranteed fair treatment in accordance with the relevant provisions of the Universal Declaration of Human Rights and other relevant international agreements in force at all stages

of the investigation and eventual prosecution and trial.

Article 17

1   Acts constituting enforced disappearance shall be considered a continuing offence as long as the perpetrators continue to conceal the fate and the whereabouts of persons who have disappeared and these facts remain unclarified.

2   When the remedies provided for in article 2 of the International Covenant on Civil and Political Rights are no longer effective, the statute of limitations relating to acts of enforced disappearance shall be suspended until these remedies are re-established.

3   Statutes of limitations, where they exist, relating to acts of enforced disappearance shall be substantial and commensurate with the extreme seriousness of the offence.

Article 18

1   Persons who have, or are alleged to have, committed offences referred to in article 4, paragraph 1, shall not benefit from any special amnesty law or similar measures that might have the effect of exempting them from any criminal proceedings or sanction.

2   In the exercise of the right of pardon, the extreme seriousness of acts of enforced disappearance shall be taken into account.

Article 19

The victims of acts of enforced disappearance and their family shall obtain redress and shall have the right to adequate compensation, including the means for as complete a rehabilitation as possible. In the event of the death of the victim as a result of an act of enforced disappearance, their dependants shall also be entitled to compensation.

Article 20

1   States shall prevent and suppress the abduction of children of parents subjected to enforced disappearance and of children born during their mother's enforced disappearance, and shall devote their efforts to the search for, and identification of, such children and to the restitution of the children to their families of origin.

2   Considering the need to protect the best interests of children referred to in the preceding paragraph, there shall be an opportunity, in States which recognize a system of adoption, for a review of the adoption of such children and, in particular, for annulment of any adoption which originated in enforced disappearance. Such adoption should, however, continue to be in force if consent is given, at the time of the review mentioned above, by the child's closest relatives.

3   The abduction of children of parents subjected to enforced disappearance or of children born during their mother's enforced disappearance, and the act of altering or suppressing documents attesting to their true identity, shall constitute an extremely serious offence, which shall be punished as such.

4   For these purposes, States shall, where appropriate, conclude bilateral and multilateral agreements.

Article 21

The provisions of the present Declaration are without prejudice to the provisions enunciated in the Universal Declaration of Human Rights or in any other international instrument, and shall not be construed as restricting or derogating from any of the provisions contained therein.

APPENDIX 7   **PRINCIPLES ON THE EFFECTIVE PREVENTION AND INVESTIGATION OF EXTRA-LEGAL, ARBITRARY AND SUMMARY EXECUTIONS** (adopted by the UN Economic and Social Council on 24 May 1989 in resolution 1989/65 and endorsed by the UN General Assembly on 15 December 1989 in resolution 44/162)

Prevention

1   Governments shall prohibit by law all extra-legal, arbitrary and summary executions and shall ensure that any such executions are recognized as offences under their criminal laws, and are punishable by appropriate penalties which take into account the seriousness of such offences. Exceptional circumstances including a state of war or threat of war, internal political instability or any other public emergency may not be invoked as a justification of such executions. Such executions shall not be carried out under any circumstances including, but not limited to, situations of internal armed conflict, excessive or illegal use of force by a public official or other person acting in an official capacity or a person acting at the instigation, or with the consent or acquiescence of such person, and situations in which deaths occur in custody. This prohibition shall prevail over decrees issued by governmental authority.

2   In order to prevent extra-legal, arbitrary and summary executions, Governments shall ensure strict control, including a clear chain of command over all officials responsible for the apprehension, arrest, detention, custody and imprisonment as well as those officials authorized by law to use force and firearms.

3   Governments shall prohibit orders from superior officers or public authorities authorizing or inciting other persons to carry out any such extra-legal, arbitrary or summary executions. All persons shall have the right and the duty to defy such orders. Training of law enforcement officials shall emphasize the above provisions.

4   Effective protection through judicial or other means shall be guaranteed to individuals and groups who are in danger of extra-legal, arbitrary or summary executions, including those who receive death threats.

5   No one shall be involuntarily returned or extradited to a country where there are substantial grounds for believing that he or she may become a victim of extra-legal, arbitrary or summary execution in that country.

6   Governments shall ensure that persons deprived of their liberty are held in officially recognized places of custody, and that accurate information on their custody and whereabouts, including transfers, is made promptly available to their relatives and lawyer or other persons of confidence.

7   Qualified inspectors, including medical personnel, or an equivalent independent authority, shall conduct inspections in places of custody on a regular basis, and be empowered to undertake unannounced inspections on their own initiative, with full guarantees of independence in the exercise of this function. The inspectors shall have unrestricted access to all persons in such places of custody, as well as to all their records.

8   Governments shall make every effort to prevent extra-legal, arbitrary and summary executions through measures such as diplomatic intercession, improved access of complainants to intergovernmental and judicial bodies, and public denunciation. Intergovernmental mechanisms shall be used to investigate reports of any such executions and to take effective action against such practices. Governments, including those of countries where extra-legal, arbitrary and summary executions are reasonably suspected to occur, shall co-operate fully in international investigations on the subject.

Investigation

9   There shall be a thorough, prompt and impartial investigation of all suspected cases of extra-legal, arbitrary and summary executions, including cases where complaints by relatives or other reliable reports suggest unnatural death in the above circumstances. Governments shall maintain investigative offices and procedures to undertake such inquiries. The purpose of the investigation shall be to determine the cause, manner and time of death, the person responsible, and any adequate autopsy, collection and analysis of all physical and documentary evidence, and statements from witnesses. The investigation shall distinguish between natural death, accidental death, suicide and homicide.

10   The investigative authority shall have the power to obtain all the information necessary to the inquiry. Those persons conducting the investigation shall have at their disposal all the necessary budgetary and technical resources for effective investigation. They shall also have the authority to oblige officials allegedly involved in any such executions to appear and testify. The same shall apply to any witness. To this end, they shall be entitled to issue summons to witnesses, including the officials allegedly involved, and to demand the production of evidence.

11   In cases in which the established investigative procedures are inadequate because of lack of expertise or impartiality, because of the importance of the matter or because of the apparent existence of a pattern of abuse, and in cases where there are complaints from the family of the victim about these inadequacies or other substantial reasons, Governments shall pursue investigations through an independent commission of inquiry or similar procedure. Members of such a commission shall be chosen for their recognized impartiality, competence and independence as individuals. In particular, they shall be independent of any institution, agency or person that may be the subject of the inquiry. The commission shall have the authority to obtain all information necessary to the inquiry and shall conduct the inquiry as provided for under these Principles.

12   The body of the deceased person shall not be disposed of until an adequate autopsy is conducted by a physician, who shall, if possible, be an expert in forensic pathology. Those conducting the autopsy shall have the right of access to all investigative data, to the place where the body was discovered, and to the place where the death is thought to have occurred. If the body has been buried and it later appears that an investigation is required, the body shall be promptly and competently exhumed for an autopsy. If skeletal remains are discovered, they should be carefully exhumed and studied according to systematic anthropological techniques.

13   The body of the deceased shall be available to those conducting the autopsy for a sufficient amount of time to enable a thorough investigation to be carried out. The autopsy shall, at a minimum, attempt to establish the identity of the deceased and the cause and manner of death. The time and place of death shall also be determined to the extent possible. Detailed colour photographs of the deceased shall be included in the autopsy report in order to document and support the findings of the investigation. The autopsy report must describe any and all injuries to the deceased including any evidence of torture.

14   In order to ensure objective results, those conducting the autopsy must be able to function impartially and independently of any potentially implicated persons or organizations or entities.

15   Complainants, witnesses, those conducting the investigation and their families shall be protected from violence, threats of violence or any other form of intimidation. Those potentially implicated in extra-legal, arbitrary or summary executions shall be removed from any position of control or power, whether direct or indirect, over complainants, witnesses and their families, as well as over those conducting investigations.

16   Families of the deceased and their legal representatives shall be informed of, and have access to, any hearing as well as to all information relevant to the investigation, and shall be entitled to present other evidence. The family of the deceased shall have the right to insist that a medical or other qualified representative be present at the autopsy. When the identity of a deceased person has been determined, a notification of death shall be posted, and the family or relatives of the deceased immediately informed. The body of the deceased shall be returned to them upon completion of the investigation.

17   A written report shall be made within a reasonable period of time on the methods and findings of such investigations. The report shall be made public immediately and shall include the scope of the inquiry, procedures and methods used to evaluate evidence as well as conclusions and recommendations based on findings of fact and on applicable law. The report shall also describe in detail specific events that were found to have occurred, and the evidence upon which such findings were based, and list the names of witnesses who testified, with the exception of those whose identities have been withheld for their own protection. The Government shall, within a reasonable period of time, either reply to the

report of the investigation, or indicate the steps to be taken in response to it.

Legal proceedings

18   Governments shall ensure that persons identified by the investigation as having participated in extra-legal, arbitrary or summary executions in any territory under their jurisdiction are brought to justice. Governments shall either bring such persons to justice or co-operate to extradite any such persons to other countries wishing to exercise jurisdiction. This principle shall apply irrespective of who and where the perpetrators or the victims are, their nationalities or where the offence was committed.

19   Without prejudice to Principle 3 above, an order from a superior officer or a public authority may not be invoked as a justification for extra-legal, arbitrary or summary executions. Superiors, officers or other public officials may be held responsible for acts committed by officials under their hierarchical authority if they had a reasonable opportunity to prevent such acts. In no circumstances, including a state of war, siege or other public emergency, shall blanket immunity from prosecution be granted to any person allegedly involved in extra-legal, arbitrary or summary executions.

20   The families and dependents of victims of extra-legal, arbitrary or summary executions shall be entitled to fair and adequate compensation within a reasonable period of time.

APPENDIX 8   AMNESTY INTERNATIONAL 14-POINT PROGRAM
                 FOR THE PREVENTION OF "DISAPPEARANCES"

The "disappeared" are people who have been taken into custody by agents of the state, yet whose whereabouts and fate are concealed, and whose custody is denied. "Disappearances" cause agony for the victims and their relatives. The victims are cut off from the world and placed outside the protection of the law; often they are tortured; many are never seen again. Their relatives are kept in ignorance, unable to find out whether the victims are alive or dead.

The United Nations has condemned "disappearances" as a grave violation of human rights and has said that their systematic practice is of the nature of a crime against humanity. Yet thousands of people "disappear" each year across the globe, and countless others remain "disappeared". Urgent action is needed to stop "disappearances", to clarify the fate of the "disappeared" and to bring those responsible to justice.

Amnesty International calls on all governments to implement the following 14-Point Program for the Prevention of "Disappearances". It invites concerned individuals and organizations to join in promoting the program. Amnesty International believes that the implementation of these measures is a positive indication of a government's commitment to stop "disappearances" and to work for their eradication worldwide.

1   **Official condemnation**

The highest authorities of every country should demonstrate their total opposition to "disappearances". They should make clear to all members of the police, military and other security forces that "disappearances" will not be tolerated under any circumstances.

2   Chain-of-command control

Those in charge of the security forces should maintain strict chain-of-command control to ensure that officers under their command do not commit "disappearances". Officials with chain-of-command responsibility who order or tolerate "disappearances" by those under their command should be held criminally responsible for these acts.

3   Information on detention and release

Accurate information about the arrest of any person and about his or her place of detention, including transfers and releases, should be made available promptly to relatives, lawyers and the courts. Prisoners should be released in a way that allows reliable verification of their release and ensures their safety.

4   Mechanism for locating and protecting prisoners

Governments should at all times ensure that effective judicial remedies are available which enable relatives and lawyers to find out immediately where a prisoner is held and under what authority, to ensure his or her safety, and to obtain the release of anyone arbitrarily detained.

5   No secret detention

Governments should ensure that prisoners are held only in publicly recognized places of detention. Up-to-date registers of all prisoners should be maintained in every place of detention and centrally. The information in these registers should be made available to relatives, lawyers, judges, official bodies trying to trace people who have been detained, and others with a legitimate interest. No one should be secretly detained.

6   Authorization of arrest and detention

Arrest and detention should be carried out only by officials who are authorized by law to do so. Officials carrying out an arrest should identify themselves to the person arrested and, on demand, to others witnessing the event. Governments should establish rules setting forth which officials are authorized to order an arrest or detention. Any deviation from established procedures which contributes to a "disappearance" should be punished by appropriate sanctions.

7   Access to prisoners

All prisoners should be brought before a judicial authority without delay after being taken into custody. Relatives, lawyers and doctors should have prompt and regular access to them. There should be regular, independent, unannounced and unrestricted visits of inspection to all places of detention.

8   Prohibition in law

Governments should ensure that the commission of a "disappearance" is a criminal offence, punishable by sanctions commensurate with the gravity of the practice. The prohibition of "disappearances" and the essential safeguards for their prevention must not be suspended under any circumstances, including states of war or other public emergency.

9   Individual responsibility

The prohibition of "disappearances" should be reflected in the training of all officials involved in the arrest and custody of prisoners and in the instructions issued to them. They should be instructed that they have the right and duty to refuse to obey any order to participate in a "disappearance". An order from a superior officer or a public authority must never be invoked as a justification for taking part in a "disappearance".

10   **Investigation**

Governments should ensure that all complaints and reports of "disappearances" are investigated promptly, impartially and effectively by a body which is independent of those allegedly responsible and has the necessary powers and resources to carry out the investigation. The methods and findings of the investigation should be made public. Officials suspected of responsibility for "disappearances" should be suspended from active duty during the investigation. Relatives of the victim should have access to information relevant to the investigation and should be entitled to present evidence. Complainants, witnesses, lawyers and others involved in the investigation should be protected from intimidation and reprisals. The investigation should not be curtailed until the fate of the victim is officially clarified.

11   **Prosecution**

Governments should ensure that those responsible for "disappearances" are brought to justice. This principle should apply wherever such people happen to be, wherever the crime was committed, whatever the nationality of the perpetrators or victims and no matter how much time has elapsed since the commission of the crime. Trials should be in the civilian courts. The perpetrators should not benefit from any legal measures exempting them from criminal prosecution or conviction.

12   **Compensation and rehabilitation**

Victims of "disappearance" and their dependants should be entitled to obtain fair and adequate redress from the state, including financial compensation. Victims who reappear should be provided with appropriate medical care or rehabilitation.

13   **Ratification of human rights treaties and implementation of international standards**

All governments should ratify international treaties containing safeguards and remedies against "disappearances", including the International Covenant on Civil and Political Rights and its first Optional Protocol which provides for individual complaints. Governments should ensure full implementation of the relevant provisions of these and other international instruments, including the UN Declaration on the Protection of All Persons from Enforced Disappearance, and comply with the recommendations of intergovernmental organizations concerning these abuses.

14   **International responsibility**

Governments should use all available channels to intercede with the governments of countries where "disappearances" have been reported. They should ensure that transfers of equipment, know-how and training for military, security or police use do not facilitate "disappearances". No one should be forcibly returned to a country where he or she risks being made to "disappear".

AMNESTY INTERNATIONAL 14-POINT PROGRAM
FOR THE PREVENTION OF EXTRAJUDICIAL
EXECUTIONS

Extrajudicial executions are fundamental violations of human rights and an affront to the conscience of humanity. These unlawful and deliberate killings, carried out by order of a government or with its complicity or acquiescence, have been condemned by the United Nations. Yet extrajudicial executions continue, daily and across the globe.

Many of the victims have been taken into custody or made to "disappear" before being killed. Some are killed in their homes, or in the course of military operations. Some are assassinated by uniformed members of the security forces, or by "death squads" operating with official connivance. Others are killed in peaceful demonstrations.

The accountability of governments for extrajudicial executions is not diminished by the commission of similar abhorrent acts by armed opposition groups. Urgent action is needed to stop extrajudicial executions and bring those responsible to justice.

Amnesty International calls on all governments to implement the following 14-Point Program for the Prevention of Extrajudicial Executions. It invites concerned individuals and organizations to join in promoting the program. Amnesty International believes that the implementation of these measures is a positive indication of a government's commitment to stop extrajudicial executions and to work for their eradication worldwide.

1   **Official condemnation**

The highest authorities of every country should demonstrate their total opposition to extrajudicial executions. They should make clear to all members of the police, military and other security forces that extrajudicial executions will not be tolerated under any circumstances.

2   **Chain-of-command control**

Those in charge of the security forces should maintain strict chain-of-command control to ensure that officers under their command do not commit extrajudicial executions. Officials with chain-of-command responsibility who order or tolerate extrajudicial executions by those under their command should be held criminally responsible for these acts.

3   **Restraints on use of force**

Governments should ensure that law enforcement officials use force only when strictly necessary and only to the minimum extent required under the circumstances. Lethal force should not be used except when strictly unavoidable in order to protect life.

4   **Action against "death squads"**

"Death squads", private armies, criminal gangs and paramilitary forces operating outside the chain of command but with official support or acquiescence should be prohibited and disbanded. Members of such groups who have perpetrated extrajudicial executions should be brought to justice.

5   **Protection against death threats**

Governments should ensure that anyone in danger of extrajudicial execution, including those who receive death threats, is effectively protected.

6   **No secret detention**

Governments should ensure that prisoners are held only in publicly recognized places of detention and that accurate information about the arrest and detention of any prisoner is made available promptly to relatives, lawyers and the courts. No one should be secretly detained.

7   **Access to prisoners**

All prisoners should be brought before a judicial authority without delay after being taken into custody. Relatives, lawyers and doctors should have prompt and regular access to them. There should be regular, independent, unannounced and unrestricted visits of inspection to all places of detention.

8   **Prohibition in law**

Governments should ensure that the commission of an extrajudicial execution is a criminal offence, punishable by sanctions commensurate with the gravity of the practice. The prohibition of extrajudicial executions and the essential safeguards for their prevention must not be suspended under any circumstances, including states of war or other public emergency.

9   **Individual responsibility**

The prohibition of extrajudicial executions should be reflected in the training of all officials involved in the arrest and custody of prisoners and all officials authorized to use lethal force, and in the instructions issued to them. These officials should be instructed that they have the right and duty to refuse to obey any order to participate in an extrajudicial execution. An order from a superior officer or a public authority must never be invoked as a justification for taking part in an extrajudicial execution.

10   **Investigation**

Governments should ensure that all complaints and reports of extrajudicial executions are investigated promptly, impartially and effectively by a body which is independent of those allegedly responsible and has the necessary powers and resources to carry out the investigation. The methods and findings of the investigation should be made public. The body of the alleged victim should not be disposed of until an adequate autopsy has been conducted by a suitably qualified doctor who is able to function impartially. Officials suspected of responsibility for extrajudicial executions should be suspended from active duty during the investigation. Relatives of the victim should have access to information relevant to the investigation, should be entitled to appoint their own doctor to carry out or be present at an autopsy, and should be entitled to present evidence. Complainants, witnesses, lawyers, judges and others involved in the investigation should be protected from intimidation and reprisals.

11   **Prosecution**

Governments should ensure that those responsible for extrajudicial executions are brought to justice. This principle should apply wherever such people happen to be, wherever the crime was committed, whatever the nationality of the perpetrators or victims and no matter how much time has elapsed since the commission of the crime. Trials should be in the civilian courts. The perpetrators should not be allowed to benefit from any legal measures exempting them from criminal prosecution or conviction.

12   **Compensation**

Dependants of victims of extrajudicial execution should be entitled to obtain fair and adequate redress from the state, including financial compensation.

13   **Ratification of human rights treaties and implementation of international standards**

All governments should ratify international treaties containing safeguards and remedies against extrajudicial executions, including the International Covenant on Civil and Political Rights and its first Optional Protocol which provides for individual complaints. Governments should ensure full implementation of the relevant provisions of these and other international instruments, including the UN Principles on the Effective Prevention and Investigation of Extra-Legal, Arbitrary and Summary Executions, and comply with the recommendations of intergovernmental organizations concerning these abuses.

14   **International responsibility**

Governments should use all available channels to intercede with the governments of countries where extrajudicial executions have been reported. They should ensure that transfers of equipment, know-how and training for military, security or police use do not facilitate extrajudicial executions. No one should be forcibly returned to a country where he or she risks becoming a victim of extrajudicial execution.

> *The 14-Point Programs for the Prevention of "Disappearances" and Extrajudicial Executions were adopted by Amnesty International in December 1992 as part of the organization's worldwide campaign for the eradication of "disappearances" and political killings. A similar program is available on the prevention of torture.*

INDEX